ACTIVE KOREAN

A FUNCTIONAL APPROACH

ACTIVE KOREAN

by Namgui Chang
Yong-chol Kim

HOLLYM
Elizabeth, NJ · Seoul

About the Authors

NAMGUI CHANG was born in Korea in 1925. He was educated at Seoul National University (B.A. in Sociology) before coming to the United States. He received a Ph.D. in Linguistics from the University of California, Berkeley. For many years Dr. Chang directed the basic Korean course development of the Defense Language Insititute in Monterey, California. Dr. Chang wrote *Functional Korean* (1989) (with Yong-chol Kim). He is residing in Monterey, California.

YONG-CHOL KIM was born in Korea in 1931. He majored in English at Seoul National University (B.A. and M.A) and later obtained his M.A. degree in English from the University of Hawaii. He received a Ph.D. in English Literature from the University of California, San Diego. During the 1970's he directed an intermediate Korean course development project at the Defense Language Institute in Monterey, California. Dr. Kim was Professor of English at Sungkyunkwan University in Seoul until his retirement in 1994. He is now residing in Monterey, California.

Active Korean: A Functional Approach

First published in 1996
Fifth printing, 2002
by Hollym International
18 Donald Place, Elizabeth, New Jersey 07208, U.S.A.
Tel: (908)353-1655 Fax: (908)353-0255
http://www.hollym.com

Published simultaneously in Korea
by Hollym Corporation; Publishers
13-13 Kwanchol-dong, Chongno-gu, Seoul 110-111, Korea
Tel: (02)735-7551~4 Fax: (02)730-5149, 8192
http://www.hollym.co.kr

ISBN: 1-56591-059-1
Library of Congress Catalog Card Number: 95-76494
Illustations by Hyesun Chang

Printed in Korea

PREFACE

Active Korean is an introductory textbook for a course in both spoken and written Korean leading up to an intermediate level. It is intended primarily for the English-speaking persons who desire to use Korean as they interact with native Koreans in ways appropriate to contemporary Korean life. The book stresses the importance of authentic language use in purposeful situational settings (discourse and communicative functions). It also emphasizes the awareness of cultural information and of contemporary scenes, appropriate to the learner's communicative needs.

This book is designed for a two-semester or three-quarter course with the teacher, but it may also be used for self-instruction by individual learners who already possess some basic knowledge of Korean but wish to advance, by reviewing some fundamentals, to more functional and culturally appropriate levels.

The varieties of Korean introduced in this book are largely based on the standard Korean, the speech used by the educated middle class in Seoul today. Furthermore, this book has incorporated many colloquial expressions as used by young Korean speakers today. Some of these expressions reflect recent language changes, which are not generally incorporated in other Korean language textbooks.

One of the innovative features of this book is an early introduction of style variations, generally known as "levels of politeness," which are one of the most distinctive characteristics of Korean. The three major levels of politeness, called here the high, the mid, and the low, are relatively simple and systematic, and an early introduction of the levels of politeness is not as difficult as it is often regarded. The primary reasons for this approach are (1) that the authentic use of Korean in realistic as well as classroom situations frequently demands level shifts, (2) that an immediate application and exercise of the learned material must involve speaking with adult speakers (e.g., the teacher) as well as with the peers (e.g., classmates), and (3) that the learner needs to be aware of, if not accustomed to, the importance of manipulation of speech levels and variations, which are so typical of Korean.

A total of approximately 1,500 lexical entries are included in this book, and there are also over 200 additional entries, labeled "personalized vocabulary," which may be left to the individual learner's needs and initiatives. It is strongly recommended that the teacher introduce for each lesson a few more additional vocabulary items (perhaps as an optional requirement) that are associated with each communicative situation. Such entries may be used in exercises, but not necessarily required of all students in the class. We believe that vocabulary expansion—though people often neglect this obvious fact—is the key to communicative efficacy. Grammar is of course important, but it is not a shortcut to learning a language.

Active Korean begins with "Hangul: Its Letters and Sounds,"a chapter that introduces the pronunciation and writing system of the Korean language together. In the first five lessons we have provided a romanization system, hoping that it will ease the learning experience of the beginning student. Once the learner gets used to the sound values of Korean symbols through Roman letters—though we are not unaware of a theory that the use of Roman letters only delays the learning of the Korean symbols—we hope that the learner will soon be able to pronounce Korean sounds without the aid of the romanization.

Each lesson has the following parts:

*Frames of Communicative Exchanges
*Vocabulary Study in Context
*Exercises of Various Types
*Grammar Explanations on Selected Features
*Reading and Writing Exercises with Authentic Materials
*Vocabulary Summary
*Answers to Exercises

Each lesson is centered on a simulated situation or a topic, and it is illustrated by four or five sets of conversational exchanges. Generally, the first three frames except the last one use the high or mid level of politeness, which is the all-important speech style for students to learn. The last frame on the low level of politeness is a model for exercises to be used between peers. This frame may be either lightly covered as cultural learning material or may even be skipped for those adult learners who may feel that peer-talk situations may not arise for them.

Frames of conversational exchanges should be considered as models for further variations and expansions. The teacher must be always ready and alert to supply additional words on the board in order to satisfy individual students' needs to express themselves in each specific situation. Exercises provided in this book are varied in type, but they are never meant to be sufficient. The teacher must provide additional ones. One recommended method for the teacher is to keep stock of prototype exercises at hand so that additional exercises may readily be made available at ease. We believe that no dogmas are needed in creating various types of exercises so long as they encourage students to freely take risks in expressing themselves, and more importantly, to keep them from being bored in their learning experience.

TABLE OF CONTENTS

Lesson 8. Coming to Korea

Lesson 9. Shopping

Lesson 10. Getting Around

제11과 새 학기

제12과 기차 여행

제21과 가족 이야기

제22과 친구집 방문

제23과 친구를 만나서 하는 이야기

제24과 한가한 오후

HANGŬL: ITS LETTERS AND SOUNDS

1. What is Hangŭl?

The Korean writing system is called Hangŭl. It is a phonetic system like the alphabet. Hangŭl is simple, systematic, and easy to learn. It consists of ten vowel symbols and fourteen consonant symbols that are variously combined to form syllables, which are then strung together to form words and phrases.

In South Korea today, certain authors mix Chinese characters (ideographic symbols borrowed from Chinese) within their Hangŭl writings. North Korea has eliminated the use of Chinese characters altogether since 1945.

2. Vowels

Although there are ten vowel symbols according to traditional counting (which will be explained later), there are only eight simple vowels in the Seoul dialect. Their sound values are shown in the McCune-Reischauer system (MR) and in the International Phonetic Alphabet (IPA) below.

HANGŬL	MR	IPA	Cautionary Notes	Approximate English Sounds
아	a	a		father
어	ŏ	ə	Lips not rounded	word
오	o	o	Lips rounded	more
우	u	u	Lips rounded	two
으	ŭ	ɯ	Lips not rounded	could
이	i	i		feet
애	ae	ɛ	Mid-low front	air
에	e	e	Mid-high front	end

CAUTION! 1. Korean vowels are sustained without gliding into a higher position (like "go" [gou] in English).
2. None of the English approximations above are perfect matches for Korean vowels.
3. Each of the eight vowels has a range of variations, especially the vowel 어 varies from [ə] to [ɔ].

3. Positions of Consonants

Look at the vowel symbols again. You will notice that all of them have a small circle "ㅇ." The small zero symbol means the absence of a consonant in the initial position of a syllable, and it also comes with long and short sticks (ㅏ, ㅗ, etc.), which are the real vowel symbols. However, neither a vowel symbol nor a consonant symbol is used independently of each other. They are always found together combined in syllables, i.e., a written syllable always begins with a consonant followed by a vowel. Even when a vowel is found alone in speech, the zero symbol (meaning the absence of an initial consonant) must be used.

4. Consonants

Each of the following consonants may replace the zero symbol to form written syllables. The fourteen consonants shown below are arranged in the traditional sequence, which is used in dictionaries. From this point on, unless otherwise noted, all romanization symbols are those of the McCune-Reischauer system.

ㄱ k(g)	ㄴ n	ㄷ t(d)	ㄹ r(l)	ㅁ m	ㅂ p(b)	ㅅ s
ㅇ ø(ng)	ㅈ ch(j)	ㅊ ch'	ㅋ k'	ㅌ t'	ㅍ p'	ㅎ h

These consonants are shown again below, each combined with the vowel [a]. Korean children are taught to memorize the sequence in order to be able to use dictionaries. Repeat after your teacher, and memorize the sequence, so that you can also use Korean dictionaries.

ka - na - ta - ra - ma - pa - sa - a

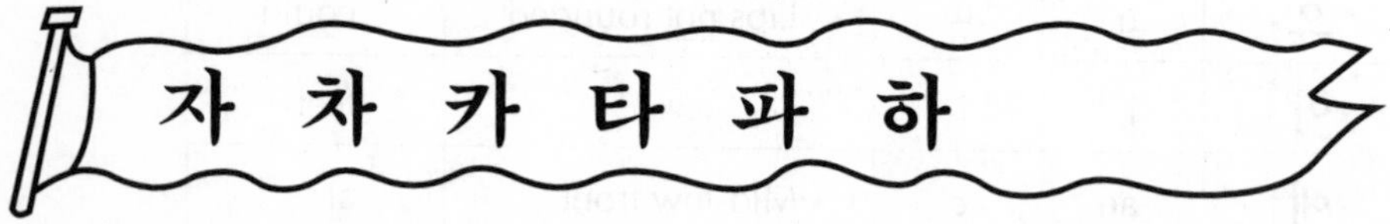

cha - ch'a - k'a - t'a - p'a - ha

The pronunciations of these consonants will be explained more in detail a little later. For now, let us have simple reading and writing exercises.

EXERCISE 1 Listen to your teacher's pronunciation and repeat after him/her while copying the following words.

a. 개	"dog"	e. 머리	"head"	i. 저	"I"	m. 파티	"party"
b. 네	"yes"	f. 비	"rain"	j. 차	"tea"	n. 하나	"one"
c. 다	"all"	g. 스키	"ski"	k. 코	"nose"		
d. 우리	"we"	h. 애기	"baby"	l. 타이	"necktie"		

5. Syllable-final Consonants

A consonant may be placed at the end of a syllable, and in such cases, it is placed directly below the combination of a consonant and a vowel, as you see in the next exercise.

CAUTION! A syllable-final consonant in Korean is never released (unless a vowel follows). The closure at a point in the mouth is held.

EXERCISE 2 Read aloud the following words while copying them.

a. 책	"book"	c. 달	"moon"	e. 밥	"rice"	g. 미국	"U.S.A"
b. 눈	"eye"	d. 금	"gold"	f. 한국	"Korea"	h. 서울	"Seoul"

The "zero" consonant symbol ㅇ, however, plays two different roles. In the initial position of a syllable, it means "no consonant," but at the end of a syllable, the same symbol stands for the sound of ng.

EXERCISE 3 Read aloud the following words while copying them.

a. 강	"river"	c. 궁	"palace"	e. 핑퐁	"ping-pong"
b. 창	"window"	d. 공	"ball"	f. 한강	"the Han River"

CAUTION! The sound of [ng] symbolized by ㅇ in Korean is a single consonant. The g of ng is not to be pronounced even when a vowel follows. In romanization, when ng is followed by a vowel, an apostrophe is placed after it to avoid confusion between ng and the combination of n and g as in the following examples.

공이	kong'i	"ball" (as subject)
강아지	kang'aji	"puppy"

6. Three Series of Stop Consonants

The stop consonants in Korean are quite different from their English counterparts. There are three series, which we will call "plain," "aspirated," and "double."

Plain	ㄱ [k(g)]	ㄷ [t(d)]	ㅂ [p(b)]	ㅈ [ch(j)]
Aspirated	ㅋ [k']	ㅌ [t']	ㅍ [p']	ㅊ [ch']
Double	ㄲ [kk]	ㄸ [tt]	ㅃ [pp]	ㅉ [tch]

a. Plain Stops: In the word-initial position, they do not accompany a heavy puff of air (aspiration). In this respect, they are like voiced stops in English, but not voiced. However, between vowels or after a voiced consonant (m, n, ng), they are voiced [g, d, b, j]. In each of the examples below, the same stop consonant occurs twice, but they are pronounced differently depending on their positions.

가게	[kage]	"store"	둘 다	[tul da]	"both"
바보	[pabo]	"fool"	제주도	[Chejudo]	"Cheju Island"

b. Aspirated Stops: Aspirated stops in Korean are similar to English voiceless stops in the word-initial position. They accompany a heavy puff of air when released and are never voiced in any positions. Compare the following pairs of words.

공	[kong]	"ball"	들	[tŭl]	"field"	불	[pul]	"fire"
콩	[k'ong]	"bean"	틀	[t'ŭl]	"frame"	풀	[p'ul]	"grass"
자	[cha]	"to sleep"						
차	[ch'a]	"tea"						

c. Double Consonants: There are five consonants that are not directly represented in the traditional consonant sequence. They are all represented by "double" symbols: ㄲ [kk], ㄸ [tt], ㅃ [pp], ㅉ [tch], and ㅆ [ss]. They are pronounced with the point of stricture in the mouth a fraction of a second longer than their plain counterparts. They are then released suddenly <u>without</u> a puff of air. Compare the following triplets of words.

개	[kae]	"dog"	달	[tal]	"moon"	발	[pal]	"foot"
캐	[k'ae]	"dig"	탈	[t'al]	"trouble"	팔	[p'al]	"arm"
깨	[kkae]	"sesame"	딸	[ttal]	"daughter"	빨	[ppal]	"to wash"
자	[cha]	"ruler"	살	[sal]	"flesh"			
차	[ch'a]	"tea"	쌀	[ssal]	"rice"			
짜	[tcha]	"salty"						

7. Unique Character of ㄹ [l/r]

In native Korean words, the consonant ㄹ occurs only between vowels or in the final position of a syllable. It does not occur word-initially. In recent loan words, however, it occurs word-initially, and is pronounced as shown below.

a. Between vowels, ㄹ is a flap sound similar to the English <u>r</u> in "three," or to the Spanish <u>r</u>.

나라	[nara]	"nation"	소리	[sori]	"sound"
다리	[tari]	"bridge"	우리	[uri]	"we"

b. In the final position of a syllable (when not followed by a vowel), ㄹ is a lateral sound <u>l</u>. It is a "clear" l, like that of French or Spanish.

말	[mal]	"language"	술	[sul]	"alcoholic drink"
서울	[sŏul]	"Seoul"	둘	[tul]	"two"

c. In recent loan words and foreign proper nouns, it occurs initially and is pronounced like <u>r</u>.

라이타	[rait'a]	"lighter"	라디오	[radio]	"radio"
레코드	[rek'odŭ]	"record"	레벨	[rebel]	"level"

EXERCISE 4 Read aloud the geographical names in the map below.

1. Hanguk
2. Chungguk
3. Taeman
4. Hongk'ong
5. P'illip'in
6. Ilbŏn
7. Rŏsia

8. Diphthongs

There are three kinds of diphthongs: the y-series (those beginning with y), the w-series (those beginning with w), and one unique diphthong 의. (See the note below.) All diphthongs may be regarded as combinations of two successive vowels, since most instances of two successive vowels are contracted. The y-series are obtained by adding an extra short stick (ㅑ, ㅛ, etc.), and the w-series by putting two vowel symbols within one syllable.

Y-series					W-series				
이 + 아	⇨	야	[ya]		오 + 아	⇨	와	[wa]	
이 + 어	⇨	여	[yŏ]		오 + 애	⇨	왜	[wae]	
이 + 오	⇨	요	[yo]		우 + 어	⇨	워	[wŏ]	
이 + 우	⇨	유	[yu]		우 + 에	⇨	웨	} [we]	
이 + 애	⇨	얘	[yae]		오 + 이	⇨	외		
이 + 에	⇨	예	[ye]		우 + 이	⇨	위	[wi]	
					으 + 이	⇨	의	[ŭi]	

NOTE: a. Possible diphthongs [yŭ], [yi], and [wo] do not occur.
b. Two diphthongs 웨 and 외 are normally pronounced the same in Seoul.
c. 의 is often pronounced [e], [u], or [i] in different contexts.

9. Dictionary Sequence of Vowels

The y-series of diphthongs are traditionally considered "vowels" and each of the diphthongs are placed immediately after the vowel which is the first component of a given diphthong. Memorize the sequence so that you will be able to use Korean dictionaries later.

아 야 어 여 오 요 우 유 으 이

EXERCISE 5 Read aloud the following words.

a. 여기 "here"
b. 용산 "Yongsan" (place name)
c. 영어 "English"
d. 학교 "school"
e. 컴퓨터 "computer"
f. 안녕하세요? "How are you?"

10. Reduction in Syllable-final Consonants

In writing, any consonant may be found at the end of a syllable. However, because Korean does not allow release of a consonant at the end of a syllable, some consonants cannot be fully pronounced with their basic values. Consonants, other than nasals and ㄹ, are reduced to [k], [t], or [p] in pronunciation.

ㄱ, ㅋ, ㄲ ⇨ k	ㄷ, ㅌ, ㄸ, ㅅ, ㅆ, ㅈ, ㅊ, ㅉ ⇨ t	ㅂ, ㅍ, ㅃ ⇨ p

EXERCISE 6 Read aloud the following words.

a. 박 "Pak" (name)
b. 밖 "outside"
c. 부엌 "kitchen"
d. 옷 "clothes"
e. 빚 "debt"
f. 낮 "daytime"
g. 입 "mouth"
h. 잎 "leaf"

* Romanization is given for your reference, but in the reverse order: h. [ip], g. [ip], f. [nat], e. [pit], d. [ot], c. [puŏk], b. [pak], a. [pak].

11. Moving a Consonant to the Next Syllable (Liaison)

When a syllable-final consonant is followed by a vowel, it is often pronounced in the next syllable. In English, "at all" is sometimes pronounced "a tall." In Korean, it is a "must" within a word, but between words it happens only in fast speech.

SPELLING		PRONUNCIATION	
집에	chip/e	⇨ chi/be	"home-SUFFIX"
영어	yŏng/ŏ	⇨ yŏ/ngŏ	"English language"
물을	mul/ŭl	⇨ mu/rŭl	"water-SUFFIX"

EXERCISE 7 Read aloud the following pairs of words, observing the rule of liaison.

a. 앞	"front"	d. 중국	"China"
앞에	"in front"	중국어	"Chinese language"
b. 한국	"Korea"	e. 서울	"Seoul"
한국에	"to Korea"	서울에	"to Seoul"
c. 옷	"clothes"	f. 미국	"America"
옷이	"clothes-SUFFIX"	미국인	"American"

* Romanization is given for your reference in the reverse order: f. [Miguk-Migugin] e. [sŏul-Sŏure], d. [chungguk-chungug'ŏ], c. [ot-oshi], b. [hanguk-hanguge], a. [ap-ap'e]

12. Syllables to Words and Phrases

a. Words: A string of syllables without any spaces between them, right to left as in English, or top to bottom, will form a word. In most cases, we will be using the right-to-left arrangement.

"teacher"

선 | 생 → or 선 / 생 ↓

"student"

학 | 생 → or 학 / 생 ↓

b. Suffixes: There are many suffixes to nouns and verbs. They are added to words without any space.

학교에 "to school"

c. Between words and phrases: A space is placed between two words or phrases.

저	학교에	가요.	"I go to school."
"I"	"school-to"	"go."	

d. Lines: When you write from left to right, lines proceed the same way as in English. Most modern writings are written in this way. However, the traditional arrangement, top-to-bottom, is still used (especially in newspaper articles). In this case, the reading of lines proceeds from right to left.

Horizontal lines
(As in English)
START →

Vertical lines (Traditional)
(right to left)
← START

한국식 록음악 대표

최근 우리말로 된 음반을 발매하면서 일본으로 진출하는데 성공한 「서태지와 아이들」이 랩·힙합·헤비메탈류의 음악을 하면서도 독창적인 면모를 보여줘 한국식 록음악을 대표하는것으로 소개되고 있다. 「서태지와 아이들」은 근착 타임지와의 인터뷰에서 "외국과 유럽에서도 한국의 젊은이들이 생각하는 바를 알게하기 위해 외국으로 진출한 것"이라고 말했다.

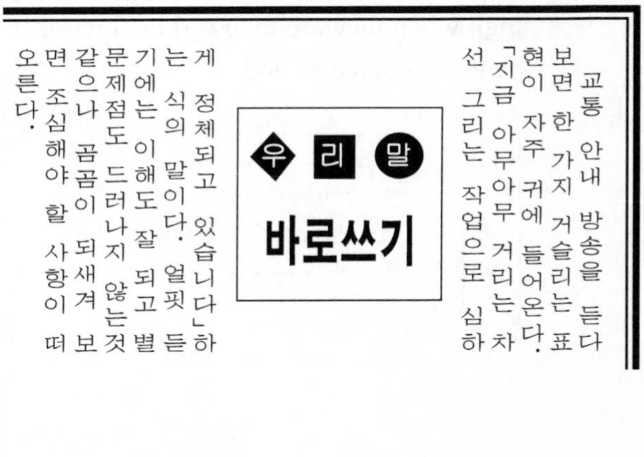
우 리 말
바로쓰기

교통 안내 방송을 듣다
보면 한 가지 거슬리는 표
현이 자주 귀에 들어온다.
「지금 아무아무 거리는 차
선 그리는 작업으로 심하
게 정체되고 있습니다」하
는 식의 말이다. 얼핏 들
기에는 이해도 잘 되고 별
문제점도 드러나지 않는 것
같으나 곰곰이 되새겨 보
면 조심해야 할 사항이 떠
오른다.

13. Various Sound Changes (for Later Reference Only)

> You may use this section as a reference resource later as you encounter pronunciation and spelling problems in the lessons that follow.
>
> The back slash \ is used to show the syllabic divisions where the sound changes occur, and the arrow ⟶ means "becomes" or "is pronounced."

a. Palatalization by [i] and [y]:

(1) ㅅ and ㅆ: The consonant ㅅ and ㅆ are palatalized, or they become sounds similar to sh of short, sheet, etc. in English when they are followed by [i] or [y].

도시	[toshi]	"city"	씨	[ssi]	"seed"
셔츠	[shŏch'ŭ]	"shirt"	쇼핑	[shop'ing]	"shopping"

Note: In the McCune-Reischauer system of romanization, shi and shy... is not always used; i.e., 도시 may be romanized either [tosi] or [toshi].

(2) ㄷ and ㅌ: The syllable-final consonant ㄷ or ㅌ is palatalized (ㄷ ⟶ ㅊ [ch']), when it is followed by a suffix beginning with 이.

해돋이	[haetot/i] ⟶	[haeto/ji]	"sunrise"
같이	[kat'/i] ⟶	[ka/ch'i]	"together"

b. Combination of Two Consonants

Combination of two consonants often occur between two syllables, and such combinations are subject to various sound changes.

(1) Double Consonants of ㄴ/ㄴ, ㅁ/ㅁ and ㅂ/ㅂ: The sequences of ㄴ/ㄴ, ㅁ/ㅁ, and ㅂ/ㅂ found between syllables, are pronounced with the point of closure held slightly longer than their single consonant counterpart.

안녕하세요?	[an/nyŏng haseyo]	"How are you?"
삼만	[sam/man]	"thirty thousand"
물론	[mul/lon]	"of course"

(2) Nasalization: Syllable-final obstruents are nasalized, or they become ([m], [n], [ng]) when they are followed by a nasal (ㄴ or ㅁ). Obstruents include all consonants except nasals and ㄹ.

* ㄱ, ㅋ, ㄲ ⟶	[ng]
* ㄷ, ㅌ, ㄸ / ㅈ, ㅊ, ㅉ / ㅅ, ㅆ ⟶	[n]
* ㅂ, ㅍ, ㅃ ⟶	[m]

Example

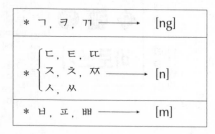

학문	[hak/mun]	⟶	[hang/mun] "learning"
있는	[iss/nŭn]	⟶	[in/nŭn] "existing"
앞문	[ap'/mun]	⟶	[am/mun] "front gate"

(3) Clusters with ㄹ: The consonant ㄹ changes to [n] after another consonant (except ㄴ or ㄹ). Then, the nasalization rule, described above in (2), applies. Note in the examples below that there are two changes in the consonant clusters with ㄹ.

독립 ⟶ [tok/nip]	→ [tong/nip]	"independence"
십리 ⟶ [sip/ni]	→ [sim/ni]	"ten ri" (unit of distance)

(4) Clusters with ㄴ and ㄹ: The combinations of ㄴ and ㄹ in any order (whether ㄴ/ㄹ or ㄹ/ㄴ) are pronounced as [ll].

일년	[il/nyŏn] →	[il/lyŏn]	"one year"
신라	[sin/la] →	[sil/la]	"Silla" (ancient Korean kingdom)

(5) Aspiration by ㅎ: The consonants (ㄱ, ㄷ, ㅂ and ㅈ) become aspirated before or after ㅎ.

약혼	[yak/hon]	⟶	[ya/k'on]	"betrothal"
좋지요.	[choh/chiyo]	⟶	[cho/ch'iyo]	"It's good."
많다	[manh/ta]	⟶	[man/t'a]	"to be many"

(6) Consonant Clusters at the End of a Syllable: Some words end in two different consonants. The two consonants of such a cluster are pronounced only when followed by a suffix vowel. If no suffix vowel follows, one of them is silent.

ㅂ/ㅅ ⟶ ㅂ	as in 없다	[ŏp/ta]	"not to exist"
ㄴ/ㅈ ⟶ ㄴ	as in 앉다	[an/ta]	"to sit down"
ㄹ/ㄱ ⟶ ㄱ	as in 닭	[tak]	"chicken"
ㄹ/ㅂ ⟶ ㄹ	as in 넓다	[nŏl/ta]	"to be wide"

14. Intonation

Standard Korean does not have a tonal or accentual system that distinguishes the meanings of words. Spoken phrases and sentences are relatively flat in intonation, without contrasts of ups and downs or syllables of prominence that one finds in English. The student should try not to place two or more stresses in one spoken phrase or sentence.

One characteristic tonal feature of Korean that the beginning student should note is a sharp rising tone (indicated by ↗ below) at the end of a question, which does not contain an interrogative word.

김선생님 계십니까? ↗ "Is Mr. Kim in?"

A question that contains an interrogative word does not have this sharp rising tone. It has a neutral tone, or a slight rise or fall, as in a declarative sentence.

누구십니까? ↘ "Who is there, please?"

The sharp rising tone is also associated with some types of sentence endings (e.g., –는데요! an exclamatory ending), and it sometimes plays crucial roles in distinguishing somewhat similar but still different types of sentences. (See Grammar notes in Lessons 13, 14, and 15).

LESSON 1
GREETING AND LEAVE-TAKING

FRAME 1

Greeting a Teacher, a Friend, an Acquaintance or a Stranger

김: 안녕하세요? [annyŏnghaseyo]	Kim: How are you?
박: 네, 안녕하세요? [ne annyŏnghaseyo]	Pak: Fine. How are you?

NOTE: A greeting is normally accompanied by a bow. Among friends or acquaintances, a nod will suffice.

VOCABULARY STUDY

- 안녕하세요? [annyŏnghaseyo] How are you?

  This is a greeting phrase used when one sees a friend or an acquaintance for the first time on a given day.

  안녕 [annyŏng] means "peace," and the sentence 안녕하세요? [annyŏnghaseyo] literally means "Are (you) in peace?" with "you" omitted. It is used to inquire about someone's well-being. A typical response is simply to acknowledge with 네 [ne], meaning "yes" and then repeat the same question.
- 네 [ne] yes

FRAME 2

Greeting a Friend in a Familiar Manner

조: 안녕하세요, 미스터 김? [annyŏnghaseyo misut'ŏ kim]	Cho: How are you, Mr. Kim?
김: 조 선생, 안녕하십니까? [cho sŏnsaeng annyŏnghashimnikka]	Kim: Ms. Cho, how are you?
조: 오래간만입니다. [oraeganmanimnida]	Cho: It's been a long time.
김: 네, 오래간만입니다. [ne oraeganmanimnida]	Kim: Yes, it's been a long time.

VOCABULARY STUDY

- 미스터 김 [misŭt'ŏ kim] Mr. Kim
- 조 선생 [cho sŏnsaeng] Mr. Cho/Ms. Cho

  선생 [sŏnsaeng] means "teacher." Here it is used as a title (Mid Level) suffixed to a person 's name.
- 안녕하십니까? [annyŏnghashimnikka] How are you?

  This longer version is slightly more formal than 안녕하세요? [annyŏnghaseyo] but the two forms of greeting are generally interchangeable.
- 오래간만입니다. [oraeganmanimnida] It's been a long time.

  The expression may be taken as an idiomatic phrase at this point. 오래 [orae] means "a long time."

❖ ADDRESSING A TEACHER OR A SENIOR ADULT (High Level)

On the High Level, the honorific suffix -님 [-nim] is attached to a title such as 선생 [sŏnsaeng], meaning "teacher." A surname may precede the title as in the second example below.

선생님 [sŏnsaengnim]	A teacher or a senior adult
김 선생님 [kim sŏnsaengnim]	Mr. Kim

EXERCISE 1 Replace the surname Kim with the surnames listed below or any other surname that you know. Common anglicized spellings are given next to the pronunciation.

Common Surnames

김	[kim]	Kim	이	[i:]	Yi or Lee or Rhee
박	[pak]	Park or Pak	정	[chŏng]	Chung

조	[cho]	Cho	한	[han]	Han
권	[kwon]	Kwon	서	[sŏ]	Suh or Seo
유	[yu]	Yu or Ryu	최	[ch'oe]	Choi or Choe

❖ ADDRESSING A COLLEAGUE OR AN ACQUAINTANCE (Mid Level)

Once colleagues or acquaintances have become better acquainted with each other, the speech may be lowered to the Mid Level. In such cases, the honorific suffix -님 [nim] is dropped.

선생	[sŏnsaeng]	A teacher, or an adult equal or lower in age and social status
유 선생	[yu sŏnsaeng]	Mr. Yu

❖ ADDRESSING YOUR CLASSMATE IN A FORMAL MANNER (Mid Level)

The titles below are used among relatively young people, who are not close enough to call each other by their first names.

조 형	[cho hyŏng]	Mr. Cho
미스터 박	[mistŏ pak]	Mr. Pak
미스 김	[misŭ kim]	Miss Kim
민 양	[min yang]	Miss Min

NOTE: 형 [hyŏng] means "elder brother" (of a male sibling) and as such it is used like a title among males. The female equivalent 언니 [ŏnni], meaning "elder sister" (of a female sibling), is used by a younger female student addressing or referring to an older female student.

EXERCISE 2 Greet the classmate seated next to you by using his or her surname and an appropriate title. Do not forget that you should be a little formal (Mid Level) when you are not well acquainted with your classmate, and this means that you would give a slight nod or bow when you greet.

Model: 박 형, 안녕하세요? [pak hyŏng annyŏnghaseyo]
네, 안녕하세요, 이 형? [ne annyŏnghaseyo i hyŏng]

❖ ADDRESSING A FRIEND IN A FAMILIAR MANNER (Mid Level)

Given names may be used among close friends as in English, but in Mid Level speech the use of the suffix -씨 [-ssi] still maintains a degree of formality.

매리 씨	[maeri ssi]	혜숙 씨	[hesuk ssi]
제임스 씨	[jeimsŭ ssi]	영철 씨	[yŏngch'ŏl ssi]

EXERCISE 3 Greet your classmates, using their first names.

EXERCISE 4 Perform each of the following tasks.

a. Say hello to your teacher.
b. Greet a male classmate next to you.
c. Greet a female classmate next to you.
d. Say that it's been a long time.

EXERCISE 5 Imagine you are working in an office. Greet one of your colleagues, and say that it's been a long time since you saw him last.

EXERCISE 6 Listen to your teacher greeting his or her colleagues, and write down the surnames of the person that you hear in his or her speech.

FRAME 3

Leave-Taking

조 : 그럼, 안녕히 가세요! [kŭrŏm annyŏng'i kaseyo]	Cho: Well, good-bye! (Please go in peace.)
김 : 네, 안녕히 계세요! [ne annyŏng'i kyeseyo]	Kim: O.K., good-bye! (Please stay in peace.)

VOCABULARY STUDY

•그럼	[kŭrŏm]	well, then
•안녕히	[annyŏng'i]	in peace, safely, in good health
•가세요!	[kaseyo]	Please go! (a polite request form)
•계세요!	[kyeseyo]	Please be or stay! (a polite request form)

EXERCISE 7 It is the end of the day. Say good-bye to each of the following persons, using an appropriate expression for each situation.

a. The teacher is staying in the classroom and you are going home.
b. The teacher is also leaving the classroom.
c. Say good-bye to your close friend as you leave his or her home.
d. Say good-bye to your close friend who is leaving.

❖ ADDRESSING A CLOSE FRIEND BY HIS/HER GIVEN NAME (Low Level)

Low Level speech is primarily used in the following three situations: (1) when an adult speaks to a child, (2) when children speak among themselves, and (3) when close friends speak intimately.

On this level, when you address someone, you simply use given names without the polite suffix -씨 [-ssi]. However, given names are usually extended by an extra syllable. The vowel 아 [a] is added to names ending in a consonant, and 야 [ya] to those ending in a vowel.

Given names	*Basic form*	*Addressing form*
Ending in a consonant	동훈 [donghun] 명숙 [myŏngsuk]	동훈아 [donghuna] 명숙아 [myŏngsuga]
Ending in a vowel	영자 [yŏngja] 정호 [chŏngho]	영자야 [yŏngjaya] 정호야 [chŏnghoya]

EXERCISE 8 Imagine that you have Korean friends with common given names such as shown below. Call each of them by his or her first name.

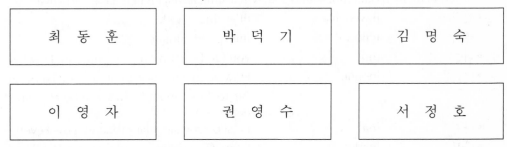

최 동 훈	박 덕 기	김 명 숙
이 영 자	권 영 수	서 정 호

EXERCISE 9 The teacher will assign a Korean name to each student unless he or she already has one. Each student will make a personal name card and display it. Call the attention of your classmate next to you by using his or her given name.

FRAME 4

Greeting a Close Friend

덕기: 영숙아! 잘 있니? [yŏngsuga chal inni]	Tŏkki : Yŏngsuk! How's it going? (Are you O.K.?)
영숙: 응, 좋아. 너는? [ŭng chowa nŏnŭn]	Yŏngsuk : Yeah, I'm doing fine. How about you?
덕기: 나도 괜찮아. [nado kwench'ana]	Tŏkki : I'm O.K., too.

VOCABULARY STUDY

- 잘 있니? [chal inni] How's it going? Are you O.K.?

  A Low Level greeting, equivalent to 안녕하세요 or 안녕하십니까. It literally means "Are you well?" 잘 [chal]=well, safely, 있니? [inni]=are you?
- 응 [ŭng] yeah (a Low Level equivalent to 네)

  응 is actually nasal grunt sound somewhat similar to a French nasalized vowel.
- 괜찮아 [kwench'ana] (It's) alright, O.K.
- 좋아 [chowa] fine, good, alright
- 너 [nŏ] you (2nd person singular pronoun, Low Level)
- 너는? [nŏnŭn] How about you? (-는 [-nŭn] is a suffix, meaning "as for" or "about." This will be explained in detail later.)
- 나 [na] I (1st person singular pronoun, Low Level)
- 나도 [nado] I, too. (The suffix -도 [-do] means "too.")

EXERCISE 10 Imagine that you have just run into two friends of yours. One is a very close friend that you see every day, and the other is his older sister. Greet both of them. Normally you are expected to greet the older person first.

EXERCISE 11 Greet your friend seated next to you, using his or her first name. Use Frame 4 as a model.

EXERCISE 12 You see your teacher and a close friend of yours walking toward you on the street. Greet them.

FRAME 5

Parting

영수 : 그럼 잘 가 ! [kŭrŏm chal ga]	Yŏngsu : Well, good-bye! (Go safely.)
순이 : 응, 잘 있어 ! [ŭng chal issŏ]	Suni : O.K., good-bye! (Stay safely.)
안녕 ! [annyŏng]	So long!

VOCABULARY STUDY

• 가!	[ka]	Go! (a Low Level request form)
• 잘 가!	[chal ka]	Good-bye! (an informal greeting to a friend leaving)
• 있어!	[issŏ]	Be/stay! (a Low Level request form)
• 잘 있어!	[chal issŏ]	Good-bye! (an informal greeting to a friend staying)
• 안녕!	[annyŏng]	So long! Good-bye! (an informal greeting simulated to children's speech)

EXERCISE 13 Express yourself in a way most appropriate for each of the following situations.

a. Greet your classmate, with whom you are on the first-name terms.
b. Imagine that it is the end of the day. Say good-bye to your friend who is also leaving.
c. Say good-bye to two friends of yours who are leaving the room. One of them is someone you met rather recently, and the other a very close friend of the same age.
d. You are about to leave your friend's house. This friend of yours is older than you. Say good-bye to your friend.

GRAMMAR

1. Three Levels of Speech

It is important to distinguish the levels of politeness in Korean. How you say something depends on the relationship you have with the one you are speaking to. In this course, we will distinguish three levels of speech: High Level, Mid Level, and Low Level. The descriptions below are not complete but are tentative guides for introductory purposes.

	WHEN YOU SPEAK TO	CHARACTERISTICS
HIGH LEVEL	Adults senior to you in age and social status	Honorific forms are used for the addressee (2nd person).
	Acquaintances, colleagues, or strangers with formality	

MID LEVEL	Friends and colleagues equal in age and social status	No honorific forms are used for the addressee (2nd person), but polite forms are used.
	People junior to you in age and social status	
LOW LEVEL	Close friends speaking on a first-name basis	No honorific and polite forms are used.
	Children or those who are considerably younger than you	

NOTE: The term "honorific" is applied to those forms which express the speaker's respect to the subject of a sentence. The term "polite" is applied to those forms which express the speaker's respect to the addressee. These terms will be explained more in detail later.

2. Korean Names and Terms of Address

The full name of a Korean consists of a surname (family name) and a given name arranged in that order. No space is usually placed between the surname and the given name.

Surname	*Given Name*	
박	영수	a typical name of a male person
[pak yŏngsu]		
김	명숙	a typical name of a female person
[kim myŏngsuk]		

Almost all Korean surnames are in one syllable, e.g., 김, 박, etc., but given names are generally in two syllables as in 영수, 명숙.

Terms of address are summarized below. We will use the two full names shown above, 박영수 (male) and 김명숙 (female), to show how these titles are used. (M=male, F=female, M/F=male or female.)

HIGH LEVEL	MID LEVEL	LOW LEVEL
박 선생님 [pak sŏnsaengnim] (M/F)	박 선생 [pak sŏnsaeng](M/F) 박 형 [pak hyŏng] (M) 미스터 박 [misŭtŏ pak] (M) 미스 김 [misŭ kim] (F) 김 양 [kim yang] (F) 영수 씨 [yŏngsu ssi] (M/F)	영수야 [yŏngsuya] (M/F) ⇧ -야 after a vowel, -아 after a consonant

NOTE : The suffix -씨 [-ssi] are also used with a full name (e.g., 박영수 씨) or with a surname only (e.g., 박 씨), but such uses generally sound somewhat impersonal and not very friendly.

3. Interjections

There are only two sets of interjections for "yes" and "no." The High and Mid Levels use the same set while the Low Level another.

	HIGH LEVEL/MID LEVEL	LOW LEVEL
yes	네 [ne]	응 [ŭng]
no	아니오 [anio]	아니 [ani]

4. Personal Pronouns

In Korean, the uses of personal pronouns are limited to the first person ("I") on all levels and to the second person ("you") on the Low Level. Where personal pronouns are not available, names and/or titles are used in place of pronouns as indicated in the list below. For example, on the High Level, the 2nd and 3rd person expressions are made with 선생님 "Teacher," 김 선생님 "Mr. Kim," etc. Although not all pronouns are introduced yet, the list of pronouns is provided below to give you a general picture.

	HIGH LEVEL	MID LEVEL	LOW LEVEL
*1st Person Singular I	저 [chŏ]	나 [na]	
*1st Person Plural we	저희(들) [chŏi(dŭl)]	우리(들) [uri(dul)]	
*2nd Person Singular you	Appropriate name and/or title		너 [nŏ]
*2nd Person Plural you			너희(들) [nŏi(dŭl)]

READING & WRITING

1. Names for "Korea"

한국: The word for Korea currently used in South Korea is 한국. The name 한 comes from an ancient word referring to the southern region of the Korean peninsula 한반도, where three old kingdoms 삼국 existed in the third century. When South Koreans today refer to South Korea and North Korea separately, they use the expressions 남한 "South Korea" and 북한 "North Korea."

조선: North Koreans today use 조선 to refer to Korea. The word 조선 is also an ancient name for Korea, and it was used again during Korea's last kingdom, 이씨 조선 the "Yi Dynasty" (1392-1910). Literally, 조선 means "Morning Brightness" or "Morning Calm."

고려: The English word "Korea" comes from the name of a medieval kingdom called 고려 (918-1392), which preceded 조선. 고려 literally means the "Highlands Grace."

EXERCISE 14 In the spaces below, write in Hangŭl the names for Korea during the different historical periods.

	Ancient Times	*Koryŏ Dynasty* (918-1392)	*Yi Dynasty* (1392-1910)	*Today* (1910-)
North:				
South:				

2. Three Rules of Pronunciation in 안녕하십니까

There are three rules of pronunciation and spelling that you can learn in 안녕하십니까? [annyŏnghashimnikka] "How are you?"

a. Pronunciation of Double Consonants

Double consonants (in spelling) are pronounced differently from single consonants. The double consonants, such as [nn], [mm], and [ll], are pronounced with the point of closure in your mouth held longer than for the single consonants. 안녕 involves two L consonants, so it is pronounced [an/nyŏng].

EXERCISE 15 Read the following words aloud.

a. 언니	elder sister	c. 몰라요.	I don't know.
b. 금메달	gold medal	d. 올림픽	Olympics

b. Palatalization of ㅅ and ㅆ

The consonant ㅅ and ㅆ are palatalized when followed by the vowel 이 or y-diphthong. The syllables 시 and 씨 are pronounced like [shi] and [ssi] respectively. The romanization may not always reflect this.

EXERCISE 16 Read the following words aloud.

a. 김 씨	Mr. Kim	c. 가십시오.	Please go.
b. 다시	again	d. 시간	time

c. Nasalization of ㅂ in 하십니까

The consonant ㅂ of 하십니까 is pronounced [m] because it is followed by [n]. This is called "nasalization."

EXERCISE 17 Read the following words aloud.

a. 한국말	the Korean language	c. 옷만	clothing only
b. 중국말	the Chinese language	d. 압니다.	I know.

3. The Pronunciation of 계 [ke]

In ordinary speech, there is no difference between 게 and 계 in pronunciation: both are pronounced [ke]. In this lesson, you had one example in 계십시오 [keshipshio] "Please stay" (High Level).

4. Dictionary Arrangement of Words

In order to use a Korean dictionary, it is necessary to understand the traditional sequence of consonants and vowels.

EXERCISE 18 Complete the following dictionary sequence of the consonants combined with the vowel 아.

가	나	다					아	자					하

EXERCISE 19 Rearrange the following words in the dictionary sequence.

선생 고려 한국 반도 조선 오래

VOCABULARY SUMMARY

Vocabulary items in each category are arranged as in the standard Korean dictionary. The speech levels are specified only for certain items by symbols: Ⓗ=High Level, Ⓜ=Mid Level, and Ⓛ=Low Level. When the speech level is not specified for a given item, it means that the item is used on any level. Answers are provided only for those exercises that would have uniform answers.

Nominals

고려		Koryŏ (medieval Korean kingdom)
나	ⓂⓁ	I (pronoun)
남한		South Korea
너	Ⓛ	you (pronoun)
미스터		Mr.
미스		Miss
반도		peninsula
북한		North Korea
선생		teacher; Mr.
선생님	Ⓗ	teacher; Mr.
-씨	Ⓜ	Mr./Miss
조선		Korea (used in North Korea)
한국		Korea (used in South Korea)
형		elder brother of a male sibling; Mr.

Verbs

가.	Go.
가세요.	Please go.
계세요.	Please stay.
괜찮아.	I'm O.K.
좋아.	I'm fine.

Adverbs

안녕히	Ⓗ	safely, in peace	잘		well, safely
오래		a long time			

Suffixes

-는		a topic marker as in 너는? "How about you?"	-아/야	Ⓛ	an extra vowel added to the given name { -야 after a vowel; -아 after a consonant }
-도		also, too			

Interjections

그럼		well, then	응	Ⓛ	yeah
네	Ⓗ Ⓜ	yes			

Expressions of Greeting and Leave-Taking

High/Mid Level	Low Level	
안녕하세요?	잘 있니?	How are you?
안녕하십니까?		How are you?
안녕히 가세요.	잘 가!	Good-bye! (Go safely.)
안녕히 계세요.	잘 있어!	Good-bye! (Stay well.)
	안녕!	Good-bye! (Children's speech)
오래간만입니다.	오래간만이야.	It's been a long time.

ANSWERS TO EXERCISES

Exercise 7. a. 안녕히 계세요. b. 안녕히 가세요. c. 잘 있어. d. 잘 가.

Exercise 14.

	Ancient Times	Koryo Dynasty	Yi Dynasty	Today
North :	조선	고려	조선	조선
South :	한			한국

Exercise 18. 가 나 다 라 마 바 사 아 자 차 카 타 파 하

Exercise 19. 고려 - 반도 - 선생 - 오래 - 조선 - 한국

LESSON 2

MEETING PEOPLE

FRAME 1

Introducing People

박: 친구 소개합니다. [ch'ingu sogaehamnida]	Pak : I'd like to introduce my friend.
이분이 홍기수 씨입니다. [ibuni hongkisu ssiimnida]	This is Mr. Hong Kisu.
홍: 처음 뵙습니다. [ch'ŏŭm poepsŭmnida]	Hong : I am glad to meet you.
저 홍기수입니다. [chŏ hongkisuimnida]	I'm Hong Kisu.

VOCABULARY STUDY

•친구	[ch'ingu]	friend
•소개합니다.	[sogaehamnida]	I'd like to introduce....
•이분	[ibun]	this person
이-	[i-]	this
-분	[-bun]	person (gentleman, lady)

This noun -분 is never used without a modifier before it.

It is a polite term. The vowel 이 following 분 is a subject-marking suffix.

•홍기수 씨	[hong kisu ssi]	Mr. Hong Kisu
•-입니다.	[-imnida]	is/are....

NOTE: The hyphen "-" before or after a word, as in -입니다 or -분 means that the form cited is never used independently of something preceding or following.

- 처음 [ch'ŏŭm] for the first time
- 뵙습니다. [poepsŭmnida] I am seeing/meeting....

  처음 뵙습니다. I'm glad to meet you.

  This is an idiomatic greeting phrase. It literally means "I meet you for the first time."
- 저 [chŏ] I (1st person pronoun)
- 홍기수입니다. [hongkisuimnida] I'm Hong Kisu.

❖ HOW TO USE EQUATIONAL SENTENCES

When you introduce someone by name or occupation, you may use the following construction.

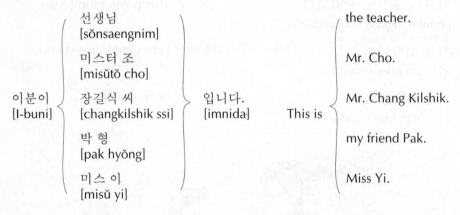

	선생님 [sŏnsaengnim]			the teacher.
	미스터 조 [misŭtŏ cho]			Mr. Cho.
이분이 [I-buni]	장길식 씨 [changkilshik ssi]	입니다. [imnida]	This is	Mr. Chang Kilshik.
	박 형 [pak hyŏng]			my friend Pak.
	미스 이 [misŭ yi]			Miss Yi.

NOTE: 형, denoting "an older brother," is also used to mean "buddy" or "pal" between intimate friends. In direct address, the surname often precedes the term 형, thus 오 형, 김 형 or 박 형.

EXERCISE 1 Suppose you are with a group of people who need to be introduced to one another, how would you meet the following needs?

a. Introduce yourself by stating your name.
b. Introduce your teacher to the rest of the group.
c. Introduce one of your classmates to the group.
d. To the person who has just been introduced to you, say that you are glad to meet him or her.

FRAME 2

Asking People's Names

김 : 성함이 어떻게 되십니까? [sŏnghami ŏttŏke toeshimnikka]	Kim : May I ask your name?
죤즈: 제 이름은 톰 죤즈입니다. [che irŭmŭn tom jonzŭimnida]	Jones: My name is Tom Jones.
잘 부탁합니다. [chal put'ak hamnida]	Happy to be your friend. (Please do me a favor.)

VOCABULARY STUDY

- 성함 [sŏngham] full name (used only for 2nd or 3rd person)
  성함이 어떻게 되십니까? What is your name?
  This is the most polite way of asking someone's name.
  The Ⓜ equivalent to this is 이름이 무엇입니까? [irŭmi muŏshimnikka]
- 제- [che-] my (a polite possessive form of 저)
- 이름 [irŭm] name
- -은 [-ŭn] a topic-marking suffix
- 잘 [chal] well, favorably
- 부탁합니다. [put'akhamnida] I'd like to ask a favor of you.
  The implied meaning of this highly social expression is : "I ask you to treat me as a good friend, because I need your help."

EXERCISE 2 Exchanging names is a common means of social introduction. Let us go about that task.

a. Give your name as you introduce yourself.
b. Ask politely the name of the person you are meeting.
c. Say that you would like to be his or her good friend.

FRAME 3

Visiting an Office

권 : 백 선생님 계십니까? [paek sŏnsaengnim keshimnikka]	Kwon : Is Mr. Paek in?
접수: 네, 계십니다. [ne keshimnida]	Chŏpsu : Yes, he is.
누구십니까? [nugushimnikka]	May I ask who you are?
권 : 제 이름은 권기태입니다. [che irŭmŭn kwonkit'aeimnida]	Kwon : My name is Kwon Kitae.
저는 학생입니다. [chŏnŭn haksaengimnida]	I'm a student.
접수: 잠깐 기다리세요. [chamkkan kidariseyo]	Chŏpsu : Please wait for a little while.

VOCABULARY STUDY

- 계십니까? [keshimnikka] Is (he) there? Is (he) in?

  계시다, a High Level term, means "to be, stay."
- 접수 [chŏpsu] receptionist
- 계십니다. [keshimnida] (He) is.
- 누구 [nugu] who
- 누구십니까? [nugushimnikka] May I ask who you are?

  The insertion of -시 [-shi] makes the expression more polite.
  This marker, called the "honorific" marker, will be explained later.
- 학생 [haksaeng] student
- 잠깐 [chamkkan] a little while
- 기다리세요. [kidariseyo] Please wait.

FRAME 4

Visiting a Friend's Home

정: 조 형 있습니까? [chohyŏng issŭmnikka]	Chŏng : Are you in, Mr. Cho?
조: 누구세요? [nuguseyo]	Cho : Who is this?
정: 정유산입니다. [chŏngyusanimnida]	Chŏng : I'm Chŏng Yusan.
조: 네, 잠깐 기다리세요. [ne chamkkan kidariseyo]	Cho : O.K. Wait for a second, please.

VOCABULARY STUDY

- 있습니까? [issŭmnikka] Is (he) there? Are (you) there?

  The verb 있다 means "to be, stay." Its Ⓗ form is 계시다. The verb 있다 is used only to indicate that someone or something is present at a certain time or place. Do not use this verb to indicate the identity of something or someone, as in "I am Hong Kisu." or "He is my teacher." For that, the verb 이다 is used.

- 누구세요? [nuguseyo] Who is this / it?

  This expression is slightly less polite than 누구십니까? even though it is polite enough for ordinary communication.

  NOTE : All Korean verbs consist of at least one stem and one ending. The verb stem helps to give its lexical meaning while the ending serves to determine the verb's mood. For now, we will deal with only the so-called "long" verb in two kinds of mood : the declarative (for certainty) and the interrogative (for uncertainty or question). For more details see Grammar in Lesson 3.

LEVEL	DECLARATIVE	INTERROGATIVE
High/Mid	Vowel + ㅂ니다 Consonant + 습니다	Vowel + ㅂ니까? Consonant + 습니까?

EXERCISE 3 You are visiting your teacher in his/her office. Your partner will play the role of receptionist. Greet her, identify yourself and ask her if your teacher is in.

EXERCISE 4 You are invited to the apartment of your classmate. What do you say at the door? Carry on an initial conversation at the door.

> *Special Note on English Translations:* In Korean, the subject is often missing from a sentence, and the English translation for such a sentence still shows a pronoun subject appropriate for the context. For simplicity, hereafter, we will select one pronoun without parentheses in such cases. As a rule, a Korean verb *does not* change its form by person (1st, 2nd, or 3rd), nor by number (singular or plural). A verb (in a particular shape) may be used with any subject, so long as it is compatible with the given speech level.

FRAME 5

Visiting a Friend

존 : 철수야, 있니? [ch'ŏlsuya inni]	John : Ch'ŏlsu, are you there?
철수: 누구야? [nuguya]	Ch'ŏlsu : Who is it?
존 : 나야. 존이야. [naya joniya]	John : It's me. John.
철수: 아, 존, 오래간만이야. [a jon oreganmaniya]	Ch'ŏlsu : Oh, John, it's been a long time.
어서 들어 와! [ŏsŏ tŭrŏ wa]	Come right in.

- 있니? [inni] Are (you) there? / Are (you) in?

  This is an Ⓛ question form of the verb 있다 [itta] "to be or stay."
- 누구야? [nuguya] Who is it?
- 나야. [naya] It's me.
- 오래간만이야. [oreganmaniya] It's been a long time.

  -야 (after a vowel) or -이야 (after a consonant) is equivalent to the English copula verb "to be." See Grammar for more details.
- 어서 들어와! [ŏsŏ tŭrŏwa] Come right in! (Ⓛ form)

  어서 [ŏsŏ] please, kindly ; quickly (used only in urging)

  들어와! [tŭrŏwa] Come in!

  This is a command form of the verb 들어오다 [tŭrŏoda] "to come in."

EXERCISE 5 You are about to make an unannounced visit to a good friend of yours. You and your partner are on first-name terms. Carry on an initial conversation at the door.

EXERCISE 6 The comparative list below of sentences on three speech levels is incomplete. Complete it by filling in the blank spaces.

HIGH	MID	LOW
( )	누구입니까?	누구야?
오래간만입니다.		( )
안녕하세요?		( )
어서 들어오세요.		( )
( )		잠깐 기다려.

EXERCISE 7 Convert the following polite expressions into those of Low Level speech.

A. 인철 씨, 계십니까? ______________________

B. 누구십니까? ______________________

A. 저입니다. 마이클입니다. ______________________

B. 네, 어서 들어오세요. ______________________

A. 안녕하십니까? ______________________

B. 네, 오래간만입니다. ______________________

EXERCISE 8 The vowel 이 of the equational verb is often omitted as in 누구야? (<누구이야?). Explain when it is omitted by giving examples.

GRAMMAR

1. The Korean Verb and Its Dictionary Form

The Korean verb comes at the end of a sentence, and often a sentence consists of a verb only. The verb in Korean is made up of at least one STEM and one ENDING, none of which can stand by itself. For example, let's look at a sentence in Frame 4.

조 형 있습니까? [chohyŏng issŭmnikka]	Is Mr. Cho there?

The verb stem is 있-, meaning "to exist, to be there" and the ending is -습니까, which denotes a polite question.

When any verb is discussed, cited, or listed, it is shown in the "dictionary form" (also known as the "citation form"), which consists of the STEM and the ENDING -다, as in 있다 [itta] "to be, stay."

2. Two Kinds of "Be" in English

The English verb "be" (am, is, are, etc.) has, among others, two distinct functions: one to state EXISTENCE and the other EQUATING two nominals.

a. EXISTENCE: Expressing existence or presence of something or someone at some location.

There *are* thirty people in our office.
The gas station *is* around the corner.

b. EQUATING: The subject noun is equated to another nominal: X is Y.

I *am* a student.
My name *is* Alice Harding.

Unlike English, Korean has two entirely different verbs for expressing EXISTENCE of something (있다) and for EQUATING two nominals (-이다).

3. Equating Verb: -이다

The equating verb -이다 attaches itself to the preceding nominal as though it is a mere appendix.

SUBJECT	PREDICATE	
X	Y -입니다. *-imnida*	X is Y.

• 저 [chŏ	*학생입니다.* haksaeng'imnida]	I am a student.
• 이분이 [ibuni	*김 선생입니다.* kim sŏnsaeng'imnida]	This (person) is Mr. Kim.
• 제 이름은 [che irŭmŭn	*죤 테일러입니다.* jon teilŏ imnida]	My name is John Taylor.

• 죤이야. (It's) John.
[jon iya]

Note that the stem -이 is *normally dropped* whenever the preceding nominal ends in a *vowel*. For example,

접니다. [chŏmnida]	(< 저입니다)	(It's) me.
나야. [naya]	(< 나이야)	(It's) me.

CAUTION! In English, "who" in "Who is he?" is not the subject, but the predicate. It is placed in the beginning of a sentence as all question words in English (who, what, why, when, where, etc.) are placed in the beginning. In Korean, however, the question word 누구 [nugu] is placed in the predicate.

SUBJECT	PREDICATE
이분이 [ibuni]	누굽니까? [*NUGU*-mnikka] 누구십니까? [*NUGU-shi*mnikka]

PREDICATE	SUBJECT
WHO is	this person?

The addition of 시 in the second Korean sentence above makes the expression even more polite. The suffix -시 is called an "honorific" marker, which will be explained in Section 5.

4. Existence Verb: 있다

The verb 있다 expresses the existence or presence of the subject at some location. The "honorific" form of this verb is 계시다 [keshida].

• 김 선생님 계십니까? Is Mr. Kim there?
[kim sŏnsaengnim keshimnikka]

• 계십니다. He is (there).
[keshimnida]

• 박 선생 있습니까? Mr. Pak, are you there?
[pak sŏnsaeng issŭmnikka]

• 있습니다. I am (here).
[issŭmnida]

• 영숙이 있니? Is Yŏngsuk there?
[yŏngsugi inni]

• 잘 있어! Good-bye! (Stay well.)
[chal issŏ]

5. "Honorific" Forms

There are two separate but related systems of politeness in Korean. One is the speech levels (HIGH, MID and LOW) that you already know. The other is marking a special respect to the subject of a sentence, which is called the "honorific" marking. Note the following difference between the two systems.

SPEECH LEVELS: Speaker's respect to the addressee (2nd person)
HONORIFIC FORM: Speaker's respect to the subject of a sentence (2nd or 3rd person)

What are the markers for honorific forms?

- For Verbs: The marker is -(으)시 suffixed to the stem for most verbs. (There are a small number of exceptions, such as 계시다.)

  NOTE : The vowel -(으)시 means that 으 is present only when the stem ends in a consonant. The marker also takes the form of -(으)세 as a result of combining with the ending -어요, as in 안녕하세요.

- For Nominals: The suffix -님 is suffixed to a title as in 선생님.

이 선생님 계세요?	[yi sonsaengnim keseyo]	Are you there, Mr. Yi?

- Difference between High and Mid Levels

  Basically, the honorific forms may be used on *any* level, since the subject of a sentence is not necessarily the addressee. However, when the addressee is at the same time the subject of a sentence ("you"), then the High Level speech always requires the use of HONORIFIC forms.

High Level: Honorific forms are used whenever the second person ("you") is the subject of a sentence.

Mid Level: Honorific forms are not generally used for the second person (with the exceptions noted below.)

* Exceptions:

In making a request or in greeting phrases, the honorific markers are commonly used even on the Mid Level.

안녕하세요?	How are you? (Greeting)
어서 들어오세요.	Please come right in. (Request)

READING & WRITING

1. Names of Persons

The full name (성명 Ⓜ and 성함 Ⓗ) of a person consists of the family name or surname (성) and the given name arranged in that order. Typical Korean family names are in one syllable, and there are only a handful of Korean surnames in two syllables. Korean given names are generally in two syllables. This means that the great majority of Korean full names are in three syllables; e.g., 김성기, 박민환. In each instance, the first syllable is the surname and the next two the given name. Generally no space is placed between the family name and the given name.

CAUTION! When Korean names are put into English, people use either the English order of placing the given name before the surname, such as Minho Kim, or the Korean way of placing the surname before the given name, such as Kim Minho.

2. Common Family Names in Korea

The family names (성 or 성씨) for Koreans are relatively limited in variety. There are about 300 different 성씨, of which only 40 to 50 names predominate. All family names are in Sino-Korean (loan words from Old Chinese). Listed below are common 성씨 with their common English spellings:

김	Kim	이	Lee/Yi/Rhee	박	Pak/Park	최	Choi/Choe
정	Chung	강	Kang	조	Cho	윤	Yun/Yoon
장	Chang	임	Im/Yim/Lim	한	Han	오	Oh
신	Shin	서	Suh/Soh/Seo	권	Kwon	황	Hwang
송	Song	안	Ahn/An	유	Yu/Yoo/Ryu	홍	Hong

3. Given Names in Korea

Unlike in English, given names (이름) in Korean are rich in variety. This is because 이름 is typically created by combining two Chinese characters (syllables) with preferred meanings. It is not always possible to tell a person's gender by a given name. However, names for females (여자) commonly ends with -순, -숙, -자, and -옥. Brothers often share a common syllable. For example, 인철 may very well be the brother of 순철.

- Typical names for males (남자):
  철수, 영섭, 기호, 태성, 인철
- Typical names for females (여자):
  복순, 정숙, 순자, 경옥, 선애

EXERCISE 9 The list below contains the names of Korean singers. Copy at least five names, and explain how you can tell that they are names of persons.

이번 주 ◎ Top 10 레코드

순위	제 목	가 수
1	하여가 (1)	서태지와 아이들
2	널 사랑하니까 (2)	신승훈
3	애모 (3)	김수희
4	그래도 이제는 (4)	김종서
5	너를 사랑해 (5)	한동준
6	연인 (6)	정석원
7	세상은 요지경 (9)	신신애
8	사는게 뭔지 (8)	이무송
9	이승환라이브 (7)	이승환
10	서편제 (10)	김수철

1. __________
2. __________
3. __________
4. __________
5. __________

4. Pronunciation of 외

The typical Seoul-dialect pronunciation today makes no distinction between 외 and 웨. Both are pronounced [we]. However, the standard pronunciation of 외 is considered to be [oe], which is pronounced with a lip-rounding, similar to French œ or German ü. You may pronounce the vowel either way.

EXERCISE 10 Repeat after your teacher while copying the following words.

a. 회	meeting	d. 됩니다.	It becomes ....
b. 교회	church	e. 뵙습니다.	I see ....
c. 외국	foreign country	f. 쇠	iron

5. Aspiration by ㅎ

The consonant ㅎ placed before or after another consonant creates an aspirated consonant, if that consonant is "aspiratable," e.g., 어떻게 [ŏttŏk'e] "how."

EXERCISE 11 Read aloud the following words or phrases, paying close attention to the effect of the consonant ㅎ.

a. 어떻게	how	c. 북한	North Korea
b. 안녕히 계세요.	Good-bye.	d. 박 형	Mr. Pak

6. Dictionary Arrangement of Words

In dictionaries and vocabulary lists, words are arranged according to the traditional sequence of consonants and vowels. We will review here the vowel sequence.

EXERCISE 12 Complete the dictionary sequence of vowels below.

아	야	어	여						이

EXERCISE 13 Rearrange the words below in the dictionary sequence.

a. 누구 - 나 - 너 - 기다리다 - 가다
b. 남자 - 여자 - 이름 - 미국 - 있다

EXERCISE 14 The sentences below contain one unknown word in each. Find the meanings of the unknown words, using your dictionary or the glossary at the end of this textbook. Then, give English equivalents to the sentences.

a. 아저씨가 기다립니다.
b. 제 동생을 소개합니다.
c. 교수님 계십니까?

VOCABULARY SUMMARY

Nominals

남자		male person	이름		name
누구		who	이분	Ⓗ	this person
성		surname	저	Ⓗ	I (pronoun)
성명	Ⓜ	full name	제	Ⓗ	my
성함	Ⓗ	full name	친구		friend
여자		female person	학생		student

Verbs

From this point on, each verb will be given in the "dictionary form," which consists of a stem and the ending -다. When a verb has an important variant form, it will be listed after a slash. For example, in 들어오다/들어와, the first entry 들어오다 is the dictionary form, and the second form 들어와 is a form used in Low Level speech.

계시다	to be there, exist (honorific)
기다리다	to wait
들어오다/들어와	to come in, enter
뵙다/뵈워	to see, meet (someone)
부탁하다	to ask a favor (of someone)
소개하다	to introduce
-이다/-이야	to be ... (equating)
있다	to be there, exist (existence)

Adverbs

어서	quickly (used only in urging)
잠깐	for a moment, for a short while
처음	for the first time

Idioms

성함이 어떻게 되십니까?	What is your name, please?
잘 부탁합니다.	Happy to be your friend.
처음 뵙습니다.	I'm happy to meet you.

ANSWERS TO EXERCISES

Exercise 6.

HIGH	MID	LOW
(누구십니까)	누구입니까?	누구야?
	오래간만입니다.	(오래간만이야.)
	안녕하세요?	(잘 있니?)
	어서 들어오세요.	(어서 들어와.)
	(잠깐 기다리세요.)	잠깐 기다려.

Exercise 7. A: 인철아, 있니?
B: 누구야?
A: 나야. 마이클이야.
B: 응, 어서 들어와.
A: 잘 있어?
B: 응, 오래간만이야.

Exercise 8. When the preceding noun ends with a vowel, the vowel 이 of the verb -이다 is commonly dropped. For example, 철숩니다.

Exercise 9. You can tell that they are names by the number of syllables: three syllables. Then you can determine whether the first syllable is indeed a family name. (You may check the list of common family names in Korea on page 25.)

Exercise 10. 아 야 어 여 오 요 우 유 으 이

Exercise 13. a. 가다 - 기다리다 - 나 - 너 - 누구
b. 남자 - 미국 - 여자 - 이름 - 있다

Exercise 14. a. My uncle is waiting.
b. I'd like to introduce my younger brother.
c. Is the professor in?

LESSON 3

COMING AND GOING

FRAME 1

Inviting a Guest in

권: 어서 이리 들어오세요. [ŏsŏ iri tŭrŏ oseyo]	Kwŏn: Please come in this way.
이리 앉으세요. [iri anjŭseyo]	Please sit down here.
신: 네. [ne]	Shin : Yes.
권: 커피 한 잔 하시겠어요? [kŏp'i han chan hashigessŏyo]	Kwŏn: Would you like to have a cup of coffee?
신: 네, 감사합니다. [ne kamsahamnida]	Shin : Yes, thank you.

VOCABULARY STUDY

- 들어오세요. [tŭrŏ oseyo] Please come in. (a polite request form of the verb 들어오다 "to come in/enter")
- 이리 [iri] this way, here (an adverb denoting a movement in the direction of the speaker)

•앉으세요.	[anjŭseyo]	Please sit down. (a polite request form of 앉다 "to sit down")
•커피 한 잔	[kŏp'i han chan]	a cup of coffee (커피=coffee, 한 잔=one cup)
•하시겠어요?	[hashigessŏyo]	Would you like to have...? (a polite question form asking the 2nd person's intention.) The verb 하다 "to do" means here "to eat, drink."
•감사합니다.	[kamsahamnida]	Thank you.

PERSONALIZED VOCABULARY

The words listed below are optional items for personalized exercise. Students are encouraged to commit themselves to learning at least three words that they think they encounter frequently in real life.

커피
[k'ŏp'i] coffee

사이다
[saida] soft drink (uncola)

차
[ch'a] tea

홍차
[hongch'a] Lipton tea

과일
[kwail] fruit

과자
[kwaja] sweets, confectionary

콜라
[k'olla] Coca-Cola

인삼차
[insamch'a] ginseng tea

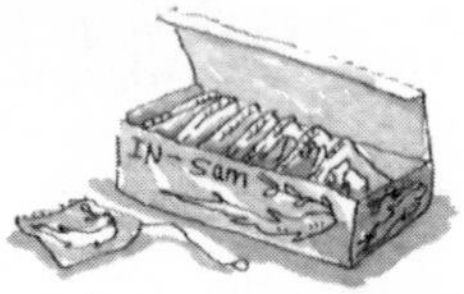

EXERCISE 1 A good friend of yours has just visited you. Greet your friend, and ask him/her to step in. Offer a seat, and ask the person if he/she would like to have something you can serve.

EXERCISE 2 You see a new verb form in the expression: 커피 한 잔 하시겠어요? Between the verb stem and the ending, you see two markers. One is the "honorific marker" and the other is the "intention marker." Show which is which by drawing arrows (⟶) below.

하 시 겠 어요?

HONORIFIC MARKER INTENTION MARKER

EXERCISE 3 Say appropriate Korean equivalents to the following English sentences.

a. Would you like to wait for a minute?
b. Are you going?
c. Would you like to come in, sir?
d. Would you like to stay?

FRAME 2

Going for an Outing

권: 주말에 무엇 하세요? [chumare muŏt haseyo]	Kwon: What are you doing this weekend?
신: 서울에 가요. [sŏure kayo]	Shin : I'm going to Seoul.
선생님은요? [sŏnsaengnimŭnyo]	How about you, ma'am?
권: 저는 인천에 가요. [chŏnŭn inch'ŏne kayo]	Kwon: I'm going to Inch'ŏn.

VOCABULARY STUDY

- •주말 [chumal] weekend
- •-에 [e] a suffix marking the time, equivalent to "at" or "in" in English.
- •무엇 [muŏt] what (The final consonant ㅅ is pronounced like [t] when it is not followed by a vowel.)
- •하세요 [haseyo] An honorific form of 하다 "to do" is 하시다.

When 하시 is followed by a common ending -어요, the result is 하세요. Here, the verb ending indicates a question even though it may indicate a statement or a request elsewhere.

•서울	[sŏul]	Seoul, the capital city of South Korea.
•-에	[e]	a suffix marking the place of destination, equivalent to "to" in English.
•가요.	[kayo]	a plain (or non-honorific) form of the verb 가다 "to go." In this case, the verb ending indicates a statement even though it may indicate a question or a request in other instances.
•선생님은요?	[sŏnsaengnimŭnyo]	How about you, sir/ma'am?

This expression is not a full sentence. It is a topic phrase with the suffix -은. The suffix -은 is a topic marker. The addition of -요 makes the phrase "polite."

•저는	[chŏnŭn]	I (1st person)

The topic marker -는 has two forms: -는 after a vowel, and -은 after a consonant.

•인천	[inch'ŏn]	Inch'ŏn, a port city near Seoul

EXERCISE 4 The instructor will read with a natural speed six sentences (in the next page). As you listen to each of them, match it with one of the following English equivalents and write in the letter a, b, c, d, e or f before the correct equivalent.

[ ] Please sit down.
[ ] Are you going?
[ ] Please wait.
[ ] Please do (have).
[ ] Are you there?
[ ] Are you waiting?

❖ IMPORTANT DISTINCTION BETWEEN 가세요 AND 가요

We will call the verb forms ending with -요, as in 가세요 [kaseyo] and 가요 [kayo], SHORT FORMS for convenience. Both verb forms (가세요 and 가요) may be used as a statement, a question, or a request. The former is honorific but the latter is plain. It means that 가세요 is used only with the 2nd or 3rd person subject, and 가요 with any person (1st, 2nd, or 3rd). Remember the honorific form (가세요) should never be used with the 1st person subject.

EXERCISE 5 Listen and repeat after your teacher.

HONORIFIC	*PLAIN*	
하세요	해요	do
가세요	가요	go
오세요	와요	come
들어오세요	들어와요	come in/enter
기다리세요	기다려요	wait
앉으세요	앉아요	sit down
계세요	있어요	stay (be there)

EXERCISE 6 Ask your partner if he/she is going to take an action, using each of the verbs listed above. Your partner will respond affirmatively.

EXAMPLE: Question: 가세요? Are you going?
Response: 네, 가요. Yes, I'm going.

SENTENCES FOR EXERCISE 4. Listening Comprehension

a. 하세요.	c. 계세요?	e. 가세요?
b. 앉으세요.	d. 기다리세요?	f. 기다리세요.

FRAME 3

Going to the Store

안: 미스 유, 집에 가요? [misŭ yu chibe kayo]	An: Miss Yu, going home?
유: 아니오, 아직 안 가요. [anio ajik an gayo]	Yu: No, not yet.
안: 그럼, 어디 가요? [kŭrŏm ŏdi kayo]	An: Then, where are you going?
유: 지금 상점에 가요. [chigŭm sangjŏme kayo]	Yu: I'm going to a store now.

VOCABULARY STUDY

- 집 [chip] home, house
- 아니오 [anio] no (interjection)
- 아직 [ajik] yet, still
- 안 가요. [an gayo] I'm not going.

  All verbs, except 있다 and -이다, may be negated by the prefix 안-, which is placed before the verb stem.
- 어디 [ŏdi] where
- 상점 [sangjŏm] store

EXERCISE 7 Ask your partner where he/she is going. Your partner will respond by choosing one of the places listed below.

집 [chip]	house	학교 [hakkyo]	school
상점 [sangjŏm]	store	식당 [sikttang]	restaurant
교회 [kyohoe]	church	극장 [kŭkchang]	theater

EXERCISE 8 You see your friend going on an errand. Choose a place from the list below, and ask your friend if he/she is going to the same place that you have picked from the list. Your partner will answer negatively, and will tell you specifically where he/she is headed.

① 집	[chip]	⑤ 호텔	[hot'el]
② 학교	[hakkyo]	⑥ 식당	[siktang]
③ 교회	[kyohoe]	⑦ 상점	[sangjŏm]
④ 극장	[kŭkchang]		

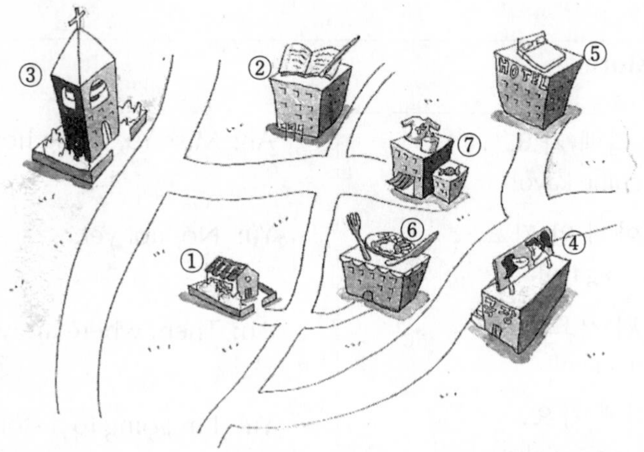

EXERCISE 9 One of your classmates will engage in small talk with your teacher (using the scripts given in the Answers to Exercises section). The rest of the class will listen and write down in English the place where he/she is going.

a. ________________ d. ________________
b. ________________ e. ________________
c. ________________ f. ________________

EXERCISE 10 You run into a friend of yours on the street. Greet your friend and then carry on short conversation, using Frame 3 as a model. (Replace the names of places as you please.)

EXERCISE 11 This time, you run into your teacher on the street. Carry on the same sort of conversation with your teacher. (Remember to take a bow and use High Level speech.)

FRAME 4

After School

미란: 순희야, 집에 안 가? [suniya chibe an ga]	Miran: Suni, aren't you going home?
순희: 응, 같이 가. [ŭng kach'i ka]	Suni : Yeah, let's go together.
미란: 너 오늘 저녁에 뭐 해? [nŏ onŭl chŏnyŏge mwŏ hae]	Miran: What are you doing this evening?
순희: 아무것도 안 해. [amugŏtto an hae]	Suni : I won't be doing anything.
미란: 그럼, 같이 극장 가자. [kŭrŏm kachi kŭchang kaja]	Miran: Then, let's go to the movies.
순희: 응, 그래. [ŭng kŭrae]	Suni : Yeah, let's do that.

VOCABULARY STUDY

•같이	[kach'i]	together
•오늘 저녁	[onŭl chŏnyŏk]	this evening (오늘=today, 저녁=evening)
•해	[hae]	a Ⓛ statement form of 하다 "to do."
•아무것도	[amugŏtto]	anything (used only in a negative sentence)
•극장	[kŭkchang]	theater, movie theater

The destination marker -에 is often omitted in spoken Korean when the noun denotes a place.

❖ SHORT VERB FORMS AND LOW LEVEL SPEECH

The suffix -요 is a polite marker. When you remove -요 from a polite short form, you get a blunt short form used in Low Level speech. Short forms may be used in any mood (either as a statement, a question or a request) with appropriate intonations.

POLITE	BLUNT	
있어요	있어	there is/are...
해요	해	do
가요	가	go
와요	와	come
들어와요	들어와	come in/enter
기다려요	기다려	wait
앉아요	앉아	sit down

EXCEPTION: The equation verb -이다 has different vowels in Polite and Blunt Short forms.

-이에요	- 이야	X is Y.

EXERCISE 12 Two classmates will engage in a series of conversation according to the scripts in the Answers to Exercises section. As you listen to each utterance, match it with one of the following English equivalents and write in the letter a, b, c, d, e, f, g or h before the correct equivalent.

[ ] Will enter the room.
[ ] Going to a restaurant.
[ ] Waiting for a friend.
[ ] Not going to school.
[ ] Will sit down.
[ ] Will not have coffee.
[ ] Staying home.
[ ] Doing nothing.

EXERCISE 13 Ask your partner in Low Level speech what he/she is doing. Your partner will respond by choosing any one of the actions listed below.

a. Waiting for a friend.
b. Going to a store.
c. Going home.
d. Doing nothing.
e. Going to movies.
f. Having coffee.

EXERCISE 14 Ask your partner if he/she is doing one of the actions listed above. Your partner will respond negatively.

EXERCISE 15 A close friend of yours has just come to visit you. Ask him/her to come in, offer him/her a seat, and ask if he/she would like to have one of the things listed below.

a. tea
b. Coca-Cola
c. ginseng tea
d. fruit
e. coffee
f. sweets

GRAMMAR

1. Verb Endings

There are two kinds of verb forms: the short and the long. The long forms are generally used in a specific mood (a statement, a question, or a request), but the short forms are versatile, and may be used in any sentence mood with appropriate intonations.

LONG FORMS	SHORT FORMS	
커피 하십니까? [k'ŏp'i hashimnikka]	커피 하세요? [k'ŏp'i haseyo]	Are you having coffee?
커피 하십니다. [k'ŏp'i hashimnida]	커피 하세요. [k'ŏp'i haseyo]	He is having coffee.
	커피 하세요. [k'ŏp'i haseyo]	Please have coffee.

2. Short Forms

The basic rules for making short forms are not very complicated, but they have a few irregularities. At this point, you will simply learn the short forms of the verbs you have covered. You will learn the rules later with more verbs.

	POLITE		BLUNT
	HONORIFIC	*PLAIN*	
Equation be	-이세요 [-iseyo]	-이에요 [-ieyo]	-이야 [-iya]
Existence be	계세요 [kyeseyo]	있어요 [issŏyo]	있어 [issŏ]
do	하세요 [haseyo]	해요 [haeyo]	해 [hae]
go	가세요 [kaseyo]	가요 [kayo]	가 [ka]
come	오세요 [oseyo]	와요 [wayo]	와 [wa]
enter	들어오세요 [tŭrŏoseyo]	들어와요 [tŭrŏwayo]	들어와 [tŭrŏwa]
wait	기다리세요 [kidariseyo]	기다려요 [kidaryŏyo]	기다려 [kidaryŏ]
sit	앉으세요 [anjŭseyo]	앉아요 [anjayo]	앉아 [anja]

❖ GENERAL CHECKUP: SHORT FORMS

a. All honorific forms end with -세요 but the verb 앉다 "to sit down" has an extra vowel -으. Guess why before you look at the answer given below.

---

b. If you remove -요 from polite plain forms, you get the blunt forms. There is one exception here. Which one?

---

c. Almost all blunt forms end with the vowel 어 or 아 except two verbs. What are they?

and

---

d. In blunt forms, the last vowel is basically 어. Under certain conditions, the last vowel changes to 아. Can you guess what conditions they are?

> Answers to Questions Above
>
> a. The verb stem 앉- ends with a consonant. The honorific suffix requires the insertion of 으 before it if the verb stem ends in a consonant. See Grammar in Lesson 2.
> b. The equational verb is an exception. After removing -요, you must change the vowel 에 to 야 to get the blunt form. Remember also that the stem vowel -이 is normally dropped when another vowel precedes.
> c. The equational verb -이야 "to be" and 해 "to do."
> d. The basic shape of the blunt form is STEM + 어, but the vowel changes to 아 if the verb stem has 아 or 오 in its last syllable. Examples: 가다 "to go," 오다 "to come," etc. The exception to the above is 하다, which becomes 해.

3. The Polite Suffix -요 Attached to a Nominal

The suffix -요 is not only attached to verbs but also to any phrases (nominals, adverbs, etc.). In Frame 2, you had a fragment of a sentence (without a verb), 선생님은요? The suffix -은 is a topic marker, and -요 is added to make the phrase polite. When you say something without a verb on HIGH or MID LEVEL, you normally add -요 at the end.

HIGH/MID LEVEL	LOW LEVEL	
어디 가세요? [ŏdi kaseyo]	어디 가? [ŏdi ka]	Where are you going?
집에요. [chibeyo]	집에. [chibe]	Home.

저 친구 기다려요. [chŏ ch'ingu kidaryŏyo]	나 친구 기다려. [na ch'ingu kidaryŏ]	I'm waiting for a friend.
누구요? [nuguyo]	누구? [nugu]	Who?

4. How to Negate a Verb

All verbs may be negated by placing 안- before the stem. It will be called the "negative prefix." There are important exceptions: the equational verb -이다 and the existence verb 있다, which will be introduced soon.

정 선생님 안 계세요. [chŏngsŏnsaengnim an keseyo]	Mr. Chŏng is not (here).
서울에 안 가요? [sŏure an kayo]	Aren't you going to Seoul?
아무것도 안 해. [amugŏtto an hae]	I'm not doing anything.
그 분 이리 안 오세요. [kŭ bun iri an oseyo]	He is not coming here.
안 앉아요? [an anjayo]	Aren't you going to sit down?
안 좋아. [an chowa]	It isn't good.

5. Postpositions or Suffixes to Nominals

Korean extensively uses suffixing. Among many suffixes, there are some that define the roles of nominals in a sentence, such as the subject, object, place, time, etc. Some suffixes are roughly equivalent to prepositions in English, but some don't have any equivalents in English. We will call such suffixes "postpositions," since they always come after nominals. In this lesson, three postpositions are introduced: the topic marker, the time marker and the destination marker.

a. Topic marker postposition

It is not easy to explain the nature of topic-marking, since in English there is no device for marking a topic. The following is a general tentative definition of the topic, but a more detailed explanation will be given later.

> The topic is a nominal that sets the premise for the rest of the sentence where the main information is given.

A topic is generally the subject of a sentence. However, the subject is not always a topic. The topic marker has two shapes: nominals ending in a consonant take -은, and those ending in a vowel -는.

선생님은 서울에 가세요? — Are you going to Seoul?
[sŏnsaengnimŭn sŏure kaseyo]

네, 저는 서울에 가요. — Yes, I am going to Seoul.
[ne chŏnŭn sŏure kayo]

영숙 씨는? — How about you, Miss Yŏngsuk?
[yŏngsukssinŭn]

b. Postposition -에 marking the time or the destination

The postposition -에 marks the time or the destination of a travel. It must be noted, however, that some phrase expressing the time and place such as 오늘 [onŭl] "today" and 어디 [ŏdi] "where," do not take -에.

주말에 뭐 하세요? — What do you do on the weekend?
[chumare mwo haseyo]

저녁에 집에 오세요. — Please come to my house tonight.
[chŏnyŏge chibe oseyo]

나 서울에 가. — I'm going to Seoul.
[na sŏure ka]

6. How to Express Intention

The expressions of intention do not require any special marking, and a simple verb (usually called the "present tense") may be used to express one's intention. However, there is also a specific intention-marking suffix in Korean, similar to "will" or "would" in English. It is placed after a verb stem with or without the honorific marker -으시.

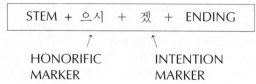

STEM + 으시 + 겠 + ENDING

(으시 ↑ HONORIFIC MARKER; 겠 ↑ INTENTION MARKER)

기다리시겠어요? — Would you like to wait?
[kidarishigessŏyo]

네, 기다리겠어요. — Yes, I would.
[ne kidarigessŏyo]

집에 있겠어? — Are you going to stay home?
[chibe ikkessŏ]

집에 있겠어. — I'm going to stay home.
[chibe ikkessŏ]

READING & WRITING

1. Major Cities in South Korea

- 서울: The capital city of South Korea is called 서울. The name originally comes from a common noun meaning "the capital." It has been known to the West with the spelling "Seoul," but make sure that you pronounce it in two syllables: [sŏ\ul]. 서울 is the only city in Korea with a name of native Korean origin. All other cities have names consisting of two or three Sino-Korean characters. 서울 has been the capital of Korea for more than six hundred years after it became the capital during the Yi Dynasty Era 이조 시대, and it abounds with historical buildings and remains among modern high-rise buildings. With a population of over ten millions, it is one of the largest cities in the world.

Downtown Seoul

- 인천: A principal port city lying to the west of 서울, 인천 has played an important role in Korea's trade with China. It became famous for the U.N. Forces landing operation during the Korean War, 육이오 사변 [yugio sabyŏn] (1950-1953).
- 수원: Situated about 20 miles south of 서울, 수원 is the capital of the Kyŏnggi Province (경기도). It is noted for old city gates.
- 대전: A provincial capital in the central region, 대전 is better known to the world as the site of the Expo 93.
- 대구: A third largest city in South Korea, 대구 is an important center for industry and education.
- 경주: An ancient city near the southeastern coast, 경주 was the capital of the kingdom of Shilla (신라), one of the three kingdoms in the third century, which eventually unified Korea in 668 A.D. A magnificent old Buddhist temple, Pulguksa (불국사), is located in its vicinity.

• 광주: A provincial capital and the largest city of the southwestern region, 광주 is an important center for agriculture, industry and education.
• 부산: The second largest city and a major port city in South Korea, 부산 is located on the southeastern tip of the Korean peninsula. It has been the most important foreign trade center.

EXERCISE 16 Write in the names of the Korean cities.

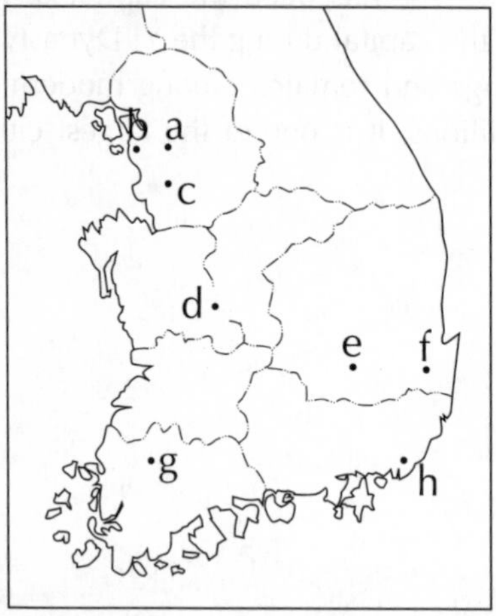

a. Seoul ------------------------------------
b. Inch'ŏn ---------------------------------
c. Suwon-----------------------------------
d. Taejŏn ----------------------------------
e. Taegu------------------------------------
f. Kyŏngju----------------------------------
g. Kwangju ---------------------------------
h. Pusan------------------------------------

2. Words Ending in ㅅ

Words ending in ㅅ, such as 무엇 "what," 아무것 "anything," etc. have the following peculiarities:

a. When nothing follows or when a suffix beginning with a consonant follows, ㅅ is not released and pronounced like [t].

무엇	[muŏt]	what
아무것	[amugŏt]	anything

b. When a suffix beginning with the vowel is attached, ㅅ is fully pronounced as [s] or [sh].

무엇이	[muŏshi]	what-(SUFFIX)
아무것이나	[amugŏshina]	anything-(SUFFIX)

EXERCISE 17 Read aloud the following words, paying close attention to the pronunciation of ㅅ.

a. 무엇	what
b. 이것	this thing
c. 아무것도 아닙니다.	It's nothing. (HIGH/MID)
d. 아무것이나 좋아요.	Anything will do. (HIGH/MID)
e. 무엇이	what
f. 이것이	this thing

3. Compound Vowels in Korean Dictionaries

The traditional sequence of vowels (아, 야, 어, 여, 오, 요, 우, 유, 으, 이) does not include some vowels and diphthongs, such as 애, 에, 와, etc. It is because they are considered compound vowels consisting of two or more vowels. Therefore, it is necessary for you to know what these compound vowels are made up of.

애 = 아+이	얘 = 야+이	에 = 어+이	예 = 여+이
와 = 오+아	왜 = 오+애	외 = 오+이	
워 = 우+어	웨 = 우+에	위 = 우+이	
의 = 으+이			

In dictionaries and vocabulary lists, words consisting of compound vowels are placed after the first vowel of the given compound vowel. For example, 애, consisting of 아 and 이, is placed after all words beginning with 아 are exhaustively listed.

EXERCISE 18 Rearrange the compound vowels below in the dictionary sequence.

외 - 에 - 위 - 왜 - 예 - 애

EXERCISE 19 Rearrange the words below in the dictionary sequence.

쉬다 - 색 - 쇠 - 괜찮다 - 계시다 - 과일

4. Double Consonants in Korean Dictionaries

Where is 까 found in a Korean dictionary? It is found after all words beginning with the syllable 가 are exhaustively listed. In other words, when you look for a word beginning with a double consonant, you have to take the first syllable as a unit rather than the first consonant.

EXERCISE 20 The sentences below contain one unknown word in each. Find the meanings of unknown words using your dictionary or the glossary at the end of this textbook. Then, give English equivalents to the sentences.

a. 개 있습니까?
b. 커피 또 하세요?
c. 빨리 오세요.

VOCABULARY SUMMARY

Nominals

극장	theater
무엇	what
상점	store
서울	Seoul (the capital of South Korea)
아무것도	anything (used only in a negative sentence)
어디	where
오늘	today
저녁	evening

주말	weekend	집	house, home
커피	coffee	한 잔	one cup

Personalised Vocabulary

과일	fruit	과자	cookies, sweets
교회	church	사이다	soft drink (uncola)
식당	restaurant	인삼차	ginseng tea
차	tea	콜라	Coca-Cola
호텔	hotel	홍차	Lipton tea

Verbs

앉다 / 앉아	to sit down	오다/와	to come
하다/해	to do; to have (eat/drink)		

Adverbs

같이	together	아직	yet, still
이리	this way	지금	now

Others

감사합니다.	Thank you.	아니오	no (Ⓛ: 아니)
안-	a negative prefix	-에	in/at/on (time marker); to (destination maker)
-은 / 는	a topic marker		

ANSWERS TO EXERCISES

Exercise 2. HONORIFIC MARKER → 시 INTENTION MARKER →겠

Exercise 3.
a. 잠깐 기다리시겠어요?
b. 가시겠어요?
c. 들어오시겠어요?
d. 계시겠어요?

Exercise 4.
[b] [a]
[e] [c]
[f] [d]

Exercise 9.
a. 선생: 지금 어디가요?
학생: 식당에 가요.
b. 선생: 집에 가요?
학생: 아니오. 교회에 가요.
c. 선생: 주말에 서울에 가요?
학생: 아니오. 서울에 안 가요.
선생: 그럼, 어디 가요?
학생: 인천에 가요.
d. 선생: 상점에 가요?
학생: 아니오. 학교에 가요.
e. 선생: 미스 유, 어디 가요?
학생: 저 지금 극장에 가요.
f. 선생: 집에 안 가요?
학생: 네. 선생님은 안 가세요?
선생: 나도 집에 가요.
학생: 안녕히 가세요.

Exercise 12. a. 학생 A: 어디 가?
학생 B: 식당에 가.
b. 학생 A: 지금 학교에 가?
학생 B: 아니, 아직 안 가.
c. 학생 A: 누구 기다려?
학생 B: 친구 기다려.
d. 학생 A: 영식아, 오래간만이야.
학생 B: 응, 오래간만이야.
학생 A: 이리 앉아.
e. 학생A: 커피 한 잔 하겠어?
학생B: 나 커피 안 해.
f. 학생A: 오늘 무엇 해?
학생B: 아무것도 안 해.
g. 학생A: 오늘 저녁에 어디 가?
학생B: 집에 있어.
h. 학생A: 미란아, 잘 있니?
학생B: 어서 들어와.
학생A: 응.

[h]
[a]
[c]
[b]
[d]
[e]
[g]
[f]

Exercise 16. a. 서울
b. 인천
c. 수원
d. 대전
e. 대구
f. 경주
g. 광주
h. 부산

Exercise 18. 애-에-예-왜-외-위

Exercise 19. 계시다-과일-괜찮다-색-쇠-쉬다

Exercise 20. a. dog b. again c. quick(ly)

LESSON 4
LOOKING FOR THINGS

FRAME 1

Looking for Something

양선: 선주 씨, 연필 있으세요? [sŏnjussi yŏnp'il issŭseyo]	Yangsŏn: Do you have a pencil, Miss Sŏnju?
선주: 없어요. 제 볼펜 쓰세요. [ŏpsŏyo che polp'en ssŭseyo]	Sŏnju : I don't. Use my ballpoint pen, please.
여기 있어요. [yŏgi issŏyo]	Here it is.
양선: 고맙습니다. [komapsŭmnida]	Yangsŏn: Thank you.
잠깐 쓰겠어요. [chamkkan ssŭgessŏyo]	I'll use it for a minute.

VOCABULARY STUDY

- 연필 [yŏnp'il] pencil
- 있으세요? [issŭseyo] Do you have...?

  When the verb 있다 is used in the sense of "have," the honorific form is 있으세요, not 계세요.
- 없다 [ŏptta] there isn't / don't have

This is the negative of 있다 "to have."

•볼펜	[polp'en]	ballpoint pen
•쓰다/써	[ssŭda/ssŏ]	to use; to write
•고맙습니다.	[komapssŭmnida]	Thank you. (=감사합니다)
•여기	[yŏgi]	here

NOTE ON VERB CITATION: In citing stem-changing verbs (such as 쓰다/써 above), the blunt form will be listed after the dictionary form and a slash. See Grammar on how to use this information.

❖ 있으세요/있어요/없어요. "DO YOU HAVE … / DON'T HAVE"

The existence verb 있다 [itta] and its negative 없다 [ŏptta] have an important secondary meaning: "one has …/ one does not have …" If the verb 있다 or 없다 is used for this secondary meaning, the sentence will have actually two subjects—subject 1 being the person who "has …" and subject 2 the thing that the person has.

SUBJECT 1	SUBJECT 2	VERB	
선주 씨 [sŏnjussi	연필 yŏnp'il	있으세요? issuseyo]	Do you have a pencil, Miss Sŏnju?
저 [chŏ	연필 yŏnp'il	없어요. ŏpsŏyo]	I don't have a pencil.

CAUTION! The honorific form of 있다 in this usage ("have") is 있으세요, not 계세요.

EXERCISE 1 Ask your partner if he/she has any of the things below. Your partner will respond factually.

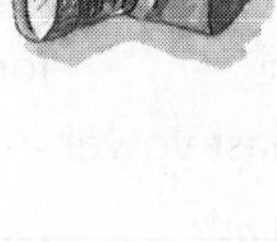

EXERCISE 2 Choose one of the objects shown above, and ask your partner if he/she is using it. Your partner will respond negatively and then make an offer, saying "Please use mine."

EXAMPLE: 카메라 쓰세요?
[k'amera ssŭseyo]

아니오, 안 써요. 제것 쓰시지요.
[anio an ssŏyo chekkŏt ssŭshijiyo]

> NOTE: The verb 쓰다 drops its vowel 으 whenever it is followed by a vowel. Note the different vowels between the polite form and the plain form.
>
> 쓰세요 (POLITE) 써요 (PLAIN)
> [ssŭ-seyo] [ssŏyo]

FRAME 2

Looking for Today's Paper

유: 오늘 신문 있어요? [onŭl shinmun issŏyo]	Yu : Do you have today's paper?
김: 아니오, 없어요. [anio ŏpsŏyo]	Kim : No, I don't.
유: 저것은 무엇입니까? [chŏgŏsŭn muŏshimnikka]	Yu : What is that one?
오늘 것이 아닙니까? [onŭl kkŏsi animnikka]	Isn't that today's?
김: 어제 것입니다. [ŏje kkŏshimida]	Kim : That's yesterday's.

VOCABULARY STUDY

- 신문 [shinmun] newspaper
- 저것은 [chŏgŏsŭn] that (with the topic marker -은)
- -것 [-gŏt/kkŏt] (a certain) thing
- 오늘 것 [onŭl kkŏt] today's one (= a certain thing)

The last vowel -이 in 오늘 것이 is the nominative marker.

- 아닙니까? [animnikka] Isn't it?
- 어제 [ŏje] yesterday
- 어제 것 [ŏje kkŏt] yesterday's one

❖ 이것이/저것이 무엇입니까? "WHAT IS THIS/THAT?"

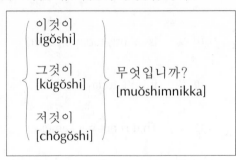

이것이 [igŏshi] 그것이 [kŭgŏshi] 저것이 [chŏgŏshi]	무엇입니까? [muŏshimnikka]	What is this? / that? (near you) / that? (over there)

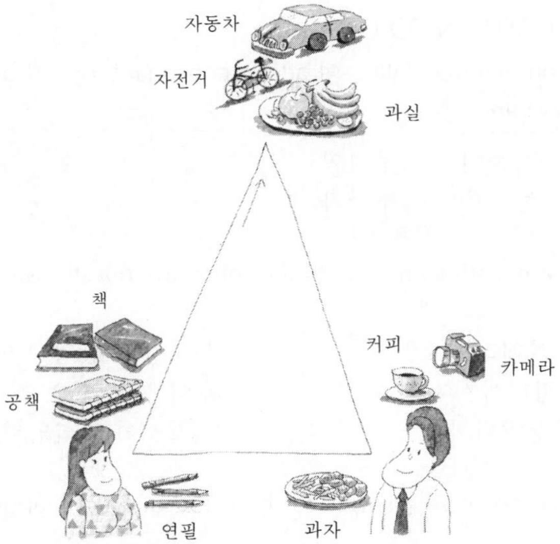

EXERCISE 3 Place various objects (or pictures) that you can name in Korean in three different locations: one near you, another near your partner, and still another away from both of you. Engage in the question-answer practice to identify things.

EXAMPLE: 이것이 무엇입니까?
그것은 연필입니다.

NOTE: The subject marker (-이) may or may not be used. If this is not used, the last consonant ㅅ must be pronounced like [t].

❖ NEGATIVE OF EQUATION VERB: 아니다

The negative of an equation sentence has a unique construction as shown below. Ⓟ below stands for an appropriate postposition, e.g., 은, 는, 이, 가.

SUBJECT	PREDICATE		
X + Ⓟ	Y + Ⓟ	아니다	X is not Y.

저분은 [chŏbunŭn	선생님이 sŏnsaengnimi	아니십니다. anishimnida]	Ⓗ	That person is not a teacher.
이것 [igŏt	오늘 신문 onŭl shinmŭn	아닙니까? animnikka]	Ⓗ Ⓜ	Isn't this today's paper?
	오늘 것이 [onŭl kkŏshi	아니예요. aniyeyo]	Ⓗ Ⓜ	It isn't today's.
저것 [chŏgŏt	내 카메라가 nae k'ameraga	아니야. aniya]	Ⓛ	That is not my camera.

❖ WHAT POSTPOSITION TO USE

The predicate nominal may take -이 after a consonant, or -가 after a vowel, just like the subject. For example,

선생님<u>이</u>, 신문<u>이</u>, 무엇<u>이</u>
카메라<u>가</u>, 선주<u>가</u>, 누구<u>가</u>

EXERCISE 4 Give negative answers to the following questions, using the long form 아닙니다.

a. 이것 미스 리 카메라예요?
b. 저 사람 학생입니까?
c. 저 분이 박 선생입니까?
d. 오늘 주말입니까?
e. 이 신문이 오늘 것입니까?
f. 저것이 교회입니까?

EXERCISE 5 Give negative answers to the same questions above, using the short form (아니예요).

FRAME 3

Talking on an English Magazine

조: 이것 영어 잡지 아니예요?
[igŏt yŏng'ŏ chapchi aniyeyo]
Cho: Isn't this an English magazine?

한: 네. 보세요.
[ne poseyo]
Han: Yes, it is. Take a look.

조: 나 영어 못 읽어요.
[na yŏng'ŏ mot ilgŏyo]
Cho: I can't read English.

영어 공부해요?
[yŏng'ŏ kongbuhaeyo]
Are you learning English?

한: 네, 그런데 아직 잘 못합니다.
[ne kŭrŏnde ajik chal mot' amnida]
Han: Yes. But I can't speak it well yet.

VOCABULARY STUDY

- •영어 [yŏng'ŏ] English (language)
- •잡지 [chapchi] magazine
- •보다/봐 [poda/pwa] to see, look at, take a look
- •못- [mod/mot-] can't, be unable to

  This is a negative prefix, which precedes the verb, e.g., 못 하다, 못 보다.
- •읽다 [iktta] to read

  The consonant ㄹ of 읽 is pronounced only when a vowel follows the stem.
- •공부하다/해 [kongbu hada/hae] to study, learn

  공부 is also a noun denoting the act or process of studying.
- •그런데 [kŭrŏnde] but; by the way

❖ NAMES OF LANGUAGES (Personalized Vocabulary)

The name of a language is obtained by adding 말 or -어 (both meaning "language" or "speech") to the name of a country. But some languages are usually shortened, as in 영어 and 불어.

COUNTRY		LANGUAGE			
한국 [hanguk]	Korea	한국어 [hangug-ŏ]	or	한국말 [hangung-mal]	Korean
중국 [chungguk]	China	중국어 [chungug-ŏ]	or	중국말 [chunggung-mal]	Chinese
일본 [ilbon]	Japan	일본어 [ilbon-ŏ]	or	일본말 [lbon-mal]	Japanese
미국 [miguk]	USA	영어 [yŏng-ŏ]	or	미국말 [migung-mal]	English (American)
영국 [yŏngguk]	England	영어 [yŏng-ŏ]	or	영국말 [yŏnggung-mal]	English (British)
프랑스 [p'ŭrangsŭ]	France	불어 [pur-ŏ]	or	프랑스말 [p'ŭrangsŭ-mal]	French
독일 [togil]	Germany	독일어 [togil-ŏ]	or	독일말 [togil-mal]	German

EXERCISE 6 Ask your partner if he/she speaks any of the above languages.

EXAMPLE: 한국어 하세요? [hangugŏ haseyo]

네, 좀/조금 해요. [ne chom/chogŭm haeyo]
아뇨, 못합니다. [anyo mot'amnida.]

EXERCISE 7 Ask your partner if he/she reads any of the languages listed above.

EXERCISE 8 Ask your partner if he/she is studying Korean, and if he/she speaks it.

FRAME 4

Talking on a French Book

미란: 이거 불어책 아니야? Miran: Isn't this a French book?
[igŏ purŏ chaek aniya]
불어 읽어? Do you read French?
[purŏ ilgŏ]
순희: 잘 못 읽어. Suni : I can't read it well.
[chal mot ilgŏ]
미란: 말 좀 해? Miran: Do you speak a little?
[mal chom hae]
순희: 조금만. Suni : Just a little.
[chogŭmman]

VOCABULARY STUDY

- 이거 [igŏ] this (a contracted form of 이것)
  The final ㅅ of -것 and of 무엇 is commonly dropped in colloquial speech, as in 이거, 그거, 저거, and 무어.
- 불어 [purŏ] French (language)
- 책 [chaek] book
- 말 [mal] speech, word, language

- 말하다/해 [malhada/hae] to speak
  The verb 하다 alone without 말 is used to mean "speak" when the context makes it clear. For example, 영어(를) 하다.
- 좀/조금 [chom/chogŭm] a little, somewhat
- -만 [man] just, merely, only

EXERCISE 9 Practice the same items contained in Exercises 6, 7 and 8 in Low Level speech.

GRAMMAR

1. Subject and Topic

In Korean, the subject of a sentence is freely omitted whenever it is obviously understood. However, when the subject is mentioned, there are three forms that it may possibly take.

a. Bare Nominal: In the conversational style (as opposed to the written), the subject of a simple sentence is generally a bare nominal taking no postposition.

김 형 서울에 가세요. — Mr. Kim is going to Seoul.
[kim hyŏng sŏure kaseyo]

b. Focused Subject: When the subject carries the main point of message (i.e., when the predicate is understood), it takes the subject postposition.

SUBJECT	ending in a consonant: - 이 ending in a vowel: - 가

김 형이	서울에 가세요.	Mr. Kim is going to Seoul.
[kim hyŏng'i	sŏure kaseyo]	(It is Mr. Kim who is going to Seoul.)
⇧	⇧	
MESSAGE (Focused)	BACKGROUND (Someone is going to Seoul.)	

c. Topical Subject: When the subject is the topic at the same time, it takes the topical postposition.

TOPIC	ending in a consonant: -은 ending in a vowel: -는

김 형은	서울에 가세요.	Mr. Kim is going to Seoul.
[kim hyŏng'ŭn	sŏure kaseyo]	(As for Mr. Kim, he is going to Seoul.)
⇧	⇧	
BACKGROUND	MESSAGE (Focused)	

- *What is a topic?* The topic is a word that sets the premise or background for the rest of the sentence. This means that (1) the topic is NOT a focal point of message but (2) it is either new in the immediate context or a reminder of the topic for the addressee.

2. Negative Verbs : A Summary

Four negative forms are so far introduced: 안-, 못-, 아니다, and 없다. The first two negatives may be used with almost all verbs except the equation verb and the existence verb.

a. Flat Negation: **안 + VERB**

This prefix simply negates all verbs but those that express equation and existence.

아직 <u>안</u> 가요? [ajik an kayo]	Aren't you going yet?
나 아무것도 안 해. [na amugŏtto an hae]	I'm not doing anything.

b. Lack of Ability: **못 + VERB**

This prefix is equivalent to "can't" or "be unable to" in English.

지금 상점에 <u>못</u> 가요. [chigŭm sangjŏme mot kayo]	I can't go to the store now.
불어 <u>못</u> 합니다. [purŏ mot hamnida]	I can't speak French.

CAUTION! The consonat ㅅ of 못- is always pronounced like ㄷ.

c. Negative Equation Verb:

X + Ⓟ	Y + Ⓟ	아니다

To negate the equation verb, a unique negative construction is required. The predicate nominal (Y above) takes the same postposition as the subject marker (-이 after a consonant, and -가 after a vowel), and the negative verb 아니다 is used.

이것<u>은</u> 오늘 신문<u>이</u> 아닙니다. [igŏsŭn onŭl shinmuni animnida]	This is not today's newspaper.
저것<u>이</u> 제 카메라<u>가</u> 아니예요. [chŏgŏshi che k'ameraga anyieyo]	That isn't my camera.
저분<u>이</u> 박민수 씨<u>가</u> 아닙니까? [chŏbuni pakminsussiga animnikka]	Isn't that Mr. Minsu Pak?
저 아이<u>가</u> 영철<u>이</u> 아니야? [chŏ aiga yŏngch'ŏri aniya]	Isn't he Yungchŏl?

d. Negative Existence Verb: **없다**

The negative of 있다 is expressed by 없다. The consonant of ㅅ is pronounced only when a vowel follows the stem.

연필 없어요. [yŏnp'il ŏpssŏyo]	I don't have a pencil.

민주 씨 여기 없어요. Minju is not here.
[minjussi yŏgi ŏpssŏyo]

3. Double Subjects for the 있다/없다 Construction

The verb 있다, which denotes that there *is* someone or something, may be also used to state that someone *has* .... Likewise the verb 없다 may be used to state that someone *has not* .... The 있다/없다 construction with this secondary meaning has two subjects: the first subject refers to the *person* who has/has not and the second subject to the *thing* being had.

SUBJECT 1	SUBJECT 2	VERB		
선생님 [sŏnsaengnim	연필 yŏnp'il	있으세요? issŭseyo]	Ⓗ	Do you have a pencil?
	커피 [k'ŏp'i	없어요? issŏyo]	Ⓜ	Don't you have coffee?
너 [nŏ	볼펜 polp'en	있어? issŏ]	Ⓛ	Do you have a ballpoint pen?

CAUTION! When the verbs 있다 and 없다 are used in the original sense ("be"), the honorific forms are 계시다 and 안계시다. But when the verbs are used in the sense of "have," the honorific forms are 있으시다 and 없으시다, respectively.

HONORIFIC FORMS	(1) "to be"	(2) "to have"
Affirmative	계시다	있으시다
Negative	안 계시다	없으시다

선생님 안 계세요. He isn't here.
[sŏnsaengnim an geseyo]

선생님 자동차 없으세요? Don't you have a car?
[sŏnsaengnim chadongch'a ŏpsŭseyo]

4. Verb Forms: A Summary

A Korean sentence ends with a verb, which in turn ends with one of many types of verb endings. Now that you have covered a fair number of verbs, it is time to review and summarize verb forms. It has already been noted that there are long and short forms. Long forms are used with specific modes: -ㅂ니다 and -습니다 for statements, and -ㅂ니까 and -습니까 for questions. On the other hand, short forms are used in any mood (as a statement, a question, or a request) with appropriate intonations.

a. General Rules for LONG FORMS

(1) When a consonant precedes, add -습니다 or -습니까?
(2) When a vowel precedes, add -ㅂ니다 or -ㅂ니까?

Since there are very few irregularities in long forms, examples are given below rather than an exhaustive listing.

어디 가십니까?	Where are you going?
저분 고 선생 아닙니까?	Isn't that Mr. Ko?
친구 소개합니다.	I'd like to introduce my friend.
고맙습니다.	Thank you.
커피 하시겠습니까?	Would you like to have coffee?

b. General Rules for SHORT FORMS

(1) Add the ending	-어요 for High or Mid Level -어 for Low Level
(2) Change -어 to -아, if the last vowel of the stem is 아 or 오.	

Vowel contractions: Since the ending -어요 may be suffixed to a stem ending in a vowel, it often entails a succession of two vowels (after the above rules). Such successions of two vowels are generally contracted into one syllable, as you see in the list of short forms below. There are, of course, some irregular verbs.

❖ LIST OF VERBS IN SHORT FORMS

		Honorific	Plain	Blunt
(1) Equation and Existence Verbs				
-이다 [-ida]	be	-이세요 [-iseyo]	-이에요 [-ieyo]	-이야 [-iya]
아니다 [anida]	not be	아니세요 [aniseyo]	아니예요 [aniyeyo]	아니야 [aniya]
있다 [itta]	exist	계세요 [keseyo]	있어요 [issŏyo]	있어 [issŏ]
	have	있으세요 [issŭseyo]	있어요 [issŏyo]	있어 [issŏ]
없다 [ŏptta]	not exist	안계세요 [ankeseyo]	없어요 [ŏpssŏyo]	없어 [ŏpssŏ]
	not have	없으세요 [ŏpssŭseyo]	없어요 [ŏpssŏyo]	없어 [ŏpssŏ]
(2) Action Verbs				
하다 [hada]	do	하세요 [haseyo]	해요 [haeyo]	해 [hae]
가다 [kada]	go	가세요 [keseyo]	가요 [kayo]	가 [ka]
오다 [oda]	come	오세요 [oseyo]	와요 [wayo]	와 [wa]

들어오다 [tŭrŏoda]	enter	들어오세요 [tŭrŏoseyo]	들어와요 [tŭrŏwayo]	들어와 [tŭrŏwa]
보다 [poda]	see	보세요 [poseyo]	봐요 [pwayo]	봐 [pwa]
앉다 [antta]	sit down	앉으세요 [anjŭseyo]	앉아요 [anjayo]	앉아 [anja]
읽다 [iktta]	read	읽으세요 [ilgŭseyo]	읽어요 [ilgŏyo]	읽어 [ilgŏ]
쓰다 [ssŭda]	use;write	쓰세요 [ssŭseyo]	써요 [ssŏyo]	써 [ssŏ]
기다리다 [kidarida]	wait	기다리세요 [kidariseyo]	기다려요 [kidaryŏyo]	기다려 [kidaryŏ]

(3) "하다" Verbs: Even though these verbs are classified separately, they are actually compounds of a noun and the verb 하다. Accordingly, their conjugations are the same as that of the verb 하다, one of the ation verbs above.

부탁하다 [put'akáda]	ask a favor
소개하다 [sogaehada]	introduce
공부하다 [kongbuhada]	study, learn
말하다 [malhada]	speak, say

5. Why List the Blunt Form

Problems in learning verb forms are mostly for those verbs that change the shapes of the stems, especially when the ending -어요 or -어 is used as in 하세요, 해요 and 해. Let us call such verbs "stem-changing" verbs. Some changes are regular and some irregular. However, for ease of learning, we will list two basic forms (the dictionary form and the blunt form) whenever a new stem-changing verb is introduced in the Vocabulary Study section. For example,

쓰다/써 — to use; to write

↙ ↘

DICTIONARY FORM — *BLUNT FORM*

The first is the dictionary form showing that 쓰 is the basic form of the stem, and the second 써- is the blunt form. This means that you will use 쓰- for most cases except when the ending begins with the vowel 어, as in -어요 and -어.

READING & WRITING

1. The East: 동양

For Koreans in the past, the world 세계 [sege] was supposed to be divided into two large parts: the East 동양 [tong'yang] and the West 서양 [sŏyang]. The word 동양 literally means "Eastern Seas." It is also called 아세아 [asea] "Asia" or 동아 [tong'a] "East Asia."

EXERCISE 10 Read aloud the names of countries in the map below, and write them in Hangŭl.

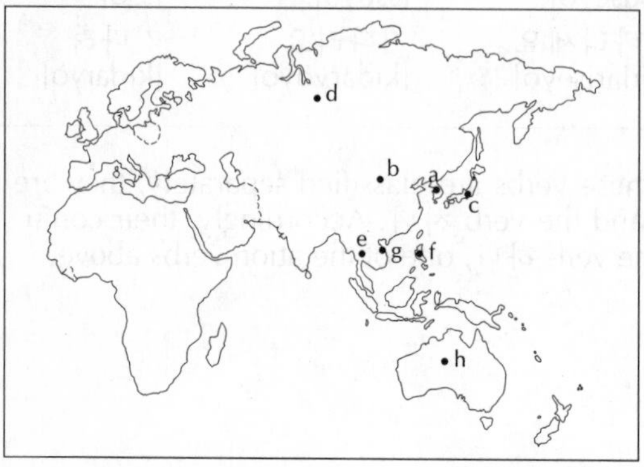

a. Korea__________________________

b. China __________________________

c. Japan __________________________

d. Russia__________________________

e. Taiwan__________________________

f. The Philippines ______________

g. Vietnam _______________________

h. Australia______________________

2. The West : 서 양

The term 서양 "West" literally means "Western Seas," and it vaguely refers to Europe and America. By Koreans Europe is called 구라파 [kurap'a] or 유럽 [yurŏp], and America is called 미국 [miguk] or 아메리카 [amerik'a].

EXERCISE 11 Read aloud the names of countries in 서양, and write them in Hangŭl.

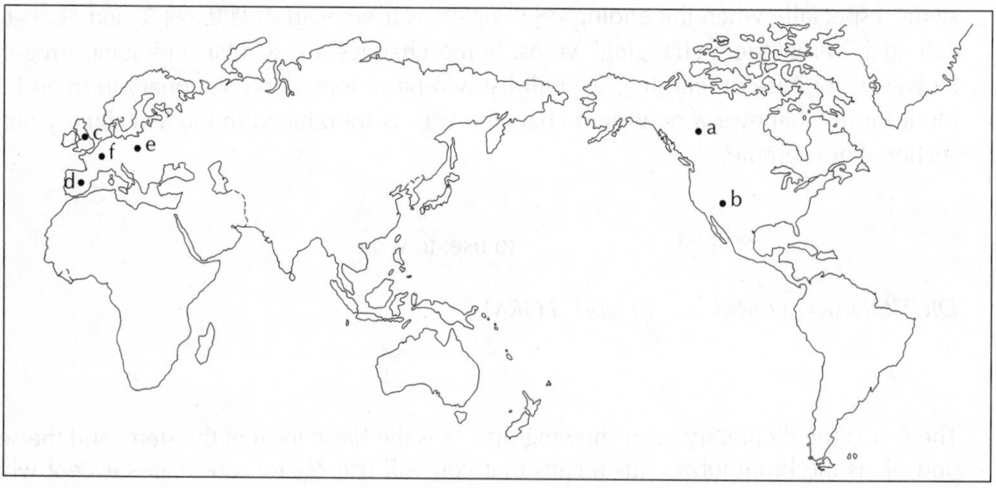

a. Canada _____________________ c. England ________________ e. Germany ______________

b. U.S.A. ______________________ d. Spain __________________ f. France _________________

3. Names of Languages

The word for "language" is 언어 [ŏnŏ] or more informally 말. The name of a language is formed simply by suffixing -어 or -말 to the country's name. Both -어 and -말 means "speech" or "language." The former is somewhat more formal than the latter.

한국어	[hangugŏ]	or	한국말	[hangungmal]	Korean
중국어	[chunggugŏ]	or	중국말	[chunggungmal]	Chinese
일본어	[ilbonŏ]	or	일본말	[ilbonmal]	Japanese

The foreign languages 외국어 [oegugŏ] are taught from secondary schools in Korea. (Some elementary schools in large cities have started English programs.) The first 외국어 that students learn in schools is English, and the second 외국어 for students is French, German, Chinese or Japanese.

EXERCISE 12 Complete the following sentences by filling in the spaces provided. The suffix - 에서 means "in."

a. 미국에서 ______ 씁니다.
b. 독일에서는 ______ 합니다.
c. 프랑스에서 ______ 해요.
d. 중국에서 ______ 써요.
e. 카나다에서 ______ 씁니다.
f. 멕시코에서 ______ 해요.

4. Verb Stems Ending in Two Consonants

Some verb stems end in two consonants in spelling. In such cases, one of the two consonants is silent unless a vowel follows. When a suffix beginning with a vowel follows, the last consonant is moved to the next syllable in pronunciation. You have learned three verbs of this type so far. The backslashes in the following indicate syllabic divisions.

DICTIONARY FORMS	MEANING	LONG FORMS	SHORT FORMS	
없다 [ŏp\ta]	not exist	없습니다 [ŏp\sŭm\ni\da]	없어요 [ŏp\sŏ\yo]	없으세요 [ŏp\sŭ\se\yo]
읽다 [ik\ta]	read	읽습니다 [ik\sŭm\ni\da]	읽어요 [il\gŏ\yo]	읽으세요 [il\gu\se\yo]
앉다 [an\ta]	sit	앉습니다 [an\sŭmnida]	앉아요 [an\ja\yo]	앉으세요 [an\jŭ\se\yo]

CAUTION! Which of the two consonants is silent is determined by the particular combination of consonants. It is not always the last of two that is silent.

5. Pronunciation of 못-

The pronunciation of ㅅ in the negative prefix 못- is [t/d] except when followed by another ㅅ.

못갑니다	[motkamnida]	can't go
못기다립니다	[motkidarimnida]	can't wait
못합니다	[mot'amnida]	can't do
못옵니다	[modomnida]	can't come

못읽습니다	[modiksŭmnida]	can't read
못있습니다	[modissŭmnida]	can't stay
못씁니다	[mossŭmnida]	can't use/write

EXERCISE 13 Complete the following list of verbs by filling in the missing forms (Honorific and Plain) on HIGH and MID Levels.

DICTIONARY FORMS	LONG FORMS *Honorific*	LONG FORMS *Plain*	SHORT FORMS *Honorific*	SHORT FORMS *Plain*
-이다	-이십니다			-이에요
아니다	아니십니다		아니세요	
있다		있습니다	계세요	
없다	안계십니다		없으세요	
하다	하십니다			없어요
가다		갑니다	가세요	
오다	오십니다			와요
보다		봅니다	보세요	
앉다	앉으십니다		앉으세요	
읽다		읽습니다		읽어요
쓰다		씁니다	쓰세요	
기다리다	기다리십니다			기다려요

VOCABULARY SUMMARY

Nominals

공책	notebook	어제	yesterday
구라파/유럽	Europe	여기	here, this place
동양	East, Orient	연필	pencil
무엇	what	영어	English
볼펜	ballpoint pen	잡지	magazine
서양	West	책	book
신문	newspaper	한국어/한국말	Korean language

Personalized Vocabulary

• Personal possessions

개	dog	자전거	bicycle
라디오	radio	카메라	camera
자동차	automobile	컴퓨터	computer

• Languages

독일어	German	언어	language
불어	French	외국어	foreign language
세계	world	일본어	Japanese
-어	language (suffix)	중국어	Chinese

Verbs

공부하다/해	to study, learn
말하다/해	to speak
보다/봐	to see, look at
쓰다/써	to use; to write
아니다	nagative of -이다
없다	negative of 있다 (ㅅ of 없 is pronounced only when a vowel follows the stem.)
읽다	to read (ㄹ of 읽 is pronounced only when a vowel follows the stem.)

Adverbs

좀/조금	a little, somewhat

Others

고맙습니다	Thank you. (= 감사합니다)
-것	thing (always preceded by a modifier)
그-	that... (pointing to something near the addressee)
그런데	but, however, by the way
-만	just, merely, only (postposition)
못-	cannot, unable to (negative prefix)
이-	this... (pointing to something near the speaker)
저-	that... (pointing to something away from the speaker)

ANSWERS TO EXERCISES

Exercise 4.
a. 이것 미스 리 카메라 아닙니다.
b. 저 사람 학생 아닙니다.
c. 저분 박선생 아닙니다.
d. 오늘 주말 아닙니다.
e. 이 신문 오늘 것 아닙니다.
f. 저것 교회 아닙니다.

Exercise 5.
a. 이것 미스리 카메라 아니예요.
b. 저 사람 학생 아니예요.
c. 저분 박선생 아니예요.
d. 오늘 주말 아니예요.
e. 이 신문 오늘 것 아니예요.
f. 저것 교회 아니예요.

Exercise 10. a. 한국 b. 중국 c. 일본 d. 러시아 e. 대만 f. 필린핀 g. 월남 h. 호주

Exercise 11. a.카나다 b.미국 c.영국 d.스페인 e.독일 f.프랑스

Exercise 12. a.영어 b.독일어 c.불어/프랑스어 d.중국어 e.영어 f.스페인어

Exercise 13.

DICTIONARY FORMS	LONG FORMS Honorific	Plain	SHORT FORMS Honorific	Plain
-이다	-이십니다	-입니다	-이세요	-이예요
아니다	아니십니다	아닙니다	아니세요	아니에요
있다	계십니다	있습니다	계세요	있어요
없다	안 계십니다	없습니다	안 계세요	없어요
하다	하십니다	합니다	하세요	해요
가다	가십니다	갑니다	가세요	가요
오다	오십니다	옵니다	오세요	와요
보다	보십니다	봅니다	보세요	봐요
앉다	앉으십니다	앉습니다	앉으세요	앉아요
읽다	읽으십니다	읽습니다	읽으세요	읽어요
쓰다	쓰십니다	씁니다	쓰세요	써요
기다리다	기다리십니다	기다립니다	기다리세요	기다려요

LESSON 5
LEARNING A FOREIGN LANGUAGE

FRAME 1

Attending a Language School

최: 미스 한, 저녁에 바쁘세요?
[misŭ han chŏnyŏge pappŭseyo]

한: 네, 요즈음 좀 바빠요.
[ne yojŭŭm chom pappayo]

외국어 학원에 다녀요.
[oegugŏ hagwŏne tanyŏyo]

최: 그래요? 어느 나라 말 배우세요?
[kŭraeyo ŏnŭ nara mal paeuseyo]

한: 중국어요.
[chunggugŏyo]

71Ch'oe: Are you busy in the evening, Miss Han?

Han : Yes, I'm rather busy lately.

I attend a foreign language school.

Ch'oe: Really? What language are you learning?

Han : Chinese.

VOCABULARY STUDY

- 바쁘다/바빠 [pappŭda/pappa] to be busy

  Note that any verb stem ending with the vowel 으 loses the vowel 으 whenever it is followed by another vowel. For example, 쓰+어요→써요 "I use"; 바쁘+어요→바빠요 "I am busy."
- 요즈음 [yojŭŭm] lately
- 외국어 [oegŭgŏ] foreign language (외국 = foreign country)
- 학원 [hagwon] school, institute

  학원 refers to an educational institution, especially one devoted to technical fields such as foreign languages.
- 다니다/다녀 [tanida/tanyŏ] to attend, go (regularly)

  This verb expresses one's regular or repeated goings to a place, such as a school (as a student), a work-place (as an employee).
- 그래요? [kŭraeyo] Really? Is that so?
- 어느 [ŏnŭ] which, what (interrogative)
- 나라 [nara] country, nation
- 말 [mal] language, speech
- 배우다/배워 [paeŭda/paewo] to learn, study (=공부하다)

  배우다 has a broader sense, meaning any kind of learning, while 공부하다 usually denotes a formal study. Since 공부 is a noun and originally the object of 하다, 공부하다 may be used by itself (meaning "doing a study"), but 배우다 requires an object (e.g., English, French, etc.) in its immediate context.

EXERCISE 1 Listen to your teacher narrating five stories based on the scripts given in the Vocabulary Summary section. As you listen, write down the following key points of information from each story.

	What language?	Where?	When?
a.			
b.			
c.			
d.			

EXERCISE 2 Based on the information you wrote down above for Exercise 1, conduct short conversations with your partner. One of you will ask if your partner is busy lately, what foreign language he/she is learning, and what school he/she is attending, etc. Your partner will use the information that he/she wrote down for each segment of conversation above.

FRAME 2

Talking about the Class

최: 반에 학생이 몇이 있어요? [pane haksaeng'i myŏch'i issŏyo]	Ch'oe: How many students are there in the class?
한: 우리 반에 일곱이 있어요. [uri pane ilgobi issŏyo]	Han : There are seven in our class.
최: 반이 별로 안 크네요. [pani pyŏllo an k'ŭneyo]	Ch'oe: The class is not very big.
한: 네, 작아요. 그래서 좋아요. [ne chagayo kŭraesŏ chowayo]	Han : No, it's small. So, it's good.

VOCABULARY STUDY

- 반 [pan] class
- 몇 [myŏt] how many

  ㅊ is fully pronounced as [ch'] only when a postposition beginning with a vowel follows.

  CAUTION! Grammatically, 몇 is not a modifier but a nominal that may take a postposition (-이 or -가 here).

- 우리 [uri] we, us; our (when followed by a noun)
- 일곱 [ilgop] seven
- 별로 [pyŏllo] particularly, especially (not)

  CAUTION! This adverb is used only in a negative sense.

- 크다/커 [k'ŭda/k'ŏ] to be big, large (stative verb)
- -네요 [-neyo] an exclamatory verb ending

This is a verb ending expressing the speaker's discovery of a fact, rather than stating any new information. Its function is similar to that of exclamatory sentences in English, but the ending is used rather casually without a real sense of exclamation.

• 작다	[chakda]	to be small (stative verb)
• 그래서	[kŭraesŏ]	so, therefore

❖ WHY IS 네 TRANSLATED AS "NO" SOMETIMES?

The functions of the Korean interjections (네 and 아니오) are quite different from those of English counterparts "yes" and "no," even though they may seem to coincide with the English counterparts in most situations. Note the true meanings of the Korean and English interjections below.

KOREAN	ENGLISH
네 means: *YOU* ARE RIGHT.	"YES" means: THE *AFFIRMATIVE* SENTENCE IS RIGHT.
아니오 means: *YOU* ARE WRONG.	"No" means: THE *NEGATIVE* SENTENCE IS RIGHT.

In Korean, it doesn't matter whether the preceding sentence is affirmative or negative.

In English, it doesn't matter whether you agree or disagree with your conversation partner.

EXERCISE 3 Look at the following exchanges and fill the spaces with 네 or 아니오.

a. 반이 큽니까?
_____, 커요.

b. 집에 안 가요?
_____, 지금 못갑니다

c. 영어 하세요?
_____, 잘 못해요

d. 오늘 신문 없어요?
_____, 없어요.

e. 반이 작네요.
_____, 안 작아요.

f. 아무 것도 안 하세요?
_____, 아무 것도 안 합니다

❖ COUNTING ONE TO TEN:

1 하나 [hana]	2 둘 [tul]	3 셋 [set]	4 넷 [net]	5 다섯 [tasŏt]
6 여섯 [yŏsŏt]	7 일곱 [ilgop]	8 여덟 [yŏdŏl]	9 아홉 [ahop]	10 열 [yŏl]

CAUTION! Note the spelling of 여덟. The last consonant ㅂ is normally silent, although it is pronounced when 덟 is followed by a vowel.

EXERCISE 4 Count aloud the following groups of five numbers.

하나 - 둘 - 셋 - 넷 - 다섯
여섯 - 일곱 - 여덟 - 아홉 - 열

❖ 몇/몇이 …? "HOW MANY…?"

X - {이 / 가}	몇 [myŏt] / 몇이 [myŏch'i]	있어요? [issŏyŏ]	How many X's are there?

The question word 몇 "how many" may or may not take the subject marker postposition. Note the pronunciation of the last consonant ㅊ of 몇, which is fully pronounced as [ch'] only when a postposition begins with a vowel.

EXERCISE 5 In each of the following groups of commodities, count the item(s) by using Korean numbers such as 하나, 둘, 셋, etc.

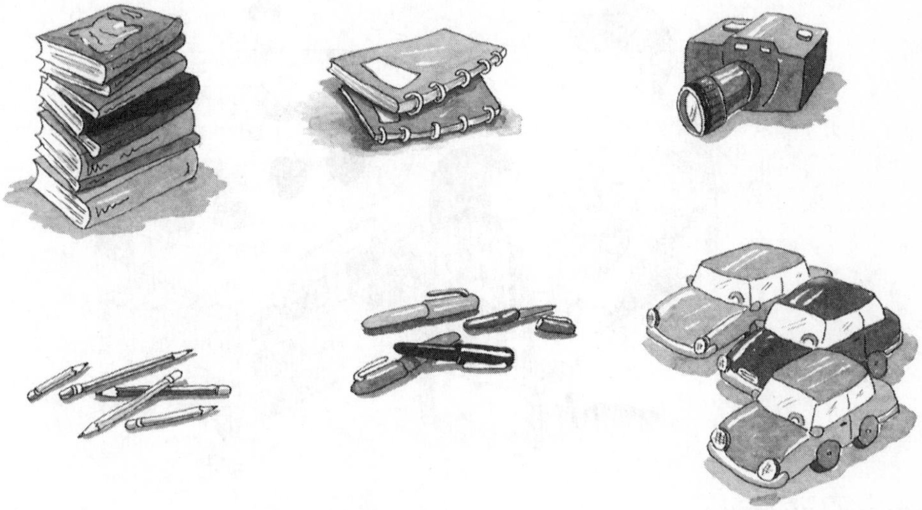

FRAME 3

People in the Class

최: 선생님은 어느 나라 사람입니까?
[sŏnsaengnimŭn ŏnŭ nara saramimnikka]

한: 중국 사람이에요.
[chungguk saramieyo]

최: 학생들은 다 한국사람이에요?
[haksaengdŭrŭn ta hanguk saramieyo]

한: 미국 사람이 한 명 있어요.
[miguk sarami hanmyŏng issŏyo]

최: 반에 남자가 더 많아요? 여자가 더 많아요?
[pane namjaga tŏ manayo yŏjaga tŏ manayo]

한: 남자가 더 많아요.
[namjaga tŏ manayo]

Ch'oe: What's the nationality of your teacher?

Han : He is a Chinese.

Ch'oe: Are the students all Koreans?

Han : There is one American.

Ch'oe: Are there more men or more women in the class?

Han : There are more men.

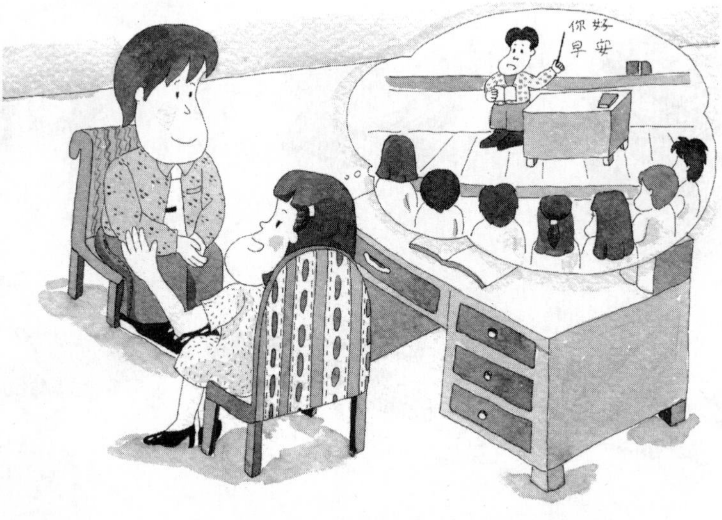

VOCABULARY STUDY

•사람	[saram]	person
•어느 나라 사람	[ŏnŭ nara saram]	What nationality...? (Which country person...?)
•-들	[dŭl]	a plural marker (See Grammar.)
•다	[ta]	all
다 follows, rather than precedes, a nominal.		
•남자	[namja]	male person (man/boy)
•여자	[yŏja]	female person (woman/girl)
•더 많다/많아	[tŏ mant'a/mana]	to be more, greater in number (stative verb)

❖ INTONATION IN THE "CHOICE" QUESTION

When you ask a "choice" question (either X or Y), two questions are placed one after another without any connective. However, there is a special intonation for it: The tone of voice goes up at the and of the first question(↗), and down at the end of the second(↘).

남자가 더 많아요? 여자가 더 많아요? Are there more men or women?
[namjaga tŏ manayo ↗ yŏjaga tŏ manayo ↘]

EXERCISE 6 Ask the following questions of your partner. Make sure to use the right intonations.

a. 바쁩니까? 안 바쁩니까?
b. 반이 커요? 작아요?
c. 자동차가 있어요? 없어요?
d. 중국어 배워요? 일본어 배워요?

EXERCISE 7 Say the following choice question utterances in Korean.

a. Is he a Korean or a Japanese?
b. Are you busy or not busy?
c. Is your teacher a man or a woman?
d. Is there or isn't there?

EXERCISE 8 You will hear the sentences that contain Korean numbers. As you listen, put the numbers in Arabic numerals.

a. ____ b. ____ c. ____ d. ____ e. ____ f. ____ g. ____ h. ____ i. ____ j. ____

EXERCISE 9 As you respond to your partner's question, identify the numbers of the objects you are asked of.

Example: 학생이 몇이 있어요?
다섯이 있어요.

EXERCISE 10 Now engage in the same question-and-answer exercise about your actual classroom. Identify the numbers of the objects for which you know the Korean words.

FRAME 4

Showing the Classroom

영희: 여기가 우리 교실이야. 들어와. [yŏgiga uri kyoshiriya tŭrŏwa]	Yŏnghi: This is our classroom. Come on in.
동우: 꽤 크네! [kkwae k'ŭne]	Tong'u: It's quite large!
영희: 안 작아. [anchaga]	Yŏnghi: Not small.
동우: 너는 어디 앉니? [nŏnŭn ŏdi anni]	Tong'u: Where do you sit?
영희: 나는 늘 저 의자에 앉아. [nanŭn nŭl chŏ ŭijae anja]	Yŏnghi: I always sit on that chair.

VOCABULARY STUDY

•교실	[kyoshil]	classroom
•꽤	[kkwae]	quite (adverb)
•-네	[-ne]	an exclamatory ending (blunt form)
•늘	[nŭl]	always
•저	[chŏ]	that over there (prenominal)

A prenominal means a word that is always placed before a nominal and used as a modifier of the the nominal.

GRAMMAR

1. Adjectives Working as Verbs

In this course, "adjectives" are called "stative verbs" because in Korean they function like verbs. They are placed at the end of a sentence, taking more or less the same verb endings, and not preceded by any copula verb ("be" in English).

자동차가 좋아요! [chadongch'aga chowayo]	Ⓗ Ⓜ	The car is good!
선생님 바쁘세요? [sŏnsaengnim pappŭseyo]	Ⓗ	Are you busy, sir?
이 나라는 작아요. [i naranŭn chagayo]	Ⓗ Ⓜ	This country is small.
교실이 커. [kyoshiri k'ŏ]	Ⓛ	The classroom is big.

•PRENOMINAL FORM: Adjectives are also used as noun-modifiers placed before a noun both in English and Korean. We will call such uses "prenominal" since it is placed *before* a nominal. The penominal ending (for stative verbs) is -은.

좋은 자동차 [choŭn chadongch'a]	a good car
바쁜 사람 [pappŭn saram]	a busy person
작은 나라 [chagŭn nara]	a small country
큰 교실 [k'ŭn kyoshil]	a big classroom

NOTE: Any suffix beginning with the vowel -으, as in 은, drops 으 whenever it is preceded by a vowel. For example,

크 + 은 ⟶ 큰
k'ŭ ŭn k'ŭn

2. Quantified Nominals

Unlike in English, and contrary to the normal rule of sequence for the modifier and the modified, the quantity expression in Korean (하나, 둘, 몇, 다, 좀, etc.) generally follows the nominal rather than precedes it.

NOMINAL + Ⓟ	QUANTITY + Ⓟ

Ⓟ = an appropriate postposition

자동차 둘 있어요. [chadongch'a *tul* issŏyo]	We have two cars.
의자가 몇이 있습니까? [ŭijaga *myŏch'i* issŭmnikka]	How many chairs are there?
한국말 좀 합니다. [hangungmal *chom* hamnida.]	I speak Korean a little.
학생들은 다 남자예요? [haksaengdŭrŭn *ta* namjayeyo]	Are the students all men?

3. "Choice" Questions

A question for the addressee to pick one or the other (either X or Y) between two choices is made simply by asking two questions one after another. Naturally, the subject and the object are not repeated in the second question. However, there is a special intonation for the "choice" question: the tone of voice goes up at the end of the first question [↗], and down at the end of the second[↘].

그것이 영업니까? 불업니까? [kŭgŏshi yŏng'ŏmnikka↗ purŏmnikka↘]	Is that English or French?
교실이 커요? 작아요? [kyoshiri k'ŏyo↗ chagayo↘]	Is the classroom big or small?

가? 안 가? Are you going or not?
[ka⤴ an ka⤵]

4. Plural Marker: -들

As you have already noticed, plurality (-s or -es in English) is not generally marked in Korean. A Korean noun (without any plural marking) may mean either singular or plural. However, a plural marker (-들) is used in certain cases. Compare the following pair of sentences from Frame 3.

학생이 몇이 있습니까? How many students are there?
[haksaeng'i myŏch'i issŭmnikka]

학생들은 다 한국 사람이에요? Are the students all Koreans?
[haksaengdŭrŭn ta hanguk saramieyo]

The plural marker (-들) is normally used when a nominal refers to specific people that the speaker and the hearer are aware of in a given context (a situation where you would use "the" in English). In the first sentence above, 학생 does not refer to any specific people, since the speaker does not even know how many there are. On the other hand, 학생들 in the second sentence is already assumed to be "specific"or "definite" since they are identified in the context. So the plural marker is used.

5. Plural Pronouns

The personal pronouns are by definition "definite" nominals in the sense explained above. Therefore, plural pronouns are clearly distinguished from singular pronouns as shown below.

<table>
<tr><th></th><th></th><th>HIGH LEVEL</th><th colspan="2">MID LEVEL / LOW LEVEL</th></tr>
<tr><td rowspan="2">1ST PERSON</td><td>singular</td><td>저
[chŏ]</td><td colspan="2">나
[na]</td></tr>
<tr><td>plural</td><td>저희(들)
[chŏi(dŭl)]</td><td colspan="2">우리(들)
[uri(dŭl)]</td></tr>
<tr><td rowspan="2">2ND PERSON</td><td>singular</td><td>TITLE-님
... [nim]</td><td>TITLE
...</td><td>너
[nŏ]</td></tr>
<tr><td>plural</td><td>TITLE-님들
... [nim dŭl]</td><td>TITLE-들
... [dŭl]</td><td>너희들
[nŏi(dŭl)]</td></tr>
</table>

NOTE: The parentheses surrounding as in -(들) means that the use of -들 is optional. The use of -들 after 저희, 우리, and 너희 is redundant but is not uncommon.

❖ THIRD PERSON PRONOUNS IN KOREAN

There are no third person pronouns in spoken Korean (equivalent to *he, she, it,* and *they* in English). The closest Korean equivalents to the third person pronouns in English are made in the following phrases:

ENGLISH	HONORIFIC	PLAIN	
he/she	그분 [kŭ bun]	그 이 [kŭ i]	그 사람 [kŭ saram]
they (persons)	그분들 [kŭ bundŭl]	그 이들 [kŭ idŭl]	그 사람들 [kŭ saramdŭl]
it/they (inanimate)		그 것 [kŭ gŏt]	

NOTE: When a phrase denotes two or more persons who are already mentioned in its context (equivalent to "they"), the plural suffix -들 must be used. However, for inanimate objects in plural, the plural suffix -들 is not normally used. Other phrases often used in referring to persons include 그 남자 "the man," 그 남자들 "the men," 그 여자 "the woman," and 그 여자들 "the women." In written Korean, the following three third person pronouns are commonly used: 그 for "he," 그녀 for "she," 그들 for "they (persons)," and 그녀들 for "they (female persons)."

READING & WRITING

1. Major Landmarks in Seoul

Kimpo Airport (김포공항) is the gateway to 서울. Through this airport most visitors arrive in 한국. You would take a taxi and go west about 40 minutes to get to the heart of the city (도심지).

서울 도심지 (Map of Central Seoul)

Perhaps, the first landmark with which you may orient yourself may be the South Gate (남대문), the main city gate of the old capital (수도), which finds itself today in the middle of 서울. The South Gate is located at the foot of the Namsan Hill (남산). From a tower on top of the Namsan Hill (남산탑) you may have a bird's-eye view of the city. The old 서울 is surrounded by three hills, and you see the Han River (한강) in the south. Seoul Railroad Station (서울역) is located just south of 남대문. The City Hall (시청) is within a walking distance. Further north through the avenue named 세종로, you see a seat of the royal palace called 경복궁. Right across from the City Hall Plaza (시청앞 광장) is a small palace called 덕수궁. From there eastward, you can walk through a crowded business section and the downtown shopping area, which is called 명동.

EXERCISE 11 Names of places often end with a common noun indicating geographical features. Guess the nouns for the following features, and write them in Hangŭl.

a. The word for "mountain": ____
b. The word for "river": ____
c. The word for "palace": ____
d. The word for "gate": ____

2. Syllable-final ㅎ

Some verb stems end with the consonant ㅎ (e.g., 좋다 "to be good"). Such ㅎ is almost never pronounced as [h], but has the effects on the next syllable.

a. When a vowel follows, ㅎ is silent.

좋아요.	[chowayo]	It's fine.
NOTE: The verb 좋다 is a unique case: [w] is inserted between [o] and [a].		
많아요.	[manayo]	There are many.
괜찮아요.	[kwench'anayo]	It's all right.

b. When a consonant (ㄱ, ㄷ, ㅂ, or ㅈ) follows, ㅎ causes the next consonant to become aspirated.

좋지요?	[choch'iyo]	Isn't it nice?
많지요?	[manch'iyo]	Aren't there many?
괜찮지요?	[kwaench'anch'iyo]	Isn't it all right?

c. When ㅅ or ㄴ follows, it causes the next consonant to become doubled in pronunciation: [ss] and [nn] respectively.

좋습니다.	[chossŭmnida]	It's good.
좋네요.	[chonneyo]	It's good, isn't it?
많습니다.	[manssŭmnida]	There are many.
많네요.	[manneyo]	There are many, aren't there?
괜찮습니다.	[kwaench'anssŭmnida]	It's all right.
괜찮네요.	[kwaench'anneyo]	It's all right, isn't it?

EXERCISE 12 The following verbs are spelled as pronounced, but they are wrong. Rewrite them with the correct spellings.

a. 조와요. ____________ d. 괜차나요. ____________

b. 조치요? ____________ e. 조씁니다. ____________

c. 만네요. ____________ f. 만씁니다. ____________

3. On Reading Vocabulary Review

In order for you to acquire additional vocabulary for reading and writing, occasional review sections will be provided. The "reading" vocabulary is simply a label for those words that are introduced in the Reading and Writing section. They are used in conversation as well with few exceptions. Some items of reading vocabulary are, however, more common in writing than in speech.

EXERCISE 13 Write three words referring to "Korea."

a.________________ b.________________ c.________________

EXERCISE 14 Complete the following sentences by filling in the blank spaces with words listed in the box. Then, give an English equivalent to each Korean sentence.

산	강	수도	도시	시청	공항	동양	외국어

a. 한국 ____는 서울입니다. ------------------------------

b. 서울에는 ____이 많습니다. ------------------------------

c. 한강은 큰 ____입니다. ------------------------------

d. 오늘 친구가 ____에 옵니다. ------------------------------

e. 하와이에 ____ 사람이 많아요. ------------------------------

f. 저는 ____를 처음 배웁니다. ------------------------------

g. 이 ____ 이름이 무엇입니까? ------------------------------

h. 열한 시에 ____에 오십시오. ------------------------------

VOCABULARY SUMMARY

Nominals

강	river	반	class
공항	airport	사람	person, human
광장	plaza, open space	여자	female person, girl
교실	classroom	외국어	foreign language
궁	palace	우리	we; us
나라	country, nation	의자	chair
남자	male person, boy	저희 Ⓗ	we; us
너희 Ⓛ	you (as plural)	학원	institute (educational)
도심지	heart of the city	시청	city hall
문	gate, door	역	railroad station
산	hill, mountain	탑	tower
말	language; word		

Personalize Vocabulary

시계	clock, watch	칠판	chalkboard
유리창	window	텔레비전	television
책상	desk		

Numbers

하나	one	여섯	six
둘	two	일곱	seven
셋	three	여덟	eight
넷	four	아홉	nine
다섯	five	열	ten

Action Verbs

다니다/다녀	to go, attend	배우다/배워	to learn, study

Stative Verbs

많다/많아	to be many, numerous	작다/작아	to be small
바쁘다/바빠	to be busy	크다/커	to be big, large

Adverbs

그래서	so, therefore	더	more
꽤	quite	별로	particularly (not)
늘	always	요즈음/요즘	lately, recently
다	all		

Others

그래요? Ⓜ	Is that so?	몇	how many
-네요	an exclamatory ending	어느	which
-들	a plural marker		

Scripts For Exercises

Exercise 1.
a. 저 바빠요. 한국말 배웁니다. 저녁에 교회 다녀요.
b. 나 요즈음 외국어 학원 다녀요. 불어 공부합니다.
c. 나 주말에 학교 다닙니다. 영어 배워요.
d. 저 아직 중국어 못해요. 집에서 배우겠어요.

Exercise 8.
a. 카메라가 둘 있습니다.
b. 반에 여자가 여섯이 있어요.
c. 남자가 많아요. 열명 있어요.
d. 일본사람이 넷이 옵니다.
e. 반에 한국 사람이 여덟이 있어요.
f. 자동차가 셋이 갑니다.
g. 저는 잡지 둘 봐요.
h. 친구 다섯이 기다립니다.
i. 여기 연필이 아홉 있어요.
j. 우리 학교에 컴퓨터가 일곱 있습니다.

ANSWERS TO EXERCISES

Exercise 1.	a. Korean - church - evening		c. English - school - weekend		
	b. French - school - lately		d. Chinese- home - future		
Exercise 3.	a. 네 b. 네 c. 아니오 d. 네 e. 아니오 f. 네				
Exercise 7.	a. 저 사람 한국 사람입니까? 일본 사람입니까?				
	b. 바쁘세요? 안 바쁘세요?				
	c. 선생님이 남자분이세요? 여자분이세요?				
	d. 있어요? 없어요?				
Exercise 8.	a. 2	c. 10	e. 8	g. 2	i. 9
	b. 6	d. 4	f. 3	h. 5	j. 7
Exercise 11.	a. 산	b. 강	c. 궁	d. 문	
Exercise 12.	a. 좋아요.	c. 많네요.	e. 좋습니다.		
	b. 좋지요?	d. 괜찮아요.	f. 많습니다.		
Exercise 13.	a. 한국	b. 조선	c. 고려		
Exercise 14.	a. 수도	c. 강	e. 동양	g. 도시	
	b. 산	d. 공항	f. 외국어	h. 시청	

LESSON 6
DINING OUT

FRAME 1

It's Lunch Time.

한: 점심 식사하러 가십시다.	Han: Let's go to have lunch.
민: 지금 몇 시예요?	Min: What time is it now?
한: 열두시 반입니다.	Han: It's twelve thirty.
민: 벌써요? 나가십시다.	Min: Already? Let's go out.

• From this lesson on, the romanization will not be given except where there are unpredictable gaps between sounds and letters.

VOCABULARY STUDY

• 점심   lunch

점심 is a common shortened form for "lunch." 식사 denotes "meal."

• -으러   in order to…

The connective ending -으러 is preceded by the verb stem. When the verb stem ends in a consonant -으러 follows (e.g., 읽으러, 앉으러), but with the verb stem ending in a vowel 으 is dropped (e.g., 보러, 하러).

CAUTION! This ending is used only with the verbs of locomotion, such as 가다 "to go," 오다 "to come," and similar verbs.

- -으십시다. Let's ….
  This is a Ⓗ suggestive form. When the verb stem ends in a consonant, -으십시다 follows, as in 앉으십시다. When the verb stem ends in a vowel, 으 is dropped, as in 가십시다. If you drop the honorific marker -으시, you get -ㅂ시다 which is the Ⓜ form. For example, 가십시다 Ⓗ and 갑시다 Ⓜ.
- 지금 now (adverb/noun)
- 몇 시 what time
- 열두 시 twelve o'clock
- 반 half
- 벌써 already
- 나가다/나가 to go out

❖ TELLING TIME

Hours of the day are expressed by the suffix -시 (meaning "time" or "hour") added to the numbers. There are two important points you should bear in mind when you express hours in Korean.

a. The numbers beyond ten, such as 11 and 12, are expressed simply by compounding 열 "ten" and the number in the second digit. For example, 열 하나 "eleven" and 열 둘 "twelve."

11	열하나	[yŏlhana]	16	열여섯	[yŏlyŏsŏt]
12	열둘	[yŏlttul]	17	열일곱	[yŏlilgop]
13	열셋	[yŏlset]	18	열여덟	[yŏlyŏdŏl]
14	열넷	[yŏllet]	19	열아홉	[yŏlahop]
15	열다섯	[yŏlttasŏt]			

b. The first four numbers (1-4) are shortened by dropping the last sound (a consonant or vowel) before -시.

한 시	[hanshi]	one o'clock	네 시	[neshi]	four o'clock
두 시	[tushi]	two o'clock	열한 시	[yŏlhanshi]	eleven o'clock
세 시	[seshi]	three o'clock	열두 시	[yŏlttushi]	twelve o'clock

EXERCISE 1 Voice aloud the hours from one o'clock to twelve o'clock as you look at the face of your clock.

EXERCISE 2 The teacher will point at an hour on the clock. Ask your partner what time it is now. Your partner will answer according to the time pointed to by the teacher.

FRAME 2

Picking the Place to Eat

민: 어디가 좋아요? 저는 이 근처 잘 몰라요. 선생님 잘 아시지요?	Min: Which place do you recommend? I don't know this area well. You know it well, don't you?
한: 네. 한국 음식 잡수시겠어요, 중국 음식 잡수시겠어요?	Han: Yes. Would you like Korean food or Chinese food?
민: 한국 음식 먹겠어요.	Min: I would have Korean food.
한: 네. 제가 좋은 데 알아요.	Han: I see. I know a good place.

VOCABULARY STUDY

- 어디 — where, which place, what place

  CAUTION! The question words 어디 "where" is an adverbial like its English equivalent, but it is also used nominally (like a noun). Thus, 어디 is equivalent here to "what place" or "which place."
- 근처 — vicinity
- 아시지요? — You know, don't you?

  With the new ending -지요? in his speech the speaker expects an agreement from the addressee. (See Grammar.)
- 알다/알아/아세요 — to know; to become aware of

  This verb is represented here by three forms to show its peculiar conjugation.
- 모르다/몰라 — do not know (the negative of 알다)

  CAUTION! The negative 안- is not used for 알다.
- 음식 — food

- 먹다 Ⓜ to eat
- 잡수시다 Ⓗ to eat (an honorific form of 먹다)
- 좋은 데 a good place

  데 means "place," but it is always used with a prenominal modifier.
  좋은 is a prenominal form of 좋다.
- 제가 The first person singular pronoun ("I") with the subject marker -가 (focused). Note the change of the vowel in this form.

❖ 알다/모르다 "TO KNOW/NOT TO KNOW"

a. The verb 알다 drops ㄹ when it is followed by certain types of suffixes. The rules for this type of conjugation will be explained more later. For now simply memorize the following forms.

Ⓗ Ⓜ FORM	아세요. 아십니다. 아시지요? 압니다.	[aseyo] [ashimnida] [ashijiyo] [amnida]	알겠습니다. 알지요? 알아요.	[algessŭmnida] [aljiyo] [arayo]
Ⓛ FORM	아니? 아네.	[ani] [ane]	알지? 알아.	[alji] [ara]

b. The verb 모르다 "not to know" is the negative of 알다. This verb becomes irregular only when it is followed by any suffix beginning with the vowel or when it occurs in such forms as 몰라 or 몰라요 as shown below.

Ⓗ Ⓜ FORM	모르세요. 모르십니다. 모르시지요? 모릅니다.	[morŭseyo] [morŭshimnida] [morŭshijiyo] [morŭmnida]	모르겠습니다. 모르지요? 몰라요.	[morŭkessŭmnida] [morŭjiyo] [mollayo]
Ⓛ FORM	모르니? 모르네.	[morŭni] [morŭne]	모르지? 몰라.	[morŭji] [molla]

EXERCISE 3 Say appropriate Korean equivalents to the following English sentences.

a. Do you know?
b. You know, don't you?
c. I don't know him well.
d. Let's go to see the teacher.
e. What time is it now?
f. What place would you recommend?
g. I know one good place.
h. Is it already five thirty?

FRAME 3

Ordering Dishes

웨이터: 어서 오십시오. 몇 분이십니까?	Waiter: Come right in. How many of you, sir?
한 : 세 사람.	Han : Three people.
웨이터: 이리 앉으시겠어요? 뭐 하시겠어요?	Waiter: Would you like to sit here? What would you like to have?
한 : 나는 냉면.	Han : Naengmyŏn for me.
김 : 나도 같은 것.	Kim : The same for me.
민 : 나는 만두국.	Min : Manduguk for me.
웨이터: 냉면 두 그릇하고 만두국 한 그릇. 감사합니다.	Waiter: Two bowls of naengmyŏn and one bowl of manduguk. Thank you, sir.

VOCABULARY STUDY

- 웨이터 waiter
- 뭐 =무엇 (a common contraction in conversation)
- 냉면 cold noodles

  This Korean-style noodle menu is generally served with meat and vegetables in a big bowl of cold beef broth.
- 그릇 bowl, dish
- 같다 to be the same (stative verb)

  같은 것 "the same thing"
- 만두국 dumpling soup

  Small balls of dough, stuffed with meat and vegetables, are served in a ball of hot beef broth.

• -하고　　　　　and (connective postposition)

CAUTION! This connective is used only between two nominals, and it is a post position suffixed to the first nominal, as in: X-하고 Y.

CULTURAL ENCOUNTER In Korea the four most popular types of restaurants are the traditional Korean (한식집), the Chinese (중국집), the Japanese (일식집), and the Western (양식집). Lunch menus are served mostly à la carte. The following is a typical Korean lunch menu.

• 점심 메뉴 (Personalized Vocabulary)

비빔밥 pibimbap	A little meat and a variety of cooked vegetables are served on top of steamed rice.
불고기 pulgogi	Thin-sliced and marinaded beef, broiled over charcoal fire. It is served with steamed rice and cooked vegetables.
갈비 kalbi	Broiled short ribs served in the same way as 불고기.
냉면 naengmyŏn	Noodles in a bowl of cold beef broth with vegetables and meat.
만두국 manduguk	Dumplings stuffed with meat and vegetables in hot beef broth.
찌개 백반 tchigaepaekban	Spicy stew of fish (생선), tofu (두부), or meat mixed with vegetables. This is usually served with steamed rice.

NOTE: Coming together with any of the dishes above is 김치 [kimch'i]. This popular side dish is pickled cabbage seasoned with red pepper and garlic. Also well known is 깍뚜기 [kkakttugi], pickled radish seasoned with red pepper and garlic.

EXERCISE 4 Form small groups of three or four students. In each group, one will be chosen to play the waiter or waitress. The waiter or waitress will welcome the customers, seat them at a table, take orders from the menu above. After taking the orders, the waiter or waitress will confirm all the orders by citing what items and how many of them have just been ordered.

EXERCISE 5 Ask your partner what he/she would like to eat. Your partner will choose one item from the menu above.

EXAMPLE: 뭐 잡수시겠어요?
　　　　저는 _____ 먹겠어요.

EXERCISE 6 Say the following utterances in Korean, paying attention to the -으시지요 ending.

a. You are busy, aren't you?
b. He speaks English, doesn't he?

c. You don't have a car, do you?
d. You are a Korean, aren't you?
e. This restaurant is good, isn't it?

EXERCISE 7 It's lunch time now in your office. As you go out with one of your colleagues for lunch, ask the person what kind of food he/she prefers, and ask the person if he/she knows a decent place in the vicinity.

EXERCISE 8 Ask your partner the following questions. Your partner will respond factually.

a. 몇 시에 아침 식사 하세요?
b. 몇 시에 학교에 오세요?
c. 몇 시에 커피 하시겠어요?
d. 몇 시에 점심 하러 가세요?
e. 몇 시에 저녁 식사 잡수세요?
f. 몇 시에 저녁에 공부하세요?
g. 몇 시에 집에 가세요?

FRAME 4

Going for Breakfast

양: 아침 식사 하러 가자.	Yang: Let's go out for breakfast.
박: 너무 일러.	Pak : It's too early.
양: 지금 몇 시야?	Yang: What time is it now?
박: 저기 시계 봐.	Pak : Look at the clock there.
양: 벌써 여덟 시야.	Yang: It's already eight.
박: 그래. 이 근처 좋은 데 알아?	Pak : O.K. Do you know a good place in this area?
양: 내가 좋은 데 알아. 한국 음식 먹지?	Yang: I know a good place. You'll have Korean food, won't you?
박: 그래.	Pak : Sure.

VOCABULARY STUDY

- 아침 식사 — breakfast (아침=morning; 식사=meal)
- 너무 — too (excessively, extremely)
- 이르다/일러 — to be early (stative verb)
- 저기 — over there
- 그래 — O.K., that's right

The verb 그렇다/그래 is a stative verb, meaning "to be so." It is used in the following phrases.

그러세요? Ⓗ 그래요? Ⓜ 그래? Ⓛ		Really? Is that so?
그러세요. Ⓗ 그래요. Ⓜ 그래. Ⓛ		O.K. Let's do that.
•내가		The 1st person pronoun with the subject postposition -가. Used in Ⓜ Ⓛ speech. (See Grammar.)

GRAMMAR

1. More on the Topic

Even though the subject of a sentence is often the topic at the same time (Lesson 4, Grammar), the topic does not have to be the subject. The topic is simply a background or premise setter for a sentence, and so it may have no direct "case" role (such as subject, object, location, time, etc.) in a sentence. In Frame 3, we have an interesting example in ordering food.

김: 나도 같은 것.	Kim: The same for me. (*Me too*, the same.)
민: 나는 만두국.	Min: Dumpling soup for me. (*Me*, it's dumplings.)

The topic 나는 has no case role in the sentence. It merely shows what the speaker is talking about.

2. Contrastive Topics

There are three situations in which the topic is mentioned: (a) when the topic has not yet been established, (b) when the speaker believes a reminder is needed, and (c) when the topic abruptly shifts from one to another. The first two instances represent the basic use of the topic, but the third is somewhat different in that the topic is "contrasted" to the immediately preceding topic.

By "contrasted" it is meant that *something different* will be said about the new topic in contrast to the topic immediately preceding. For example, in the exchange above, *someone* (the earlier topic) is having "noodle," but the new topic 나는 (민) will rather have "dumplings." Below are some more examples.

A: 주말에 뭐 하세요?	What will you be doing during the weekend?
B: 인천에 갑니다. 선생님은요?	I'm going to Inchŏn. How about you? (CONTRASTED to B's going to Inch'ŏn)
A: 형도 영어 배워요?	Are you also learning English?
B: 아니오, 나는 안 배워요.	No, I'm not learning it. (CONTRASTED to A's learning English)

3. Tag Questions

The ending -지요? (Polite) and -지? (Blunt), *with a sharp rising tone,* is equivalent to a "tag" question in English. A sentence with -지요/-지? is not a real question. It expresses the speaker's belief and his/her expectation of the addressee to agree with the statement.

바쁘시지요?	Ⓗ	You are busy, aren't you?
이것 선생님 자동차지요?	Ⓗ	This is your car, isn't it?
저 여자 학생이지?	Ⓛ	She is a student, isn't she?
한국 음식 먹지?	Ⓛ	You will have Korean food, won't you?

CAUTION! If the sentence is a negative, it is the negative sentence that the speaker expects the addressee to agree with.

카메라 없지요?	Ⓜ	You don't have a camera, do you?
한국 사람 아니지요?	Ⓜ	He isn't a Korean, is he?

4. More pointer words

In Lesson 4, you have learned how to point at something in three ways: 이- "this" for something *near the speaker,* 그- "that" for something *near the addressee,* and 저- for something *away from both* the speaker and the addressee. This three-way distinction is also made in pointing at places. In pointing at places, however, there are two sets, one that involves movements to places, and another that does *not* involve movements.

	MOVEMENT	NON-MOVEMENT
Near the speaker	이리 this way	여기 here
Near the addressee	그리 that way	거기 there
Away from both	저리 that way over there	저기 over there

이리 앉으세요	Please sit down *here.*
연필이 여기 있어요	The pencil is *here.*

Note that the English adverb "here" translates differently in the above examples.

CAUTION! 그- "that," 그리 "that way," and 거기 "there" have an additional important use: REFERENCE TO SOME DEFINITE NOMINAL understood in the context (equivalent to the English definite article "the").

그 사람 아세요?	Do you know the man?
거기 언제 가세요?	When do you go there?
그리 못갑니다.	You can't go there (that way).

5. Long Forms in Four Basic Moods

The long forms of a verb (used in HIGH and MID LEVELS) express *four* specific sentential moods. We have now covered all four.

MOOD	LONG FORM	EXAMPLE
Declarative (Statement)	C-습니다 V-ㅂ니다	먹습니다. 갑니다.
Interrogative (Question)	C-습니까? V-ㅂ니까?	있습니까? 합니까?
Imperative (Request)	C-으십시오 V-십시오	앉으십시오. 하십시오.
Suggestive (Suggestion)	C-으십시다 V-ㅂ시다	앉으십시다. 갑시다.

NOTE: (1) C - means "after a consonant," and V- means "after a vowel."
(2) The imperative form generally has the honorific marker -으시 incorporated on MID LEVEL. However, the suggestive form need not have the honorific marker on the MID LEVEL.

6. Sound Changes in Pronouns : A Summary

Three pronouns, 저 (1st person HIGH, "I"), 나 (1st person Ⓜ/Ⓛ, "I"), and 너 (2nd person Ⓛ, "you"), change their vowels in the "focused" subject form and in the possessive form.

Basic	Focused Subject	Possessive (Prenominal)
저	제가	제 - NOUN
나	내가	내 - NOUN
너	네가	네 - NOUN

NOTE: See Grammar, Lesson 4 on the "focused" subject.

제가 좋은 데 압니다. Ⓗ
내가 좋은 데 압니다. Ⓜ } I know a good place.

FOCUSED

네가 좋은 데 알지? Ⓛ You know a good place, don't you?

제 친구입니다. Ⓗ
내 친구야. Ⓛ } This is my friend.

네 책이니? Ⓛ Is this your book?

7. How to Connect Two Nominals

The English conjunction "and " is so versatile that it can connect any two or more words, phrases, or sentences. In Korean there is no single word that connects all these different sentence elements. To connect two nominals, the connective postposition -하고 is added to the first nominal. You will learn how to connect other sentence elements later.

냉면 둘하고 만두국 하나.	Two naengmyŏns and one manduguk.
미스 고는 영어하고 불어 배워요.	Miss Ko is learning English and French.

To connect more than two nominals, -하고 may be placed after each nominal (even the last nominal sometimes).

책하고 잡지하고 신문이 있어요.	We have books, magazines and papers.
(or 책하고 잡지하고 신문하고 있어요.)	
서울하고 부산하고 대전에 가요.	I'll go to Seoul, Pusan and Taejŏn.

READING & WRITING

1. Types of Restaurants in Korea

The generic term for "restaurant" is 음식점, consisting of 음식 "food" and the suffix -점 "store." Another popular term for "restaurant" is 식당. Common types of restaurants in Korea are those serving Korean food (한국 음식), Chinese food (중국 음식), and Japanese food (일본 음식). The different ethnic types of food are often referred to as 한식 (Korean style), 중식 (Chinese style), and 일식 (Japanese style). The suffix -식 means "style."

EXERCISE 9 The class will scan the following advertisements and circle the words that are recognized. The one who recognizes the largest number of words is the winner.

a.

한국 식당
바닷가에서 일몰을 바라보며
한국음식을 드시지 않겠습니까?
≪단체예약 환영≫
전화: (408) 372-2526

b.

• 전통 중국 음식 전문 업소 •
중 화 각
中 華 閣
◎ 전통 중국 음식
◎ 관광단체손님 할인우대

c.

명동 하우스
◐ 한국 전통 음식점 ◑
삼계탕 *영양 족발 * 산게찜
명동 칼국수 *조개찜 *해물 전골
≫ 예약 환영 ≪
영업시간: 월~일11:00~11:00

d.

◔ 韓國의 집 ◔
한국 전통 한식 전문
- 주방장 경력 10년을 바탕으로 주인이 직접 요리해서 여러분을 모십니다. 박찬홍입니다
전화: 408/249-0808

EXERCISE 10 Write the names of the four restaurants, and the types of food they serve.

	RESTAURANT NAMES	TYPES OF FOOD SERVED
a.		
b.		
c.		
d.		

EXERCISE 11 The word 전통 is recurring a few times in the advertisement on page 96. Look up the word in the dictionary, and write down its meaning.

2. Assimilation of [t] to the Following Consonant [s]

The combination of [t] and [s] is pronounced as [ss]. The [t], in this case, may be any of the written consonants (ㄷ, ㄸ, ㅌ, ㅈ, ㅉ, ㅊ, ㅅ, ㅆ) at the end of a syllable, not followed by a vowel.

받습니다 I receive. ⟶ pat · sŭmnida ⟶ passŭmnida
못써요 I can't use. ⟶ mot · ssŏyo ⟶ mossŏyo
같습니다 It's the same. ⟶ kat · sumnida ⟶ kassŭmnida

EXERCISE 12 Complete the following sentences by filling in the blank spaces with words listed in the box. Then, give an appropriate English equivalent to each sentence.

a. 한국은 ____ 입니다. ....
b. 저 학생 ____을 압니까? ....
c. 복순은 ____ 이름입니다. ....
d. 한 선생은 오늘 ____에 갑니다. ....
e. 중국은 ____에서 제일 큽니다. ....
f. 미국과 영국은 ____가 같습나다. ....

이름
여자
반도
세계
언어
유럽

EXERCISE 13 Complete the following list of verbs by filling in the missing forms (Honorific and Plain) on HIGH and MID LEVELS.

DICTIONARY FORM		LONG FORM *Honorific*	LONG FORM *Plain*	SHORT FORM *Honorific*	SHORT FORM *Plain*
알다	know	아십니다		아세요	
모르다	not know		모릅니다		몰라요
먹다	eat	잡수십니다			먹어요
그렇다	be so		그렇습니다	그러세요	
이르다	be early	이르십니다		이르세요	
같다	be same	같으십니다			같아요

EXERCISE 14 You found a note on your desk. Apparently, someone left it while you were away. Though the note contains some unknown words, you should be able to get the gist.

> 선생님,
> 점심 식사 아직 안하셨지요? 오늘은
> 저희들하고 같이 점심 하십시다.
> 아래층 일식 식당에서 기다리겠습니다.
> 곧 그리 오십시오.
> 박창식
> 신승일

a. Write the gist of the note in English.

b. Find the meanings of the unknown words in the note by using a dictionary.

VOCABULARY SUMMARY

Nominals

그릇	bowl, dish	웨이터	waiter
냉면	cold noodles	음식	food
동네	vicinity	점심	lunch
만두	dumplings	식당	restaurant; dining hall
몇 시	what time	음식점	restaurant
뭐	a contraction of 무엇	일식	Japanese food
반	half	중식	Chinese food
식사	meal	한식	Korean food

Personalized Vocabulary

깍두기	pickled radish	메뉴	menu
갈비	short ribs	불고기	broiled meat
김치	pickled cabbage	찌개	thick stew
백반	"white rice" dish		

Bound Nouns

-데	place

Action Verbs

나가다/나가	to go out	알다/아세요	to know
먹다	to eat	잡수시다	to eat (honorific)
모르다/몰라	not to know		

Stative Verbs

같다	to be the same	이르다/일러	to be early

Adverbs

너무	too, excessively	곧	immediately, right away
벌써	already		
지금	now	아직	yet, still

Pronouns

내가 Ⓜ Ⓛ	I	저희/저희들 Ⓗ	we
제가 Ⓗ	I		

Pointer Words

여기	here	저기	over there
거기	there		

Postpositions

-하고	and

Verb Endings

-으러	in order to	-으십시오. Ⓗ	Please do ....
-으십시다. Ⓗ	Let's		

ANSWERS TO EXERCISES

Exercise 3.
a. 아세요/알아요/알아?
b. 아시지요/알지요/알지?
c. 그 사람 잘 모르시지요/모르지요/모르지?
d. 선생님 보러 가십시다/갑시다.
e. 지금 몇 시예요/몇 시야?
f. 어디가 좋아요/좋아?
g. 좋은 데 하나 압니다/알아.
h. 벌써 5시 반이에요/반이야?

Exercise 6.
a. 바쁘시지요/바쁘지요/바쁘지?
b. 저분 영어 하시지요/저 사람 영어 하지요?
c. 자동차 없으시지요/없지요?
d. 한국 분이시지요/한국 사람이지요?
e. 이 식당 괜찮지요?

Exercise 10.
a. 한국 식당 - 한식
b. 명동 하우스 - 한식
c. 중화각 - 중식
d. 한국의 집 - 한식

Exercise 11.	전통 tradition; traditional				
Exercise 12.	a. 반도	c. 여자	e. 세계		
	b. 성	d. 구라파/유럽	f. 언어		
Exercise 13.	알다	아십니다	압니다	아세요	알아요
	모르다	모르십니다	모릅니다	모르세요	몰라요
	먹다	잡수십니다	먹습니다	잡수세요	먹어요
	그렇다	그러십니다	그렇습니다	그러세요	그래요
	이르다	이르십니다	이릅니다	이르세요	일러요
	같다	같으십니다	같습니다	같으세요	같아요

Exercise 14. a. We'd like to have lunch with you today. We'll be waiting for you at the Japanese restaurant downstairs.

b. 아직 yet, 저희 we Ⓗ, 곧 immediately

아래층 downstairs

LESSON 7
MAKING AN APPOINTMENT

FRAME 1

A Lunch Appointment

박: 미스 조, 오늘 점심 같이 하십시다.

조: 미안해요. 저 점심 약속이 있어요. 점심 후에 만나십시다.

박: 그러세요. 몇 시가 좋아요?

조: 세 시가 어때요?

박: 좋습니다. 어디서요?

조: 신라호텔 커피숍에서 만납시다.

박: 네, 그럼 이따 뵈요.

Pak : Miss Cho, let's have lunch together today.

Cho: I'm sorry. I have an engagement for lunch. Let's meet after lunch.

Pak : All right. What time is good for you?

Cho: How about three o'clock?

Pak : Fine. Where?

Cho: Let's meet at the coffee shop of Hotel Shilla.

Pak : O.K. Well then, see you later.

VOCABULARY STUDY

- 같이 — together
- 미안하다/-해 — to be sorry (used in apology)
- 약속 — engagement, appointment ; promise

- -후에 after…
- 만나다/만나 to meet, encounter
- 그러세요. Ⓗ Let's do that; All right.
- 어때요? How about…? How is…?

  The verb 어떻다/어때 is a stative verb denoting "how it is."
- 신라 호텔 Hotel Shilla
- 커피숍 coffee shop

CULTURAL ENCOUNTER There are two types of coffee shops in Korea : 다방 and 커피숍. 다방 "tea room" is an establishment where people get together and leisurely enjoy conversation over tea or coffee. In gereral 다방 serves beverages only, no food. 커피숍 is an American-style shop, which is growing more popular, gradually replacing the old-fashion 다방 in cities today. 커피숍 serves snacks and ice cream as well as beverages.

- 어디서요? Where (at)?

  CAUTION! The particle -서 must be added to a location word or phrase, when it denotes a place of an *action* or *event*, as opposed to the *existence*. (See Grammar.)
- 그럼 well, then
- 이따/이따가 later, after a while
- 뵙다 Ⓗ to see (someone)

  The verb 뵙다 is a "humble" form of 보다 "to see." With the "humble" form the speaker humbles himself so much that the speech level naturally becomes high.

  이따 뵙겠어요. Ⓗ I'll see you later.

  처음 뵙겠습니다. Ⓗ I'm glad to meet you.

CULTURAL ENCOUNTER How does a man talk to a woman in Korea? There are no special styles or speech features for men and women in talking to members of the opposite sex, except for a slight tendency to maintain more formality compared to similar situations in the United States. This means that typically Ⓗ speech is held longer between men and women than between members of the same sex. Classmates, colleagues, social acquaintances, and even lovers often maintain Ⓗ speech. This tendency is probably a vestige of the Confucian influence.

EXERCISE 1 Invite your friend to a dinner, and discuss the time and the place to meet.

EXERCISE 2 Each pair of your classmates will perform in front of the class the same conversation practiced in EXERCISE 1. The rest of the class will take notes on the key information exchanged. After each conversation, the class will compare notes.

FRAME 2

Being Late for an Appointment

조:	늦어서 미안합니다. 오래 기다리셨어요?	Cho:	I'm sorry for being late. Did I keep you waiting long?
박:	아니오. 저도 조금 전에 왔어요. 길에 차가 많았지요?	Pak :	No. I got here just a while ago myself. A lot of cars on the streets, weren't there?
조:	정말 많았어요. 그래서 좀 늦었어요.	Cho:	Really there were a lot. That's why I am a little late.
박:	커피 하시겠어요?	Pak :	Would you like coffee?
조:	아니오. 저 오후에는 커피 안 마셔요.	Cho:	No. I don't drink coffee in the afternoon.
박:	주스 어떻습니까?	Pak :	How about juice?
조:	네, 주스 시키십시다.	Cho:	O.K., let's order juice.

VOCABULARY STUDY

•늦어서 — because I am late

The general use of this connective -어서 will be reintroduced later.

•늦다 — to be late

This is a process verb. See Grammar on this type of verbs.

•오래 — for long (adverb)

•기다리셨어요? — Did you wait? (honorific past tense of 기다리다)

•-전에 — before... ; ... ago (antonym of -후에 "after...")

•왔어요. — (I/He) came (past tense of 오다)

•길 — street, road

•차 — car, vehicle

•정말 — really (adverb)

•오후 — afternoon (antonym: 오전 "before noon")

•마시다 — to drink

•주스 — juice

•시키다 — to place an order

❖ DESCRIBING PAST EVENTS

The basic rule for marking the past tense of a verb is to suffix the past marker -었 after the stem and the honorific marker.

PAST TENSE FORM : STEM + (으시) + 었 + ENDING

The honorific past stems always have the form: STEM + 으셨 + ending (where 시 and 어 are fused in one syllable).

가셨습니다.	[kasyŏssŭmnida]	He went/is gone.
읽으셨지요?	[ilgŭsyŏjjiyo]	You read it, didn't you?

The plain (non-honorific) past stems, on the other hand, involve the same sound changes that you saw in the short blunt form (STEM-어) because the past marker begins with the vowel 어. This means that to obtain the plain past tense form, you need to recall the short blunt form (STEM-어) and add ㅆ to it.

DICTIONARY FORM		SHORT BLUNT FORM	PLAIN PAST FORM	
하다	do	해	했습니다	did
있다	exist	있어	있었어요	existed
기다리다	wait	기다려	기다렸어요	waited
가다	go	가	갔어요	went
오다	come	와	왔습니다	came
모르다	don't know	몰라	몰랐어요	didn't know

The only exceptions to the above are the equation verbs (both the affirmative and the negative) which have different vowels in the plain past tense form from those of short blunt forms.

DICTIONARY FORM		SHORT BLUNT FORM	PAST TENSE FORM	
-이다	be	-이야	-이었어요	was/were
아니다	be not	아니야	아니었어요	wasn't/weren't

EXERCISE 3 With your partner engage in short question-answer exchanges using an honorific past form for a question and plain (non-honorific) form in a response.

EXAMPLE : 읽으셨어요? — Did you read?
네, 읽었어요. — Yes, I did (read).

a. 기다리셨어요?
b. 지금 오셨습니까?
c. 아셨어요?
d. 모르셨습니까?
e. 그 사람 보셨지요?
f. 차가 없으셨어요?
g. 식사 하셨습니까?
h. 서울에 안가셨어요?

NOTE: If you are unsure of the plain past tense forms of any verbs, check the list of past tense forms in the Grammar section.

EXERCISE 4 Say appropriate Korean equivalents to the following English sentences.

a. I'm sorry for being late.
b. No, you weren't late.
c. We didn't wait long.
d. There were a lot of people on the streets.
e. Did you order coffee?
f. I already drank two cups of coffee.
g. I don't drink coffee in the afternoon.
h. It was really good.

FRAME 3

At the Tea House

박 : 아가씨! 여기 주스 하나하고 커피 한 잔 주세요.	Pak : Young lady! Give us one juice, and a cup of coffee.
아가씨 : 예, 알았습니다. 곧 갖다 드리지요.	Waitress: All right, sir. I'll bring them right away.
박 : 그리고 물도 주세요.	Pak : And some water, too.
아가씨 : 예, 알았습니다.	Waitress: All right, sir.

VOCABULARY STUDY

- 아가씨 — young lady (unmarried); waitress (in this case)
- 주다 — to give
- 예 — yes

  예 [ye] is the standard form of affirmative or consenting reply. 네 is a colloquial form used in Seoul.
- 알았습니다. — I understand; All right.

  A typical response used by a waiter/waitress to express approval or agreement.

  CAUTION! Note the use of the past marker -았. In addition to the meaning "to know," the verb 알다 may also mean "come to understand" or "become aware of." The past marker here indicates that the "understanding" took place. It is similar to "I got it" in colloquial English.

- 곧 — immediately, right away (adverb)

• 갖다 드리지요. Ⓗ I will bring (them) (to you).

CAUTION! The ending -지요 in this case means "I'll..." and it has a falling tone ↘.

• 그리고 and (a sentence connective)
• 물 water

❖ 주다/드리다: VERBS OF GIVING

The verb 주다 "to give" changes the stem entirely to 드리다 when the receiver is given a special respect. Note the exchange between Mr. Pak and the waitress.

커피 한 잔 주세요.	Give me a cup of coffee.
갖다 드리지요.	I'll bring them (and give) to you.

The receiver is "me" (Mr. Pak himself) in the first sentence, and the plain form 주다 is used. However, in the second sentence, the receiver is the customer (Mr. Pak), and she uses the form: 드리다. Note also the pronouns ("me" and "you") are not normally expressed in Korean unless there is a real need to clarify the receiver.

❖ SUGGESTED LEARNING METHOD FOR 주다 AND 드리다

> You might remember the verb 드리다 as "give respectfully" in your mind. 드리다, of course, is never so translated, but it is useful to remember that the expression shows the speaker's respect toward the receiver.

The verb 갖다 주다 "to bring something to someone" is a compound verb consisting of 갖다 "bring" and 주다/드리다 "give."

의자 갖다 주세요	Please bring me a chair.
갖다 드리겠습니다.	I'll bring it to you.

EXERCISE 5 Ask your partner for an item from the pictures below. Your partner will say that he/she will comply.

EXERCISE 6 Place various objects (or pictures) on the table in the center. The teacher will call upon each student, and ask him or her to bring an object to the teacher. Each student will in turn pick up the object and bring it to the teacher, saying "He/She will bring the object to you."

FRAME 4

The Weekend Vacation

순옥: 주말 어떻게 지냈니?	Sunok : How was your weekend?
명주: 경주에 갔지.	Myŏngju: I went to Kyŏngju.
순옥: 왜? 구경하러?	Sunok : Why? For sightseeing?
명주: 응. 미국에서 손님이 왔어.	Myŏngju: Yeah. We had visitors from America.
순옥: 누가?	Sunok : Who?
명주: 아버지 친구분들이.	Myŏngju: My Dad's friends.
순옥: 언제 돌아왔니?	Sunok : When did you come back?
명주: 일요일 밤에.	Myŏngju: Sunday night.

VOCABULARY STUDY

•어떻게	how
•지내다/지내	to get along, spend (time)
•경주	Kyŏngju (a city on the southeastern coast, the old capital of the Shilla Kingdom)
•왜	why
•구경하러	(in order) to sightsee
•-에서	from (postposition)
•누가	who (as subject)

CAUTION! The question word 누구 "who" is shortened when the subject marker -가 is added.

•아버지	father
•손님	guest, visitor; customer
•언제	when
•돌아오다/돌아와	to return, come back
•일요일 밤	Sunday night

❖ DAYS OF THE WEEK

The days of the week are expressed by seven Sino-Korean characters followed by -요일, meaning "day of the week." The seven characters are: 일 for "sun," 월 for "moon," 화 for "fire," 수 for "water," 목 for "tree," 금 for "gold," 토 for "earth."

㉠일 요 일	월 요 일	화 요 일	수 요 일	목 요 일	금 요 일	토 요 일
Sunday	Monday	Tuesday	Wednesday	Thursday	Friday	Saturday

日 SUN	月 MON	火 TUE	水 WED	木 THU	金 FRI	土 SAT
	1 근로자의 날	2	3	4	5 어린이날	6 입하
7 부처님 오신날	8 어버이날	9	10	11	12	13

EXERCISE 7 Say what day of the week it is, as the teacher points to days on the calendar.

CULTURAL ENCOUNTER Hanja or Chinese characters are loan elements from Old Chinese and they generally are word-builders but not words by themselves. They are comparable to Greek or Latin elements in English, such as com- meaning "together," par- "equal," and -able "possible." Many Korean words are made up of Hanja, and it will be useful to learn and recognize Sino-Korean elements in them.

EXERCISE 8 Invite your friend to lunch, and discuss the day (of the week), time and the place to meet.

EXERCISE 9 You are late for an appointment at a coffee shop. Apologize to your friend and tell him/her why you were late. Discuss with your friend what to order.

EXERCISE 10 Discuss with your partner how he/she will/did spend each day of the week. Your partner will say what he/she actually will do or did. You may select some activities shown below.

•집에 있었어.	Stayed home.	•피크닉 갔어.	Went picnicking.
•아무 것도 안 했어.	Didn't do anything.	•쇼핑 했어.	Did shopping.
•책 읽었어.	Read books.	•스키 타러 갔어.	Went skiing.
•한국말 공부했어.	Studied Korean.	•...에 갔어.	Went to ....

GRAMMAR

1. How to Describe What Happened in the Past

The basic rule for marking the past tense of a verb is to suffix the past marker -었 after the stem with or without the honorific marker.

PAST TENSE FORM : STEM + (으시) 었 + ENDING

If the honorific marker is present, it is always fused with the past marker, thereby resulting in -으셨-.

계셨습니다.	Ⓗ	He was there.
가셨어요?	Ⓗ	Did you go?
읽으셨습니까?	Ⓗ	Did you read?

CAUTION! The verb 알다 "to know" loses ㄹ before the honorific marker.

아셨어요? Did you know?/Did you understand?

If the honorific marker is not present, the vowel 어 (or 었) is subject to the influence of the last vowel of the stem, just like the short blunt form (STEM +어). This means that the same sound changes for the blunt ending -어 apply to the past marker.

(1) The vowel 어 changes to 아 when the last vowel of the stem is 아 or 오.
(2) A succession of two vowels are contracted (to form one syllable).

Compare the blunt form and the past tense stem of the sample verbs below. A complete list of verbs in the past tense is given at the end of this section.

DICTIONARY FORM		SHORT BLUNT FORM	PAST TENSE FORM	
하다	do	해	했...	did
가다	go	가	갔...	went
앉다	sit	앉아	앉았...	sat
읽다	read	읽어	읽었...	read

This is the reason why a new irregular verb is listed in two or three verb forms (as in 하다/해 "to do" or 알다/아세요/알아 "to know") in the vocabulary section of each lesson. The last form is generally the short blunt form (STEM + 어), to which you add ㅆ to obtain the past tense stem. There are, of course, always some exceptions to any rule. Luckily, however, there are only two exceptions: -이다 and 아니다, which are perfectly regular in the past tense: -이었다 and 아니었다 even though the blunt forms are -이야 and 아니야, respectively. For your reference, a complete list of verbs introduced so far in the short blunt form and the past tense form is given on the next page.

DICTIONARY FORM	BLUNT FORM	PAST STEM (Plain)	PAST STEM (Honorific)	MEANING (Past)
가다	가	갔···	가셨···	went
같다	같아	같았···	같으셨···	was the same
그렇다	그래	그랬···	그러셨···	was so
나가다	나가	나갔···	나가셨···	went out
늦다	늦어	늦었···	늦으셨···	was late
다니다	다녀	다녔···	다니셨···	attended
드리다	드려	드렸···	드리셨···	gave (humble form)
들어오다	들어와	들어왔···	들어오셨···	came in
마시다	마셔	마셨···	마시셨···	drank
만나다	만나	만났···	만나셨···	met
많다	많아	많았···	많으셨···	were many
먹다	먹어	먹었···	잡수셨···	ate
바쁘다	바빠	바빴···	바쁘셨···	was busy
배우다	배워	배웠···	배우셨···	learned
보다	봐	봤···	보셨···	saw
뵙다	뵈워	뵈웠···	뵈우셨···	saw (humble form)
쓰다	써	썼···	쓰셨···	used; wrote
시키다	시켜	시켰···	시키셨···	ordered
아니다	아니야	아니었···	아니셨···	was not(equation)
앉다	앉아	앉았···	앉으셨···	sat down
알다	알아	알았···	아셨···	knew
어떻다	어때	어땠···	어떠셨···	was how
없다	없어	없었···	안계셨··· 없으셨···	was not (existence)
-이다	-이야	-이었···	-이셨···	was (equation)
이르다	일러	일렀···	이르셨···	was early
읽다	읽어	읽었···	읽으셨···	read
있다	있어	있었···	계셨··· 있으셨···	was there
작다	작아	작았···	작으셨···	was small

좋다	좋아	좋았…	좋으셨…	was good
주다	주어	주었…	주셨…	gave
지내다	지내	지냈…	지내셨…	spent (time)
크다	커	컸…	크셨…	was big
하다	해	했…	하셨…	did

2. Implications of the Past Tense in Korean

The past tense of Korean verbs has broader implications than its English counterpart does. It denotes some event *completed,* and its effect still *remains to the present.* It is generally equivalent to both the simple past and the present perfect in English. Thus,

김 선생님 집에 갔어요. means (1) Mr. Kim went home.
(2) Mr. Kim has gone home.

Sometimes, depending on the peculiar nature of the action or stative verb, the past tense of a Korean verb may even be equivalent to the present tense in English.

알았습니다. I understand. (I have understood you.)
늦었어요. I am late. (I have become late.)

3. Places of Activities

Nominals expressing the location of something is marked by the postposition -에, but if the location has something to do with an activity, an addition of -서 or -에서 is required.

미스터 박 어디(에) 있어요? Where is Mr. Pak?
미스터 박 어디서 기다려요? Where is Mr. Pak waiting?
순옥 씨는 집에 있습니다. Miss Sunok is at home.
순옥 씨는 집에서 공부해요. Miss Sunok is studying at home.

4. Verbs of Giving

The verb 주다 "to give" changes the stem entirely to 드리다 when respect is shown to the *receiver* (indirect object). In other words, the verb 드리다 means "give respectfully" rather than simply "to give." The expression of this kind is called a "humble" forms.

물 좀 주세요. Give me some water, please.
드리지요. (Humble form) I'll give it (to you).

The verb 갖다 주다 "to bring (and give)" is a compound verb consisting of 갖다 "bring" and 주다 "give." Here again, the verb 주다 must be replaced with 드리다 when the speaker shows respect to the *receiver.*

메뉴 갖다 주세요. Bring me a menu.
메뉴 갖다 드리겠습니다. (Humble form) I'll bring a menu (to you).

CAUTION! Although the verb 갖다주다 or 갖다드리다 is translated as "to bring," remember that a part of its meaning is "to give something to someone." This verb should *not* be used when one simply "bring" something along with oneself, in which case, an entirely different verb (가지고 오다) is used.

그 책 가지고 오세요.	Bring the book (with you).

5. Two Uses of -지요.

The verb ending -지요 (-지 in the LOW LEVEL) has several uses in conversation. Two uses are introduced here.

a. Tag question (with a *sharp rising* tone).

좋지요?	It's nice, isn't it?
안 바쁘시지요?	You aren't busy, are you?

b. Emphatic response with certainty or intention (with a *falling* tone)

가시겠어요?	Would you like to go?
네, 가지요.	Yes, I certainly would.
물 좀 주시겠어요?	Could you give me some water?
네, 갖다 드리지요.	Yes, I will bring it right away.
미스 강 아시지요?	You know Miss Kang, don't you?
알지요.	Of course, I do.

6. What is a Process Verb?

Most verbs introduced so far are ACTION and STATIVE verbs. ACTION verbs typically express some actions by human subjects, while STATIVE verbs express some state or quality of the subject. There is yet another type of verbs that express some processes not under the direct control of human subjects. We will call this type of verbs "PROCESS" verbs. We have two process verbs in this lesson: 알다 "come to be aware of" and 늦다 "get/become late." Special grammatical properties of process verbs will be introduced later.

7. A Summary of Sentence Endings

Below is a list of verb endings that are used to conclude sentences.

HIGH LEVEL → Honorific, Plain; MID LEVEL → Plain; LOW LEVEL → Blunt

	Honorific	Plain	Blunt
GENERAL (used in all moods)	-으세요.	-어요.	-어.

(Used in specific moods)

Declarative	-으십니다.	V-ㅂ니다. C-습니다.	
Interrogative	-으십니까?	V-ㅂ니까? C-습니다.	-니?
Imperative	-으십시오.		
Suggestive	-으십시다.	-읍시다.	
Exclamatory	-으시네요.	-네요.	-네.
Tag Question	-으시지요?	-지요?	-지?
Emphatic Response	-으시지요.	-지요.	-지.

READING & WRITING

1. Numbers with Counters

Unlike in English, a number usually comes after the noun in Korean, as in 학생 하나 "one student." (See Lesson 5.) Also, a number is often followed by a particle, as in 커피 두 잔 "two cups of coffee." In this case, 잔 happens to be a noun meaning "cup." However, they are particles, not nouns by themselves, that are suffixed to numbers so that they may indicate the kinds of nouns being counted. We will call such nouns or particles "counters." Some of the most common counters are:

•PEOPLE:	(Honorific)	-분	•CUPS/GLASSES:	-잔
	(Plain)	-사람	•MACHINES:	-대
	(Plain)	-명	•SHEETS OF PAPER:	-장
•YEARS OF AGE:		-살	•HOURS:	-시
•ANIMALS:		-마리	•OCCURRENCES:	-번
•SMALL OBJECTS:		-개	•WORDS:	-마디
•KINDS OF OBJECTS:		-가지	•BOOKS:	-권

CAUTION! Remember that the numbers below are shortened before a noun or a counter.

• 하나 > 한...
• 둘 > 두...
• 셋 > 세...

• 넷 > 네...
• 스물 > 스무...
(twenty)

EXERCISE 11 Fill the spaces below with appropriate counters.

a. 의자 다섯 ______ 갖다 주세요.
b. 한국에 네 ______ 갔습니다.
c. 자동차 두 ______ 있습니다.
d. 책 한 ______ 읽었지요.
e. 손님 세 ______ 오셨어요.
f. 저는 스무 ______ 입니다.

EXERCISE 12 Translate the following phrases into Korean.

a. Two cups of tea: ________
b. Seven guests: ________
c. One English word: ________
d. Eight books: ________
e. Twenty years old: ________
f. Three automobiles: ________
g. Four pencils: ________
h. Six different objects: ________

2. Days of the Week

The days of the week are all Sino-Korean (words of Chinese origin) in three syllables. The first syllable of each symbolizes one of the seven basic elements: 일, 월, 화, 수, 목, 금, 토. The last two syllables, -요일 means "day of the week."

CAUTION! With one exception of 금 ("gold"), none of all these syllables are words to be used by themselves. As a rule, Sino-Korean elements are word-formants, but not words.

EXERCISE 13 Read each of the newspaper clippings below, and answer the questions.

An English class schedule is announced here. Check ( ) the class day in English, and write in the time for each session.

영어학습

화요일 – 저녁 6시

금, 토요일 – 저녁 6시

일요일 – 오후 2시

	Day	Time
( )	Monday	________
( )	Tuesday	________
( )	Wednesday	________
( )	Friday	________
( )	Saturday	________
( )	Sunday	________

EXERCISE 14 This is an announcement of a new publication (발행) date of a newspaper. Scan the headlines, and write the answers to the questions given below.

일 요 신 문 1995년 7월 18일 (화요일)

〈매주 수요일 발행〉

위의 업소에서 매주 수요일 (일부 지역은 목요일)부터 일요신문을 판매합니다.

Reading Vocabulary

- 매주 every week
- 발행 publication, issue
- 판매 sale

a. What is the name of the publication in English? ________________

b. The headline announces a new date of the publication. What is the new date? ________________

c. In some districts (일부지역) the same publication is sold on a different day. What is that date? ________________

EXERCISE 15 Writing a note for your friend. You want to invite your colleague to lunch at a Chinese restaurant. Leave a note, asking him/her to come to the tea house, downstairs (아래층) at 11:30. Add that you will be waiting there until 12:00 (열두 시까지).

VOCABULARY SUMMARY

Nominals

경주	Kyŏngju (city)	아가씨	young lady (unmarried)
길	street, road, way	아버지	father
누가	who (as the subject)	약속	promise, engagement
다방	tea house	주스	juice
물	water	차	car, motor vehicle
발행	publication	커피숍	coffee shop
손님	guest, visitor, customer	판매	sale

Time/Week Days

밤	night	수요일	Wednesday
오전	before noon (a.m.)	목요일	Thursday
오후	afternoon (p.m.)	금요일	Friday
주말	weekend	토요일	Saturday
월요일	Monday	일요일	Sunday
화요일	Tuesday		

Stative Verbs

미안하다/미안해	to be sorry (an expression of apology)
어떻다/어때	to be how

Action Verbs

갖다 주다	to bring (something) to (someone) (Plain form)
갖다 드리다	to bring (soemthing) to (someone) (Humble form)
구경하다/해	to sightsee
드리다	to give (Humble form)
돌아오다/-와	to return, come back
마시다	to drink
만나다/만나	to meet
뵙다	to see, meet (someone) (Humble form)
시키다	to place an order
주다	to give (Plain form)
지내다/지내	to get along, spend (time)

Process Verbs

늦다	to be late

Adverbs

같이	together	오래	for a long time
곧	immediately, right away	왜	why
매주	every week	이따/이따가	later, after a while
어떻게	how	정말	really
언제	when		

Postpositions

-에서	from; at (marking the place of an activity)
-전에	before (some event)
-후에	after (some event)

Idiomatic Phrases

그러세요.	Let's do that.
알았습니다.	I understand; All right.

Interjections

예	yes (Formal, standard version of the colloquial 네.)

Verb Endings

-지(요)	an ending with a falling tone, used in giving an emphatic, affirmative response to a question

Counters

-가지	kinds of object	-번	occurrences
-개	small objects	-분	persons (Honorific)
-권	volumes of books	-사람	persons
-대	machines	-살	years of age
-마디	words	-시	hours
-마리	animals	-잔	cups, glasses
-명	persons	-장	sheets of paper

ANSWERS TO EXERCISES

Exercise 3. a. 기다렸어요. b. 지금 왔어요. c. 알았어요. d. 몰랐어요. e. 봤어요. f. 없었어요. g. 했어요. h. 안 갔어요.

Exercise 4. a. 늦어서 미안합니다. b. 아니오, 안 늦었어요. c. 오래 안 기다렸어요. d. 길에 사람이 많았어요. e. 커피 시키셨어요? f. 벌써 커피 두 잔 마셨어요. g. 저 오후에는 커피 안 마셔요. h. 정말 좋았어요.

Exercise 11. a. 다섯 개 b. 네 번 c. 두 대 d. 한 권 e. 세 분 f. 스무 살

Exercise 12. a. 차 두 잔 b. 손님 일곱 분 c. 영어 한 마디 d. 책 여덟 권 e. 스무 살 f. 자동차 세 대 g. 연필 네 개 h. 여섯 가지

Exercise 13. Class days: Tuesday, 6 p.m., Friday/Saturday, 6 p.m., Sunday, 2 p.m.

Exercise 14. a. Sunday paper b. every Wednesday c. Thursday

LESSON 8
COMING TO KOREA

FRAME 1

On Arrival

민 : 밀러 선생, 한국에 처음 오셨어요?	Min : Mr. Miller, is this the first time for you to come to Korea?
밀러 : 아니오, 오년 전에 왔었습니다.	Miller : No, I was here five years ago.
민 : 얼마나 오래 여기 계시겠어요?	Min : How long are you going to be here?
밀러 : 약 삼주일 있을 겁니다.	Miller : I'm going to stay for about 3 weeks.
민 : 미국 어디서 오셨어요?	Min : What part of America are you from?
밀러 : 뉴욕에서 왔어요.	Miller : I've come from New York.

VOCABULARY STUDY

- 오년 — five years
- 왔었습니다. — I came/was (here).

  The past marker -었 is used here twice. (See Grammar.)
- 얼마나 오래 — how long
- 약 — approximately, about
- 삼 주일/삼주 — three weeks

• 있을 겁니다. I'm going to stay; I'll be staying.

The form -을 겁니다 is a colloquial form, meaning "one is going to..." (See Grammar).

• 어디서 from where (the short of 어디에서)

CAUTION! The postposition -에서 has two meanings: one to denote the place of activities (Lesson 7), and the other denoting the origin ("from"). In colloquial speech the vowel 에 is often dropped from 에서.

❖ TWO NUMBER SYSTEMS IN KOREAN

There are two number systems used in Korean: the native Korean and the Sino-Korean. The latter is a set of loan words from Old Chinese. The two systems are not generally interchangeable. In written Korean, numbers may be written in three ways: ① in Arabic numerals (e.g., 1, 2, 3), ② in Chinese characters (e.g., 一, 二, 三), and ③ in Hangŭl (e.g., 하나, 둘, 셋). Both arabic numerals and Sino-Korean numerals are read in the Sino-Korean way.

Arabic	1	2	3	4	5	6	7	8	9	10
Native Korean	하나	둘	셋	넷	다섯	여섯	일곱	여덟	아홉	열
Sino-Korean	일	이	삼	사	오	육	칠	팔	구	십

EXERCISE 1 Recite Sino-Korean numbers, as the teacher points at each number written in Arabic numerals.

EXERCISE 2 Read aloud the Sino-Korean numbers as the teacher points at numbers in a random order.

EXERCISE 3 A small group of learners will play a game, in which one participant will start out by asking a question (from the list below), and another will answer using any Sino-Korean number. Then the first participant will identify the number by writing down (in Arabic numerals). A correct identification of each number will earn one point. After going through all the questions by taking turns, total points earned will determine the winner.

a. 한국에 몇 주일 계실겁니까?
b. 한국말을 몇 년 배우셨어요?
c. 영어를 얼마나 오래 공부했습니까?
d. 서울에서 몇 주일 지냈습니까?
e. 미국에 몇 년 전에 갔었습니까?
f. 서울에 언제 오셨어요?

❖ COUNTING LARGE NUMBERS

Once you master small numbers, from one to ten, in the Sino-Korean system, counting up to 99 will become easy for you. Two-digit numbers are simply obtained by combining the first ten numbers.

11 (ten-one) = 십일
15 (ten-five) = 십오
20 (two-ten) = 이십
21 (two-ten-one) = 이십일
62 (six-ten-two) = 육십이
99 (nine-ten-nine) = 구십구

EXERCISE 4 Read aloud the following two-digit numbers.

30	31	42	53	64
79	70	88	91	95

EXERCISE 5 Listen to each of the sentences that your teacher reads (from the script in the Vocabulary Summary section), and write down the number you hear.

a.________ c.________ e.________ g.________ i. ________
b.________ d.________ f. ________ h.________ j. ________

FRAME 2

Sending Gifts Home

민 : 밀러 선생, 어디 다녀오셨어요?	Min : Where have you been, Mr. Miller?
밀러 : 남대문 시장에 다녀왔어요.	Miller : I have been to the Namdaemun market.
민 : 무엇을 사셨습니까?	Min : What did you buy?
밀러 : 선물이요. 보시겠어요?	Miller: Some gifts. Do you want to see?
민 : 핸드백이네요. 부인한테 보내시지요?	Min : A handbag. You're sending it to your wife, I suppose.
밀러 : 아니오. 딸한테 보낼 겁니다.	Miller: No. I'm sending it to my daughter.

VOCABULARY STUDY

- 다녀오다 — to come back (from visiting); be (back) home

  This compound verb (다니다 + 오다) is used in one of the following situations:
  ① Asking or stating where one has just been to, and ② wishing someone a safe trip including the return trip, as in 다녀오세요.

- 남대문 — The South Gate (in Seoul)

- 시장 market, market place
- -을/를 postposition marking the object

  -을 is placed after a consonant, and -를 after a vowel. (See Grammar.)
- 사다/사 to buy
- 선물 gift
- 보내다/보내 to send
- 핸드백 handbag
- 부인 wife (honorific form)
- -한테 to, for

  This is a postposition marking the dative case of human and animate nominals.) (See Grammar.)
- 딸 daughter

EXERCISE 6 You are just back from shopping. You bought some gifts to be sent to your family. Your partner is curious about what you bought, and for whom. Select shopping items from the word list below. It is recommended that you pronounce English loan words with Korean sounds and in Korean ways.

PLACES	SHOPPING ITEMS			
양품점 boutique shop	1. handbag	핸드백	6. scarf	스카프
	2. sweater	스웨터	7. stockings	스타킹
	3. blouse	블라우스	8. sun glasses	썬글래스
	4. skirt	스커트	9. shoes	구두
	5. top coat	(오버) 코트		
양복점 men's clothes store	1. suit	양복	5. shirt	셔츠
	2. jacket	자켓	6. hat	모자
	3. sport coat	스포츠 코트	7. socks	양말
	4. trousers	바지	8. shoes	구두

FRAME 3

Tidings from Home

민 : 댁에서 연락이 있으세요?	Min : Do you hear from home?
밀러 : 그럼요. 아이들한테서 전화가 자주 옵니다. 어제 아들한테서 편지 받았어요. 보세요.	Miller: Sure. I get telephone calls often from my children. I received a letter from my son yesterday. Take a look.
민 : 글을 잘 쓰네요. 몇 살입니까?	Min : He writes fine. How old is he?
밀러 : 금년에 여섯 살입니다.	Miller: He is six this year.

•댁	home, house (honorific form)
•연락	contact, touch, correspondence
•그럼요	of course, sure (an expression of emphatic affirmation)
•-한테서	from (postposition for human/animate nominals)
•자주	often
•전화	telephone; telephone call
•아들	son
•편지	letter
•받다/받아	to receive
•글	writing; sentence (as opposed to 말 "speech")
•쓰다/써	to write
•-살	a counter suffix for years of age

CAUTION! -살 is used only with native Korean numbers.

•금년	this year

EXERCISE 7 Complete the following sentences by filling in the blank spaces with appropriate postpositions from the list on your right.

a. 저녁 ____ 다방 ____ 오세요.
Come to the tea house in the evening.
b. 미스 강 ____ 편지 ____ 받았습니다.
I received a letter from Miss Kang.
c. 집 ____ 커피 ____ 없어요.
We have no coffee in the house.
d. 시장 ____ 커피 ____ 샀어요.
She bought coffee at the market.
e. 선물 ____ 아들 ____ 보냅니다.
I'm sending a gift to my son.
f. 우리는 호텔 ____ 점심 ____ 했어요.
We had our lunch at the hotel.

LIST OF POSTPOSITIONS

Subject	:	-이/-가
Object	:	-을/-를
"to/for"	:	-에/-한테
"from"	:	-에서/한테서
"at" (place)	:	-에/-에서
"at" (time)	:	-에

EXERCISE 8 Say appropriate Korean equivalents to the following English sentences.

a. Do you hear from your friend?
b. A telephone call for you.
c. I have one son and two daughters.
d. Mr. Lee is good at writing.
e. I received a letter from home.

EXERCISE 9 Suppose that there are children in your friend's house. Ask how old each of them is, using the following model.

MODEL: 그 아이가 몇 살입니까? — How old is the child?
열두 살입니다. — He/she is twelve years old.

FRAME 4

Mother from Shopping

딸 : 엄마, 어디 다녀 오세요?	Daughter: Mom, where have you been?
어머니 : 상점에 다녀와.	Mother : I've been to the store.
딸 : 뭐 사셨어요?	Daughter: What did you buy?
어머니 : 스웨터 샀어.	Mother : I bought some sweaters.
딸 : 누구 것? 제 것도 샀어요?	Daughter: Whose? Did you buy mine, too?
어머니 : 그래, 네 것도 샀지.	Mother : Yes, I bought yours, too.

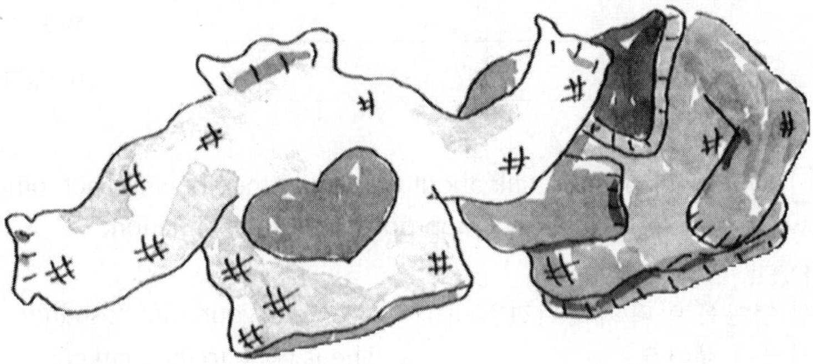

VOCABULARY STUDY

- 엄마 — Mom (a diminutive form of 어머니 "mother")
- 뭐 — what (the short for 무엇)
- 스웨터 — sweater
- 누구 것 — whose (누구 "who" + 것 "thing")
- 제 것 — mine (= my thing)
- 네 것 — yours (= your thing)

CULTURAL ENCOUNTER How do children talk to their parents? As a child begins to speak, he or she does it only on the Low Level. The polite forms (HIGH and MID LEVELS) are consciously taught by the parents as the child gets near school age (five or six). This process of acquiring polite forms varies depending on the dialect, the family tradition and outlook. Even after the child fully acquires the polite forms, some parents allow the child to use blunt forms to the senior members of the family until the child fully grows up. In the above exchanges, the daughter uses polite forms to her mother but the term of address is still 엄마 "Mom," a product of her child talk.

❖ 가족 (Personalized Vocabulary)

Expressions of family members come in two or three forms: the honorific, the plain, and occasionally the diminutive form, which denotes familiarity or endearment.

HONORIFIC	PLAIN	DIMINUTIVE	
아버님	아버지	아빠	father
어머님	어머니	엄마	mother
부인	아내 집사람		wife
바깥 어른	남편		husband
자녀분	아이	애	child
아드님	아들		son
따님	딸		daughter

EXERCISE 10 With your partner, talk about the family members of each other, using one of the following models, whichever is appropriate for your situation.

a. HIGH LEVEL

부인/바깥 어른은 어디 계십니까?	Where is your wife/husband?
아내는 시장에 갔어요.	She is gone to the market.
자녀분 많으시지요?	You have many children, don't you?

b. MID/LOW LEVEL

어머니 어디 계셔?	Where is your Mom?
아버지하고 나가셨어.	She went out with Dad.

GRAMMAR

1. A Summary of Case Postpositions

Below are the case postpositions that you have covered so far. A case postposition denotes the "role" of the nominal within the sentence. (The other type, called "context postpositions," such as -는, -도, etc. are not included here.)

Case Postpositions			English
(1) SUBJECT	NEUTRAL (no markers)	FOCUSED -이 (after a consonant) -가 (after a vowel)	(no markers)
(2) OBJECT	NEUTRAL (no markers)	FOCUSED -을 (after a consonant) -를 (after a vowel)	(no markers)
(3) PLACE	-에 / -에서	if the verb expresses the location or existence, or / if the verb expresses some state or event	in / at / on
(4) TIME (point)	- 에		in/at/on
(5) TIME (duration)	(no makers)	(-을/를 when stressed)	for
(6) DESTI-NATION	-에 / -한테	after an inanimate object / after a human/animal	to/for
(7) ORIGIN	-에서 / -한테서	after an inanimate object / after a human/animal	from

EXAMPLE SENTENCES

(1) SUBJECT

어머니 시장에 가셨어요. — Mom went to the market. [NEUTRAL]

어머니가 시장에 가셨어요. — Mom (e.g., "not sister") went to the market. [FOCUSED]

(2) OBJECT

편지 받았어요. — I received the letter. [NEUTRAL]

편지를 받았어요. — I received the letter. [FOCUSED]

(3) PLACE

우리 다방에 있었습니다. — We were in the tea house. [EXISTENCE]

우리 다방에서 만났습니다. | We met at the tea house. [ACTION]

(4) TIME
우리 아들은 금년에 두 살입니다. | My son is two years old this year. [POINT]

(5) TIME
삼 주일 있을 겁니다. | I'll be staying for three weeks. [DURATION]

(6) DESTINATION
댁에 가십니까? | Are you going home? [INANIMATE]
이 책을 미스 한한테 주세요. | Give this book to Miss Han. [HUMAN]

(7) ORIGIN
집에서 전화가 왔어요. | I got a call from home. [INANIMATE]
누구한테서 받았습니까? | From whom did you receive it? [HUMAN]

2. Asking and Stating Intentions

There are several ways of asking or stating one's intentions in Korean. You have so far learned four different ways. To say "I'm going out," or "I'll go out," you may use ⓐ the simple present, ⓑ the intention-marking suffix -겠, ⓒ the ending -지요, or ⓓ the phrasal form -을 것이다.

a. The simple present: 갑니다.
b. The intention marker -겠: 가겠습니다.
c. The ending -지요: 가지요.
d. The phrasal form -을 것이다: 갈 겁니다.

CAUTION! The ending -지요 is used in a response to a question or a request. With the form of -을 것이다, the ㅅ of 것 (originally "thing") is normally dropped in colloquial speech. It is probably closest to the English progressive form ("be + ···ing") for expressing one's intention.

무엇을 할 겁니까? | What are you going to do?
커피 할 거예요. | I'll have coffee.

편지 쓸 거예요? | Are you going to write a letter?
편지 쓸 겁니다. | I'm going to write a letter.

3. The Past of the Past: -었 었

The past marker -었 is often used twice to denote that the effect of a past event (the first use of -었) belongs to the past (the second use of -었) as well. With some verbs, however, the use of -었 sometimes implies that the effect of a past action remains to the present.

		IMPLICATIONS
그 사람 왔어요.	He has come.	So, he is here.
그 사람 왔었어요.	He came/He had come.	But, he is gone.

알았어요.	I knew/understood.	So, I know now.
알았었어요	I knew/I used to know.	But, I forgot now.

CAUTION! The second past marker 었 does not change to 았 even if the preceding vowel is 오 or 아.

READING & WRITING

1. What is Hanja?

Hanja (한자: pronounced [hanja] or [hantcha]) literally means "Han letter" or "Chinese writing." The first syllable 한 in this case does not refer to Korea, but to an ancient Chinese Empire of Han (202 B.C. - 8 A.D.). 한자 is an ideographic script, where each character (syllable) represents a "meaning" and "sound." The ideographic or pictographic writings are like Arabic numerals in English, where individual symbols signify something, as in 1, 2, 3, etc.

한자 was introduced to Korea from the earliest time of its history, and it has been used by Koreans for writing throughout its history. After the phonetic script was invented in 1446 by King Sejong (세종) and his court scholars, both scripts, 한글 and 한자, coexisted in writings. 세종, the fourth king (왕) of the Chosŏn Dynasty (조선), is regarded as the greatest ruler of the dynasty. By the middle of this century, the use of 한자 had been quite reduced. Today in South Korea, 한자 is still mixed in some types of writings. North Korea has eliminated the use of 한자 entirely since 1945.

EXERCISE 11 After reading the text, answer the questions below, which are based on the information in the text.

> 한자는 오래 전에 중국에서 한국에 들어왔습니다. 그리고 한국 사람들이 한자를 일본에 소개했습니다. 지금 한자는 동양의 세 나라, 중국, 한국, 일본에서 씁니다. 15세기에 세종이 한글을 창제하기 전에는 한국 사람들은 글을 쓰는데 주로 한문만 썼습니다.

Reading Vocabulary

- 그리고 and
- 15세기 15th century
- 글 writing
- 주로 mainly

a. When does the text say Hangŭl was created in Korea?
b. What are the three countries where 한자 is used today?
c. What did Koreans do before the creation of 한글 for writing?

NOTE: The text above contains a few unintroduced words for you. However, even without the help of the glosses given above, you should be able to understand the gist of the text.

2. Sino-Korean Words

Even though the use of 한자 is limited today, it does not mean that Chinese loan words (words of Chinese origin) are reduced in Korean. Chinese loan words that entered Korean lexicon remain today in a great quantity (over 50%), and such words are called 한자말 (Chinese character words). The numerals (숫자) in Korean are good examples. The native numerals are mostly used in smaller numbers (below 100), and the Sino-Korean numerals are mostly used in large numbers.

In counting lower numbers in daily conversation, Korean speakers primarily use the native numerals, but for some specific expressions, such as money, identification numbers, time expressions (except for "hours"), Sino-Korean numerals are used.

In writing, numbers are mostly written with Arabic numerals. Generally, written Arabic numbers are read as Sino-Korean as you see in EXERCISE 12 below.

Even though 한자 is not included within the primary objectives of this course, Sino-Korean numerals are shown below to give you some idea about them.

1: 일	2: 이	3: 삼	4: 사	5: 오
一	二	三	四	五

6: 육	7: 칠	8: 팔	9: 구	10: 십
六	七	八	九	十

EXERCISE 12 The class will scan the following advertisement and circle the words that they recognize. The one who recognizes the greatest number of words is the winner.

한국항공 전용호텔인 와이키키 리조텔에서 머무르실 경우 숙박료 및 렌트카 사용 요금을 대폭 할인해 드리고 호텔내 음식점, 선물가게에서 사용하실 수 있는 쿠폰도 드립니다.

로스엔젤레스 - 호놀룰루 주 3회
호놀룰루 - 서울 주 13회 운항으로 그리고 편리한 스케줄의 한국항공으로 꿈과 낭만의 섬, 하와이에 다녀오십시오.

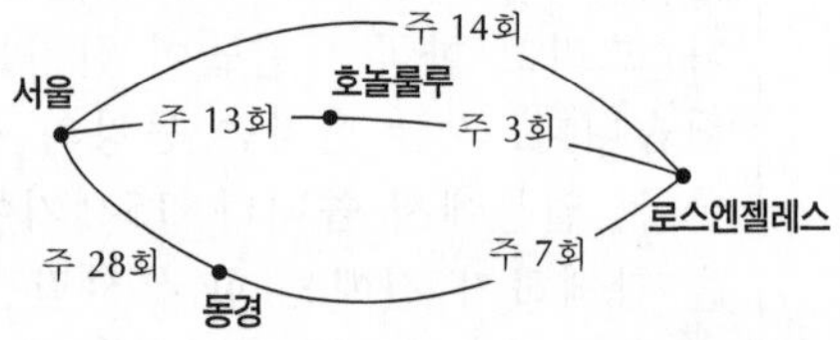

EXERCISE 13 This is an announcement of a concert (음악회). Write the date and time(s) of the event.

정통 가곡의 진수를 보여드립니다.
10월 9일 토요일 오후 2시, 저녁 8시
귀하를 초대합니다.

EXERCISE 14 Fill the spaces below with appropriate counters.

a. 주스 한 ______ 입니다
b. 자동차 두 ______ 있어요.
c. 저는 스물 다섯 ______ 입니다.
d. 시계를 세 ______ 샀어요.
e. 그 책을 네 ______ 읽었습니다.
f. 점원이 다섯 ______ 있습니다.

EXERCISE 15 Translate the following phrases into Korean.

a. Four gifts : ________
b. Six students : ________
c. Three words : ________
d. Twice (two times) : ________
e. 21 years old : ________
f. Seven computers : ________
g. Four books : ________
h. One sheet of paper : ________

EXERCISE 16 Complete the following sentences by filling in the blank spaces with the words listed on the right. Then, give an English equivalent for each Korean sentence.

a. _____을 썼습니다.
b. _____는 중국에서 왔습니다.
c. 집에 _____ 편지를 씁니다.
d. 우리는 집에서 _____ 한국말을 합니다.
e. 저는 오후에 _____ 에 다녀 오겠어요.
f. 저녁은 _____ 식당에 가십시다.

주로
매주
중식
글
한자
공항

VOCABULARY SUMMARY

Nominals

글	writing, sentence
금년	this year
남대문	the South Gate (in Seoul)
-년	counter for years of age
댁	home, house (honorific)
-살	counter for years of age
선물	gift
-세기	century
숫자	number
스웨터	sweater
시장	market place
양복점	(men's) clothes store
양품점	boutique shop
연락	contact, correspondence
전화	telephone
주일	week
편지	letter
한글	Korean script/alphabet
한자	Chinese characters
핸드백	handbag

Family Members

가족	family
남편	husband
딸	daughter
부인/아내	wife
아버님/아버지/아빠	father
아이	child
아들	son
어머님/어머니/엄마	mother

NOTE: When two or three forms are given, they are in the order of honorific-plain-diminutive. The list is by no means complete.

Verbs

다녀오다/다녀와	to have been to	사다/사	to buy
받다	to receive	쓰다/써	to write; to use
보내다/보내	to send		

Adverbs

자주	often	주로	mainly
그리고	and		

Postpositions

-을/를	the object marker (used when the object is stressed) -을 after a consonant; -를 after a vowel		
-한테	to	-한테서	from

Others

약	about (with numerals)	얼마나 오래	how long

Scripts for Exercises

Exercise 5.

a. 나는 13년 전에 한국에 왔었습니다.
b. 서울에 약 10주일 있을 겁니다.
c. 학교에서 한국말을 27주일 배웠어요.
d. 박한주 씨는 6주일 후에 올 겁니다.
e. 저는 87년에 처음 미국에 갔었어요.
f. 저는 밀러 선생을 8년 전에 뵈웠어요.
g. 미스 리는 학원에서 영어를 12주일 배웠어요.
h. 카터 씨는 하와이에서 9년 지냈습니다..
i. 미스 리는 92년에 시카고에 갔었어요.
j. 밀러 씨는 24년 전에 한국에 왔었어요.

ANSWERS TO EXERCISES

Exercise 5.

a. 13 b. 10 c. 27 d. 6 e. 87 f. 8 g. 12 h. 9 i. 92 j. 24

Exercise 7.

a. 저녁에, 다방에
b. 미스 강한테서, 편지를
c. 집에, 커피가
d. 시장에서, 커피를
e. 선물을, 아들한테
f. 호텔에서, 점심을

Exercise 8.

a. 친구한테서 연락이 있어요?
b. 선생님한테 전화가 왔어요.
c. 아들 하나하고 딸이 둘 있습니다.
d. 이 선생은 글을 잘 씁니다.
e. 집에서 편지를 받았어요.

Exercise 11. a. In the 15th century
b. They are China, Korea and Japan.
c. They used Chinese characters.

Exercise 13. October 9th, Saturday, 2 p.m. and 8 p.m.

Exercise 14. a. 한 잔 b. 두 대 c. 스물다섯 살 d. 세 개 e. 네 번 f. 다섯 명/다섯 사람

Exercise 15. a. 선물 네 개 c. (말) 세 마디 e. 스물한 살 g. 책 네 권

Exercise 15.	a. 선물 네 개	c. (말) 세 마디	e. 스물한 살	g. 책 네 권
	b. 학생 여섯 명	d. 두 번	f. 컴퓨터 일곱 대	h. 종이 한 장

Exercise 16. a. 글 b. 한자 c. 매주 d. 주로 e.공항 f. 중식

LESSON 9
SHOPPING

FRAME 1

Planning for Shopping

밀러 : 쇼핑 나갈까요?	Miller: Shall we go out for shopping?
민 : 그럽시다. 뭐 살 겁니까?	Min : Sure. What are you going to buy?
밀러 : 가방 하나 사야 해요. 가게 아직 열렸을까요?	Miller: I have to buy a suitcase. Do you think the stores are still open?
민 : 열렸을 겁니다. 지금 몇 시예요?	Min : I think they are. What time is it now?
밀러 : 여섯 시 이십오분입니다.	Miller: It's 6:25
민 : 아직 안 닫혔어요.	Min : They are not closed yet.

VOCABULARY STUDY

- -을까요? Shall we...? Do you think (it is/they are)...?
  A verb ending used in asking the addressee's opinion. (See Grammar.)
- 그러다/그래 to do so (action verb)
  CAUTION! The action verb 그러다/그래 should be distinguished from the stative verb 그렇다/그래 "to be so." In the short form (그래), both verbs become identical in form. 그럽시다 means "Let's do that."
- 가방 luggage, suitcase, briefcase
- -어야 하다. One must... / One has to... (See Grammar.)

• 가게 shop, store (=상점)
• 아직 still, yet (adverb)
• 열리다 to be opened (passive form of 열다 "to open")

As the past marker 었 is used together with this verb, it denotes a state of "being open."

가게가 열렸어요. The store is open.

• 열렸을까요? Do you think it is open?
• -을 겁니다. I think, I guess...
• -분 minutes (used only with Sino-Korean numerals)
• 닫히다 to be closed (a passive form of 닫다 "to close")

❖ HOURS, MINUTES, AND SECONDS

The hours (-시) are expressed by native Korean number words as introduced in Lesssson 6, but the minutes (-분) and seconds (-초) are expressed by Sino-Korean number words.

몇십니까?	What time is it?
한 시 사십오분입니다.	It's 1:45.

In writing, the numbers are generally written in Arabic numerals, whether they are read in the native or the Sino-Korean way.

3시 15분	Read 세 시 십오분
12시 12분	Read 열두 시 십이분

EXERCISE 1 Listen to the model voicing. As you listen, write down in Arabic numerals the time expressions.

a. ____ : ____ c. ____ : ____ e. ____ : ____ g. ____ : ____
b. ____ : ____ d. ____ : ____ f. ____ : ____ h. ____ : ____

EXERCISE 2 Say what time it is.

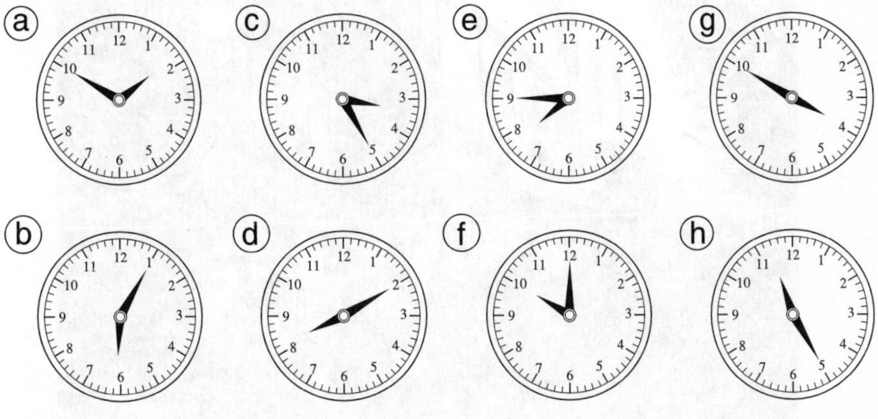

❖ ASKING AND STATING ONE'S OPINION OR CONJECTURE

A Korean asking someone's opinion or conjecture on something typically uses the ending -을까요. On the other hand, the Korean speaker's opinion or conjecture is expressed by the phrasal form -을 겁니다.

VERB STEM + (으시) + (었) +	을까요?	Do you think...?
	을 겁니다.	I think....

EXERCISE 3 With your partner, exchange opinions on what might be the case for the following situations.

EXAMPLE: Cue: 선생님 계십니까? ⟶ You say: 선생님 계실까요? ⟶ Your partner says : 선생님 계실 겁니다.

a. 사람 많습니까?
b. 아버지 오셨어요?
c. 시장이 열렸습니까?
d. 저 사람 한국 사람입니까?
e. 저 식당이 좋아요?
f. 미스 김 집에 있어요?
g. 어머니 시장에 가셨습니까?
h. 우리 안 늦었어요?

EXERCISE 4 When the ending -을까요 is used with an action verb and the 1st person subject, it is equivalent to "Shall I/we...?" Suggest to your partner the following actions. Your partner will respond with "Let's..." (-읍시다).

EXAMPLE: You say: 쇼핑 나갈까요?
Your partner says: 나갑시다.

a. 커피 한 잔 해요.
b. 잠깐 기다려요.
c. 가방 하나 사요.
d. 호텔에서 만나요.
e. 점심 같이 해요.
f. 주스 시켜요.
g. 한국 음식 먹어요.
h. 한국말 배우세요.
i. 여기 앉으세요.

FRAME 2

Buying at the Store

점원: 어서 오십시오. 뭐 찾으십니까?	Clerk : Come right in, please. What items are you looking for?
밀러: 여행 가방 있어요?	Miller: Do you have traveling bags?
점원: 예. 여기 좋은 것 많습니다.	Clerk : Yes, sir. We have many good bags here.
밀러: 네.	Miller: I see.
점원: 이것 어떻습니까?	Clerk : How about this one, sir?
밀러: 더 큰 것 없어요? 큰 것이 있어야 해요.	Miller: Don't you have bigger ones? I need to have a big one.
점원: 예, 잠깐만요.	Clerk : Yes, just a minute, sir.

VOCABULARY STUDY

- 점원 — store clerk
- 찾다 / 찾아 — to look for, search
- 여행 — trip, travel
- 가방 — luggage, suitcase
- 네. — I see. (an expression of the speaker's acknowledgement)
- 더 큰 것 — a bigger one

  더 is an adverbial form, meaning "more."
- 잠깐만요. — Just a minute, please.

  (잠깐 = little while; -만 =just, only)

FRAME 3

Paying

점원: 이거 어떻습니까?	Clerk : How about this one, sir?
밀러: 얼마입니까?	Miller: How much is it?
점원: 이것은 7만원입니다.	Clerk : This one is 70,000 won.
밀러: 그거 주세요. 그런데, 여행자 수표 받지요? 제가 한국돈이 좀 모자라요.	Miller: I'll take that. By the way, you take traveler's checks, don't you? I'm a little short of Korean money.
점원: 괜찮습니다.	Clerk : It'll be all right, sir.

VOCABULARY STUDY

- 이거 — this one (the short for 이것)

  In conversation, ㅅ is commonly dropped from 이것, 그것, 저것, and 무엇
- 얼마 — how much, how many
- 칠만원 — 70,000 won
- 그런데 — by the way, but (sentence connective)
- 여행자 수표 — traveler's check
- 돈 — money
- 모자라다/모자라 — to be insufficient, be short of... (process verb)

  Like the verb 있다 "to have," 모자라다 takes two subjects. Verbs of this kind will be shown by the formula: X가 Y가 모자라다. X is short of Y.

❖ COUNTING LARGE NUMBERS (100/1,000/10,000)

Any numbers beyond one hundred are counted in Sino-Korean numerals. The Sino-Korean numeral system is quite regular. Beyond the first two digits, there are three new units (백, 천, and 만) that are needed for most numeral expressions that you need in daily life.

The new concept that you must be accustomed to is 만 (10,000). Beyond 만, the same units repeat themselves up to a new unit called 억 (100,000,000).

100	백	1,000	천	10,000	만
308	삼백팔	5,000	오천	30,500	삼만오백
924	구백이십사	2,300	이천삼백	63,200	육만삼천이백
725	칠백이십오	6,850	육천팔백오십	170,000	십칠만
429	사백이십구	3,316	삼천삼백십육	3,900,000	삼백구십만

In all digits, zeros (0) are to be simply ignored. The concept of zero did not exist in Old Chinese (as in English). The "zero" 공 (or 영) is used today only in the digit-by-digit reading as in telephone numbers.

CAUTION! Note the pronunciation of the following number where the last digit is 6.

	SPELLED	PRONOUNCED	
6	육	육	[yuk]
16	십육	심뉵	[shim-nyuk]
26	이십육	이심뉵	[i-shim-nyuk]
36	삼십육	삼심뉵	[sam-shim-nyuk]
46	사십육	사심뉵	[sa-shim-nyuk]

EXERCISE 5 Read aloud the following numbers.

a. 130 c. 208 e. 716 g. 1,200 i. 5,724
b. 10,000 d. 85,000 f. 60,900 h. 25,600 j. 130,000

EXERCISE 6 Ask your partner how much each of the following items is. The sign ₩ stands for 원, the Korean monetary unit.

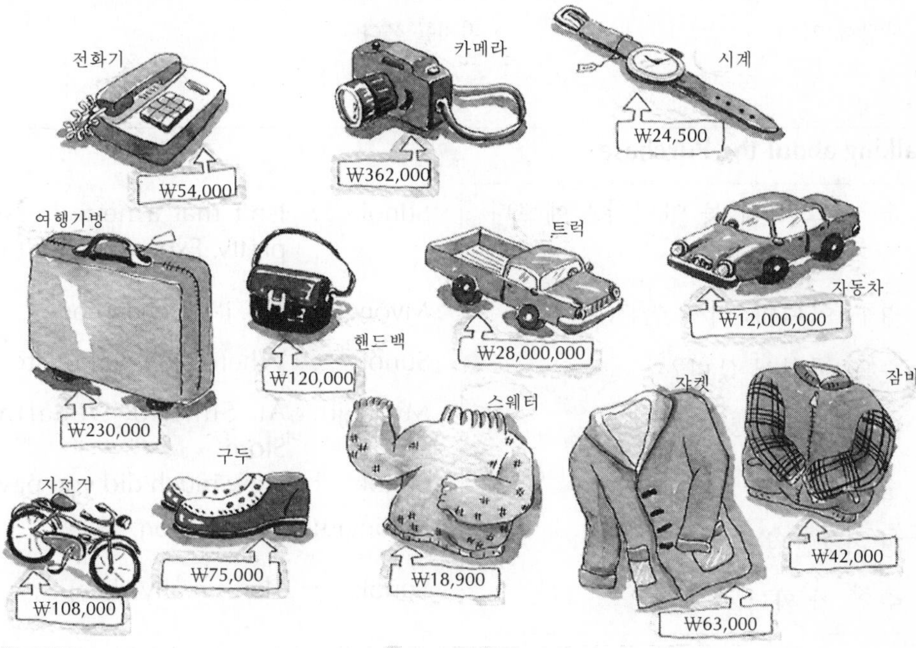

❖ -어야 하다. "ONE MUST.... / ONE HAS TO...."

The expression of necessity or obligation is made by a phrasal form: STEM +어야 하다. Its basic meaning is "It is necessary that...," but it is commonly equivalent to "must" or "have to" in English. Because this form starts with the vowel 어, the same sound changes that you have seen in the past tense form or in the short blunt form apply to this form. For example,

		SHORT BLUNT	PAST	NECESSITY
읽다	to read	읽어	읽었다	읽어야 하다
하다	to do	해	했다	해야 하다
가다	to go	가	갔다	가야 하다
쓰다	to write	써	썼다	써야 하다

EXERCISE 7 Ask your partner what he/she has to do on each day of the week. Your partner will answer factually or use some suggested activities listed below.

EXAMPLE: 월요일에 뭐 하세요? What do you do on Monday?
편지 써야 합니다. I have to write a letter.

월요일	화요일	수요일	목요일	금요일	토요일	일요일

- 공부하다
- 일하다
- 사다
- 시장에 가다
- ...을/를 보다
- ...한테 선물을 보내다
- 아파트를 찾다
- 편지를 쓰다

FRAME 4

Talking about the Purchase

순옥: 그거 새 옷 아니야? 예쁘다. 비싸지?
명주: 아니야. 이거 싼 거야.
순옥: 어디서 샀니?
명주: 성도 백화점에서.
순옥: 얼마 주었니?
명주: 2만원.
순옥: 참 싸다.

Sunok : Isn't that a new dress? It's pretty. Expensive, isn't it?
Myŏngju: No. It's a cheap one.
Sunok : Where did you buy it?
Myŏngju: At Sungdo Department Store.
Sunok : How much did you pay?
Myŏngju: 20,000 won.
Sunok : That's really cheap.

VOCABULARY STUDY

- 새 — new... (prenominal, used only before a nominal)
- 옷 — clothes, garment
- 예쁘다/예뻐 — to be pretty, beautiful (stative verb)
- 비싸다/비싸 — to be expensive (stative verb)
- -다 — a blunt declarative ending for a stative verb

CAUTION! Use it only with a stative verb now. Action verbs and process verbs require some changes.

- 싸다/싸 — to be inexpensive, cheap (stative verb)
- 백화점 — department store
- 얼마 주었니? — How much did you pay?

  CAUTION! The verb 주다 "to give" is used here to mean "pay."
- 참 — really, very (=정말)

EXERCISE 8 The students will be asked to form several groups of two or three individuals. Two teams will be asked to enact shopping scenes in front of the class, playing the roles of shopkeepers and shoppers.

PREPARATIONS: It is ideal to assemble actual clothes such as sweaters, blouses, shoes, briefcases, etc., to be displayed in the store. However, if it isn't feasible, the students may use pictures or words on cards or on the chalkboard. Attach prices (가격) in Korean currency to all items.

PERFORMANCE: As the shoppers walk in, welcome them, ask how you can help them, and show them what they want. Try to make a sale using the Frames 2 and 3. The shoppers are supposed to be close friends and so will use LOW LEVEL speech to one another.

GRAMMAR

1. Expressions of Necessity or Obligation

Expressions of necessity or obligation are made in a phrasal form with a helper verb 하다 or 되다.

VERB STEM + (으시)어야	하다 되다	It's necessary that... One must... One has to...
⇧ HONORIFIC	⇧ TENSE, etc.	

The honorific marker is incorporated in the main verb of the phrasal form, but the tense (and other modals) in the secondary verb.

The most common English translations are "must" and "have to." However, it is important to know the literal meaning, "It is necessary that...," to understand more expanded usages later.

지금 가셔야 합니까?	Do you have to go now?
네, 가야 됩니다.	Yes, I must.
오래 기다리셔야 됐어요?	Did you have to wait long?
네, 오래 기다려야 했어요.	Yes, I had to.

If no honorific marker is used, the same sound changes, such as vowel contractions and irregularities that occur in the short blunt form, apply. Compare the three verb forms of some sample verbs.

DICTIONARY FORM	SHORT BLUNT	PAST	NECESSITY
하다	해	했다	해야 하다
있다	있어	있었다	있어야 하다
가다	가	갔다	가야 하다
오다	와	왔다	와야 하다
쓰다	써	썼다	써야 하다
앉다	앉아	앉았다	앉아야 하다

CAUTION! The negative of this phrasal form is *not commonly* used, but when the negative prefix 안 is used (before the main verb), it means "must not" or "should not," but NOT "don't have to." 안 가셔야 합니다 means "You shouldn't go. (=It is necessary that you don't go.)"

2. Intention or Conjecture: An Overview

Dealing with something uncertain is part of our living. So, all languages have ways of expressing something tentative or guessing. Korean has several such forms, but each of them has two different functions depending on what the subject is. Below is an overview of the two forms introduced in this lesson. In the following sections (3 and 4), the above forms will be explained more in detail with more examples.

a. Asking one's opinion or conjecture

	WITH 1st PERSON	WITH 3rd PERSON
VERB STEM + 을까(요)?	ASKING OPINION "Shall I/we...?"	CONJECTURE "Do you think...?"
EXAMPLE: 갈까요?	Shall I go? Shall we go?	Do you think he/she will go?

b. Stating one's intention or conjecture

	WITH 1st PERSON	WITH 3rd PERSON
VERB STEM + 을 것이다	INTENTION "I'm going to..." "I will..."	CONJECTURE "I think..." "Probably..."
EXAMPLE: 갈 겁니다.	I'm going.	I think he's going.

NOTE: The consonant ㅅ of this phrasal form is normally dropped in conversation as in the above example.

3. Asking What Shall/Might Be: -을까(요)?

The basic function of -을까요 is to ask the addressee's opinion but it has two different usages:

a. Asking the addressee's opinion on what the 1st person or the 2nd person shall do. It is equivalent to "Shall I/we...?" or "Would you like to...?" In this usage, it may be taken as a gesture of persuasion or a polite request.

나가실까요?	Ⓗ	Shall we go out?
기다릴까요?	Ⓗ Ⓜ	Shall I wait?
어디서 만날까?	Ⓛ	Where shall we meet?

b. Asking the addressee's opinion or conjecture as to what might be or might have been the case. In this case, the past marker -었 can be inserted (if it is a conjecture about what might have happened), and the subject is generally the 3rd person. It is equivalent to "Do you think...?"

가게가 열렸을까요?	Ⓗ Ⓜ	Do you think stores are open?
그 사람들 뭐 할까요?	Ⓗ Ⓜ	What do you think they are doing?
비쌀까?	Ⓛ	Do you think it is expensive?
안늦을까?	Ⓛ	Don't you think we will be late?

4. Stating Intention or Conjecture: -을 것이다.

The phrasal form -을 것이다 expressing the intention (introduced in Lesson 8) may also be used to express the conjecture.

VERB STEM + (으시) + (었) + 을 것이다	{ I think... Probably...

NOTE: 것 is normally reduced to 거 in conversation.

미스 윤 바쁠 겁니다.	Miss Yun is probably busy.
미스 윤 바빴을 겁니다.	Miss Yun was probably busy.
전화할 거예요.	I think she will call me.
전화했을 거예요.	I think she called me.
영어 공부할 겁니다.	I think she will study English.
영어 공부했을 겁니다.	I think she studied English.

5. Verbs of Opening and Closing

The verbs 열다/여세요/열어 "to open" and 닫다 "to close" are action verbs like their English counterparts ("Someone opens or closes something.") However, the state of being "open" or "closed" are expressed by their passive forms in the past tense forms.

ACTIVE	PASSIVE	STATE OF BEING
• 열다 to open	• 열리다 to be opened	• 열렸다 be open
• 닫다 to close	• 닫히다 to be closed	• 닫혔다 be closed

창문 열까요?	Shall I open the window? [ACTIVE]
은행 곧 엽니다.	The bank will open soon. [ACTIVE]
은행 지금 열렸어요.	The bank is open now. [STATE]
가게를 5시에 닫아요.	They close the store at five. [ACTIVE]
가게가 6시 반에 닫혀요.	The store will close (be closed) at six thirty. [PASSIVE]
가게가 아직 닫혔습니다.	The store is still closed. [STATE]

NOTE: The passive forms in Korean are not as extensively used as in English. There are only a limited number of action verbs that have their passive counterparts. Furthermore, the uses of the passive forms in Korean usually have some additional implications such as expressing a certain state or condition.

READING & WRITING

1. Time Exprssions in Sino-Korean

The expressions of time are made with Sino-Korean numerals. One important exception is the expression of "hours" which are normally made with native numerals. For example,

YEAR >	MONTH >	DATE >	HOUR >	MINUTE >	SECOND
1984년	3월	15일	9시	30분	15초
천구백팔십사년	삼월	십오일	아홉시	삼십분	십오초
SINO-KOREAN numeral			NATIVE numeral	SINO-KOREAN numeral	

CAUTION! Unlike in English, the sequence of units always proceeds from larger elements to smaller ones in Korean.

EXERCISE 9 Read the following aloud, paying attention to the Korean convention of reading numbers.

1993년 8월 19일 9시 10분 1995년 5월 10일 5시 50분

2. Grocery Market Advertisement

There are some simple Sino-Korean characters still found in publications. One of them is 大 [대] a prefix meaning "great" as in the official name of the Republic of Korea, 대한민국. The character 대 is found below prefixed before an English loan word in an advertisement of a grocery store.

EXERCISE 10 Scan the clipping, and follow through the activities.

해 태 식 품

大 세일! 여러분의 마켓!
확실히 다릅니다!

한국 식품 일체 · 각종 밑반찬 · 각종 잔치떡

새 주인으로 바뀐 **해태** 식품은 언제나 친절하고 항상 깨끗하며 새로운 식품을 위하여 항상 노력하겠습니다.

東洋 食品店

a. List two English loan words that you find in the clipping.

 * ____________ * ____________

b. Find the meanings of the following words, using your dictionary.

 *식품 ________ *확실히 ________ *다르다 ________
 *항상 ________ *여러분 ________

c. The stative verb 다르다 is an antonym of 같다. Its short form is irregular. You can guess it, if you know the short form of another verb with a similar shape. What is that verb? And what should be the short form of 다르다?

 * A similar verb:______ / ______ * The short form of 다르다/__________

EXERCISE 11 Complete the following sentences by filling in the blank spaces with the words listed on the right. Then, give an English equivalent to each Korean sentence.

a. 오늘은 ______ 식당에 가십시다.	글
b. 우리 아버지는 ______ 바쁘세요.	다른
c. 그럼, ______, 내일 뵙겠습니다.	여러분
d. 시장 옷은 ______ 싸지요.	항상
e. 저 ______은 월요일에 닫혀요.	식품점
f. 선생님은 ______를 참 잘 쓰세요.	확실히

EXERCISE 12 There was a telephone call for Mr. Yun, from his wife. She is shopping at Tongbang department store now. She found a nice sweater for him and wants him to come to the store after work (퇴근 후). Write a telephone message for what she would have left for Mr. Yun.

VOCABULARY SUMMARY

Nominals

가게	store (=상점)	수표	check
가방	luggage, suitcase	여행	travel, trip
대한민국	Republic of Korea	여행자	traveler
돈	money	옷	garment
백화점	department store	점원	store clerk
식품	grocery item(s)		

Sino-Korean Numerals

백	hundred	만	ten thousand
천	thousand		

Action Verbs

그러다/그래	to do so	열다	to open
닫다	to close	열리다	to be opened
닫히다	to be closed		

Stative Verbs

비싸다/비싸	to be expensive	예쁘다/예뻐	to be pretty
싸다/싸	to be inexpensive	다르다/달라	to be different

Process Verbs

모자라다	to be insufficient

Interjections

네/예	yes; I see.	그런데	but; by the way

Adverbs

더	more	얼마	how much
아직	yet, still	확실히	definitely
참	very, really	항상	always (=늘)

Prenominal Adjectives

새	new	대-	great, big (prefix)

Pronouns

여러분	you (addressing to general public)

Numeral Suffixes

-분	minutes (Sino-Korean numerals required)
-원	won (Korean monetary unit; used with Sino-Korean numerals only)
-일	day (of the month)
-초	second (unit of time)
-월	month (suffix)

Sentence Endings

-을까요?	Do you think...?; Shall we/I...?
-을 겁니다	I think...
-다	a blunt declarative ending (for stative verbs)

Script for Exercise 1

a. 지금 두 시 십분입니다.
b. 한 시 반에 왔어요.
c. 일곱 시 오분에 전화가 왔어요.
d. 사십오분 기다렸어요.
e. 가게는 여덟 시 삼십분에 열어요.
f. 여섯 시 사십오분에 만납시다.
g. 벌써 다섯 시 사십분입니다.
h. 열한 시 오십분에 전화 받았어요.

ANSWERS TO EXERCISES

Exercise 1.	a. 2:10	c. 7:05	e. 8:30	g. 5:40
	b. 1:30	d. 45	f. 6:45	h. 11:50
Exercise 2.	a. 1:50	c. 3:25	e. 7:45	g. 3:50
	b. 6:05	d. 8:10	f. 10:00	h. 11:25

Exercise 3.
a. 사람 많을까요? / 사람 많을 겁니다.
b. 아버지 오셨을까요? / 아버지 오셨을 겁니다.
c. 시장이 열렸을까요? / 시장이 열렸을 겁니다.
d. 저 사람 한국 사람일까요? / 저 사람 한국 사람일 겁니다.
e. 저 식당이 좋을까요? / 저 식당이 좋을 겁니다.
f. 미스 김 집에 있을까요? / 미스 김 집에 있을 겁니다.
g. 어머니 시장에 가셨을까요? / 어머니 시장에 가셨을 겁니다.
h. 우리 안 늦었을까요? / 우리 안 늦었을 겁니다.

Exercise 4. a. 커피 한 잔 할까요? / 합시다.
b. 잠깐 기다릴까요? / 기다립시다
c. 가방 하나 살까요? / 삽시다.
d. 호텔에서 만날까요? / 만납시다.
e. 점심 같이 할까요? / 합시다.
f. 주스 시킬까요? / 시킵시다.
g. 한국 음식 먹을까요? / 먹읍시다.
h. 한국말 배울까요? / 배웁시다.
i. 여기 앉을까요? / 앉읍시다.

Exercise 5. a. 백삼십
b. 만
c. 이백팔
d. 팔만 오천
e. 칠백십육
f. 육만구백
g. 천이백
h. 이만오천육백
i. 오천칠백 이십사
j. 십삼만

Exercise 9. 천구백구십삼년 팔월 십구일 아홉 시 십분
천구백구십오년 오월 십일 다섯 시 오십분

Exercise 10. a. 세일(sale), 마켓(market)
b. groceries, always, definitely, you (the general public), different
c. 모르다/몰라 : 다르다/달라

Exercise 11. a. 다른 b. 항상 c. 여러분 d. 확실히 e. 식품점 f. 글

LESSON 10
GETTING AROUND

FRAME 1

Taking a Taxi

밀러:	택시! 용산 갑니까?	Miller:	Taxi! Can you go to Yongsan?
기사:	네, 타십시오. 용산 어디까지 가세요?	Driver:	Yes. Please get on. Where in Yongsan are you going?
밀러:	용산역 앞까지 가 주세요.	Miller:	Please go up to the front of the Yongsan Station.
기사:	네, 알겠습니다. 안전 벨트 매주세요.	Driver:	Yes, sir. I understand. Please fasten the seat belt.
밀러:	네.	Miller:	All right.

VOCABULARY STUDY

•기사	driver (professional) (an abbreviation of 운전 기사: "driving technician")
•용산	Yongsan (a northern riverside district in Seoul)
•타다/타	to ride, get on to (a vehicle, ship, airplane, etc.)
•-까지	up to; until, by (postposition marking the extent)
•역	railway station
•앞	front
•가 주세요.	Please go.
•알겠습니다.	I understand. (=알았습니다.)

CAUTION! The use of -겠 in 알겠습니다 and 모르겠습니다 should be considered idiomatic here. Except for these cases, the suffix -겠 has two basic functions: marking the intention or conjecture.

- 안전 벨트 — seat belt (안전=safety, 벨트=belt)
- 매다/매 — to tie, fasten

❖ …어 주다/드리다: "TO GIVE (HELP)"

The verb 주다/드리다 "to give" is frequently used as a helper verb expressing a service or a favor of doing something for someone. The main verb takes the short form (stem + 어).

VERB STEM + 어 { 주다 / 드리다 }

The helper verb …어 주다/드리다 has no English counterpart except in one awkward translation such as "give the service or favor of ...ing."

- 용산에 가 주세요. — Please go for me to Yongsan. (Give me the favor of going to...)
- 창문 열어 드릴까요? — Shall I open the window for you? (Shall I give you the service of...)

EXERCISE 1 Ask your classmates to do something for you. You will choose any of the actions listed below. Your classmates will respond by actually performing the action while saying "I will..."

EXAMPLE: 기다려 주세요. Please wait for me.
기다려 드리지요. I will wait for you.

a. 문을 닫아 주세요.
b. 여기 이름 써 주세요.
c. 커피 한 잔 시켜 주세요.
d. 이리 와 주십시오.
e. 그 책 이리 보내 주십시오.
f. 창문 열어 주십시오.
g. 이 글 봐 주세요.
h. 친구 소개해 주세요.

EXERCISE 2 Say the following utterances in Korean.

a. Please go to the Seoul Station.
b. Do I have to wear the seat belt?
c. I guess I have to (do).
d. Please get in the car.
e. How far have you read the book?
f. I took a taxi in front of the hotel.
g. Please send it over to me.
h. Would you mind coming over here?

FRAME 2

Arriving at the Destination

기사: 다 왔습니다.	Driver: Here we are, sir.
밀러: 얼맙니까?	Miller : How much is it?
기사: 4,000원입니다.	Driver: 4,000 won.
밀러: 고맙습니다.	Miller : Thank you.
기사: 감사합니다. 조심해서 내리세요.	Driver: Thank you. Take care as you get off.

VOCABULARY STUDY

- 다 왔습니다. Here we are. (Literally, "We are finished with this trip.")
  다 is an adverb, meaning "all, completely, entirely."
- 고맙습니다. Thank you.
  Another expression 고마워요 is not as polite as 고맙습니다 or 감사합니다.
- 조심해서 carefully
- 내리다 to get down/off

CULTURAL ENCOUNTER Tipping is not a common custom in Korea. In most tourist hotels, service charges are included in the price of the room. However, tipping taxi drivers is becoming somewhat common for two reasons: tourists from abroad often tip taxi drivers, and also making change is cumbersome on busy city streets in Seoul. If you do not want your change back, you would simply say 괜찮아요 "It's all right."

❖ 다 -었어요 "BE THROUGH WITH / BE FINISHED WITH"

To say that you are through with some project, simply use the adverb 다 "all" before a verb.

다 읽었어요?	Are you through with your reading?
편지 다 못썼어요.	I'm not finished with my letter writing.

EXERCISE 3 Say appropriate Korean equivalents to the following sentences.

a. Did you finish shopping?
b. I must finish reading this book.
c. I got off in front of the railroad station.
d. Take care as you get on the car.
e. Please come back by five o'clock.

EXERCISE 4 What are typical Korean responses to the following situations?

a. You and your friend are about to reach your destination.
b. A Korean passer-by showed you the way. Thank him/her.
c. An elderly lady did a favor for you. How do you thank her?
d. You are being asked to fasten the seat belt. There are two ways to acknowledge the request. What are they?

EXERCISE 5 Imagine yourself taking a taxi to some destination. Your partner will play the role of a taxi driver. You may freely create a situation modeled after Frames 1 and 2 (catching a taxi, getting on and off, paying, etc.).

Suggested Destinations:

서울역	Seoul Station
롯데 호텔	Hotel Lotte
신세계 백화점	Shinsege Department Store
남대문 시장	Namdaemun Market
시청	City Hall
덕수궁	Tŏksu Palace
한국은행	Bank of Korea
미국 대사관	American Embassy
국립박물관	National Museum

The Han River

FRAME 3

Asking the Way (I)

밀러: 실례합니다. 말씀 좀 묻겠습니다.	Miller : Excuse me. May I ask you a question?
행인: 네, 말씀하세요.	Passerby : Yes, you may.
밀러: 미국대사관에 어떻게 갑니까?	Miller : How do I go to the U.S. Embassy?
행인: 저기서 왼쪽으로 도세요. 그리고 그 길로 곧장 가세요. 오른쪽에 대사관이 보입니다.	Passerby : Turn to your left there. Then, go straight on that street. You will see it on your right.
밀러: 감사합니다.	Miller : Thank you.
행인: 천만에요.	Passerby : Not at all.

VOCABULARY STUDY

- 실례합니다. — Excuse me. (실례=lack of courtesy)
- 말씀 좀 묻겠습니다. — May I ask you a question?
- 묻다/물어 — to ask, inquire
- 행인 — passerby (=지나가는 사람: passing person)
- 말씀하세요. — Please speak. (말씀하다 is an honorific form of 말하다.)
- 대사관 — embassy (대사=ambassador, 관=building)
- 왼쪽으로 — to the left (왼=left, 쪽=side, 으로=toward)
- 오른쪽으로 — to the right (오른=right, 쪽=side, 으로=toward)
- 돌다/도세요/돌아 — to turn

CAUTION! The imperative form is 도세요, not 돌세요.

- 그 길로 — on that street (-으로 means "by means of" here.)
- 곧장 — straight (adverb)
- 보이다 — to be seen, visible (passive form of 보다)
- 천만에요 — Not at all; Don't mention it.

❖ -으로: "BY / IN" OR "TO/TOWARD"

The postposition -으로, is used to indicate either the means of an action or the direction of a movement. In either case, the vowel 으 is present only when it is preceded by a consonant other than ㄹ. The vowel 으 is dropped when it is preceded by another vowel or ㄹ.

(1) The means of an action

이 길로 가세요	Go by this road.
한국말로 하세요	Say it in Korean.

(2) The direction of a movement

왼쪽으로 도세요.	Turn to your left.
역 쪽으로 갔어요.	He went toward the station.

EXERCISE 6 Fill the blank spaces below with appropriate postpositions.

a. 어느 길 ____ 가야 해요?	Which street should we go by?
b. 어느쪽 ____ 갔습니까?	Which way did he go?
c. 연필 ____ 쓰십시오.	Please write with a pencil.
d. 시장 쪽 ____ 갔을 겁니다.	I believe she went toward the market.
e. 택시 ____ 갑시다.	Let's go by taxi.
f. 그것은 돈 ____ 못삽니다.	You can't buy it with money.

EXERCISE 7 Each student by turn will ask how to get to one of the places listed below. The teacher will give directions. The class will identify each location by the alphabet symbol on the map below.

a. 사보이 호텔	c. 안동역	e. 영광 교회
b. 명도 극장	d. 신한 백화점	f. 평안 시장

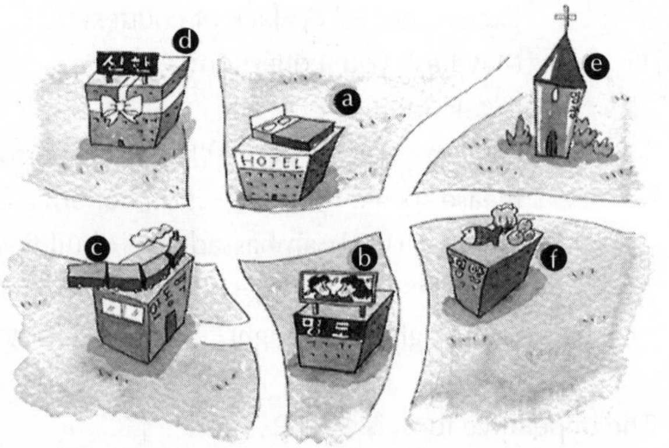

EXERCISE 8 The teacher will give directions for each student to physically move around in various directions within the classroom. You will find two new verbs in this exercise.

•일어서다/일어서	to stand up	Ex) 일어서세요.	Please stand up.
•서다/서	to stop, halt	Ex) 서세요.	Please stop.

The teacher may even use additional expressions that are not introduced. The student will make the best of the situations and guess what he or she was being told.

EXAMPLE:	알리스 씨, 일어서세요.	Miss Alice, please stand up.
	창문 쪽으로 곧장 가세요.	Go straight to the window.
	오른쪽으로 도세요.	Make a right turn.
	거기 서세요.	Stop there.

FRAME 4

Asking the Way (Ⅱ)

밀러: 학생! 이 지하도로 명동 갈 수 있나?	Miller: Young man! Can I go to Myŏngdong by this underpass?
학생: 명동에요? 갈 수 있어요. 그런데 좀 복잡해요.	Boy : To Myŏngdong? Yes, you can. But it's a little complicated.
밀러: 그럼, 어떻게 가지?	Miller: How should I go then?
학생: 아저씨, 이 길 건너가세요. 그리고 다음 길로 가세요.	Boy : Cross this street, mister. And take the next street.
밀러: 이 길 어떻게 건너가지?	Miller: How do I cross the street?
학생: 저 육교로요. 저기 저것 보이지요?	Boy : By that overpass. You see one over there, don't you?

VOCABULARY STUDY

•지하도	underpass (지=ground, 하=below, 도=road)
•명동	Myŏngdong (a shopping district in Seoul)
•-을 수 있다	can, be able to
•아저씨	uncle; mister (a way to address men whose names are not known)
•복잡하다	to be complicated, confusing (stative verb)
•다음	next
•건너가다	to go across
•육교	overpass (육=land, 교=bridge)

CULTURAL ENCOUNTER You often hear Koreans addressing a male adult as 아저씨 "uncle" and a female adult as 아줌마 "auntie" (restricted to a married woman). A young, unmarried woman is called 아가씨 "young lady" as introduced earlier.

This custom originates from the traditional "extended family" in Korea where 집안 "clan or family" means not just the parents and children but includes all male-line relatives. Within the extended family, all cousins are "brothers" and "sisters," and members of one generation above are "uncles" and "aunts."

One cautionary note! These terms belong to the Mid Level of politeness, and may be offensive to those who expect more formal and polite appellations.

❖ -을 수 있다: "ONE CAN/IS ABLE TO..."

The possibility or impossibility is expressed by the following phrasal construction:

VERB STEM + 을 수 {있다	One can.....
없다	One cannot.....

EXERCISE 9 Respond affirmatively.

EXAMPLE: 한국말 하실 수 있어요? Can you speak Korean?
네, 할 수 있어요. Yes, I can.

a. 박 선생님은 영어 하실 수 있어요?
b. 잠깐 기다리실 수 있습니까?
c. 불어를 읽을 수 있어요?
d. 저녁에 여기 올 수 있습니까?
e. 여기 앉을 수 있지요?
f. 이 차 탈 수 있어요?
g. 극장 갈 수 있어?
h. 그 책 볼 수 있어?

EXERCISE 10 Respond negatively.

EXAMPLE: 이 길로 갈 수 있어요? Can I go by this road?
아니오, 갈 수 없어요. No, you can't.

a. 중국말 할 수 있어요?
b. 오늘 쇼핑 나가실 수 있어요?
c. 오늘 저녁에 만날 수 있지요?
d. 그분의 성함 알 수 있습니까?
e. 그 식당에서 냉면 먹을 수 있어요?
f. 여기서 내릴 수 있습니까?
g. 나하고 같이 갈 수 있니?
h. 집에 다녀 올 수 있니?

EXERCISE 11 Respond factually.

a. 중국말 할 수 있어요?
b. 영어 읽을 수 있습니까?
c. 한글로 쓸 수 있어요?
d. 김치 먹을 수 있습니까?
e. 커피 마실 수 있어요?
f. 금년에 한국에 갈 수 있어요?
g. 미국에서 여행자 수표를 쓸 수 있어요?
h. 시장에서 여자옷을 살 수 있을까요?

GRAMMAR

1. Expressing the Possibility or Ability : -을 수 있다

The possibility or one's ability to do something is expressed by the following phrasal construction. -수 is a "bound" noun, meaning "possibility." It is never used as a noun independently of some modifier.

VERB STEM + -을 수 { 있다	One can/is able to...
{ 없다	One cannot/is unable to...

영어 할 수 있어요? — Can you speak English?
저 불어 좀 읽을 수 있습니다. — I can read French a little.
내일 만날 수 있습니까? — Can we meet tomorrow?
그럴 수 없어요. — It cannot be.
여기서 내릴 수 없어요? — Can't you get off here?

CAUTION! The honorific marker -으시 is normally in the main (first) verb, but it may also be used in the secondary verb, in which case it is 있으시다, not 계시다.

{ 가실 수 있어요?
가실 수 있으세요?
갈 수 있으세요? } Could you go?

CAUTION! The tense or other modal features are incorporated in the secondary verb (있다/없다).

기다릴 수 없었어요. — I couldn't wait.

CAUTION! The vowel 으 of 을, as is the case for all suffixes and endings, is dropped whenever it is preceded by a vowel. It also induces stems of some irregular verbs to change forms.

2. Doing Something as Service : -어 주다/드리다

Doing something as service for somebody is expressed by the use of the verb -어 주다/드리다. All verb markings (such as the honorific, tense, etc.) are incorporated in the helper verb (주다/드리다).

VERB STEM + 어 { 주다 / 드리다 }	to do (something) for someone's sake

The verb 주다 changes to 드리다 "to give respectfully" when the speaker shows respect toward the receiver of service.

서울역까지 가 주세요. — Please go (for my sake) to the Seoul Station.
창문 열어 드릴까요? — Shall I open the window (for you)?

CAUTION! The verb 갖다 주다/드리다 "to bring/take (something) to (someone)" has a similar construction but has a different connective (-다).

물 좀 갖다 주세요.	Bring me some water, please.
갖다 드리지요.	I'll bring it (to you).

3. The Verb of Asking (T/L Verb): 묻다/물어보다.

a. In the verb 묻다, ㄷ at the end of the stem changes to ㄹ when the stem is followed by a vowel. (Such a verb is called a T/L verb.)

묻겠습니다.	I'd like to ask.	물으세요.	Please ask.
묻지요.	I'll ask.	물었습니다.	I asked.

b. The verb is commonly used in a compound form with 보다 in conversation.

물어보세요.	Please ask him.	물어볼까요?	Shall I ask?
물어보지요.	I'll ask.	누구한테 물어봤어요?	Who did you ask?

CAUTION! Not all verbs with the stem-final ㄷ are T/L verbs. The verb 닫다 "to close," for example, is a regular verb which retains ㄷ even when a vowel follows.

문을 닫겠습니다.	I'm going to close the door.
문을 닫으세요.	Please close the door.

4. How to Express the Means and Directions: -으로

The same postpositions are often used in two or more different functions. In this lesson, you have seen the postposition -으로 used to mark either the means of doing something or the direction of a movement. In either case, the vowel 으 is present only when it is preceded by a consonant other than ㄹ. When another vowel or ㄹ precedes it, the vowel 으 is dropped.

(1) The means of an action

이 길로 갑시다.	Let's go by this road .
볼펜으로 쓰십시오.	Please write with a ballpoint pen.
자동차로 거기 갔어요.	We went there by car.

(2) The direction of a movement

어느 쪽으로 갈까요?	In which direction should we go?
여기서 왼쪽으로 돌 수 없어요.	You cannot turn to your left here.
남대문 쪽으로 갔어요.	He went toward the South Gate.

CAUTION! The direction of movement (in the sense of "toward") is normally preceded by -쪽 "side" (a "bound" noun which is always preceded by a modifier). Otherwise, the use of -으로 simply marks the destination, interchangeable with -에. Therefore, there are three common ways of expressing the destination.

{어디 / 어디에 / 어디로} 갈까요? — Where shall we go?

{서울 / 서울에 / 서울로} 갑시다. Let's go to Seoul.

READING & WRITING

1. Use of Postpositions in Writing

There are some differences between speech and writing in the use of postpositions. You have seen that in speech, subjects and objects are often without any postpositions but in writing they are normally marked by postpositions: -이/가 (for subjects), -을/를 (for objects), and -은/는 (for topics). In the advertisement below, you will find two additional differences.

a. -의 pronounced [e] is a possessive postposition equivalent to "'s" in English. It is common to leave out -의 in speech, but it is normally present in writing.

CAUTION! Some pronouns are notable exceptions: 저의 Ⓗ "my," 나의 Ⓜ "my," and 너의 Ⓛ "your." They are normally contracted to 제, 내, and 네, respectively.

b. -와/과 is a postposition equivalent to -하고 in speech. It has two meanings: "and" (connecting two nominals) and "with" (denoting accompaniment).

EXERCISE 12 Circle all the postpositions you find below. Any one who recognizes the most will be the winner.

신세계 여행사

오랜 경험과 충분한 지식을 갖춘 모든 직원들이 맡기신 일들을 시작부터 끝까지 새로운 분위기와 스타일로 가장 경제적이며 실속있게 완벽한 service를 받을 수 있도록 여행업무의 모든 것을 자신있게 도와드리겠습니다.

고향의 맛, 고향의 향취

시골집

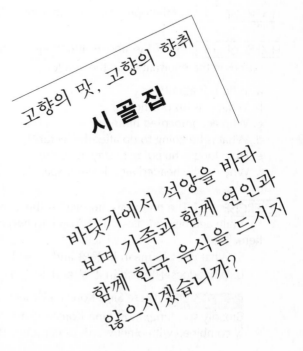

바닷가에서 석양을 바라보며 가족과 함께 연인과 함께 한국 음식을 드시지 않으시겠습니까?

EXERCISE 13 The new postposition -와/과 ("and" or "with") has two shapes. Observe the phrases where -와 and -과 are used, and guess how the two different shapes are determined.

- -와 is used when ______________________________
- -과 is used when ______________________________

2. Verbs in Written Style

Although *polite* verb forms are used in writing letters, advertisements, etc., most other types of writings such as newspaper articles, public documents, etc., are in a *blunt* form with the ending similar to, but not identical with, the dictionary form. (This form will be explained more in the next lesson.) The article below is written in a typical written style. Scan the article and follow through the exercises.

> **부시 미국 전대통령 마드리드 ____ 도착**
>
> <마드리드 통신> 8월 11일 아침______ 조지 부시 미국 전대통령______ 부인____ 같이 공항____ 도착했다. 부시 씨____ 금요일 12일 오후 2시____ 콤플루텐세 대학____ 『신세계 질서』에 대해 강의를 하고, 그후 19일____ 스페인 동해안 도시____ 구경 한 후 20일 오전 10시____ 비행기____ 파리____ 갈 예정이다.

Reading Vocabulary

•전	former	•-에 대해	concerning...
•대통령	president	•강의	lecture
•도착하다	to arrive	•동해안	east coast
•신세계 질서	new world order	•예정이다	be scheduled

EXERCISE 14 Fill the open spaces with appropriate postpositions.

EXERCISE 15 Scan the above article again, and then answer the questions which are based on the information in the article.

a. Who is it about? ______________________
b. What was his position? ______________________
c. Who accompanied him? ______________________
d. What is he going to do after the lecture? ______________________
e. How long is he going to stay in Spain? ______________________
f. Where is he headed after leaving Spain? ______________________

EXERCISE 16 The prefix 전- "former" is the same Sino-Korean element used in 조금 전에 "a while ago/before" (Lesson 7). You had two other such prefixes that you can recognize here.

a. What does 동 mean in 동양 and 동해안? __________
b. What does 신 mean in 신문 and 신세계? __________

CAUTION! These Sino-Korean elements are not "words" to be used by themselves. Broadly speaking, most Sino-Korean characters are word-builders, and they are usually combined with other words or particles. This is also true of Sino-Korean numerals.

EXERCISE 17 Complete the following sentences by filling in the blank spaces with the words listed on the right. Then, give an English equivalent to each of the Korean sentences.

a. ____가 몇 시에 있습니까?
b. 대한민국의 ____이 누굽니까?
c. 어머니는 우리한테 ____ 한국말을 쓰세요.
d. 김포공항에 예정 시간에 ____ 했습니다.
e. 동____ 에는 산이 많아요.
f. 도착시간이 같습니까, ____?

도착
강의
주로
해안
대통령
다릅니까

VOCABULARY SUMMARY

Nominals

강의	lecture
기사	driver
대사관	embassy
대통령	president (of a country)
동해안	east coast
명동	Myŏngdong (a shopping district in Seoul)
신세계	new world
오른쪽	right side (=바른 쪽)
아저씨	uncle; mister (a common term of address)
아줌마	aunt; lady (a common term of address)
안전벨트	seat belt (안전=safety, 벨트=belt)
앞	front (side)
역	railroad station
왼쪽	left side
용산	Yongsan (a Seoul district north of the Han River)
육교	overpass, land bridge
지하도	underpass, underground passage
질서	order, security

Action Verbs

건너가다/건너가	to go across	묻다/물어	to ask
내리다/내려	to get off	물어보다/물어봐	to ask
도착하다	to arrive	서다/서	to stand; to halt, stop
돌다/도세요/돌아	to turn (Intransitive)	예정이다	to be scheduled
말하다/말해	to speak	일어서다/일어서	to stand up
말씀하다/말씀해	to speak (Honorific)	타다/타	to get on, ride
매다/매	to tie, fasten		

Stative Verbs

고맙다/고마워	to be grateful
	고맙습니다. Ⓗ "Thank you."
	고마워요. Ⓜ "Thank you."
복잡하다	to be complicated, confusing

Process Verbs

보이다	to be seen; to be visible

Others

-에 대해	about, concerning

Note on Phrasal Postpositions

Phrasal postpositions ending in…해 has two other common variations: 해서 and 하여. The following three forms are generally interchangeable.

한국에 { 대해 / 대해서 / 대하여 } about/concerning Korea

ANSWERS TO EXERCISES

Exercise 1.
a. 문을 닫아 드리지요.
b. 이름을 써 드리지요.
c. 커피 한 잔 시켜 드리지요.
d. 그리 가 드리지요.
e. 이 책 그리 보내 드리지요.
f. 창문 열어 드리지요.
g. 이 글 봐 드리지요.
h. 친구 소개해 드리지요.

Exercise 2.
a. 서울역에 가주세요.
b. 안전벨트를 매야 합니까?
c. 해야 할 겁니다.
d. 자동차 타 주세요.
e. 어디까지 읽었습니까?
f. 호텔 앞에서 택시를 탔어요.
g. 그것 저한테 보내 주세요.
h. 이리 좀 와 주세요.

Exercise 3.
a. 쇼핑 다 했습니까?
b. 이 책 다 읽어야 합니다.
c. 역 앞에서 내렸습니다.
d. 자동차 조심해서 타세요.
e. 다섯 시까지 돌아오세요.

Exercise 4.
a. 다 왔습니다.
b. 고마워요.
c. 고맙습니다/감사합니다.
d. 매지요/매겠습니다.

Exercise 6.
a. 로
b. 으로
c. 로
d. 으로
e. 로
f. 으로

Exercise 9.
a. 네, 할 수 있어요.
b. 네, 기다릴 수 있어요.
c. 네, 읽을 수 있어요.
d. 네, 올 수 있어요.
e. 네, 앉을 수 있어요.
f. 네, 탈 수 있어요.
g. 응, 갈 수 있어.
h. 응, 볼 수 있어.

Exercise 10.
a. 아니오, 할 수 없어요.
b. 아니오, 나갈 수 없어요.
e. 아니오, 먹을 수 없어요.
f. 아니오, 내릴 수 없어요.

c. 아니오, 만날수 없어요. g. 아니, 갈 수 없어.
d. 아니오, 알 수 없어요. h. 아니, 다녀 올 수 없어.

Exercise 13. •-와 is used when the noun ends with a vowel.
•-과 is used when the noun ends with a consonant.

Exercise 14. 마드리드에, 아침에, 전대통령은, 부인과, 공항에, 부시 씨는, 2시에, 대학에서, 19일부터, 도시를, 10시에, 비행기로, 파리에

Exercise 15. a. Mr. George Bush c. his wife e. ten days
b. President d. sightseeing the east coast f. Paris

Exercise 16. a. east b. new

Exercise 17. a. 강의 b. 대통령 c. 주로 d. 도착 e. 해안 f. 다릅니까

제 11 과

새학기

대화 1 (FRAME 1)

날짜 이야기

박:	내일 골프 칩시다. 오후에 시간 있지요?
윤:	내일요? 내일이 며칠이지요?
박:	5월 1일입니다. 날짜도 모르세요?
윤:	아, 벌써 새 달이네요. 내일 나 시간 없어요. 일해야 돼요.

NOTE: From this lesson on, all headings will be given in Korean, with their English equivalents in parentheses. The English translation of each communicative frame will be found at the end of the lesson.

단어 공부 (*VOCABULARY STUDY*)

•내일	tomorrow
•골프	golf
•치다	to hit, strike; 골프 치다 "to play golf"
•며칠	what day; how many days
•5월	May, the fifth month
•1일	the 1st day (of a month)
•날짜	a date, a specified day

- 달 month; moon (Native Korean)
- 시간 time; hour
- 일하다/일해 to work (일=work; event)

CULTURAL ENCOUNTER Some words will be specified as *Native Korean* or *Sino-Korean* from this point on. Although this distinction is not always necessary for you in learning new words at this time, it is sometimes useful.

Generally, though there are many exceptions, *native* words are independent nouns, e.g., 달 is "moon" or "month" with or without any word accompanying. On the other hand, Sino-Korean elements are not full words to be used by themselves. They are generally word-builders, always accompanied by something else. For example, 월 meaning "moon" or "month" is always preceded by a numeral or some modifier.

❖ 년, 월, 일 : "YEARS, MONTHS, DATES"

a. Sino-Korean numerals are required for the expressions of years, months and dates.

b. The specifications of the year, month, and date are arranged differently than in English. For example,

1995년	8월	5일
(Year)	(Month)	(Date)
[천구백구십오년]	[팔월]	[오일]

c. Names of Months

일월	[irwol]	January	칠월	[ch'irwol]	July
이월	[i:wol]	February	팔월	[p'arwol]	August
삼월	[samwol]	March	구월	[kuwol]	September
사월	[sa:wol]	April	시월	[shiwol]	October
오월	[o:wol]	May	십일월	[shibirwol]	November
유월	[yuwol]	June	십이월	[shibi:wol]	December

CAUTION! Note some pronunciation changes, especially in *June* and *October.*

d. Naming and counting Years, Months, and Days

Naming and counting of years, months, and days are generally expressed by Sino-Korean numerals, but counting months is done with native numerals, as shown below.

NAMING

Question	Statement
어느 해? "What year?"	(SK) + 년
어느 달? "What month?"	(SK) + 월
어느 날? "What day?"	(SK) + 일

COUNTING

Question	Statement
몇 년? "How many years?"	(SK) + 년
몇 달? "How many months?"	(NK) + 달 (SK) + 개월
며칠? "How many days?"	(SK) + 일

SK = Sino-Korean, NK=Native Korean

CAUTION! Note the irregular spelling of 며칠, not 몇일.

연습 1. Listen to each exchange, and write (in Arabic numerals) the dates mentioned.

a. ______ c. ______ e. ______ g. ______
b. ______ d. ______ f. ______ h. ______

NOTE: The question forms for naming years and months are also done by 몇년 [myŏnnyŏn] and 몇월 [myŏdwŏl], respectively.

연습 2. When is the date of your birth (생년월일)? Ask your partner the year, month and date of his/her birth. Your partner may either tell you a factual or fictitious date.

EXAMPLE:	생년월일이 언제입니까?	When is your date of birth?
	1977년 1월 7일입니다.	It's January 7, 1977.

대화 2 (FRAME 2)

휴일과 일

박: 내일 휴일입니다. 휴일에도 일해요?

윤: 일이 많이 밀렸어요.
새 학기가 바로 시작해요. 그래서
이것 저것 준비 해야지요.

박: 그런데, 이번 학기는 언제 끝났어요?

윤: 전 주일에 끝났어요.

단어 공부 (*VOCABULARY STUDY*)

- 휴일 — non-working day, holiday (휴=rest, 일=day)
- -도 — also; even (-도 is used here in the sense of "even.")
- 많이 — a lot, many, much (adverb)
- 밀리다 — to be piled up (as of work), delayed (passive form of 밀다 "to push")

CAUTION! Note the use of 었 expressing the present state. 일이 밀렸다 "The work has been piled up/delayed."

- 학기 — semester, quarter (school term, period) (학 =study, 기=period)
- 바로 — immediately, exactly (adverb)
- 시작하다/-해 — to start, begin (시작=beginning)
- 그래서 — therefore, so
- 준비하다/-해 — to prepare (준비=preparation)
- -어야지요 — must; should (contraction of -어야 하지요)
- 이번 — this⋯, this time (이- = this, -번=occasion)

CAUTION! The English word "this" used in indicating the current or the most recent event or period (as in "this week," "this semester") is expressed in Korean by 이번 rather than 이-.

- 끝나다/끝나 — to come to the end, to be finished
  (끝 = the end, 나다/나 = to happen, occur)

❖ -도: "EVEN/ALSO"

The postpositions, -도 "even/also" and -는 (contrast marker) express a pair of opposing ideas (antonyms). For example,

일요일에도 일합니까?	Do you work even on Sunday? (in addition to other days?)
아니오, 일요일에는 일 안 해요.	No, I don't work on Sunday. (as opposed to other days.)

CAUTION! The postpositions -도 and -는 are placed after a case postposition (such as -에 or -에서), but not after the subject marker (-이/가) or object marker (-을/를).

연습 3. Respond negatively by replacing the postposition -도 "even/also" with -는.

a. 집에서도 일해요?
b. 백화점에도 갔습니까?
c. 저 사람도 학생입니까?
d. 이 길로도 갈 수 있습니까?

연습 4. Answer the following questions factually in Korean.

a. 금년이 몇 년입니까?
b. 오늘 날짜를 여기 쓰세요.
c. 휴일에도 공부합니까?
d. 다음 휴일이 언제입니까?
e. 한 달에 며칠이 있습니까?
f. 내일은 무슨 요일입니까?
g. 어제가 며칠이었어요?
h. 다음 학기가 언제 시작해요?

연습 5. Say the following sentences in Korean.

a. What day is it today?
b. I don't have time tomorrow.
c. In what month did you start the work?
d. This semester will end on 16 December.
e. Mr. Lee came to the United States in April, 1972.
f. School will start on the 14th of next month.

대화 3 (FRAME 3)

화장실을 물어본다

박: 화장실이 어딥니까?

윤: 아래 층에 있어요. 계단으로 내려 가세요.
그리고 오른쪽으로 복도 끝까지 가세요.
현관 옆입니다.

박: 네, 알았어요. 잠깐 갔다 오겠어요.

단어 공부 (*VOCABULARY STUDY*)

•화장실	restroom, bathroom
•아래층	downstairs (아래=below, -층=floor)(antonym of 위층 "upstairs")
•계단	stairway, steps
•내려가다	to go down (내리다=to get down, 가다=to go)
•복도	hallway
•끝	end (noun)
•현관	entrance, entry hall (of a house or a public building)
•갔다 오다	to go (to some place) and come back (=다녀오다)

❖ 앞, 옆, 뒤: "IN FRONT, NEXT TO, BACK OF"

Directions or relative positions are expressed in English by prepositions or adverbs (such as "in," "out," "up," "down," "in front," "behind"). These are expressed in Korean by a number of nouns indicating positions: 앞, 옆, 뒤.

These words are nouns, and often used as a modifier to another noun as in 앞 집 "front-house" (the house in front) or be placed after another as in 집 앞 "house-front" (the front of the house). When such a phrase is used as a location phrase, the postposition -에 or -에서 is attached to it.

어머니는 앞집에 가셨어요.	Mom went to the house in front.
어머니는 집 앞에 계셔요.	Mom is in front of the house.

연습 6. Where is the puppy? Respond to this question, using the proper postposition, as you look at each of the nine pictures below.

EXAMPLE:	강아지가 어디 있어요?	Where is the puppy?
	테이블 밑에 있어요.	It's under the table.

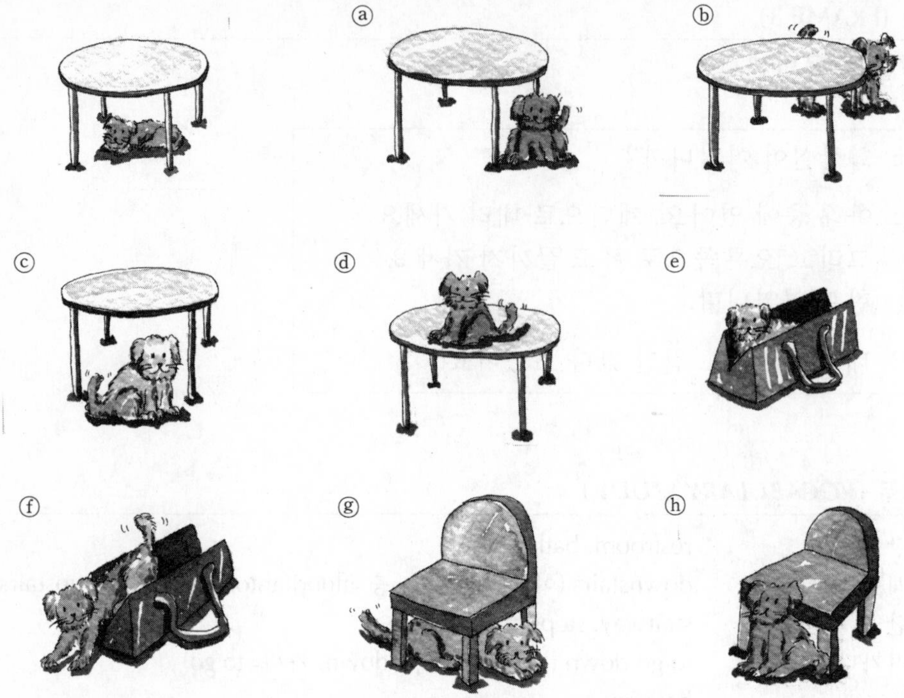

연습 7. You and your partner, now in the lobby of a hotel, want to go to one of the places in the directional guide on the right. Discuss with your partner which way to go. Use the following two verbs :

올라가다	to go up
내려가다	to go down

안 내

⇦ 다방
식당 ⇨
화장실 ⇧
⇦ 로비
계단 ⇨
⇦ 엘레베이터
주차장 ⇩

대화 4 (FRAME 4)

여름 방학의 시작

명숙: 니네 여름 방학이 언제 시작하니?
학수: 우리 19일부터 시작해. 너희들은?
명숙: 우리는 18일이다.
학수: 18일은 금요일이 아니니?
명숙: 응, 그래. 우리 금요일부터 논다.
학수: 방학동안에 여행 하니?
명숙: 그럼, 가족하고 제주도 갈 거야.

단어 공부 (*VOCABULARY STUDY*)

- 니네 — you, you guys (LOW Level 2nd person plural)

  CAUTION! 니네 is a colloquialism used among the younger generation. The formal or written style of Low Level 2nd person plural pronoun is 너희 or 너희들.

- 여름 — summer
- 방학 — school vacation (방 = release, 학 = study)
- -부터 — from, since (postposition used after a time expression)
- 논다 — have a day off (blunt declarative form of the verb 놀다 "to play"
- -동안에 — during (동안 = duration of time)
- 가족 — family
- -하고 — with, together with (someone)

연습 8. Write down the date and the event from each sentence. (The script is at the end of this lesson.)

	DATE	EVENT		DATE	EVENT
a.	________	______________	d.	________	______________
b.	________	______________	e.	________	______________

문법 (GRAMMAR)

1. The Blunt Declarative Form: STEM + (ㄴ/는)다

Let us review a few variations of declarative forms used in Low Level speech.

우리 월요일에 { 놀아. / 놀지. / 노네 / 논다. } We have Monday off.

The last form with the blunt ending -다 is particularly important because it is used not only in Low Level conversation but also in writings.

The ending -다 is also a little complex in that it requires an addition of ㄴ or 는 when it is used with action or process verbs without -었 or -겠. (It should be distinguished from the dictionary form, stem + 다, which is directly added to the stem without any changes.)

			Example
a. ACTION/ PROCESS VERBS	•If the stem ends in a vowel,	add ㄴ다.	간다 본다
	•If the stem ends in a consonant,	add 는다.	먹는다 묻는다
	•After 었/겠,	add 다.	했다 하겠다
b. ALL OTHER TYPES OF VERBS	•To the stem, or after 었/겠,	add 다.	좋다 크다 있다 있었다

CAUTION! The L verbs (such as 알다, 돌다, 열다, etc.) always drop their last consonant ㄹ when followed by ㄴ.

DICTIONARY FORM	BLUNT FORM with -다
알다	안다
돌다	돈다
열다	연다
놀다	논다

2. Context Postpositions

Sometimes, two or more postpositions may follow one nominal, as in:

휴일에도 일합니까? Do you work on holidays too?

In such cases, the first is generally a case postposition, which marks the role of the nominal within the sentence, and the second is a context postposition which relates the nominal to something in the context. A context postposition is commonly equivalent to adverbs in English such as "only," "even," etc.

Nominals	+	CASE MARKER (except -이/가 and -을/를)	+	CONTEXT MARKER

A context postposition is added to a nominal after the case postposition, but NOT after the subject or object postpositions. When a context marker is applied to the subject or the object, it is added directly to the nominal (without the case marker).

		Implications
선생님도 골프 치세요?	Do *you* play golf too?	(as well as someone mentioned before)
선생님 골프도 치세요?	Do you play golf too?	(as well as other sports)
월요일에도 골프 치세요?	Do you play golf even on Mondays?	(as well as on other weekdays)

❖ CONTEXT MARKING POSTPOSITIONS

		English
a. TOPIC MARKER	-은/는	φ
b. CONTRAST MARKER	-은/는	φ
c. PARALLEL MARKER	-도	also/too
d. EXTENT MARKER	-도	even
e. RESTRICTION MARKER	-만	only

3. The State after Completion of a Process

The so-called past marker -었 does not always express a past event, but sometimes expresses the state of being after the completion of an event. Whether it is the past action or the present state depends on the context.

	PAST ACTION	PRESENT STATE
앉았어요.	He sat down.	He is seated.
섰습니다.	He stood up.	He is standing.
결혼했어요.	He got married.	He is married.
늦었습니다.	It became late.	It is late.

When -었 is used with a passive verb (such as 열리다 "to be opened," the verb generally means the completed state.

상점이 열렸어요.	The store is open.
문이 닫혔습니다.	The door is closed.
일이 밀렸어요.	The work is piled up.

4. The Word Order: Larger to Smaller

When two or more words specify an item (time, location, name, etc.), the Korean word order is the reverse of the English one (esp. British English) : moving from larger to smaller.

		Example
a. Time Expressions		
English:	DAY < MONTH < YEAR	5th February 1993
Korean:	YEAR > MONTH > DAY	1993년 2월 5일
b. Addresses		
English:	NUMBER < STREET < CITY	56 Namchang-dong, Suwon
Korean:	CITY > DISTRICT >NUMBER	수원시 남창동 56번지
c. Full Names		
English:	GIVEN NAME < FAMILY NAME	Kwangsu Min
Korean:	FAMILY NAME > GIVEN NAME	민광수

5. Compound Verbs of Movement

Directions and manners of going and coming are expressed by compound verbs in Korean. The first verb in such compounds takes the ending -어. They are equivalent to those advervials used with verbs in English.

lst V	+ 2nd V	English	1st V	+ 2nd V	English
들어	가다	go in	건너	가다	go across
들어	오다	come in	건너	오다	come across
나	가다	go out	지나	가다	go past
나	오다	come out	지나	오다	come past
올라	가다	go up	돌아	가다	go back
올라	오다	come up	돌아	오다	come back
내려	가다	go down			
내려	오다	come down			

NOTE: The first part of each compound is an independent verb that may be used without a directional sense.

들다/들어	to get in; lodge	돌다/돌아	to turn around
나다/나	to emerge; happen	지나다/지나	to pass
오르다/올라	to rise	지나다/지나	to pass by
내리다/내려	to get off/down	건너다/건너	to cross

6. 하다 Verbs, a Productive Pattern

Loan words are used basically as *nouns* in Korean. Some of them are then converted to *verbs* simply by an addition of 하다. We will call such verbs "하다 verbs."

verbs simply by an addition of 하다. We will call such verbs "하다 verbs."

a. The first part of a 하다 verb (e.g., 공부 of 공부 하다) is a noun, and can be used as such.
   Example: 시작하다 to begin; 시작 beginning

b. The negative prefix 안- is placed before 하다, NOT before the noun.
   CORRECT: 시작 안하다 WRONG: 안 시작하다

CAUTION! The above statements apply to action and process verbs, but not necessarily to stative verbs. Not all 하다 verbs are loan words. For example, 말하다 "to speak," and 일하다 "to work" are not loan words.

읽기 · 쓰기 (READING & WRITING)

1. Sentence-endings in Written Style

Many writings, such as articles in newspapers, magazines, official documents and notices, etc. are impersonal, not addressed to specific persons. Such writings are generally written in the blunt form, -(ㄴ/는)다.

CAUTION! There are some exceptions to the above. Advertisements, letters and public signs are commonly written in polite forms.

연습 9. The blunt formal forms are generally the same as the dictionary forms with some exceptions. Look at the list of representative verbs below, and guess when they are different from the dictionary forms.

a. Add ㄴ before 다 when ____________________
b. Add 는 before 다 when ____________________

DICTIONARY FORM	BLUNT FORMAL FORM		
	Present	Past	Intent/Guess
오늘이다 있다 좋다 예쁘다	오늘이다 있다 좋다 예쁘다	오늘이었다 있었다 좋았다 예뻤다	오늘이겠다 있겠다 좋겠다 예쁘겠다
가다 오다 앉다 읽다 받다	간다 온다 앉는다 읽는다 받는다	갔다 왔다 앉았다 있었다 받았다	가겠다 오겠다 앉겠다 읽겠다 받겠다
알다 열다 놀다	안다 연다 논다	알았다 열었다 놀았다	알겠다 열겠다 놀겠다

연습 10. Rewrite the following verbs in written style.

a. 기다립니다. ______________ d. 묻습니다. ______________

b. 없어요. ______________ e. 아닙니다. ______________

c. 시작합니다. ______________ f. 돌아요. ______________

2. Loan Words in Korean

Although the great majority of loan words (외래어) used in Korean are Sino-Korean (coming from Old Chinese), there is another group of loan words that are steadily increased since 1945: English loan words. All loan words must conform to the sound structures available in Korean. As you do the exercises below, you may see if you can recognize some of the English loan words.

연습 11. Orally translate the following sentences, and then complete the statement of generalization below.

a. 오늘 컴퓨터로 편지를 썼다.
b. 오전에는 피아노 연습을 해야 한다.
c. 상점에서 초콜렛 한 상자 샀다.
d. 생일 파티에 케이크가 있어야 한다.
e. 한국 사람들은 보통 사람들 앞에서 키스 안한다.
f. 터널 앞에서 유턴 할 수 없다.

GENERALIZATION: English consonants, p, t, ch, and k (voiceless stops) are represented in Korean by ______, ______, ______, and ______, respectively.

연습 12. Orally translate the following sentences (in written style), and then complete the statement of generalization below.

a. 김 형은 기타를 잘 친다.
b. 아침에 늘 주스 한잔 마신다.
c. 서울역 뒤에서 버스를 내렸다.
d. 남산까지 드라이브 하겠다.
e. 자동차에 가솔린이 모자라겠다.
f. 백화점에서 내일부터 바겐 세일이 있다.

GENERALIZATION: English consonants, b, d, j, and g (voiced stops) are represented in Korean by ______, ______, ______, and ______, respectively.
In some cases, they are also represented by double consonants as in 빠나나 "banana."

연습 13. Orally translate the following sentences, and then complete the statement of generalization below.

a. 친구와 같이 레코드를 사러 상점에 갔다.
b. 아직 카메라에 필름이 있을 것이다.
c. 화장실은 엘레베이터 옆에 있었다.

d. 나는 호텔 로비에서 기다린다.
e. 여자 친구하고 올림픽 공원에서 점심을 먹었다.
f. 미국 캘리포니아에 한국 사람이 많이 산다.

> GENERALIZATION: Both l and r in English are represented by ____ in the word-initial position in Korean. However, between vowels the English r is represented with and l with _______.

연습 14. Translate the advertisement below, using a dictionary. There are three new words that are not yet introduced: 이미, 빠르고, and 쉽게. The last two words are derived from stative verbs.

New Words
- 이미 __________
- 빠르다/빨라 __________
- 쉽다/쉬워 __________

이미 시작했습니다

8월17일 부터

■8월 2일 - 8월 15일까지■

비디오로 영어를
빠르고 쉽게
배우십시오.

단어 정리 (VOCABULARY SUMMARY)

Nominals

가족	family	생일	birthday
계단	stairways, steps	시간	time
골프	golf	아래층	downstairs
끝	end (noun)	여름	summer
날짜	date	위층	upstairs
내일	tomorrow	이번	this time (occasion)
니네(들)	you (plural), you guys	학기	school period, semester
달	moon; month	해	sun; year
며칠	what day; how many days	현관	entrance (of a house)
방학	vacation (of a school)	화장실	restroom, bathroom
복도	hallway		

Position Words (Nominals)

뒤	behind, back	안	inside
밑	bottom, below	앞	front
밖	outside	옆	side
아래	below, lower part	위	top, upper part

Time Expressions

(Sino-Korean) + 년	year	(Sino-Korean) + 일	day (of the month)
(Sino-Korean) + 월	month (of the year)		

Action Verbs

갔다오다/-와	to have been to some place=다녀오다
끝나다/끝나	to end, be finished
내려가다/-가	to go down
놀다/노세요/놀아	to play; to have a day off
밀리다	to be pushed; be pushed aside > be delayed
시작하다/-해	to begin, start
올라가다/-가	to go up
일하다/-해	to work
준비하다/-해	to prepare
치다	to hit, strike

Stative Verbs

빠르다/빨라	to be fast, quick, swift
쉽다/쉬워	to be easy

Adverbs and Sentence Adverbials

그래서	therefore, so	바로	immediately, exactly
많이	many; much, a lot	이미	already (=벌써)

Postopositions

- 도	also; even
- 동안에	during
- 부터	from, since (Used after a time nominal)
- 하고	with (someone)

Scripts for Exercises

연습 1.
a. 오늘 며칠입니까? 7일입니다.
b. 몇 시간 일해요? 네 시간 일합니다.
c. 어느 해에 한국에 갔어요? 1988년에요.
d. 언제 학기가 시작해요? 6월 10일에요.
e. 몇 시간 일해요? 세시간 일합니다.

f. 한국에 몇 년 있었어요?　5년 있었어요.
g. 생일이 언젭니까?　12월 4일입니다.
h. 한국말을 몇 달 공부했어요?　여섯 달 공부했어요.

연습 8. a. 7월 12일에 학교가 시작합니다.　d. 1월 1일은 토요일이에요.
b. 10월 20일에 서울에 왔어요.　e. 새 상점이 9월 30일에 열립니다.
c. 2월 13일은 휴일입니다.　f. 금년 11월 8일에 부산에 갔어요.

연습문제 해답 (ANSWERS TO EXERCISES)

연습 1. a. 7　c. 1988　e. 3　g. 12-4
b. 4　d. 6-10　f. 5　h. 6

연습 3. a. 집에서는 일 안해요.　c. 저 사람은 학생이 아닙니다.
b. 백화점에는 안 갔어요.　d. 이 길로는 갈 수 없습니다/못가요.

연습 5. a. 오늘이 며칠입니까?　c. 어느 달에 일 시작했어요?
b. 내일 시간이 없어요.　d. 이 학기는 12월 16일에 끝납니다.
e. 이 선생은 1972년 4월에 미국에 왔습니다.
f. 학교는 다음달 14일에 시작합니다.

연습 6. a. 옆에　b. 뒤에　c. 앞에　d. 위에
e. 안에　f. 밖에　g. 밑에　h. 앞에

연습 8. a. July 12. School starts.　d. January 1 is Saturday.
b. October 20. I came to Seoul.　e. September 30. A new store opens.
c. February 13 is a holiday.　f. November 8. I went to Pusan.

연습 9. a. When the stem of an action/process verb ends with a vowel.
b. When the stem of an action/process verb ends with a consonant.

연습 10. a. 기다린다　b. 없다　c. 시작한다
d. 묻는다　e. 아니다　f. 돈다

연습 11. a. computer　c. chocolate　e. kiss
b. piano　d. party, cake　f. tunnel, U-turn
• Generalization: by ㅍ, ㅌ, ㅊ and ㅋ (aspirated stops)

연습 12. a. guitar　c. bus　e. gasoline
b. juice　d. drive　f. bargain sale
• Generalization: by ㅂ, ㄷ, ㅈ, ㄱ (unaspirated stops)

연습 13. a. record　c. elevator　e. Olympic
b. camera, film　d. hotel lobby　f. California
• Generalization: the initial r/l by ㄹ; the medial r with ㄹ;
the medial l with ㄹ/ㄹ.

연습 14. Already started - since August 17
From August 2 to August 15
Learn English fast and easy with videos.

Communicative Frames in English

Frame 1. What Day Is It?

Pak : Let's play golf tomorrow. You have time in the afternoon, don't you?
Yun : Tomorrow? What day is it tomorrow?
Pak : May 1st. Don't you even know tomorrow's date?
Yun : Oh, it's already a new month.
I don't have time tomorrow. I have to work.

Frame 2. Work on a Holiday?

Pak : Tomorrow is a holiday. Do you work on holidays?
Yun : I'm a lot behind in my work. (A lot of work is piled up.) The new semester will start soon. So, I've to prepare for this and that.
Pak : But, when did this semester end?
Yun : It ended last week.

Frame 3. Asking Where the Restroom Is

Pak : Where is the restroom?
Yun : It's downstairs. Go down by the stairway.
And, on your right go all the way (to the end.)
It's right in front of the entrance hall.
Pak : O.K. I understand. I'll be right back.

Frame 4. The Summer Vacation Is to Start

Myŏngsuk : When will your summer vacation start?
Haksu : Ours will start on the 19th. How about yours?
Myŏngsuk : Ours will be on the 18th.
Haksu : Isn't the 18th Friday?
Myŏngsuk : Yes, it is. We'll be off from Friday.
Haksu : Do you travel during the vacation?
Myŏngsuk : Sure. I'll be going to Chejudo with my family.

제 12 과

기차 여행

대화 1 (FRAME 1)

여행 계획

베이커	: 저 내주에 부산에 가야해요. 무엇으로 가는 것이 제일 좋습니까?
윤	: 글쎄요. 비행기보다 기차가 좋겠지요. 안전하고 경치도 보실 수 있으니까요.
베이커	: 네, 그런데 기차로 부산까지 얼마나 걸립니까?
윤	: 아마 네 시간쯤 걸릴 겁니다.
베이커	: 그거밖에 안 걸려요?
윤	: 그럴 거예요.

단어 공부 (*VOCABULARY STUDY*)

•계획	plan
•가는 것	going (nominal form of 가다) (See Grammar.)
•제일	most (adverb) (derived from 제일 "number one, topmost")
•글쎄요.	Well. (interjection expressing hesitation, doubt)
•비행기	airplane
•-보다	than (postposition)
•기차	train

- 좋겠지요. I suppose it would be good.

  The verb suffix-겠 expresses here the speaker's conjecture.

- 안전하다 to be safe (stative verb)
- -고 and (connective verb ending)
- 경치 sight, scenery
- 얼마나 how (long)

  CAUTION! 얼마나 means "just about how much," while 얼마 means "how much (exactly)." The former is used when an exact quantity is not expected, and it is often followed by a stative verb or an adverb, as in 얼마나 비싸요 "how expensive," 얼마나 자주 "how often," etc.

- 걸리다 to take (as of time), 시간이 얼마나 걸리다 "how much time is taken/consumed"; equivalent to "It takes (how much time)" in English.
- 아마 perhaps, probably

  CAUTION! The adverb 아마 must be used with a verb form expressing a conjecture (such as -을 겁니다). For example,

  CORRECT ⟶ 그것 아마 비쌀 겁니다. It might be expensive.
  WRONG ⟶ 그것 아마 비쌉니다.

- -쯤 approximately (a nominal suffix used after a quantity expression)
- -밖에 + (Negative) only/ no more than (Literally, "outside of···")

  CAUTION! The phrase, (Nominal) + 밖에 followed by a *negative* verb in Korean, is generally equivalent to "only···" in an *affirmative* sentence in English.

  우리 15분밖에 없어요. We have only fifteen minutes.
  커피 한 잔밖에 안 했어요. I only had a cup of coffee.

연습 1. Respond affirmatively.

a. 돈 이것 밖에 없어요?
b. 책밖에 안 샀어요?
c. 한국말 밖에 못합니까?
d. 이 길로 밖에 갈 수 없어요?

연습 2. Respond factually.

a. 학교에서 집까지 얼마나 걸립니까?
b. 서울에서 부산까지 얼마나 걸려요?
c. 그 일이 시간이 얼마나 걸립니까?
d. 자동차로 집까지 얼마나 걸려요?

연습 3. Discuss with your partner what activities you like (좋다 or 좋아하다) or don't like (싫다 or 싫어하다).

EXAMPLE: 책 읽는 것 좋아요/좋아해요? Do you like reading books?
책 읽는 것 좋아요/좋아해요. I like reading books.
책 읽는 것 싫어요/싫어해요. I don't like reading books.

a. 일 하는 것
b. 집에서 노는 것
c. 극장 가는 것
d. 친구 만나는 것
e. 집에서 일하는 것
f. 외국어 배우는 것

대화 2 (FRAME 2)

차표를 산다

베이커 : 실례합니다. 부산 가는 차표 어디서 삽니까?

젊은이 : 표 파는 곳 저깁니다.

베이커 : 네, 알았습니다. 감사합니다.

(매표소에서)

베이커 : 오전 10시 부산행, 특실 한 장 주세요.

매표원 : 예, 여기 있습니다.

베이커 : 열 시 정각에 떠납니까?

매표원 : 그럼요, 열 시 정각에 떠납니다.

베이커 : 몇 시에 부산에 도착합니까?

매표원 : 오후 2시 10분에 도착합니다.

단어 공부(*VOCABULARY STUDY*)

- 차표 — train ticket (차= train, car; 표= ticket)
- -는 — prenominal ending of an action/process verb

  부산 가는 차표 means a ticket for (going) to Pusan.
- 젊은이 — young man (젊다= be young, -이=person)
- 매표소 — ticket office (매=selling, 표=ticket, 소=office)
- 부산행 — Pusan-bound (-행= going)
- 특실 — first class coach (literally, "special coach")
- -장 — counter for sheets, cards (used with native numerals)
- 매표원 — ticket agent

- 정각　　　　exact hour, on the hour (suffixed to hours)

  열 시 정각 means "10 o'clock sharp."
- 떠나다／떠나　　to leave, depart

  The noun form is 출발 "departure."
- 도착하다　　to arrive

  The noun form is 도착 "arrival."

❖ -는 곳: "A PLACE FOR … -ING"

With the ending -는, an action or process verb may be converted to a noun modifier (prenominal form).

표 파는 곳	(ticket-selling place)	⟶ ticket counter
나가는 곳	(going-out place)	⟶ exit
차 타는 곳	(train-riding place)	⟶ boarding place/platform

연습 4. Read aloud each phrase and identify its English equivalent by the number.

a. ____ 모르는 사람
b. ____ 노는 날
c. ____ 책 읽는 방
d. ____ 공부하는 시간
e. ____ 점심 먹는 곳
f. ____ 일하는 사람
g. ____ 길 건너가는 데
h. ____ 기다리는 사람들

1. a place to eat lunch
2. the reading room
3. a day off (holiday)
4. people waiting
5. a place to cross the street
6. a time to study
7. the man who is working
8. a stranger

연습 5. Say appropriate Korean equivalents to the following English sentences.

a. When is the arrival time?
b. The plane bound for Chejudŏ is delayed.
c. The bus for Kyŏngju has already departed.
d. There were many people waiting in the station.
e. Going by bus will be safe and cheap.

연습 6. Fill in the vacant spaces with appropriate postpositions.

a. 박 선생님 나 ______ 커요.
   Mr. Pak is taller than me.
b. 우리는 친구들 ______ 버스 ______ 경주에 갔습니다.
   We went to Kyŏngju by bus with my friends.
c. 은행은 오전 열 시 ______ 오후 네 시 ______ 엽니다.
   The bank will be open from 10 a.m. until 4 p.m.
d. 편지 ______ 홍 씨 ______ 도 보냈어요.
   I sent a letter to Mr. Hong too.

연습 7. As you look at the bus schedule below, choose your destination, talk about the departure time and the arrival hours.

버 스	번 호	출발 시간	도착 시간
수원행	307호	오전 7:00	오전 8:15
인천행	72호	오전 8:55	오전 10:00
대전행	160호	오전 9:00	오후 1:00
대구행	245호	오후 1:25	오후 6:45

대화 3 (FRAME 3)

옆의 승객과 이야기 한다

베이커 : 어디까지 가십니까?
승객 : 저는 대전까지 갑니다. 선생님은요?
베이커 : 전 부산 갑니다.
승객 : 예... 선생님 미국분이세요?
베이커 : 네, 미국에서 왔습니다.
승객 : 어떻게 그렇게 우리 나라말 잘 하세요?
베이커 : 뭘요. 잘 못합니다. 조금 배웠죠.
승객 : 참 잘 하세요. 한국말 그렇게 잘 하시는 외국분 처음 봐요.

단어 공부 (*VOCABULARY STUDY*)

- 승객 — passenger
- 이야기하다 — to talk
- 그렇게 — so, like that (adverb)
- 우리 나라말 — our nation's language: Korean
- 뭘요. — Not at all. (In this phrase the speaker humbly declines someone's compliment paid to him. 뭘요←무엇을요)

연습 8. You are in an airplane going to Seoul, and you find a young man/woman (played by your partner) seated next to you. Engage in a casual conversation including the following topics.

a. Nationality (e.g., if he/she is a Korean.)
b. Destination, and the purpose of the travel.
c. Introduce each other.
d. Length of the stay in Seoul.
e. Ability to speak Korean.

대화 4 (FRAME 4)

언니 집에 가는 계획

순옥: 나 모레 경주 간다.
학수: 그래? 누구랑?
순옥: 오빠랑 동생이랑 다 같이 가.
학수: 뭐 하러 가니?
순옥: 놀러 가지. 거기 우리 언니가 살아.
언니도 보고 구경도 하고 ....
학수: 좋겠다.

단어 공부 (*VOCABULARY STUDY*)

- 모레 — the day after tomorrow
- -이랑 — with, along with (colloquial equivalent to -하고)

The vowel 이 of -이랑 is dropped when the preceding nominal ends with a consonant, as in 누구랑 "with whom," 나랑 "with me."

- 오빠 — elder brother (of a female person)
- 동생 — younger brother (or sister)
- 놀다/노는/놀아 — to have fun; to play; to have a day off
- 살다/사는/살아 — to live, reside

CAUTION! When the ending -으러 "in order to···" follows an L verb (such as 놀다), the vowel 으 of 으러 is absent. For example,

놀+으러 → 놀러 (in order) to have fun
열+으러 → 열러 (in order) to open

- 언니 — elder sister (of a female person)

CULTURAL ENCOUNTER In English, all siblings are eithter "brothers" or "sisters." In Korean, the age and the view point must also be considered in addition to the gender.

OLDER : brother sister

형 오빠 누나 언니

VIEWPOINT:

of a brother *of a sister* *of a brother* *of a sister*

If the sibling is younger, there is only one word 동생 "younger brother or sister." Sometimes the prefix 남- "male" or 여- "female" is added, as in 남동생 and 여동생.

연습 9. Say the follwing in Korean.

a. You have met a female classmate. Inquire about her elder brother.
b. Ask her if her elder sister speaks English.
c. You are talking to your male classmate. Ask him if he has any elder brothers.
d. Ask him how his elder sister is doing.

연습 10. With your partner, talk about each other's siblings. For example, discuss how many brothers and sisters there are in each other's family and what they do.

❖ -고: "AND"

Two or more clauses may be connected by the ending -고 at the end of the first clause.

기차가 안전하고 경치도 볼 수 있지요.
The train is safe, and you can enjoy the scenery too.

버스는 여기서 다섯 시에 떠나고 거기 일곱 시에 도착해요.
The bus will leave here at five, and arrive there at seven.

위층은 상점이고 아래층은 사무실입니다.
Stores are upstairs and offices are downstairs.

누나도 볼 수 있고 관광도 할 수 있지요.
I can see my sister and do sightseeing, too.

NOTE: When two clauses make parallel statements, with equal emphasis on both subjects/topics, the postposition -도 repeats in both clauses. For example,

부산에 가려면 버스도 있고 기차도 있다.
For Pusan we have buses as well as trains.

연습 11. Restate (orally) the sentences below by connecting each pair of sentences with the connective ending -고.

a. 길이 복잡합니다.
사람이 많아요.

b. 커피도 있습니다.
주스도 있어요.

c. 점심을 먹읍시다.
바로 떠납시다.

d. 이것이 저것보다 좋아요.
싸요.

연습 12. Respond factually.

a. 오늘이 며칠입니까?

b. 모레는 며칠이에요?

c. 내일은 무슨 요일입니까?

d. 모레는 무슨 요일이에요?

문법 (GRAMMAR)

1. Using Verbs as Noun Modifiers

Verbs are often used as a noun modifier (adjectivally) in any language. In English, noun modifiers take the form of participles (*going* prices, *spoken* words, etc.) or of infinitives (time *to go,* things *to do,* etc.). You have already learned how to use a stative verb (adjective) as a noun modifier with the ending -은, e.g., 큰 집 "a big house," 작은 차 "a small car," etc.

a. STATIVE VERBS: STEM + 은

비싼 옷	expensive clothes	같은 시간	the same time
작은 차	a small car	바쁜 시간	busy hours
예쁜 여자	a pretty girl	좋은 선물	a nice gift

b. ACTION/PROCESS VERB: STEM + 는

택시 타는 곳	a taxi stand	아는 사람	an acquaintance
나가는 곳	exit	기다리는 사람	a waiting person

NOTES:

(1) RELATIVE CLAUSES IN KOREAN
In Korean, there are no equivalents to relative clauses that you see in English or in other European languages. There are no relative pronouns (such as "that, which, who," etc.) in Korean. The Korean counterpart to the English relative clause is a phrase or clause ending with a prenominal ending (such as -는), which we will call here a "relative" clause for convenience.

(2) EXISTENCE VERB and EQUATION VERB
The existence verb 있다 takes –는 like an action verb, while the equation verb –이다 takes –ㄴ like a stative verb. For example, 여기 있는 사람 "people who are here," 학생인 사람 "a person who is a student."

(3) There are a set of four basic prenominal endings which express different tenses or aspects. They will be introduced later.

2. Using Verbs as Nominals

There are several ways to convert a verb into a nominal. One that is introduced in this lesson is to use the bound noun -것 after a prenominal form of a verb: STEM+는 것. This type of phrase often accompanies other words to form a nominal phrase or clause.

기차로 가는 것	going by train	한국말 배우는 것	learning Korean
책을 읽는 것	reading a book	집에서 일하는 것	working at home

3. Intentions or Probabilities: -겠

As introduced in Lesson 9, the verb form for expressing the speaker's *intention* is also used to express his *conjecture* in Korean. You have so far covered two forms: -겠 and -을 것이다. The distinction between intention and conjecture depends on the subject and the nature of the verb in the sentence.

a. Asking or stating intentions

{ 커피 하시겠어요? / 커피 하실 겁니까? } Are you going to have coffee? (INTENTION)

{ 네, 커피 하겠어요. / 네, 커피 할 거예요. } Yes, I'm going to have coffee. (INTENTION)

Note that the verb in this case is always of action type, and the subject is either the 2nd person in a question, or the 1st person in a statement.

b. Asking or stating conjectures or opinions

{ 괜찮겠습니까? / 괜찮을 겁니까? } Do you think it's all right? (OPINION)

{ 네, 좋겠어요. / 네, 좋을거예요. } Yes, I guess it's fine. (CONJECTURE)

Note that the subject and the verb here exclude those conditions given for ⓐ above. That is, the subject is *generally* a 3rd person, or the verb is of non-action type (processive or stative) for 1st or 2nd persons.

선생님 { 좋으시겠어요. / 좋으실 겁니다. } You must be glad.

저는 좀 { 늦겠습니다. / 늦을 겁니다. } I may be a little late.

4. Combining Two or More Clauses: -고

Sentences consisting of two or more clauses (compound and complex sentences) in Korean have a *connective ending* at the end of the first clause. A simple connective ending -고 (somewhat equivalent to "and" in English) connects any of the two verb phrases or clauses.

이것이 싸고 좋아요.
This one is cheap and nice.

점심 먹고 바로 떠납시다.
Let's have lunch and leave immediately.

이분이 신미라 양이고 저분이 이영옥 양 입니다.
This is Miss Mira Shin, and that is Miss Yŏng'ok Lee.

The modal features (moods, tenses, intentions, conjectures, etc.) are *not generally* incorporated in the connective phrase (with -고) but in the last verb. However, the honorific marker (-으시) is an exception, and it is normally incorporated in both clauses.

어머니는 시장에 가시고 아버지는 회사에 가셨어요.
HONORIFIC HONORIFIC PAST TENSE

When two clauses make parallel statements with equal emphasis on both subjects, the parallel marker -도 is often incorporated in both clauses.

누님도 보고 관광도 할 수 있지요.
I can see my sister and do some sightseeing too.

값도 싸고 품질도 좋아요.
The price is reasonable, and the quality is also fine.

5. Nominal +밖에 + Negative: "no more than"

The notion of "only" or "no more than" is expressed by a phrase, (Nominal) + 밖에 followed by a negative verb.

한 시간밖에 안 걸려요.
It takes no more than one hour.

식당에 밖에 안 갔어요.
I didn't go anywhere but the restaurant.

돈이 100원밖에 없었습니다.
He didn't have any more than 100 won.

6. Verbs and Sentence Structures

The verb is central to the sentence structure. It determines the kinds of the nominals and their case roles within a sentence. The presence of the verb "read," for example, makes you expect a human subject ("reader"), and an inanimate object ("something written") in the sentence. Most Korean verbs and their English counterparts are similar in this regard, but some are quite different.

From this lesson on, whenever a new verb is associated with the sentence structure sufficiently different from its English counterpart, such a verb will be presented along with the required sentence structure in the vocabulary section. Let us review some verbs you have already learned.

Verb Types	Structures	English Equivalents
EXISTENCE VERB:	(A- 가 B-가 있다.)	A has B.
ACTION VERBS :	(A- 가 B-를 기다리다.)	A waits for B.
	(A- 가 B-에 다녀오다.) (A- 가 B-에 갔다오다.)	A goes to B and comes back.
PROCESS VERBS :	(A- 가 열렸다.)	A is open.
	(A- 가 닫혔다.)	A is closed.
	(A- 가 보이다.)	A is visible.
	(일이 밀렸다.)	Work is piled up.
	(시간이 얼마나 걸리다.)	It takes (how much) time.
STATIVE VERBS :	(A- 가 B-가 좋다.)	A likes B.
	(A- 가 B-하고 같다.)	A is the same as B.

NOTES:

(1) Symbols A and B above represents the nominals with the postpositions to show their case roles.

(2) When a specific Korean word is used for the nominal position (e.g., 시간이 "time"), the nominal for that position is restricted to words of the same or similar category.

읽기 · 쓰기 (READING & WRITING)

1. Major Railroad Lines in Korea: 한국의 철도

The railroad (철도), which literally means "iron road," is operated by the Department of Transportation (교통부) of the Korean government. The most important lines (선) in South Korea are 경부선 and 호남선. The most heavily utilized line is 경부선, which runs between 서울 and 부산. There are three types of trains in each line: 새마을호 ("The New Community"), 무궁화호("The Hibiscus"), and 통일호 ("The Unification"). Among them, 새마을호 is the fastest.

Reading Vocabulary

- 철도 railroad (철= iron, 도=road)
- 열차 train (a technical term used in the context of railroad transportation; 기차 is nontechnical and more common in conversation.)
- 출발 departure; 출발하다 to depart (=떠나다)
- 도착 arrival; 도착하다 to arrive

연습 13. Scan the train schedule below, and write answers to the questions.

경부선 열차 시각 안내

종 별	출발 시각	종착역	도착시각	개찰구
통 일 호	06:10	부산	11:35	2
새마을호	07:30	부산	11:19	6
무궁화호	07:30	부산	12:30	3
새마을호	08:00	부산	12:16	6
통 일 호	09:20	부산	15:55	2
새마을호	09:25	부산	13:55	6

a. 서울에서 부산까지 어떻게 가는것이 제일 빠릅니까?
b. 부산에 오후 1시까지 가야 합니다. 서울역에서 몇 시 차로 떠나는 것이 좋습니까?
c. 새마을호로 서울에서 부산까지 몇 시간 걸립니까?

연습 14. At any railroad station, you will see a train fare table(열차운임표) similar to the one below. Scan the posting, and write the answers to the questions.

역명	통일호		무궁화호		새마을호	
	특실	일반실	특실	일반실	특실	일반실
대전	4,300	2,800	6,200	4,100	10,600	8,100
대구	8,000	5,500	11,100	8,000	19,200	15,000
부산	10,600	7,300	14,500	10,600	26,500	21,500

Reading Vocabulary

- 운임 fare
- 역명 station name
- 특실 special coach (=1st class)
- 일반실 general coach

a. 오늘 대전에 가야 합니다. 어떻게 가는 것이 제일 쌉니까?
b. 대구까지 새마을호로 특실 표 값이 얼마입니까?
c. 부산에 가야 합니다. 그런데 돈이 10,000원 밖에 없어요.
부산 가는 기차표를 살 수 있어요? 어느 열차표요?

연습 15. The paragraph below in Korean contains essentially the same information given in the introduction section. Scan the paragraph, and answers the questions.

> 한국의 철도
>
> 한국의 철도선 중에서 가장 중요한 것은 경부선과 호남선이다.
> 경부선은 서울과 부산 사이를 다니는 철도이고, 호남선은 서울과 목포 사이를 다니는 철도이다. 경부선에는 새마을호와 무궁화호와 통일호가 다닌다. 그중에서 새마을호가 가장 빠르다.

Reading Vocabulary

- -중에서 among
- 가장 most (=제일)
- 중요한 important
- 사이 interval

a. 호남선은 어디하고 어디 사이를 다닙니까?
b. 경부선에는 열차가 몇 가지 (kinds) 입니까?
c. 열차 중에서 어느 열차가 가장 빠릅니까?

연습 16. For each of the phrases listed below, write a phrase with an opposite meaning.

a. 안에서 ⟷ ________
b. 시작 ⟷ ________
c. 왼쪽에 ⟷ ________
d. 나가는 곳 ⟷ ________
e. 오빠의 친구 ⟷ ________
f. 도착했다 ⟷ ________
g. 닫혔어요 ⟷ ________
h. 파는 사람 ⟷ ________
i. 올라가세요 ⟷ ________
j. 여자화장실 ⟷ ________

연습 17. Complete the following sentences by filling in the blank spaces with words listed on the right. Then give an English equivalent to each Korean sentence.

a. 안전 벨트 매는 것이 ________.
b. 요즈음 비행기표 ________이 올라갔다.
c. 서울과 인천 ________에 기차가 ________.
d. 기차로 ________이 ________ 안전하다.
e.열차 ________ 새마을호가 가장 ________.
f. 비행기가 ________ 도착시각보다 좀 ________.

가는것	사이
가장	예정
가격(=값)	중에서
늦을것이다	중요하다
다닌다	빠르다

2. GUESS WHAT IT MEANS.

As in any language, Korean speakers often use old sayings in conversation. 시작이 반이다 "A beginning is a half" is one such saying. You may be able to guess what it means by the context in which it is used. See if you can guess what it means. The answer is at the end of the Answers to Exercises section.

A : 저 요새 영어 공부 시작했어요. 아직 잘 못해요.
B : 곧 잘 하실 겁니다. 시작이 반이잖아요?

단어 정리 (VOCABULARY SUMMARY)

Nominals

경치	sight, scenery	운임	price, fare
계획	plan	교통	traffic, transportation
기차	train	선	line
모레	the day after tomorrow	승객	passenger
비행기	airplane	특실	special class coach
우리 나라말	Korean language (=한국말)	열차	train (=기차)
정각	exact time, on the hour	일반실	general class coach
표	ticket	철도	railroad

Kinship Terms

형	elder brother (of a male person)	언니	elder sister (of a female person)
오빠	elder brother (of a female person)	동생	younger brother/sister
		남동생	younger brother
누나	elder sister (of a male person)	여동생	younger sister

Action Verbs

떠나다/떠나	to leave, depart	살다/사는/살아	to live, reside
도착하다	to arrive	팔다/파는/팔아	to sell
얘기하다	to talk, chat	출발하다	to depart (=떠나다)

Stative Verbs

안전하다	to be safe	중요하다	to be important

Process Verbs

걸리다	to take (as of time)

Adverbs

가장	most	얼마나	how much/long
그렇게	so, like that	제일	most (=가장)
아마	perhaps, probably		

Interjections

글쎄요	well (an expression of hesitation, doubt, pause)
뭘요	Not at all (a polite declination of a compliment)

Postpositions

-밖에	outside of, other than -밖에 + (Negative): only, no more than
-보다	than, rather than
-사이에	between (사이= space)
-이랑	with (someone) (colloquial use) (= 하고)

Suffixes and Bound Nouns

-곳	place (=데)
-장	sheet, stud (of paper)
-쯤	approximately
-행	bound for, going to (a place)

연습문제 해답 (ANSWERS TO EXERCISES)

연습 4. a. (8) c. (2) e. (1) g. (5)
b. (3) d. (6) f. (7) h. (4)

연습 5. a. 도착(하는) 시간이 언제입니까?
b. 제주도행/제주도에 가는 비행기가 늦습니다.
c. 경주 가는 버스는 벌써 떠났어요.
d. 역에 기다리는 사람이 많았어요.
e. 버스로 가는 것이 안전하고 쌉니다.

연습 6. a. 나보다 c. 열시부터 오후 네시까지
b. 친구들이랑 버스로 d. 편지를 홍 씨한테도

연습 9. a. 오빠 안녕하세요? c. 형 있어요?
b. 언니 영어해요? d. 누나 잘 있어요?

연습 11. a. 길이 복잡하고 사람이 많아요.
b. 커피도 있고 주스도 있어요.
c. 점심을 먹고 바로 떠납시다.
d. 이것이 저것보다 좋고 싸요.

연습 13. a. 새마을호로 가는 것 b. 7시 30분 새마을호 c. 3시간 20분쯤

연습 14. a. 통일호 일반실로 b. 19,200원 c. 통일호 일반실

연습 15. a. 서울과 목포 사이 b. 세가지 c. 새마을호

연습 16. a. 밖에서 c. 오른쪽에 e. 언니의 친구 g. 열렸어요 i. 내려가세요
b. 끝 d. 들어가는 곳 f. 출발했다 h. 사는 사람 j. 남자 화장실

연습 17. a. 중요하다 c. 사이, 다닌다 e. 중에서, 빠르다
b. 값 d. 가는 것, 가장 f. 예정, 늦을 것이다

ANSWER TO "GUESS WHAT IT MEANS" : 시작이 반이다 means "To have begun is half done." It stresses the importance of "getting your feet wet."

Communicative Frames in English

Frame 1. Planning for a Trip

Baker : I have to go to Pusan next week. What is the best way to go?
Yun : Well. I suppose a train would be better than an airplane.
It's safe, and you can enjoy the sights, too.
Baker : I see. But how long does it take to get to Pusan by train?
Yun : I think it'll probably take four hours.
Baker : It takes only that?
Yun : I think so.

Frame 2. Buying the Train Ticket

Baker : Excuse me, sir. Where can I buy a ticket for Pusan?
Young man : The ticket counter is over there.
Baker : I see. Thank you very much.
(At the ticket counter)
Baker : One 1st class ticket for the 10 a.m. train to Pusan, please.
Ticket agent: Yes, here it is, sir.
Baker : Does it depart exactly at 10 a.m?
Ticket agent: Of course, it'll depart at 10 a.m. sharp.

Baker : What time does it arrive in Pusan?
Ticket agent : It'll get there at 2:10 p.m.

Frame 3. Chatting with a Next Passenger.

Baker : How far are you going?
Passenger : I'm going to Taejŏn, and you, sir?
Baker : I'm going to Pusan.
Passenger : I see... Are you an American?
Baker : Yes, I'm from America.
Passenger : How come you speak Korean so well?
Baker : Not at all, I don't speak it well. I learned it just a little bit.
Passenger : You speak really well. I've never seen a foreigner speaking Korean so well.

Frame 4. Planning a Visit to Sister's Place.

Sunok : The day after tomorrow, we are going to Kyungju.
Haksu : Yeah? With whom?
Sunok : With my elder brother and my younger brother. All together.
Haksu : What are you going there for?
Sunok : To have fun. And my elder sister lives there. We will see my sister and do sightseeing, too.
Haksu : That'll be great.

제 13 과

서울의 하루

대화 1 (FRAME 1)

공항에서

한영옥: 문 선생 아니세요? 안녕하세요?

문인섭: 아이구! 영옥 씨 웬일이세요?

한영옥: 오랜만이에요. 어디 가세요?

문인섭: 아뇨. 누구 마중 나왔어요.
친구가 미국에서 와요. 영옥 씨는요?
어떻게 공항에 나왔어요?

한영옥: 제 동생이 일본에 가요.
그애 전송하러 나왔어요.

문인섭: 네. 영옥 씨 시간 있으면 차나 한 잔 합시다.

한영옥: 네, 좋아요.

단어 공부 (*VOCABULARY STUDY*)

- 하루 — a day
- 아이구! — Oh my! (interjection expressing surprise)
- 웬일이세요? — What brought you here?
  An idiom used when one meets someone unexpectedly.
  웬일 literally means "what kind of event or business."
- 오랜만입니다. — It's been a long time. (=오래간만입니다.)
- 어디 가세요? — Are you going somewhere?

CAUTION! 어디 and 누구 in this exchange are not interrogative pronouns. They are indefinite pronouns, "somewhere" and "someone," respectively. (See Grammar.)

- 마중 나오다 — to come out to greet
  A -가 B-를 마중 나오다. — *A* comes out to meet *B*.
- 그애 — that kid
  A term of endearment used by an older member of a family to refer to a younger one; 애 is the short for 아이 "child."
- 전송하다 — to send off someone (on a trip)
- 있으면 — if you have...
  - 으면 is a connective ending meaning "if" or "when." (See Grammar.)
- 차나 — tea or something (See below for -이나.)

❖ -이나: "EITHER...OR..."

Two nominals expressing alternatives are connected by the postposition -이나 attached to the first nominal. The vowel –이 of –이나 is dropped when the preceding nominal ends in a vowel.

여섯 시나 일곱 시에	either at six or seven o'clock
형이나 동생	an elder brother or a younger brother
사이다나 주스	cider or juice
기차나 버스로	either by train or by bus

Sometimes, a nominal with –이나 is not followed by another nominal. In such cases, the nominal expresses a "weak" and noncommittal choice by the speaker.

커피나 하십시다.	Let's have coffee (or something).
책이나 읽지요.	I'll read a book (or something).

연습 1. Express two or more alternative choices based on the pictures below. Add an appropriate verb phrase for each.

a.

c.
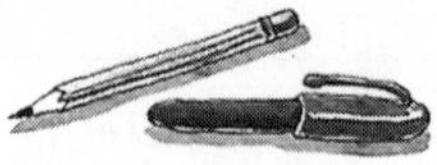

e.

b.
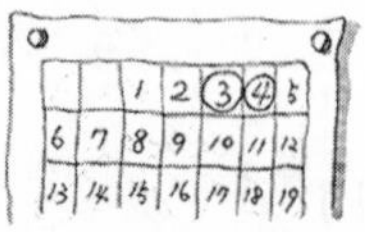

d.

f.

연습 2. Restate the sentences below by making the choice non-committal.

a. 극장에 가겠어요.
b. 커피 한 잔 시킵시다.
c. 골프 칠까요?
d. 신문을 읽지요.

연습 3. You have run into a friend at the train station. Exchange greetings and talk about why you are there by choosing one of the reasons shown below.

a. 아버지 마중 나왔어요.
b. 우리 형을 전송하러 나왔어요.
c. 아는 사람 만나러 왔어요.
d. 친구들이랑 경주에 가요.
e. 수원에 갔다왔어요.
f. 점심 먹으러 왔어요.

대화 2(FRAME 2)

레스토랑에서

문: 커피 하겠어요?

한: 아니오. 전 오후에는 커피 안 해요.

문: 왜요?

한: 오후에 커피 마시면 밤에 못잡니다.
사이다나 주스 하죠. 목이 좀 말라요.

문: 식사는 하지 않겠어요? 난 배가 좀 고파요.

한: 저는 식사는 일러요. 선생님 시장하시면
식사 주문하세요. 전 주스 하나 시켜 주세요.

문: 그래요? 그럼, 나도 커피나 시키죠.
아가씨! 여기 주문 받아요.

단어 공부 (*VOCABULARY STUDY*)

- 레스토랑 — restaurant (particularly Western-style)
- 전 — the short for 저는
  The postposition -는 is commonly contracted to ㄴ in colloquialism.
- 자다 — to sleep, to go to bed

CAUTION! The honorific form of 자다 is irregular: 주무시다.
안녕히 주무세요. Good night. (Sleep well.)

- 사이다 — "cider" drink (a clear soft drink more like 7-Up in America)
- 목(이) 마르다/말라 — to be thirsty (stative verb) (목=throat, 마르다=to be dry)
- -지 않다 — long negative form. (See Grammar.)
  하지 않아요?＝안 해요? Won't you do?

• 배 고프다/고파	to be hungry (stative verb) (배=stomach)
A-가 배 고프다.	*A* is hungry.
• 난	the short for 나는
• 주문 받아요.	Please take an order.

❖ -지 않겠어요/않아요? "WON'T YOU ...?"

The long negative form is generally interchangeable with the short form (안 + verb). The honorific marking and other modals (tense, mood, etc.) are incorporated in the final verb (않다). However, the honorific marker may also be incorporated in the first verb.

가지 않으세요?	Aren't you going?	싸지 않습니다.	It's not cheap.
가시지 않으세요?	(HONORIFIC)	가지 않았어요.	I didn't go.
하지 않겠어요?	Won't you do?		

연습 4. Respond negatively, using the long negative form.

a. 그 옷 비싸지요?
b. 편지 받았습니까?
c. 오늘 은행에 가세요?
d. 어제 놀았어요?

연습 5. Restate the questions with the long negative form.

a. 안 가세요?
b. 음식 안시키셨어요?
c. 돈이 안 모자랐습니까?
d. 커피 안 하시겠어요?

❖ HOW TO USE THE CONDITIONAL CLAUSE

The connective ending -으면 makes a clause a conditional one, equivalent to "if" or "when" in English. The vowel 으 of -으면 is absent whenever it is preceded by a vowel or ㄹ. The dependent clause always precedes the main clause.

시간이 있으시면 커피 합시다.	If you have time, let's have coffee.
배가 고프면 식사 주문하세요.	If you are hungry, order a meal.
오른쪽으로 돌면 보입니다.	If you turn to your right, you'll see it.

연습 6. Complete the following sentences.

a. 커피 _____면 오렌지 주스 한 잔 __________.
If you don't have coffee, give me a glass of orange juice.

b. 내일 _____면 우리 집에 오세요.
If you have a day off tomorrow, come to my house.

c. 목이 _____면 주스 _____ 물을 마시세요.
If you are thirsty, drink some juice or water.

d. 여기서 표를 _____면 왜 _____ 가세요?

If they sell tickets here, why do you go to the station?

e. 지금 _____면 거기 세 시 _____ 도착할 수 있어요.

If you leave now, you can get there by three.

대화 3 (FRAME 3)

날씨 이야기

문: 오늘 날씨가 좋지요?
한: 네, 이제 봄이 됐어요. 아침에도 춥지 않아요.
문: 그래요. 요새 낮에는 더워요.
한: 네,… 그럼 저는 일어서야겠어요.
문: 벌써 갈 시간이 됐나요?
한: 네, 그럼, 선생님 조심해서 들어 가세요.
부인한테 안부 전해 주시고.
문: 네. 그리고 한번 우리 집에 놀러 오세요.
한: 네, 찾아가 뵙겠습니다. 안녕히 가세요.
문: 잘 가요. 또 봅시다.

단어 공부 (*VOCABULARY STUDY*)

- 날씨 — weather
- 이제/인제 — now (adverb)

CAUTION! Note the difference between 지금 and 이제, both of which are usually translated "now" in English. 지금 "now" had *no* special implication. 이제 "now" implies a *change* from the past to the present time. For example,

인제는 날씨가 좋아요. The weather is fine now (though it had been bad before).

- 봄 — spring (season)
- 되다/돼 — to become

CAUTION! The pronunciation of 외 varies in different dialects. The official standard one is [oe], a simple rounded mid-vowel, similar to the French *eu*, but in Seoul today [we] is the most common pronunciation. Thus, the three diphthongs(외, 웨, 왜) may all be pronounced [we]

- 춥다/추워 — to be cold (used of weather, but not to describe tangible objects such as water, food, etc.)

•낮	day time (as opposed to 밤 "night")
•덥다/더워	to be warm, hot
•요새	nowadays, lately (synonym : 요즈음)
•-어야겠어요	common contraction of -어야 하겠어요, where the verb stem 하- is often dropped.
•갈 시간이 되다	to be-become time to go
•조심해서 들어가세요.	Good-bye and take care.
•(누구)-한테 안부 전하다.	to give one's regards to (someone) (안부=inquiry of someone's health; 전하다=to convey)
•한번	once

-번 is a counter for occurrences, as in 한번 "once", 두번 "twice", etc.

•찾아가 뵙다	to go to visit with (someone) (Humble form)
•잘 가요. Ⓜ	Good-bye.
•또	again

연습 7. Respond factually.

a. 오늘 날씨가 좋습니까?
b. 어제 날씨는 어땠어요?
c. 요새 아침에 추워요? 더워요?
d. 지금 배가 고프지 않아요?
e. 목이 마르면 뭐 마십니까?
f. 선생님 댁에 찾아가 뵈었어요?

연습 8. Listen to the model voicing. As you listen, fill in the blanks with the correct words.

a. I'm going to visit with _______ ________.
b. Give my best regards to ________.
c. It's too _______. Please ________.
d. When it's _______, it'll probably be very _______.
e. I went to visit with _______ _______ before.

연습 9. Say the follwing utterances in Korean.

a. Is it time to go already?
b. Give my regard to your brother.
c. Come to see me again sometime.
d. I went to visit with my teacher yesterday.
e. See you again.

대화 4 (FRAME 4)

영화 구경

순희: 오늘 밤 나랑 극장 가자.

영옥: 그래. 어디서 좋은 영화 하니?

순희: 신문 있어? 신문 보자.

영옥: 여기 있어… 너 "첫사랑" 봤니?
중앙 극장에서 한다.

순희: 그 영화 좋아?

영옥: 아주 좋아. 그거 보자.

순희: 어떻게 알아?

영옥: 나 봤어. 그저께.

순희: 그럼 너 같은 거 두 번 보니?

영옥: 왜? 좋으면 또 보지. 빨리 가자.

단어 공부 (*VOCABULARY STUDY*)

•-자.	Let's... (a blunt ending equivalent to -읍시다.)
•영화	movie, cinema
•구경	seeing, viewing
•첫사랑	first love (첫= first, 사랑=love)
•중앙	Central (proper noun)
•아주	very, extremely
•그저께	the day before yesterday
•빨리	quickly, promptly

연습 10. Listen to the model voicing. As you listen, fill in the blanks with the correct words.

a. How many _______ did you see _______?
b. _______ for the first time is _______?
c. It's not _______ any more. Isn't it _______ now?
d. I _______ last night at _______.
e. I read _______ _______.

연습 11. Respond factually.

a. 요새 좋은 영화 봤어요?
b. 그 영화 지금 어디서 합니까?
c. 영화가 좋으면 두 번 보겠어요?
d. 누구랑 영화 보러 가요?
e. 어제가 무슨 요일이었어요?
f. 그저께가 무슨 요일이었어요?

연습 12. Talk with your partner about a movie that you have seen recently. Tell him/her how good it was, where it is shown, and whether or not you want to see it again.

문법 (GRAMMAR)

1. Somebody, Somewhere, Sometime

All question words (누구, 어디, 언제, etc.) with one exception of 왜 may be used as indefinite pronouns ("some…").

밖에 누가 왔어요.	Someone came outside.
누구를 만나야 돼요.	I have to meet somebody.
어디 갑시다.	Let's go somewhere.

This could potentially create confusion in interpreting question sentences, but in reality it doesn't because the *intonation* makes it clear which way a given sentence is intended. For example, the two question sentences below are quite different in intonation.

(a) 뭐 하세요?	What are you doing?
(b) 뭐 ↗ 하세요? ⤴	Are you doing something?

Question (a) has no special intonation to be noted except the tone at the end either goes slightly up or down.

On the other hand, question (b) has unique intonation features as indicated by arrows above: a little break between 뭐 and 하세요 with a rising tone [↗] after 뭐 (something), and a sharp rising tone [⤴] at the end of the sentence. Observe the same pattern below.

어디 가세요?	Where are you going?
어디 ↗ 가세요? ⤴	Are you going somewhere?
돈 얼마 있어요?	How much money do you have?
돈 얼마 ↗ 있어요? ⤴	Do you have some money?
한국에 언제 가세요?	When will you go to Korea?
한국에 언제 ↗ 가세요? ⤴	Will you go to Korea sometime?

The above patterns of intonation are due to a general rule which requires the "either-or" question (without a question word) to have a sharp rising tone [↗], while a question with a question word (누가, 무엇, etc.) has the same intonation as the statement: a slight rise or fall at the end of the sentence.

NOTE: The above intonations are typical of Seoul speech, but there are other variations.

2. Long Negatives

The two negative forms (안- and 못-) introduced earlier are both prefixes (placed before a verb stem). They may also take phrasal forms, which we will call "long" negatives. The short and long negatives are generally interchangeable.

	Short Negative	Long Negative
a. Simple Negative	안 + VERB	STEM + 지 않다
b. Inability	못 + VERB	STEM + 지 못하다

SHORT NEGATIVE	LONG NEGATIVE	
안 갑니다.	가지 않습니다.	I'm not going.
이리 못가요.	이리 가지 못해요.	You can't go this way.
저 안 바쁩니다.	저 바쁘지 않습니다.	I'm not busy.
안 추워요.	춥지 않아요.	It's not cold.

3. The Sequence of Verb Markers

In long negatives and most compound verb constructions, all verb markers (honorific, tense, conjecture, etc.) are normally incorporated in the *last verb*. Such verb markers are in the following sequence:

STEM + 지	않 (으시)	(었)	(겠)다
	Honorific	Tense	Conjecture

나가지 않으세요.	[Honorific]	He isn't going out.
읽지 않으셨어요?	[Honorific + Past]	Didn't you read it?
팔지 못하실 겁니다.	[Conjecture]	He will not be able to sell.

However, the honorific marking is sometimes repeated in both verbs of the compound which naturally makes the expression extra polite.

저하고 가시지 않으시겠어요? Won't you go with me?

When the honorific form is irregular, i.e., 계시다 "to be," 잡수시다 "to eat," and 주무시다 "to sleep," the honorific marker is found in both verbs of the compound.

점심 잡수시지 않으셨어요? Didn't you have your lunch?
잘 주무시지 못하셨어요? Couldn't you sleep well?

4. If and When: -으면

The clause expressing the condition ("if" or "when") for the main (last) clause has the connective ending -으면.

시간이 있으면	커피 한 잔 하십시다
If you have time,	let's have a cup of coffee.
일이 끝나면	전화해 주세요.
When the work is over,	please give me a call.
목이 마르면	오렌지 주스 한 잔 하세요.
If you are thirsty,	have a glass of orange juice.
세 시에 거기 떠났으면	여기 곧 도착할 겁니다.
If she left there at 3,	she should arrive here soon.

Note that the dependent clause precedes the main clause in formal styles (although in speech they are sometimes reversed). This is true of all complex sentences in Korean.

CAUTION! The vowel 으 of -으면 is absent when preceded by a vowel or ㄹ. The L verb (with a stem ending in ㄹ) retains ㄹ and is directly connected to 면:

알면	if you know	돌면	if you turn

5. Alternatives: A 이나 B

Two or more alternatives are connected by the postposition -이나. The vowel 이 of -이나 is present only when the preceding noun ends with a consonant.

커피나 주스 하시지요.	Why don't you have coffee or juice?
이것이나 저것을 사지요.	I'll buy either this or that.
아들이나 딸이 있을겁니다.	I think he has a son or a daughter.

The connective -이나 may be placed after a case postposition (except the subject or the object).

기차로나 비행기로	by train or by plane
학교에서나 집에서	in school or at home

Sometimes, the connective -이나 may be placed after both nouns for emphasis.

너나 나나 가야 해.	You or I must go. (LOW)

6. A Weak Commitment: X or Something

A nominal with the postposition -이나 may *not* be followed by another nominal. In such cases, it implies a weak commitment on the part of the speaker in selecting the particular nominal, similar to the English expression, "X or something (like it)."

커피나 합시다	Let's have coffee (or something).
대구나 갈까요?	Shall we go to Taegu (or somewhere)?

7. Double Subject Sentences

Unlike English, Korean allows two subjects with one verb in a sentence.

임 선생은 자동차가 있어요.	Mr. Yim has a car.
저는 냉면이 좋아요.	I like naengmyŏn.
영옥 씨, 배가 고파요?	Are you hungry, Yŏng'ok?

These sentences represent one major type of sentences, not isolated exceptions to the general rules in Korean. The structure (SUBJECT + SUBJECT + VERB) is one of the basic sentence types where the first subject is followed by a predicate, which in turn consists of a subject and a predicate. In other words, a Korean predicate can be a small clause consisting of (SUBJECT+PREDICATE) again.

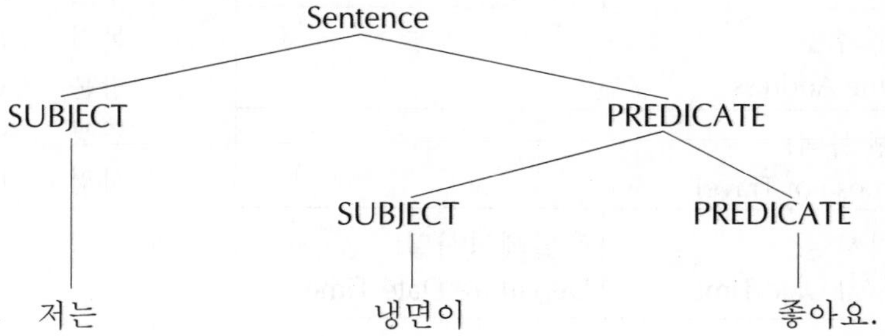

NOTE : The double subject sentences are generally determined by the meanings and the types of verbs (mostly *process* or *stative verb* types, but *not action verb* type). This kind of information for a new verb will be presented with the notation (A-가 B-가 + Verb) in the Vocabulary Summary section whenever a verb or a verb phrase calls for it.

읽기 · 쓰기 (READING & WRITING)

1. Kimpo Airport: 김포공항

Kimpo Airport is the gateway to Seoul. It is located in the western outskirt (about 30 kilo meters) of Seoul. As you come out from the arrival area, you will see many signs, most of which are both in English and Korean. For the convenience of Chinese and Japanese, signs are also in Chinese characters (한자). The following are some of the signs that you will encounter first.

입국 심사 (入國審査) Passport Control
- 입국 = entering the country
- 심사 = examination, inquiry

세관 신고 (稅關申告) Customs Declaration
- 세관 = customs
- 신고 = reporting

외국인 (外國人) Alien, Foreigner
- 외국 = foreign country

내국인 (內國人) Korean Nationals
- 내국/국내 = domestic

연습 13. Pretend that you have just arrived at Kimpo. You now have an entry card to fill out similar to the one below. Complete the form as much as possible in Korean.

입국 신고 (Entry Record Card)	
성명: Full Name	성별:남☐ 녀☐ Sex: Male/Female
국적: Nationality	여권번호: Passport Number
생년월일: Date of Birth	직업: Occupation
본국 주소: Home Address	
여행 목적: Purpose of Travel	
도착시일: Arrival Date/Time	출발예정시일: Departure Date/Time

Reading Vocabulary

성명	full name
여권	passport
번호	number
직업	occupation
주소	address
목적	purpose
방문	visit
관광	sightseeing
사업	business

2. Airline Advertisement

The clipping below is an airliner's advertisement printed in a Korean language newspaper for Korean-American clients in the U.S.A.

서울 일류 호텔 2박 + 왕복 비행기

두 분이 함께 다녀오실 수 있는 티켓을 한장 가격에 드립니다.

12월 31일까지 펼치는 특별 보너스—
퍼스트/비지니스 클래스 항공권을 구입하시는 분께는
동반자 1인에게 같은 클래스의 항공권을 무료로 드립니다.

Reading Vocabulary

일류	first-class
2박	two nights stay
왕복	round-trip
함께	together
가격	fare, price
다녀오다	to have a trip (to go and come back)

연습 14. Scan the advertisement given above and answer the questions.

a. What city is the destination?
b. How many nights can you stay in a hotel?
c. What kinds of discount or benefit are included in the package deal?
d. Until when is this package deal valid?
e. Find at least three English loan words in the advertisement.

연습 15. For each word, find a paraphrase from the list on the right, that may define the word. Identify it by the number. For example, the number for a. 공항 is 7.

a. 공항	(7)	1. 사는 곳
b. 여객	( )	2. 내일 다음 날
c. 방문	( )	3. 여행하는 사람들
d. 가격	( )	4. 갔다 오는 것
e. 왕복	( )	5. 하는 일
f. 주소	( )	6. 여기 저기 구경 다니는 것
g. 직업	( )	7. 비행기가 떠나고 내리고 하는 곳
h. 모레	( )	8. 누구하고 같이
i. 함께	( )	9. 누구를 찾아가는 것
j. 관광	( )	10. 값

연습 16. For each phrase below, write a phrase with an opposite (반대) meaning (뜻).

a. 도착 시간: ____________	e. 파는 사람: ____________
b. 낮에: ____________	f. 내려가면: ____________
c. 끝에: ____________	g. 위층으로: ____________
d. 추운 날씨: ____________	h. 달라요: ____________

연습 17. Write a postcard to your family. Imagine that you have been visiting Korea and enjoying the sights for a week now. You may include the time and date of arrival, where you are staying, the places you have seen, what you have been doing and whom you have seen, etc.

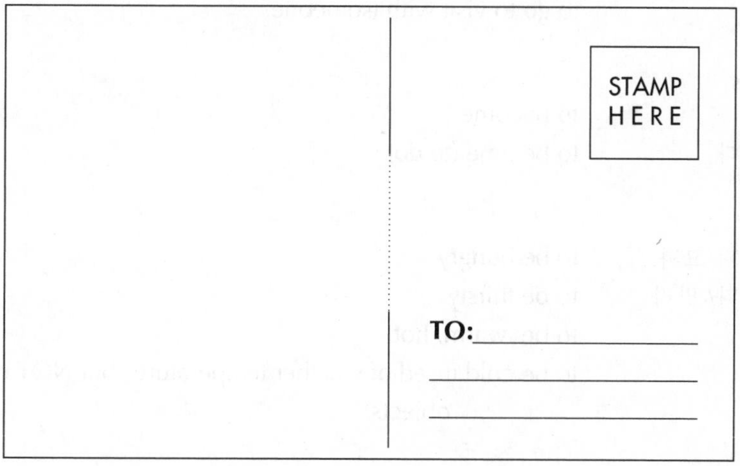

NOTE: For this activity, students may form pairs or small groups to work together.

단어 정리 (VOCABULARY SUMMARY)

Nominals

그저께	the day before yesterday	관광	sightseeing
그애	that child (애 is the short for 아이)	목적	purpose
		-박	staying overnight
날씨	weather	방문	visit
낮	daytime	번호	number (serial)
목	throat	사업	business, enterprise
배	stomach	여권	passport
봄	spring (season)	왕복	round trip
사이다	cider (soft drink)	일류	first-class
영화	movie (cinema)	주소	address
주문	order (buyer's)	직업	occupation
첫사랑	first love	하루	a day
가격	price (=값)		

Action Verbs

마중 나오다	to come out to meet
안부 전하다	to give regards to (someone)
자다	to sleep (HONORIFIC: 주무시다)
전송하다	to send off (someone)
주문을 받다	to take an order (from a buyer)
찾아가다	to go to visit with (someone)

Process Verbs

되다/돼	to become
시간이 되다	to be time (to do)

Stative Verbs

배가 고프다/고파	to be hungry
목이 마르다/ 말라	to be thirsty
덥다/더워	to be warm, hot
춥다/추워	to be cold (used of weather/temperature, but NOT of tangible objects)

Adverbs

또	again	이제/인제	now
아주	very, extremely	빨리	quickly
요새	recently, nowadays	함께	together (=같이)

Interjections

아이구!	Oh my!

Verb Endings

-으면	if, when	-자	let's (Blunt)

Postpositions

-이나	or

Counters

-번	a counter fo occurrences

Idioms

웬 일이세요?	What brought you here? What's going on?

Scripts for Exercises

연습 8.
a. 모레 선생님 찾아가 뵙겠어요.
b. 형님한테 안부 전해 주세요.
c. 여기 너무 더워요. 창문 좀 여세요.
d. 여름이 되면 아주 더울 겁니다.
e. 전에 박 선생을 두 번 찾아 갔었어요.

연습 10.
a. 그 영화 몇 번 봤어요?
b. 처음 사랑하는 것이 첫사랑입니다.
c. 인제 춥지 않아요. 인제 봄이 아니예요?
d. 난 어제 밤에 열두 시에 잤어요.
e. 저는 같은 책을 세 번 읽었어요.

연습문제 해답 (ANSWERS TO EXERCISES)

연습 1.
a. 커피나 사이다
b. 삼일이나 사일
c. 연필이나 볼펜
d. 자동차나 비행기
e. 형이나 누나
f. 컴퓨터나 전화

연습 2.
a. 극장에나 가겠어요.
b. 커피나 한 잔 시킵시다.
c. 골프나 칠까요?
d. 신문이나 읽지요.

연습 4.
a. 비싸지 않아요.
b. 받지 않았습니다.
c. 가지 않습니다.
d. 놀지 않았어요.

연습 5.
a. 가지 않으세요?
b. 시키지 않으셨어요?
c. 모자라지 않았어요.
d. 하지 않겠어요?

연습 6.
a. 없으면, 주세요.
b. 놀면 /노시면
c. 마르면, 주스나
d. 팔면, 역에
e. 떠나면, 세 시까지

연습 8.	a. teacher, the day after tomorrow		d. summer, hot	
	b. your brother		e. Mr. Pak, twice	
	c. hot, open the window			
연습 9.	a. 벌써 갈 시간이 됐어요?		d. 어제 선생님 찾아가 뵈었어요.	
	b. 오빠한테 안부 전해 주세요.		e. 또 봅시다.	
	c. 언제 한번 또 놀러 오세요.			
연습 10.	a. times, the movie		d. went to bed, twelve	
	b. to love, the first love		e. the same book, three times	
	c. cold, spring			
연습 14.	a. Seoul		c. 2 persons for the price of one	
	b. two nights		d. 31 December	
	e. hotel, ticket, bonus, first/business class, class			
연습 15.	a. (7), b. (3), c. (9), d. (10), e. (4), f. (1), g. (5), h. (2), i. (8), j. (6)			
연습 16.	a. 출발 시간	c. 시작에	e. 사는 사람	g. 아래층으로
	b. 밤에	d. 더운 날씨	f. 올라가면	h. 같아요.

Communicative Frames in English

Frame 1. At the Airport

Han : Isn't this Mr. Mun? How are you?
Mun : Well! Miss Yong'ok, what brought you here?
Han : Haven't you seen you long! Are you going somewhere?
Mun : No. I came out here to meet someone. A friend of mine is coming from America. What about you, Miss Yong'ok?
Han : My younger brother is going on a trip to Japan. I am out here to send him off.
Mun : I see... Miss Yong'ok, if you have time, let's have a cup of coffee.
Han : O.K. Fine.

Frame 2. At the Restaurant

Mun : Would you like to have coffee?
Han : No, I don't drink coffee in the afternoon.
Mun : Why not?
Han : If I drink coffee in the afternoon, I can't sleep at night. I'll have some cider drink or juice. I'm a little thirsty.
Mun : Don't you want to have a meal? I'm a little hungry.
Han : A meal is too early for me. If you are hungry, why don't you order a meal? You can order a juice for me.
Mun : Really? Then, I'll have coffee too.
Young lady! Take an order here. please.

Frame 3. Talking about the Weather

Mun : A nice day today, isn't it?
Han : Yeah, it's spring now. It isn't cold even in the morning.
Mun : Right. It's warm in the daytime.
Han : Yes... Well, I'll have to get up and go.
Mun : Is it time to go already?
Han : Yes. Now, good-bye and take care.
Please give my regards to your wife, and...

Han	:	Yes. I'll go for a visit with you. Good-bye.
Mun	:	So long. See you again.

Frame 4. Going to the Movies

Sunhi	:	Let's go to the theater tonight with me.
Yong'ok	:	O.K. Where are they showing good movies?
Sunhi	:	Do you have a newspaper? Let's see the newspaper.
Yong'ok	:	Here it is... Did you see "First Love"? It's shown at the Chung-ang Theater.
Sunhi	:	Is it good?
Yong'ok	:	Very good. Let's see that.
Sunhi	:	How do you know?
Yong'ok	:	I saw it the day before yesterday.
Sunhi	:	Well, do you see the same movie twice?
Yong'ok	:	Why not? When it's good, I'll see it again. Let's hurry.

제 14 과

미국에서 오는 손님

대화 1 (FRAME 1)

손님을 마중 나간다

문　: 카슨 선생. 어서 오세요. 반갑습니다.
카슨 : 아이구. 문 선생 이렇게 나와 주셔서
　　　감사합니다. 그동안 안녕하셨어요?
문　: 네, 저희들 잘 지냅니다. 짐 많습니까?
카슨 : 아뇨. 이것이 다입니다.
문　: 이건 제가 들지요. 자, 가십시다.
카슨 : 고맙습니다.
문　: 고단하시죠?
카슨 : 네, 좀 그렇네요. 잠을 잘 못자서.
문　: 그렇죠. 비행기 안에서는 잠이 잘 안 오죠.
　　　자, 저기가 택시 타는 데입니다.
　　　저기 가서 서십시다.

단어 공부 (*VOCABULARY STUDY*)

- 반갑다/반가워 — to be glad (to see someone or hear good news)
- 이렇게 — like this, so (adverb derived from 이렇다)

ADVERBS Derived from Stative Verbs of Demonstration

•이렇게	like this/so	← 이렇다
•그렇게	like that/so (pointing near the addressee)	← 그렇다
•저렇게	like that/so (pointing something away)	← 저렇다

•나와 주셔서 — for having come out (-어서=because) (See Grammar.)
•그동안 — during the time, all the while
When 그동안 is used with the greeting expression(안녕하셨어요?) it is best translated as "since I saw you last."
•짐 — luggage, load
•이것이 다입니다. — This is all. (The contracted form is 답니다.)
•들다/드는/들어 — to lift up, hold something in hand
•자 — well (interjection used in urging)
•고단하다 — to be tired
•잠을 자다 — to sleep (= 자다) (잠 is a nominal form of 자다 "to sleep.")
•잠이 오다 — to become sleepy
•가서 — go and (-어서=and) (See Grammar.)

❖ -어서: "BECAUSE, FOR..."

CAUSE ⋯-어서	EFFECT
나와 주셔서 For coming out for me,	감사합니다. I thank you.
더워서 Because it was hot,	창문을 열었습니다. I opened the window.
늦어서 For being late,	미안합니다. I am sorry.

CAUTION!

•No tense marker is used with -어서, even if it expresses a past event.

•-어서 is NOT used if the main clause is a request or a suggestion.

연습 1. Listen to each voicing, and identify the cause for the main clause by the number.

a. I have to go
b. I couldn't buy
c. I went to that eatery
d. I didn't buy that
e. I'm tired

(1) because I didn't have money.
(2) because I was hungry.
(3) because my friend is waiting.
(4) because it's too expensive.
(5) because I couldn't sleep well.

연습 2. Ask your partner the following questions. Your partner will give an answer by selecting one of the possible reasons on the right, or make up one.

	Possible Reasons
a. 왜 늦었어요?	•돈이 없어서
	•어제 잠을 못자서
b. 그 옷 왜 사지 않았어요?	•길에 차가 많아서
	•일을 너무 해서
c. 왜 공항에 갔습니까?	•미국에서 친구가 와서
	•너무 비싸서
d. 왜 고단해요?	•약속이 있어서
e. 왜 벌써 가십니까?	•날씨가 추워서

연습 3. Each of the following sentences contains a cause and an effect. Combine the sentences using the connective -어서.

a. 배가 고파요. 만두 먹겠어요.
b. 너무 비쌉니다. 사지 않겠어요.
c. 늦었습니다. 미안합니다.
d. 자동차가 없었어요. 버스로 갔어요.
e. 약속이 있어요. 가야해요.
f. 잠을 못잤어요. 좀 고단합니다.

연습 4. Say appropriate Korean equivalents to the following English sentences..

a. How have you been?
b. I'm really glad (to see you).
c. Is this all?
d. Let's go there, and stand.
e. I don't get sleepy at night.
f. Can you hold the bag for me?

대화 2 (FRAME 2)

택시로 호텔에 간다

문 :	(운전기사한테) 동아 호텔요.
기사 :	네, 알았습니다. 이거 손님의 짐이지요?
카슨 :	네, 이것하고 저거 둘입니다. 다 실을 수 있죠?
기사 :	그럼요. 트렁크에 다 들어갑니다. 자, 타시죠.
카슨 :	(문 씨에게) 호텔에 예약해주셨지요?
문 :	그럼요. 동아 호텔에 예약했습니다. 거기가 시내에 가까워서 편리해요.
카슨 :	네. 도와주셔서 감사합니다.
문 :	그런 말씀하지 마세요.

•기사한테	to the driver (-한테=to)
•동아 호텔	Tong'a Hotel (동아= East Asia)
•-의	...'s (possessive postpostion) (See Grammar.)
•싣다/실어	to load

NOTE: ㄷ changes to ㄹ when the stem is followed by a vowel.

•트렁크	trunk (of a car)
•예약하다	to make a reservation (예약=reservation)
•시내	downtown area
•가깝다/가까워	to be near, close by (stative verb) (antonym : 멀다/멀어 "to be far, distant")
•편리하다	to be convenient
•돕다/도와	to assist, help

This verb is commonly used in the compound form, 도와 주다/도와드리다.

•그런	such (prenominal form of 그렇다 "to be so")
•-지 마세요	Please don't... (See Grammar.)

연습 5. Pick one of the places listed below, and ask whether the place is near or far from your partner's home.

EXAMPLE: 학교가 집에서 가까워요? — Is your school close to your home?
아니오, 집에서 멀어요. — No, it's far from home.

a. 시장	c. 교회	e. 시내	g. 우체국
b. 절	d. 극장	f. 은행	h. 역

❖ - 지 마세요/-지 맙시다: "PLEASE DON'T.../LET'S NOT..."

STEM + 지 | 말다

가지 마십시오	Ⓗ	
가지 마세요.	Ⓜ	Please don't go.
가지 말아/마.	Ⓛ	
가지 마십시다.	Ⓗ	
가지 맙시다.	Ⓜ	Let's not go.
가지 말자.	Ⓛ	

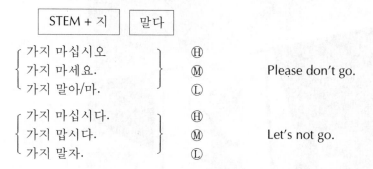

연습 6. Respond to the following questions by negative requests or suggestions. Keep the same level of speech as in the questions.

EXAMPLE : 기다릴까요? — Shall I wait?
아니오. 기다리지 마세요. — No, please don't wait.

a. 전화할까요?	Ⓜ	d. 내가 짐을 들까요?	Ⓜ
b. 호텔 예약할까요?	Ⓜ	e. 지금 떠날까?	Ⓛ
c. 택시 탈까?	Ⓛ	f. 좀 기다릴까?	Ⓛ

❖ -고/-어서: "AND"

Two actions, one followed by another, are connected either with -고 or -어서, depending on the type of the verb.

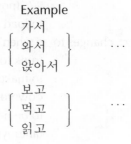

FIRST ACTION		Example
a. Verbs of locomotion or posture	-어서	가서 / 와서 / 앉아서 …
b. Others	-고	보고 / 먹고 / 읽고 …

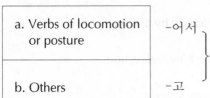

연습 7. Combine each pair of sentences, using -고 or -어서.

a. 저기 갑시다. 앉으십시다.
b. 준비해요. 나오겠어요.
c. 집에 옵니다. 밥 먹어요.
d. 방에 들어오세요. 기다리세요.
e. 점심 먹어요. 곧 떠나요.
f. 호텔 예약했어요. 돌아왔어요.

연습 8. Say the following sentences in Korean

a. My elder brother helped me.
b. Is this your luggage?
c. Can you load up everything?
d. Can you hold the big one?
e. It's safe and convenient.
f. Please don't mention it.

대화 3 (FRAME 3)

카슨의 가족 이야기

문	왜 부인하고 함께 오지 않으셨어요?
카슨	집사람은 여름 학기에 가르칩니다. 그 사람 고등학교에서 영어를 가르치지 않습니까? 그래서 이번에는 저 혼자 나왔죠.
문	아, 그러세요? 아드님은 대학 졸업하셨나요?
카슨	내년에 졸업합니다.
문	따님은요?
카슨	학교 졸업하고 작년에 결혼했어요.
문	벌써 그렇게 됐습니까? 세월도 빠르지요.

단어 공부 (*VOCABULARY STUDY*)

•함께	together (=같이)
•집사람	wife (used by her husband)
•가르치다	to teach
•고등학교	high school (고=high, 등=class)
•이번	this time
•혼자(서)	by oneself, alone
•아드님	son (honorific form of 아들)
•졸업하다	to graduate (from)
•내년	next year (=다음 해) (내=coming, 년=year)
•따님	daughter (honorific form of 딸)
•작년	last year
•결혼하다	to marry
•벌써	already

- 그렇게 됐습니까? Is that so?
- 세월 time; years and months (the passage of time)
- 빠르다/빨라 to be rapid, fast (stative verb)

❖ -지 않아요? EMPHATIC STATEMENT

A negative question (with the long negative form) is often used to make an emphatic and affirmative statement.

그 사람 영어 가르치지 않습니까?	She teaches English, you know.
호텔이 가깝지 않아요?	The hotel is close by, you see.
제 아들은 작년에 결혼하지 않았어요?	My son got married last year, you know.

연습 9. Restate the following sentences, using the negative question form.

a. 아드님이 영어 잘 하세요.
b. 제 동생이 내년에 졸업합니다.
c. 집사람은 상점에서 일해요.
d. 딸이 고등학교에 들어갔어요.
e. 오늘 날씨가 좋습니다.
f. 아들은 아직 혼자 있어요.

연습 10. Mr. Pak has one son and two daughters. Listen to each paragraph, and write answers to the questions.

Paragraph 1.
a. When did his son graduate from college? ______________
b. Where is he working now? ______________
c. When will he get married? ______________

Paragraph 2.
a. When did she get married? ______________
b. When did she graduate from college? ______________
c. What does her husband do? ______________

Paragraph 3.
a. What does his second daughter do? ______________
b. What will she do next year? ______________
c. Will she get married soon? ______________

대화 4 (FRAME 4)

시험 이야기

학수: 시험 잘 쳤니?
영옥: 난 두 문제 틀렸어. 넌?
학수: 잘 모르겠어. 3번 문제 답이 뭐니?
영옥: 이십사(24) 아니니?
학수: 그래? 그럼 나도 맞았다.
영옥: 아마 그거 맞을거야.
학수: 시험이 생각보다 쉬웠지?
영옥: 그래. 별로 어렵지 않았어.

단어 공부 (*VOCABULARY STUDY*)

- 시험 — test, examination; 시험을 치다 "to take a test"
- 문제 — question, problem
- 틀리다 — to get/turn wrong (process verb)

CAUTION! The completion marker -었 is used to form a stative expression: e.g., 이것은 틀렸다. "This one is wrong."

- 답 — answer
- 맞다 — to get right; to fit (process verb)

CAUTION! Like its antonym 틀리다, the completion marker must be used to make a stative expression: e.g., 이것은 맞았다. "This is right."

- 생각 — thought, idea; 생각하다 "to think"
- 생각보다 — than I thought
- 쉽다/쉬워 — to be easy
- 어렵다/어려워 — to be difficult

연습 11. Listen to the model voicing. As you listen identify the correct translation by choosing the number on your right.

a. ________	d. ________	(1) It was too difficult.	(4) I'm sure I was right.
b. ________	e. ________	(2) I think so.	(5) That's a good idea.
c. ________	f. ________	(3) Your answer was wrong.	(6) You are probably correct.

연습 12. Say the following sentences in Korean.

a. You are right.
b. Do we have to take the test again?
c. Do you think so?
d. It was easier than I thought.
e. That's a good idea.
f. How many problems were there?

문법 (GRAMMAR)

1. Expressing Cause and Effect: A-**어서** B

Two clauses expressing cause and effect are linked by the connective -어서. There are two important RESTRICTIONS for this connective.

<CAUSE> + 어서	<EFFECT>
No tense marker (었) is used with -어서 even if it expresses a past event.	No request or suggestion is used.

이렇게 나와 주셔서 For coming out like this,	감사합니다. I am grateful.
학교가 가까워서 The school is very close, and so	걸어갑니다. he walks to it.
택시가 많아서 Because there are many taxis,	오래 걸리지 않아요. it doesn't take long.
잠을 잘 못자서 Since I couldn't sleep well,	좀 고단합니다. I'm a little tired.

2. Two Actions in Sequence: -어서 and -고

The sequence of two (or more) actions are connected either by -어서 or by -고, depending upon the type of the first verb in such compounds.

VERB TYPE	
Verbs of locomotion (go, come, etc.) Verbs of posture (sit, stand, lie, etc.)	STEM + 어서...
All other verbs	STEM + 고...

가서 보십시다.	Let's go and see it.
보고 가십시다.	Let's see it and (then) go.
우리는 앉아서 먹었어요.	We sat down and ate.
우리는 먹고 앉았어요.	We ate and (then) sat down.
그 사람이 와서 일했어요.	She came and worked.
그 사람이 일하고 왔어요.	She worked and came here.

3. Negative Requests and Suggestions: -지 말다

Requests and suggestions for not to do something are made by the use of the verb 말다 in the long negative form. The verb 말다 means "stop doing something," but is not commonly used as an independent verb.

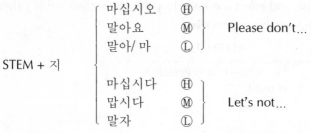

STEM + 지	마십시오	Ⓗ	Please don't...
	말아요	Ⓜ	
	말아/ 마	Ⓛ	
	마십시다	Ⓗ	Let's not...
	맙시다	Ⓜ	
	말자	Ⓛ	

나가지 마십시오.	Please don't go out.
더 기다리지 맙시다.	Let's not wait any more.
날짜를 잊지 마세요.	Please don't forget the date.
여기 있지 마십시다.	Let's not stay here.

4. Negative Questions for Emphatic Affirmation

Negative questions (generally with the long form with -지 ⋯) are often used in making emphatic and affirmative expressions in Korean. It is commonly used to remind or inform one of something. In this case, since the *negative* is used only as a rhetorical device, it does not carry the typical question intonation (with a sharp rise: ↗). Compare the sentences' final tones below.

•REAL QUESTION : 영어가 어렵지 않아요? ↗ Isn't English difficult?
•RHETORICAL QUESTION: 영어가 어렵지 않아요? ↘ English is difficult, *you see.*

홍 선생이 늘 도와 주시지 않아요?	Mr. Hong alway helps me, *you know.*
제가 마중 나가지 않았습니까?	I went out to meet her, *you see.*
어제 시험 치지 않았어?	We took a test yesterday, *you know.*
나한테 너무 어렵지 않아?	It's too difficult for me, *you know.*

NOTE: This rheteorical question is particularly common among the younger generation today, and the ending -지 않아? is often shortened to -잖아? : e.g., 좋잖아? [choch'ana] "It's good, isn't it?"

***5.* The L Verbs**

The L verbs, whose stems end with the consonant ㄹ, are unique among irregular verbs in the following points:

•All verbs whose stems end with ㄹ conjugate in the same pattern WITHOUT EXCEPTION. (This is not true of other irregular verbs.)

알다	to know	들다	to hold
열다	to open	살다	to live
팔다	to sell	멀다	to be far
돌다	to turn	길다	to be long

•For all L verbs, the vowel 으 of any ending must be removed in applying the following rules for dropping or retaining the stem-final ㄹ:

(1) If the ending begins with ㄴ, ㅂ, or ㅅ ⟶	drop ㄹ.
(2) Otherwise ⟶	retain ㄹ.

Example: 알다

•아는 •아세요?
•아니? •압시다.
•압니까? •아십니까?

•알고 •알면
•알지요. •알러
•알겠지요. •알아요.
•알았습니다.

EXCEPTION: 알 +을 ⟶ 알

NOTE: Other irregular verbs will be summarized later.

6. A Nominal Modifying Another Nominal

A nominal may be freely used as a modifier of another nominal in Korean. You have seen many such examples:

• 한국말	Korean language ← (Korea language)
• 대학교 학생	university student
• 차표	train ticket
• 김 선생님 딸	Mr. Kim's daughter ← (Mr. Kim daughter)
• 집사람	my wife ← (house person)

Pronouns (with some exceptions noted below) are also used as a modifier.

• 우리 집	our house ← (we house)
• 누구 것	whose thing ← (who thing)
• 어느 나라 사람	what nationality ← (which country person)

CAUTION! The notable excepetions are 1st and 2nd person possessive forms shown below.

• 제 아저씨	(BUT NOT 저 아저씨)	my uncle
• 내 책	(BUT NOT 나 책)	my book
• 네 가방	(BUT NOT 너 가방)	your bag

These possessive pronouns are originally contracted forms of pronouns with the possessive postposition -의.

• 저의 → 제
• 나의 → 내
• 너의 → 네

The pronunciation of -의 varies from dialect to dialect, but it is commonly pronounced [e] today.

The 2nd person possessive 네 (Low Level) is further changed to 니 in colloquialism.

For ease of reference, we will call it the "possessive" postposition, but it marks a prenominal modifier for another nominal. As you have noted, the use of -의 is not very extensive since any noun may be used as a modifier without -의 anyway.

❖ GUESS WHAT IT MEANS: 생각 없어요.

It's a common colloquial expression. Guess what it means, using the context of the conversation, and check A, B, C, or D.

윤식 : 점심하러 갑시다.
순자 : 저 지금 생각없어요.

A: I have no idea.
B: I don't feel like having it.
C: I never thought of it.
D: I forgot it.

The answer is found in the Answers to Exercises section.

읽기 · 쓰기 (READING & WRITING)

1. Travel Agency: 여행사

There are sizable Korean communities (한인 사회) in Hawaii, Los Angeles and New York. In Korean newspapers for such communities you often see advertisements (광고) of travel agencies such as the one below, soliciting Korean residents with special discount fares for trips back to their mother country (고국/모국).

대성 여행사

아름다운 와이키키 해변에서
2박 3일 관광 하시고
날로 발전하는 수도 서울을 직접 보시고
1년안에 언제라도 돌아오실 수 있는
고국 방문과 하와이 관광 여행을
파격적 가격으로
두 분께서 함께 다녀 오시지 않겠습니까?

■ 각국 대사관 각종 민원업무
■ 여행지 호텔 예약
■ 경제적이며 실속있는 관광여행
지금 곧 전화주십시오.

자세히 안내해 드리겠습니다.

445-9990

• Reading Vocabulary

아름다운	beautiful <아름답다	언제라도	anytime
해변	beach (=바닷가)	파격적	unprecedented, exceptional
날로	daily, every day (=매일)	-께서	honorific subject postposition (=-이/가)
발전 하는	developing		
직접	directly, first hand (Antonym: 간접)	안내하다	to guide, escort

연습 13. Answer the following questions based on the above advertisement.

a. Write the gist of the package tour deal offered.

____

____

b. How many days and how many nights do clients stay in Hawaii?

____

c. According to this deal, the clients must use the return tickets within a certain period. How long is that period?

____

d. Find the meanings of two words, using your dictionary.
경제적: ______________ 자세히: ______________

e. 언제라도 means "anytime" (used in affirmative sentences). What do the following phrases mean?
어디라도________, 무엇이라도________, 누구라도 ________

2. More on Loan Words

Not only the sounds but also the meanings of loan words are often changed from those of the source words. The meanings of loan words are generally narrow, specific, and sometimes unexpectedly changed. Their shapes are often shortened or truncated for ease. This is because all loan words are naturalized to different degrees in the host language. In the exercises below, you will see a few examples of such loan words.

연습 14. Each of the sentences below contain English loan words. Orally translate them into English.

a. 아침에 수퍼마켓에 갔다 왔다.
b. 백화점에 가서 텔레비전을 한대 샀다.
c. 오후에 커피를 마시면 밤에 잠이 안 온다.
d. 아파트에 스팀이 들어와서 춥지 않다.
e. 금년 안에 사면 티켓을 싸게 살 수 있다.
f. 다섯 시 뉴스 들었어요?

연습 15. The last consonant *t* of English loan words, such as *market, ticket, jacket, apart* (ment), etc. are represented two different ways in the examples above. Show the two different ways of representing *t* in Hangŭl.

연습 16. Complete the following paragraphs by filling in the blank spaces with words listed on the right. Then answer the questions based on each paragraph.

a. 요즈음 여행사들이 관광여행 광고를 많이 한다. 미국에 사는 한인들이 _______을 많이 방문하기 때문이다. 그래서 고국으로 가는 사람들은 가는 길에 싼 ______으로 하와이도 구경할 수 있고 고국에 가서 날로 _____하는 서울도 직접 보고 일년_____에 언제 _____ 돌아올 수가 있다.

가격
고국
라도
발전
내

Question 1. Who are these advertisements aimed at?
Question 2. What are passengers able to do on their way?
Question 3. How long are the return tickets valid?

b. 아버님께서 어제 신문에서 여행사 ______를 보시고 제주도행 비행기표를 두 장 사셨다. 아버님께서는 오래간만에 어머님과 함께 _______ 여행을 하실 생각이다. 제주도에서는 누님이 사셔서 누님 집에서 _______ 하게 계실 수 있고 또 누님이 여기 저기 ______ 해 드릴 것이다.

관광
광고
안내
편안

Question 1. What did his father buy?
Question 2. What are his parents′ plans?
Question 3. Where will they stay when they get there?
Question 4. Who will be their travel guide in Cheju-do?

연습 17. For each of the phrases listed below, write a phrase with an opposite meaning.

a. 함께 ⟷ _________
b. 맞다 ⟷ _________
c. 시작 ⟷ _________
d. 배우다 ⟷ _________
e. 쉽다 ⟷ _________
f. 다르다 ⟷ _________
g. 멀다 ⟷ _________
h. 도착 ⟷ _________

단어 정리 (VOCABULARY SUMMARY)

Nominals

고등학교	high school	잠	sleep (noun)
그동안	during that time	집사람	wife (Humble form)
답	answer	아드님	son (Honorific form)
따님	daughter (honorific form)	고국	mother country
문제	problem, question	광고	advertisement
상가	shopping district	날로	daily
생각	thought, idea	사회	society, community
세월	time, years	여행사	travel agency
시험	test, examination	해변	beach (=바닷가)
운전기사	driver	한인	Korean national (=한국인)
이번	this time		

Action Verbs

가르치다	to teach	예약하다	to make a reservation
결혼하다	to marry	잠(을) 자다	to sleep (=자다)
돕다/도와	to help, assist	치다 (시험을)	to take (a test)
들다/드는/들어	to hold, carry	발전하다	to develop
싣다/실어	to load	안내하다	to guide, escort

Stative Verbs

가깝다/가까워	to be close	쉽다/쉬워	to be easy
고단하다	to be tired	어렵다/어려워	to be difficult
멀다/멀어	to be far	편리하다	to be convenient
반갑다/반가워	to be glad	아름답다/아름다워	to be beautiful
빠르다/빨라	to be fast	획기적이다	to be unprecedented

Process Verbs

맞다	to be correct	틀리다	to be wrong
잠이 오다	to be(come) sleepy		

Adverbs

이렇게	so, like this	언제라도	anytime
함께	together (=같이)	직접	directly
혼자(서)	alone		

Interjections

자	well (expression of urging)

Postpositions

-의	…'s (possessive)	-께서	honorific subject marker

Scripts for Exercises

Exercise 10.
Para. 1. 아들은 금년에 대학을 졸업하고 은행에서 일합니다. 아직 결혼 안했어요. 내년 삼월에 결혼할 겁니다.
Para. 2. 큰 딸은 작년에 이화여대 졸업하고 바로 결혼했어요. 남편은 지금 고등학교에서 중국어 가르칩니다.
Para. 3. 작은 딸은 고등학교 다닙니다. 내년에 졸업해요. 아직 결혼 생각 없어요.

Exercise 11.
a. 네 답은 틀렸어.
b. 그거 좋은 생각이다.
c. 나 맞았을꺼야.
d. 그거 너무 어려웠어.
e. 너 맞았을 거다
f. 그렇게 생각해.

연습문제 해답 (ANSWERS TO EXERCISES)

Exercise 1.
a. (3) 친구가 기다려서 가야돼요.
b. (1) 돈이 없어서 사지 못했어요.
c. (2) 배가 고파서 식당에 갔어요.
d. (4) 너무 비싸서 안 샀습니다.
e. (5) 잠을 못자서 고단해요.

Exercise 3.
a. 배가 고파서 만두 먹겠어요.
b. 너무 비싸서 사지 않겠어요.
c. 늦어서 미안합니다.
d. 자동차가 없어서 버스로 갔어요.
e. 약속이 있어서 가야해요.
f. 잠을 못자서 좀 고단합니다.

Exercise 4.
a. 안녕하셨어요?
b. 반갑습니다.
c. 이것이 답니까?
d. 저기 가서 서십시다.
e. 밤에 잠이 안 와요.
f. 가방 들어 주실 수 있어요?

Exercise 6.
a. 전화하지 마세요.
b. 호텔 예약하지 마세요.
c. 택시 타지 말아.
d. 짐 들지 말아요.
e. 지금 떠나지 마.
f. 기다리지 말아.

Exercise 7.
a. 저기 가서 앉으십시다.
b. 준비하고 나오겠어요.
c. 집에 와서 밥 먹어요.
d. 방에 들어와서 기다리세요.
e. 점심 먹고 곧 떠나요.
f. 호텔 예약하고 돌아왔어요.

Exercise 8.
a. 형이 도와 주었어요.
b. 이거 선생님 짐입니까?
c. 다 실을 수 있어요?
d. 큰 거 들 수 있어요?
e. 그것이 안전하고 편리해요.
f. 그런 말씀하지 마세요.

Exercise 9.
a. 아드님이 영어 잘 하시지 않아요?
b. 제 동생이 내년에 졸업하지 않아요?
c. 집사람은 상점에서 일하지 않습니까?
d. 딸이 고등학교 들어가지 않았어요?

e. 오늘 날씨가 좋지 않습니까?
f. 아들이 아직 혼자 있지 않습니까?

연습 10. Para. 1. 아들은 금년에 대학 졸업하고 은행에서 일합니다. 아직 결혼 안 했어요. 내년 삼월에 결혼할 겁니다.
a. this year b. bank c. next year

Para. 2. 큰 딸은 작년에 이화여자대학교 졸업하고 바로 결혼했어요. 남편은 지금 고등학교에서 중국어를 가르칩니다.
a. last year b. last year c. next year

Para. 3. 작은 딸은 고등학교 다닙니다. 내년에 졸업해요. 아직 결혼 생각 없어요.
a. goes to high school b. graduate c. no

연습 11.
a. (3) 네 답은 틀렸어.
b. (5) 그거 좋은 생각이다.
c. (4) 나 맞았을 거야.
d. (1) 그거 너무 어려웠어.
e. (6) 너 맞았을 거다.
f. (2) 그렇게 생각해.

연습 12.
a. 맞았어.
b. 시험 또 쳐야 해?
c. 그렇게 생각해?
d. 생각보다 쉬웠어.
e. 그거 좋은 생각이야.
f. 몇 문제였어?

ANSWER TO "GUESS WHAT IT MEANS": B

연습 13.
a. Taesong travel agency offers a special package tour to Seoul for Korean-Americans. Clients will visit Hawaii on the way. A special discount for couples.
b. 2 nights and 3 days
c. one year
d. economical, in detail
e. anywhere, anything, anybody

연습 14.
a. supermaket
b. television
c. coffee
d. apartment, steam heater
e. ticket
f. news

연습 15. ㅅ as in a 마켓, and 트 as in 아파트

연습 16.
a. 고국을 - 가격으로 - 발전하는 - 내에 - 언제라도
1. Korean-Americans 2: visit Hawaii 3. one year

b. 광고를 - 관광여행 - 편안하게 - 안내해
1. tickets 2. do sightseeing in Chejudo 3. sister's house 4. sister

연습 17.
a. 혼자
b. 틀리다
c. 끝
d. 가르치다
e. 어렵다
f. 같다
g. 가깝다
h. 출발

Communicative Frames in English

Frame 1. Greeting a Guest from Abroad

Mun : Mr. Carson, welcome. Glad to see you.
Carson : Oh, Mr. Mun, thank you for coming out to meet me like this. Have you been well since I saw you last?
Mun : Yes, we've been getting along fine. Do you have a lot of luggage?
Carson : No, this is all.
Mun : I'll carry this one. Well, shall we go?
Carson : Thank you.
Mun : Tired, I suppose?
Carson : Yes, a little. Because I couldn't sleep well.
Mun : I know. No one can sleep well in the plane. Well, that's the taxi stand. Let's go and stand there.

Frame 2. Going to the Hotel by Taxi

Mun : (To the driver) Tong'a Hotel, please.
Driver : Yes, sir. This is your luggage, I believe?
Carson : Yes, this one and that over there; there are two. You can load all of them up, I think?
Driver : Sure. I can load them all in the trunk. Please get in.
Carson : (To Mr. Mun) You made a hotel reservation for me, right?
Mun : Of course. I made a reservation at Hotel Tong'a. It's close to the downtown area, so it's convenient.
Carson : I see. Thank you very much for helping me.
Mun : Don't mention it.

Frame 3. Talking about Mr. Carson's Family

Mun : Why didn't you come with your wife?
Carson : My wife teaches during the summer vacation. She teaches English in a high school, you know. So, this time I came by myself.
Mun : Oh, I see. Did your son graduate from college?
Carson : He'll graduate next year.
Mun : What about your daughter?
Carson : She finished school and got married last year.
Mun : Already has it become so? Time flies, doesn't it?

Frame 4. Taking about the Exams

Haksu : Did you do all right with the test?
Yong'ok : Me, I've got two questions wrong. What about you?
Haksu : I don't know. What's the answer to the third question?
Yong'ok : Isn't it 24?
Haksu : Really? Well then, I was right too!
Yong'ok : Probably that's correct.
Haksu : The test was easier than I thought, don't you think?
Yong'ok : Right. It wasn't very difficult.

제 15 과

호텔에 든다

대화 1 (FRAME 1)

호텔 프론트에서

직원 : 어서 오십시오!

카슨 : 나 카슨이라고 합니다.
방 예약했는데, 방 있죠?

직원 : 예, 잠깐만 계세요. 한 분이시죠?

카슨 : 나 혼잡니다.

직원 : 좋은 방 드리죠. 여기에 성함, 주소, 그리고
여권 번호 좀 써 주세요.
며칠 동안 계실 예정이십니까?

카슨 : 한 3주 있을 겁니다.

단어 공부 (*VOCABULARY STUDY*)

- 프론트 — front desk
- 직원 — clerk, employee
- 카슨이라고 합니다. — I'm Carson./My name is Carson. (Literally, "I call myself Carson.")
  (Nominal) -이라고 하다 is a quotation construction.
- 예약했는데 — I made a reservation, and…
  The connective ending -는데 expresses a premise for what follows. (See Grammar.)
- 방 — room
- 주소 — address (주=reside, 소=place)
- 여권 — passport (여=travel, 권=document)

- 번호 number (serial)
- -동안 for the duration of . . .
- -주 week (=주일)
- 계실 예정이십니까? Are you planning to stay?
  -을 예정이다 "to be scheduled to..." (See Grammar.)
- 한 about, approximately (=약).
  This word is always followed by a numerical expression.

연습 1. Connect the following pair of sentences by using -는데. Each pair of sentences consists of a premise statement followed by the main point of information.

a. 시간이 있어요. 커피나 한 잔 하십시다.
b. 극장에서 좋은 영화해요. 함께 갑시다.
c. 나 내일 부산에 가요. 무엇으로 가는 것이 좋아요?
d. 그 사람의 주소 모릅니다. 어떻게 가지요?

대화 2 (FRAME 2)

방을 정한다

카슨 : 온돌방 있어요? 온돌방에 들고 싶은데.

직원 : 온돌방은 빈 것이 없어요. 다 찼는데요.
침대방밖에 없어요.

카슨 : 그래요? 그럼, 침대방에 들어야죠.

직원 : 내일은 온돌방이 하나 비니까, 오늘 하루만 침대방에서 주무세요. 내일 오후에 온돌방으로 바꿔 드리지요.

카슨 : 네, 그럼 그렇게 해주세요.

단어 공부 (*VOCABULARY STUDY*)

- 정하다 to choose, decide on
- 온돌방 ondol room (a traditional Korean-style room with the heated floor)
- 들다/드는/들어 to move in, take up (a room/residence), to lodge;
  A-가 B-에 들다. *A* moves into *B*.
- -고 싶다 to want (to...); like (to...)
  The verb 싶다 "be desirous of ..." is a stative verb. It takes stative endings. (See Grammar.)
- 들고 싶은데 I want to take . . .
  This is a premise clause for the *preceding* sentence. Normally, such a clause must precede the main clause, but in conversation the normal structural order is sometimes reversed.

• 비다 — to become empty (process verb); 빈 방 "a vacant room"

• 차다 — to become full (process verb)

CAUTION! The pair of process verbs, 비다 and 차다 must be used with a completed aspect marker (었 or 은) to express a state of being empty or full.

방이 다 찼어요. — The rooms are all filled/occupied.

이 방은 비었어요. — This room is empty/vacant.

• 다 찼는데요! — They are all full!

The premise marking the connective -는데 is often used as a sentence ending with a slight exclamation. (See Grammar.)

• 침대방 — bedroom (a room with a bed)

• 바꾸다 — to change

CULTURAL ENCOUNTER 온돌 is the heated floor commonly found in a traditional Korean house. Entering a Korean house, people are expected to take off their shoes, and sit on the floor. There are no beds or chairs. Tables and chests are low, and thick mattresses are spread on the floor to sleep at night.

❖ COUNTING DAYS

There are two ways of counting days, one using *native Korean* words and the other *Sino-Korean*. Generally, small numbers are counted in *native Korean*, and large numbers in *Sino-Korean*. Although there is no rigid rule about it, Koreans, particularly older Koreans often use *native Korean* in counting up to "five days," and then shift to *Sino-Korean* in counting beyond.

	Native Korean	Sino-Korean
one day	하 루	일 일
two days	이 틀	이 일
three days	사 흘	삼 일
four days	나 흘	사 일
five days	닷 새	오 일

연습 2. Respond to the following questions in Korean.

a. 이번 주일에 휴일이 며칠 있어요?
b. 일요일이 며칠 전이었어요?
c. 일주일은 며칠입니까?
d. 여행을 며칠 동안 했습니까?
e. 이번 주일에 일했습니까?
f. 노는 날이 며칠 후입니까?

연습 3. Restate the following statements, using -고 싶다.

a. 온돌방에 들겠어요.
b. 나흘 동안 있을 거예요.
c. 커피 한 잔 하겠습니다.
d. 방에서 좀 쉬겠어요.
e. 침대방에서 잘 겁니다.
f. 말씀 좀 묻겠습니다.

대화 3 (FRAME 3)

방에 관한 이야기

카슨 : 방 값은 어떻게 됩니까?
직원 : 네, 하루에 6만원이에요.
카슨 : 방이 어떻습니까? 깨끗하겠지요?
직원 : 방은 다 깨끗합니다. 텔레비전도 있고요.
카슨 : 네, 그럼 됐어요.
직원 : 손님 방은 512 호실입니다. 키 여기 있습니다. 엘레베이터 타시고 5층으로 가셔서 왼쪽으로 도시면 바로 둘째 방입니다. 짐 곧 올려 드리죠. 편히 쉬십시오. 필요하신 것이 있으시면 알려 주세요.

단어 공부 (*VOCABULARY STUDY*)

- 값 — price (방 값=room charge)

  The consonant ㅅ is pronounced only when a vowel follows.
- 어떻게 됩니까? — How about...? What is...?

  The construction, 어떻게 됩니까? is often used in place of 무엇입니까?

  EX) 성함이 어떻게 되십니까? "What is your full name, please?"
- 하루에 — for one day, per day
- 깨끗하다 — to be (nice and) clean (antonym: 더럽다/더러워)
- 텔레비전도 있고요. — There is a television also.

  A sentence often ends with a connective in conversation as in this example. Such a sentence may be considered a displaced clause, originally meant to be a clause attached in front of the previous sentence. The polite suffix -요 is attached to such a clause in polite Ⓗ speech.
- 됐어요. — It's O.K. /all right /fine. (an expression of approval)
- 512호실 — Room 512
- 키 — key

  The native Korean word for "key" is 열쇠. In the context of the Western-style houses and buildings, the loan word 키 is more common.

- 올리다 — to send/take (something) up
- 편히 — comfortably
- 쉬다 — to rest (쉬 is pronounced like "she" in English.)
- 필요하다 — to be necessary (stative verb); A-가 B-가 필요하다. *A* needs *B*.
- 알리다 — to inform, let (someone) know (causative form of the verb 알다)

연습 4. Listen to the three segments of conversation, and write answers in English to the following questions.

1st Segment:
a. Did he have a reservation?
b. How many rooms do they need?
c. What kinds of rooms are available to them?
d. What did they decide to do?

2nd Segment:
a. How many days are they going to stay?
b. What's the room charge?
c. What's the room number?
d. How many keys did they receive?

3rd Segment:
a. 방을 왜 바꿨습니까?
b. 짐이 몇 개입니까?
c. 몇 시까지 방을 비워야 합니까?
d. 또 뭐 필요한 것이 있습니까?

연습 5. Engage in role plays with your partner, referring to the following instructions.

Segment 1. Step up to the hotel receptionist, say that you have no reservation but you need a room for two. You need to stay for four days. You prefer a traditional *ondol* room. Also, ask if they have a TV and a telephone in the room.

Segment 2. Ask what the room charges are. The clerk says they charge 80,000 won per day for an *ondol* room, but rooms with beds are cheaper (70,000 won). Tell the clerk that you changed your mind. Ask him to change your room to a room with beds.

Segment 3. The clerk gives you a key for Room 630. He says he will bring the luggage up to the room. He directs you to the room: he tells you to go up to the 6th floor, turn left, go to the end of the hallway (복도) and find the room on the right side.

대화 4 (FRAME 4)

음악 이야기

영옥 : 야, 음악 좋다. 무슨 음악이니?
학수 : 모짜르트 음악이야. 너 모짜르트 좋아하니?
영옥 : 그럼, 나도 좋아해. 모짜르트 싫어하는 사람 있니?
그런데 나 이건 못들어봤는데.
학수 : 새로 샀어. 들어 봐. 정말 좋다.
영옥 : 정말 좋은데!

단어 공부 (*VOCABULARY STUDY*)

- 야 — wow (an exclamation of surprise or pleasure)
- 음악 — music
- 무슨 — what kind of...
- 모짜르트 — Mozart
- 좋아하다 — to like, be fond of...
- 싫어하다 — to dislike
- 듣다/들어 — to listen, hear; A-가 B-를 듣다. *A* listens to *B*.

CAUTION! The object of the verb 듣다 must be something "audible" such as noises, sounds, voices or words, but NOT people. In English, one listens to or hears someone, while in Korean, one listens to someone's words: 누구의 말을 듣다.

- 못들어 봤는데 — haven't heard (i.e., had no experience of hearing)
- 새로 — newly, anew (adverb)
- 들어 봐. — Listen (and see what it is like).
- -어 보다 — to try (something)

The verb 보다, used as a helper verb in a compound, denotes experiencing something. (See Grammar.)

CAUTION! This compound form should *not* be used to express one's conscious effort to do something," which denotes an attempt at some action (without actually obtaining any result). Often the verb -어 보다 has no apparent counterpart in English.

연습 6. Listen to each sentence and match its English translation by the number.

a. ____________	(1) Have you met Miss Kang?
b. ____________	(2) I've never heard of it.
c. ____________	(3) Do you want to try my car?
d. ____________	(4) Please wait for a second.
e. ____________	(5) Listen to this one once.
f. ____________	(6) Try changing the key.

연습 7. Say the following sentences in Korean.

a. Let me know your telephone number.
b. I don't like classical music.
c. This song came out new.
d. I haven't listened to this.
e. Listen to me.

❖ GUESS WHAT IT MEANS: 비행기 태우지 마세요.

It's a humorous expression used among the younger generation, but it has nothing to do with an airplane. Guess what it means from the context of the following exchange. The answer is found at the end of the Answers to Exercises section. (태우다= give someone a ride, the causative of 타다 "to ride")

순자 : 선생님 노래 잘 하시네요.
윤식 : 비행기 태우지 마세요.

문법 (GRAMMAR)

1. Setting a Premise

The ending -는데 is one of the most frequently used connectives in Korean, but it has no English counterpart. The clause ending with -는데 sets a premise or provides background information for the main clause that follows. The common English translations may vary from "and," "but" to a semicolon (;).

PREMISE/BACKGROUND	MAIN POINT OF INFORMATION
나 방을 예약했는데 I have a reservation, and	방 있지요? you have a room (for me), don't you?
방이 하나 내일 비는데 One room will be vacant tomorrow;	선생님께 드리죠. we'll give it to you.

우리 여기서 기다렸는데 어디 있었어요?
We waited for you here; where were you?

CAUTION! The connective -는데 changes to -은데/-ㄴ데 when a stative verb or the equation verb (-이다) without 었 or 겠 following. If a stative verb has 었 or 겠, the ending is again -는데.

		Example
(a) For stative verbs or -이다/아니다 *without a tense marker*	STEM + 은데	좋은데 미국사람인데 아닌데
(b) For all cases except those noted above	STEM + (었) (겠) + 는데	가는데 있었겠는데 좋겠는데

날씨가 좋은데 우리 구경 나갑시다.
The weather is nice; let's go out sightseeing.

날씨가 좋은데 아무 데도 가지 않았어요?
The weather was nice, but didn't you go to any place?

나 베이커인데 방 있죠?
My name is Baker; you have a room for me, don't you?

The connective -는데 is also commonly used to connect two or contradicting clauses ("but").

값은 좋은데 나한테는 좀 작아요.
The price is good, but it's a little small for me.

잘 잤는데 아직도 졸려요.
I slept well, but I'm still sleepy.

2.The Use of -는데 as a Sentence Ending

a. The premise clause with -는데/-은데 is often used as a sentence ending (without a main clause following). Although no (main) clause follows -는데, it is still a "premise" statement for something else (implicit or explicit) within the immediate context.

나 방 예약했는데요. — I made a reservation. ("So I expect a room for me.")

방이 둘 필요한데. — I need two rooms. ("I wonder if you have rooms.")

b. The ending -는데/은데 has another function. It carries a slight exclamatory sense, calling the attention of the addressee. This exclamatory use of -는데/은데 has a rising tone at the end[↗], as distinguished from the original "premise" use which normally has a falling intonation.

날씨가 좋은데요!↗ — What a beautiful day!
한국 음식 먹고 싶은데요!↗ — I want Korean food!

3. Plans, Schedules or Intentions

The phrasal constructions below are used to express one's plans, schedules or intentions for some actions.

VERB STEM + 을 { 예정 / 것 } 이다.	It is my plan/schedule that... I'm going to...

며칠 동안 계실 예정입니까?	How many days are you planning to stay, sir?
한 일주일 있을 예정입니다.	I'm scheduled to stay for about one week.
집사람은 다음 주에 떠날 겁니다.	My wife is going to leave next week.

INTENTION IN CASUAL CONVERSATION: As introduced in Lesson 8, the phrasal form -을 것이다 is normally contracted to -을 겁니다 or -을 거예요 in conversation.

뭐 할 겁니까?	What are you going to do?
한 선생 만날 거예요?	Are you going to meet Mr. Han?
커피 안할 겁니다.	I am not going to have coffee.

CAUTION! A 3RD PERSON AS THE SUBJECT: When -을 겁니다 is used with a 3rd person as the subject, it expresses the speaker's idea that something is in store.

안 선생님 오실 겁니다.	I'm sure Mr. Ahn will come.
곧 비가 올 거예요.	I think it will rain soon.

4. Expressing the Desire: -고 싶다

The desire for some action is expressed by -고 싶다. This form is generally restricted to stating the speaker's desire or asking the addressee's desire. For another use on expressing the 3rd person's desire, see the note on the next page.

VERB STEM + 고	싶다	I { want / like } to...

무엇 좀 마시고 싶어요.	I want to drink something.
영어 배우고 싶습니까?	Do you like to learn English?
무슨 음식 잡수시고 싶으세요?	What kind of food would you like to eat?
선생님 만나 뵙고 싶었어요.	I wanted to meet you.

CAUTION! The verb 싶다 is a *stative* verb. You have learned a few verb endings which require different forms for stative and action/process verbs, as shown in the examples below.

- The prenominal form is -은 (NOT -는)
  : 가고 싶은 사람 one who wants to go
- The "premise" ending is -은데 (NOT-는데)
  : 가고 싶은데... I want to go; ...
- The blunt declarative ending is -다 (NOT -는다)
  : 가고 싶다. I want to go.

NOTE: A 3rd person's desire is normally expressed with an addition of 하다 : STEM + 고 싶어 하다.

미스 김이 알고 싶어해요.	Miss Kim wants to know .
선생님하고 얘기하고 싶어합니다.	He wants to talk to you.

5. Trial and Experiment: -어 보다

The phrase construction, STEM + 어 보다, expresses doing something by way of trial. The literal meaning of the phrase is "do something and see how it goes/works."

CAUTION! The accurate English translation would be "try something," NOT "try to do something." You should make a clear distinction between the two uses of the English verb "try." The first expression "try something" implies actually doing something, while "try to do something" implies a mere attempt to do something. The Korean phrase, -어 보다 means more a "doing" than an "attempting."

들어 보세요.	Listen (and see how it is).
이 옷 입어 봤어요.	I tried this dress on.
일본 음식 먹어 봤어요.	We tried (eating) Japanese food.

- This form is also commonly used to express one's past experience, and it is equivalent to the English perfect form.

구라파에 가 봤습니까?	Have you been to Europe?
여러번 가 봤지요.	I've been there many times.

- MODALS: As in most compound verbs, modals (the tense, intention, possibility, obligation, etc.) are all incorporated in the last verb 보다 in the compound. (This is a general rule that applies to most compound verbs, but there are some exceptions or irregularities.)

이 컴퓨터 써 보셔야 합니다.	You must try (using) this computer.

- NEGATIVES: The negative is incorporated in the beginning of the phrase if it is the prefix 안-, but the long negative is incorporated in the last verb.

이 책 아직 { 안 읽어 봤어요. / 읽어 보지 않았어요. }	I haven't read the book yet.

- HONORIFIC MARKING: -으시 is normally incorporated in the last verb only, but for the special honorific verbs (계시다 "to be/stay," 주무시다 "to sleep," and 잡수다/잡수시다 "to eat") the honorific marker will be used in both verbs of a compound.

여기 잠깐 계셔 보세요.	Please stay here for a moment.
온돌방에서 주무셔 보셨어요?	Have you slept in an ondol room?

CAUTION! The honorific verb 잡수시다 "to eat" is normally shortened in a compound form: 잡숴 보다.

김치 잡숴 보세요.	Try (eating) Kimchi.

6. A Summary of Connectives

We will review below some general facts regarding the connectives that you have learned so far.

a. All dependent clauses precede the main clause. However, in speech, the reverse order is also common.

미안합니다, 늦어서.	I'm sorry for being late.
식사 시키세요, 배 고프시면.	Order a meal, if you are hungry.

b. Unlike in simple short sentences, the subject and object are commonly marked (by -이/가, -를/을) in a compound or complex sentences.

c. The tenses (or any other modal markers for intention, ability, possibility, etc.) are not generally used with connectives marked *NO* in the list below (-고, -어서). For some (marked *YES*), the tense may be marked independently of the main clause. The "cause" clause has special restrictions.

	English		Lesson	Modal	Restriction
Simple	"and"	-고	(12)	NO	
Sequence	"and"	-고 -어서	(14)	NO	
Cause	"because"	-어서	(14)	NO	No request or suggestion.
Condition	"if"	-으면	(13)	YES	
Premise	";"	-는데 -은데	(15)	YES	
Contrast	"but"				

읽기 · 쓰기 (READING & WRITING)

1. Passenger Service on Air Travel: 항공 승객 서비스

A short article on a futuristic view of airline service appeared in a newspaper. Scan the article, and follow through the exercises below.

비행기내 첨단정보 서비스 시대

비행기를 탄 승객이 비행기 안에서 필요한 모든 일을 볼 수 있는 편리한 시대가 온다. 승객은 자리에 앉아서 작은 컬러 모니터에 나오는 음식 메뉴를 보고 먹고 싶은 음식을 마음대로 주문 할 수 있다. 알고 싶은 도시 안내를 받을 수 있고 쇼핑, 화폐 교환, 렌트카, 호텔 등에 대한 정보를 쉽게 얻을 수 있고 예약도 할 수 있다는 것.

연습 8. The following key words appear in the article. Find their meanings by using a dictionary.

•정보______________ •시대______________ •자리______________

연습 9. The word 승객 appears twice. From the context of the article, guess what the word means, and check one of the paraphrases that best describes its meaning.

A. 비행기표를 예약하는 손님
B. 비행기에 탄 손님
C. 비행기 안에서 일하는 사람
D. 비행기표를 파는 사람

연습 10. From the context of the article, check the kinds of services discussed in it, using the additional reading vocabulary provided.

- ☐ Buying airplane tickets
- ☐ Ordering meals
- ☐ Information on cities
- ☐ Special discount
- ☐ Shopping guide
- ☐ Local telephone calls
- ☐ Customs clearance
- ☐ Car rentals
- ☐ Hotel reservation
- ☐ Currency exchange

Reading Vocabulary

내	inside (=안)
마음대로	freely, as one wishes (마음=mind, -대로=as)
시대	era, period (historical)
자리	seat, place
첨단	very modern, most advanced
화폐 교환	currency exchange

연습 11. At what locations are these services available?

2. Flight Schedules

In train or airplane schedules, the hours of a day are expressed with twenty four hours. Koreans read them in Sino-Korean, as you see in the advertisement below.

더욱 편안하게 다녀오십시오.

미국에서 가장 이상적인 도시 샌프란시스코에서도 그리운 고국으로의 여행을 대한항공이 모십니다.

샌프란시스코에서 고국을 방문하실 때 로스앤젤레스에 들러 정다운 친지나 친구를 만나신 후 하와이에도 들러 가실 수 있습니다.

로스앤젤레스 공항에서 갈아타실 때에도 휄밀리케어 서비스로 전혀 불편함이 없습니다.

대한항공만이 가지는 다양한 서비스로 더욱 편안한 고국방문 길이 되십시오.

서울행 운항스케줄 안내

로스앤젤레스 출발 (매주 23회)

09 : 00 화 · 금 · 일 (KE061)	다음날 15:10 서울 도착
10 : 00 매일 (KE001)동경 경유	다음날 18:15 서울 도착
11 : 10 매일 (KE017)	다음날 17:20 서울 도착
14 : 00 월 · 목 · 토 (KE015)	다음날 20:10 서울 도착
19 : 30 월 · 수 · 토 (KE005)호놀룰루 경유	다음날 06:10 서울 도착

연습 12. Scan the advertisement above, and answer the questions.

a. Find the meaning of the first word "더욱" by using a dictionary, and write down its colloquial synonym (a word with the same meaning).

____

b. Translate the large-letter caption 더욱 편안하게 다녀오십시오, using a dictionary.

____

c. Imagine that you are taking a trip to Seoul. Looking at the flight schedule, choose one of the flights that you would take, and write down the departure and arrival times. Explain why you would choose the particular flight.

____

d. If you would want to arrive in Seoul early in the morning, which flight should you take?

____

연습 13. Complete the following sentences by filling in the blank spaces with the words listed on the right. Then answer each question, using the information in the text.

a. 9시 비행기에는 _____가 없어서 그 다음 것을 탔다. 그 비행기에는 _____이 생각보다 많지 않아서 _____ 쉴 수 있었다. 내가 앉은 옆_____가 비어서 누워서 잠을 잘 잤다. 서울에는 _____보다 2시간 늦어서 아침 7시 반에 _____ 했다.

예정
도착
편안하게
승객
자리

Question 1. Why did the writer miss the 9 o'clock flight?
Question 2. Was it a comfortable trip? Why?
Question 3. How long was the delay in arrival?

b. 우리들은 모든 것이 편리한 _____ 에 산다. 비행기 안에서 작은 컴퓨터를 보고 _____ 대로 알고 싶은 도시 _____를 받을 수 있고 화폐를 _____ 할 수도 있다. 지금은 정말 첨단 _____ 서비스 시대이다.

교환
시대
정보
안내
마음

Question 1. What kind of era did the writer say we are living in?
Question 2. What are the two things cited as examples.

NOTE: There are three stative verbs derived from a Sino-Korean character 便(편), which means "comfort" or "convenience."

a. 편하다 "to be comfortable" •Adverbial form: 편히, 편하게
(commonly used in colloquial speech)

b. 편안하다 "to be comfortable" •Adverbial form: 편안히, 편안하게
(slightly more formal or polite than 편하다)

c. 편리하다 "to be convenient" •Adverbial form: 편리하게

단어 정리 (VOCABULARY SUMMARY)

Nominals

값	price	자리	seat
교환	exchange	정보	information
방	room	- 주	week (=주일)
번호	number (serial)	주소	address
시대	era, period	직원	clerk, employee
여권	passport	침대방	room with beds
예정	schedule, plan	첨단	very modern, advanced
온돌방	floor-heated room	키	key (=열쇠)
음악	music	화폐	currency

Bound Nouns

-내	inside (=안)	-호실	room number...
-동안	duration (of time)		

Numbers of Days (Native Korean)

하루	one day	나흘	four days
이틀	two days	닷세	five days
사흘	three days		

Action Verbs

듣다/들어	to listen	싫어하다	to dislike
들다	to lodge	알리다	to inform
바꾸다	to change, exchange	올리다	to send up
쉬다	to rest	좋아하다	to like, be fond of...

Process Verbs

비다	to become empty	차다	to become full

Stative Verbs

깨끗하다	to be clean	필요하다	to be necessary
더럽다/더러워	to be dirty	편안하다/편하다	to be comfortable

Adverbs

새로	newly, anew	마음대로	freely
편히	comfortably		(마음= mind, heart;
한	approximately (=약)		-대로= as, according to)
더욱	more (=더)		

Prenominals

무슨...?	What kind of...?

Idiomatic Expressions

어떻게 됩니까?	What is...?	됐어요.	That's O.K.

연습문제 해답 (ANSWERS TO EXERCISES)

연습 1.
a. 시간이 있는데 커피나 한 잔 하십시다.
b. 극장에서 좋은 영화하는데 함께 갑시다.
c. 나 내일 부산 가는데 무엇으로 가는 것이 좋아요?
d. 그 사람의 주소 모르는데 어떻게 가지요?

연습 3.
a. 듣고 싶어요.
b. 있고싶어요.
c. 하고 싶습니다.
d. 쉬고 싶어요.
e. 자고 싶어요.
f. 묻고 싶습니다.

연습 4. Listening Comprehension (Scripts and answers)

Segment 1. Traveller : 나 예약하지 않았는데 방 있어요?
Clerk : 몇 분이세요?

Traveller : 세 사람인데 방이 둘 필요해요.
Clerk : 지금 온돌방 없는데 괜찮아요?
Traveller : 괜찮습니다.
a. No b. Two c. bedrooms d. to take two rooms

Segment 2. Clerk : 며칠 동안 계실 예정입니까?
Traveller : 이틀 있을 겁니다. 얼마죠?
Clerk : 온돌방은 한방에 6만원입니다.
Traveller : 네, 좋아요. 몇호실입니까?
Clerk : 312호실하고 315호실입니다. 키 넷 드립니다.
a. Two days b. 60,000 Won c. #312, #315 d. Four

Segment 3. Traveller : 그런데, 방이 좀 더러워요. 깨끗한 방 없어요?
Clerk : 네, 그럼 바꿔 드리죠. 손님 짐 몇입니까?
Traveller : 여섯입니다. 여기 있어요.
Clerk : 네, 알았습니다. 또 필요한 것 있으세요?
Traveller : 아니오. 모레 몇 시까지 방 비어야 합니까?
Clerk : 12시반까지 비우시면 됩니다.
a. They were not clean. b. six c. 12:30 d. No

연습 6. a. 키를 바꿔 보세요. (6) d. 나 그거 못들어 봤어요. (2)
b. 미스 강 만나 봤어요? (1) e. 이거 한번 들어 보세요. (5)
c. 잠깐 기다려 보세요. (4) f. 제 차 타 보시겠어요? (3)

연습 7. a. 전화 번호를 알려 주세요.
b. 클라식 음악 좋아하지 않아요/싫어해요.
c. 이 노래 새로 나왔어요.
d. 이거 못들어 봤어요.
e. 내 말 좀 들어봐요.

ANSWER TO "GUESS WHAT IT MEANS": It literally means, "Don't give me a ride on the airplane." The expression is used when the speaker feels that he/she is overly flattered to the point of embarrassment by someone's remarks.

연습 8. • 정보 information • 시대 era • 자리 seat
연습 9. B
연습 10. Ordering meals; information on cities; shopping; currency exchanges; car rentals; hotel reservation
연습 11. In the airplane
연습 12. a. 더욱 (= 더) c. (No fixed answers)
b. Have a more comfortable trip. d. Flight KE005
연습 13. a. <u>자리</u>가 - <u>승객</u>이 - <u>편안하게</u> - <u>자리</u>가 - <u>예정</u> - <u>도착</u>
Q1: No seats Q2: Yes. It wasn't crowded. Q3: 2 hours
b. <u>시대</u>에 - <u>마음</u>대로 - <u>안내</u>를 - <u>교환</u> - <u>정보</u>
Q1: The era of advanced information services
Q2: Computerized city guide information; currency exchange

Communicative Frames in English

Frame 1. At the Hotel Front Desk

Receptionist : Come right in, sir.
Carson : My name is Carson. I have a reservation. You have a room for me, I believe?
Receptionist : Yes. Hold a minute, sir. For one person, right?
Carson : I'm by myself.
Receptionist : I have a nice room for you. Please write your name. address, and your passport number here. How many days are you planning to stay, sir?
Carson : I'm going to be here for about three weeks.

Frame 2. Choosing the Room

Carson : Do you have ondol rooms? I want an ondol room.
Receptionist : Ondol rooms, I have no vacant ones. They are all taken! I have only bedrooms left.
Carson : Is that so? Well, I guess I have to take a bedroom.
Receptionist : Tomorrow I'll have one ondol room vacant; please use (sleep in) a bedroom just for one day today. Tomorrow afternoon, I'll change (move) it to an ondol room for you.
Carson : O.K., then do that for me.

Frame 3. Talking about the Room

Carson : How much do you charge for the room?
Receptionist : Well, sir. It'll be 60,000 won.
Carson : How is the room? I trust it's nice and clean.
Receptionist : All the rooms are nice and clean. They have televisions, too.
Carson : Then, it's all right.
Receptionist : Your room is #512. Here is the key.
Take the elevator and go to the 5th floor, and as you turn to your left, your room will be the second room. We'll take your luggage up right away.
Have a good rest, sir. If there is anything that you need, please let us know right away.

Frame 4. Talking about Music

Yŏng'ok : Wow, it's nice music. What kind of music is it?
Haksu : It's by Mozart. Do you like Mozart?
Yŏng'ok : Sure. I like it too. Who doesn't like Mozart? But I haven't listened to that one.
Haksu : This is a new one I bought. Listen. It's really great.
Yŏng'ok : This is really good!

제 16 과

호텔의 아침시간

대화 1 (FRAME 1)

친구와 전화 통화한다

문 :	여보세요. 카슨 선생이세요? 일어나셨어요?
카슨 :	아, 문 선생, 안녕히 주무셨어요? 지금 막 일어나서 세수하고 있었어요.
문 :	편히 주무셨습니까?
카슨 :	네, 잘 쉬었어요. 그런데 너무 일찌기 깼어요. 잠은 잘 잤지만. 그래서 침대에 누워서 책 읽고 있었지요.
문 :	시차 때문에 그러시겠지요. 제가 10시쯤 거기 가니까 기다리세요.
카슨 :	네, 나갈 준비하고 있지요. 이따 뵙겠어요.

단어 공부 (*VOCABULARY STUDY*)

- 여보세요. hello (<여기 보세요. "Please look here.")
  A word to call someone's attention. It is also used in a telephone conversation.
- 일어나다 to get up (from bed)
  Compare this to 일어서다 "to get up (from a sitting posture)."
- 막 just, at the exact moment of, only a moment ago.

This word is often used together with 지금. EX) 은행이 지금 막 열렸어요. "The bank is just opened."

•세수하다	to wash, freshen oneself (Literally, "wash hands")
•세수하고 있었어요.	I was washing. (See Grammar for -고 있다.)
•잠은 잘 잤지만	even though I slept well (See Grammar for -지만.)
•일찍이	early (adverb, often shortened to 일찍)
•깨다/깨	to wake up
•눕다/누워	to lie down
•시차	time difference (시=time, 차=difference), jet lag
•-때문에	because of, on account of...
•거기 가니까	I'm going there, so... (See Grammar for -으니까.)
•나갈 준비하다	to get ready to go out

연습 1. To express an action in progress, a phrasal construction STEM + 고 있다 is used. Ask your partner what each of the people in the pictures below is doing. Use the progressive form, -고 있다 in your questions.

EXAMPLE: 동생이 뭐 하고 있어요? — What is your brother doing?
주스 마시고 있어요. — He is drinking juice.

연습 2. Respond to each of the questions by choosing one of the possible reasons below.

Questions	Possible Reasons
a. 왜 식당에 갔어요?	(1) 상점이 가까우니까
b. 왜 집에 있습니까?	(2) 배가 고프니까
c. 어디 갈까요?	(3) 손님이 오시니까
d. 그 호텔에 방이 있어요?	(4) 예약했으니까
e. 왜 택시로 가지 않아요?	(5) 날씨가 좋으니까

연습 3. Listen to the story, and answer the questions in short phrases. Item 1-a is an example.

Segment 1. a. 이 사람이 무엇때문에 일찌기 일어났어요? 시차때문에
b. 몇 시에 깼습니까? ____________________

c. 이 사람이 아직도 고단합니까? ____________________

Segment 2. a. 뭐 하고 있었어요? ____________________

b. 친구가 몇 시에 와요? ____________________

c. 친구하고 어디서 만날 겁니까? ____________________

____

대화 2 (FRAME 2)

호텔 로비에서

직원 : 안녕히 주무셨습니까?

카슨 : 수고하십니다. 나한테 메시지 온 거 없었지요?

직원 : 잠깐만요.... 네, 없었습니다.

카슨 : 네, 알았어요. 그런데, 그럼 엽서 어디서 살 수 있어요?

직원 : 매점에서 팔 겁니다. 저기 잡지 파는 데서요.
그런데 9시 반까지 기다리셔야죠. 그때 여니까요.

카슨 : 네, 알았어요. 그런데 우체국 여기서 멀어요?

직원 : 네, 좀 먼데요. 왜 그러세요? 우표 필요하세요?

카슨 : 네, 엽서 몇 장 미국으로 보내고 싶은데.

직원 : 아, 네. 우표 여기 있습니다. 미국에 보내는 것은
300원 짜리 우표 붙이면 돼요. 몇 장 드릴까요?

카슨 : 여섯 장만 주세요.

직원 : 네.

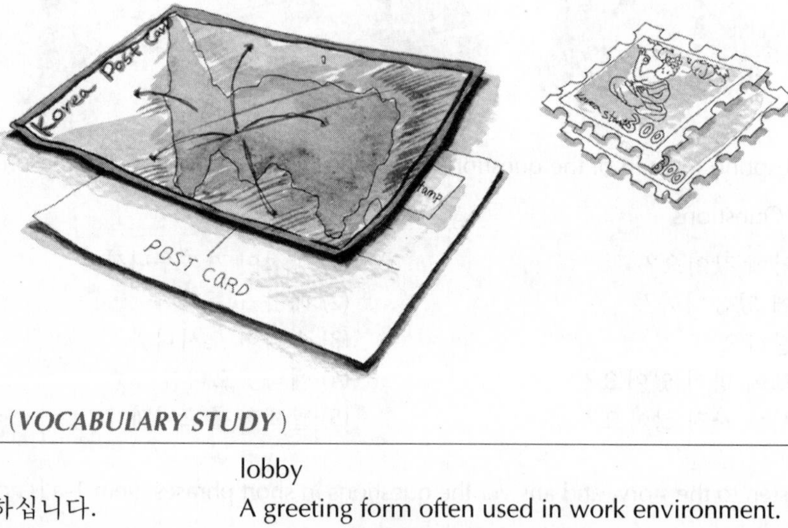

단어 공부 (*VOCABULARY STUDY*)

- 로비 — lobby
- 수고하십니다. — A greeting form often used in work environment. 수고 means "hard work."
- 메시지 온 거 — a message that is left (for me) (온 is the noun-modifying

form of 오다 in the past tense or the completed aspect.)

- 그림 picture
- 엽서 postcard
- 매점 concession shop (a small general store within public buildings such as hotels, airports, offices)
- 그때 at that time

The bound noun -때 means "time/occasion."

- 여니까 because they open ... (열 + 으니까 ⟶ 여니까)
- 우체국 post office
- 왜 그러세요? Why do you say that? What's the matter?

This is an idiomatic phrase used in politely asking the reason for the addressee's statement or behavior.

- 우표 postage stamp
- -짜리 (an item that is) worth..., of value

This suffix is always preceded by monetary amount.
EX) 100원 짜리 우표 "a 100-won stamp"

- 붙이다 to affix, paste on

붙이면 됩니다. "You just have to affix it." (Literally, "If you affix it, that will do.")

CAUTION! The verb 되다 "to become" is frequently used in Korean to mean "to be O.K./all right." EX) 그러면 됩니다. That'll do.

❖ -는/-은/-을 + NOUN

Action/process verbs have a set of three endings that form noun modifiers.

	Example	
Present/Ongoing : STEM + 는	비는 방	a room being vacated
Past/Completed : STEM + 은	빈 방	a vacant/empty room
Future/Expected : STEM + 을	빌 방	a room to be vacated

연습 4. Identify the meanings of the following phrases by the number.

a. _______ 일어날 시간 (1) A letter (that's) arrived
b. _______ 일찍이 깬 사람 (2) Time to get up
c. _______ 도착한 편지 (3) A person (who) woke up early
d. _______ 마실 것 (4) Something to drink

연습 5. Play roles with your partner as you speak with each other over the phone.

a. Your telephone is ringing. Pick up the receiver (수화기), say hello, identify yourself and ask who it is.
b. It is your friend. Your friend will ask if you are up, when you woke up, and what you are doing now, etc.
c. You ask your friend when the stores will be open, where you can obtain magazines and picture postcards, etc.

d. Ask also if the post office is nearby, where else you can get stamps from, etc. Ask your friend when he/she will come over, and where you will meet.

대화 3 (FRAME 3)

공중 전화 쓰는 법

카슨 : 또 하나 물어 볼 것이 있는데.

직원 : 네.

카슨 : 공중 전화는 한 통화에 얼마짜리 동전 넣어요?

직원 : 아니예요. 손님, 호텔 전화 쓰세요.
장거리 전화면 요금 받습니다만 시내 전화면 무료입니다.

카슨 : 그건 아는데, 전화 쓰는 법도 알아야 하니까.

직원 : 네, 아셔야죠. 한 통화에 40원입니다.
10원 짜리나 50원 짜리 동전이 있으면 됩니다.

단어 공부 (*VOCABULARY STUDY*)

- 또 하나 — another
- 공중 전화 — public telephone
- 통화 — telephone call, telephone conversation; 통화 is used here as a unit of telephone calls (통=through, 화=talk)
- 동전 — coin (동=copper, 전=coin)
- 넣다/넣어 — to put in, insert
- 장거리 — long distance (장=long, 거리=distance)
- 요금 — fee, charge (요=charge, 금=gold; money)
- 받습니다만 — We receive (charge), but...(=받지만)

  Generally the connective endings cannot incorporate levels of politeness, but -지만 "but" is one exception: -지 may be replaced by -ㅂ니다/습니다.
- 시내 전화 — local call (antonym: 시외 전화)

  The word 시내 means "the city, within the city, downtown." (시=city, 내=inside)
- 무료 — free of charge (무=none, 료=charge)
- 법 — method, means; law, regulation

연습 6. Respond factually to the following questions in Korean.

a. 가까운 데 공중전화가 있습니까?
b. 미국에서는 한 통화에 얼마입니까?
c. 장거리 전화는 언제 요금이 쌉니까?
d. 미국에서 시내 전화가 무료입니까?

❖ DENOMINATIONS OF CURRENCY AND STAMPS

-짜리 is a handy suffix to the monetary value of objects, such as coins, paper money, checks, stamps, and other commercial commodities.

십원 짜리 (동전)	a 10-won (coin)
백원 짜리 (동전)	a 100-won (coin)
천원 짜리 (지폐)	a 1,000-won (paper money)
만원 짜리 (지폐)	a 10,000-won (paper money)
십만원 짜리 (수표)	a 100,000-won (check)
이십오원 짜리 (우표)	a 25 won-(stamp)
삼백원 짜리 (우표)	a 300 won-(stamp)
팔만원 짜리 (쟈켓)	a 80,000-won (jacket)

연습 7. Each student by turn will take out all the money he/she happens to have and will announce in Korean what amount of coin/currency there is.

연습 8. Combine each pair of sentences by using one of the connectives listed below.

a. 전화로 예약했어요. 방 있습니까?
b. 우체국에 갔어요. 닫혔었습니다.
c. 전화도 있어요. 텔레비전도 있어요.
d. 늦었습니다. 미안합니다.
e. 늦었습니다. 가지 맙시다.
f. 일찍 일어났어요. 세수했어요.

▲ -고	Simple "and"
▲ -과/-는데	Sequence "and"
▲ -어서	Cause "because/for"
▲ -는데/은데	Premise " ; "
▲ -으니까	Reason "because"
▲ -지만	Contradiction "but"

연습 9. Say the follwing sentences in Korean, paying attention to the partially completed Korean sentences on the right.

a. Do you have something to ask me? ________ 것이 있어요?
b. It is time to depart. ________ 시간이 됐습니다.
c. Do you know how to use a computer? ________ 법 알아요?
d. Did you receive the postcard that I sent you? ________ 엽서 받았어요?

대화 4 (FRAME 4)

친구하고 전화한다

상빈: 여보세요. 거기 영옥이네 집이죠?
어른: 네, 그렇습니다.
상빈: 좀 바꿔주시겠어요?
어른: 잠깐만요. 영옥아! 전화 받아라.
영옥: 네에. 여보세요. 전화 바꿨습니다.
상빈: 나야, 상빈이. 잘 있었니?
영옥: 상빈아, 웬 일이니?
상빈: 응, 물어볼 게 있어서.
영옥: 뭔데?
상빈: 학수 생일 파티 초대 받았는데 날짜 잊어버렸어.
영옥: 초대 받고 날짜를 잊어 버려? 바보같이.
오는 금요일이야.
상빈: 응, 요새 바빠서 그래. 알았어. 고마워

단어 공부 (*VOCABULARY STUDY*)

- 어른 — adult (as opposed to 아이); a senior, an elder
- 네에 — an elongated form of 네 "yes": "y-e-s"
- 전화 바꿨습니다. — I'm on the line. (Literally, "I've taken over the receiver.")
  This is an expression used when one gets the phone after someone else.
- 웬 일이니? — What's up? (a blunt version of 웬 일이세요?)
- -게 — A contraction of -것이
- 뭔데? — What is it?
  The premise ending -은데 is used here as the speaker expects further expansion on the preceding remarks.
- 생일 파티 — birthday party
- 초대 — invitation; 초대하다 "to invite"
- 잊어버리다 — to forget
  잊다 means "to forget," but it is commonly used in a compound form in informal speech. 버리다 is also an independent verb, meaning "to discard/waste."
- 바보 — a fool, a stupid person (a mild derogation, often used in kid - ding someone)
- -같이 — like, as (postposition)

CULTURAL ENCOUNTER One of the outstanding characteristics of Korean culture is to place a high value in respecting old age. This value is reflected in various features of language today. 어른 does not simply mean an "adult," but it also means an older person in the family or community to whom the younger members are expected to pay respect.

연습 10. Have a short telephone conversation with your partner, as you play the role of an elder brother/sister of your friend. Include the points listed below.

- Pick up the phone.
- Ask who it is.
- Call your sister/brother.
- Ask him/her to get the phone.
- Tell him/her to hurry up.

연습 11. The teacher and a student will play roles based on the script (at the end of the Vocabulary Summary section), and the class will take notes (in English or Korean) of the key points of information (who, what, when, where, etc.).

Segment 1. ________________ Segment 2. ________________

________________ ________________

________________ ________________

❖ GUESS WHAT IT MEANS : 말도 안돼.

It's a Korean idiom, and you know all the words used in the expression. Guess what the idiom means from the context of the following exchange.

상빈 : 집에서 공부하자.
영옥 : 말도 안 돼. 날씨가 이렇게 좋은데.

The answer is found at the end of the Answers to Exercises section.

문법 (GRAMMAR)

1. Expressing an Action in Progress: -고 있다

In Korean, an action in progress may be expressed by the simple present tense. 나 책 읽어요 may mean either "I'm reading a book." or "I read a book." However, if there is a need to express clearly an action in progress, the compound form -고 있다 is used.

CAUTION! Unlike its English counterpart, the progressive form in Korean is not used to express an impending action (in the immediate future).

ACTION VERB STEM + 고	계시다 (HONORIFIC) 있다 (PLAIN)	be ... ing

지금 뭐하고 계세요? What are you doing now?

친구가 기다리고 있습니다. A friend is waiting.
저 한국말 배우고 있어요. I am learning Korean.
아무 것도 안 하고 있어. I'm not doing anything.

- MODALS: In general, as in most compound verbs, all modals (tense, honorific, possibility, obligation, etc.) are incorporated into the second verb (있다).

우리 얘기하고 있었어요. We were just chatting. (PAST)
그 사람 책 읽고 있을 겁니다. She is probably reading a book. (CONJECTURE)

- IRREGULAR HONORIFIC FORMS: The honorific markers are found in both verbs when the main verb has an irregular honorific form, i.e., 잡수시다 "to eat," 주무시다 "to sleep."

잡수시고 계십니다. He is eating. (HONORIFIC)
주무시고 계세요. He is sleeping. (HONORIFIC)

- NEGATIVE: The negative is incorporated in the beginning of the phrase if it is the prefix (안/못–), but in the second verb if it is a long negative (–지 않다).

CAUTION! The negative verb 없다 is *never* used in the progressive form.

일하고 있지 않아요. He isn't working now.
안 자고 있었어요. I wasn't sleeping

2. Expressing the Reason: –으니까

Two clauses expressing reason and consequence are connected by –으니까.

저 11시쯤에 거기 가니까 기다리세요.
I'll be there around 11; so please wait for me.

너무 비싸니까 사지 않았습니다.
Because it was too expensive, I didn't buy it.

전화를 안받으니까 집에 없을 겁니다.
Since he doesn't take telephone calls, he probably isn't home.

The connective –으니까 is often interchangeable with –어서 (which we called the "cause" connective in Lesson 14), but there are some important differences between them:

a. If the main clause is a *request* or a *suggestion*, only –으니까 is used, not –어서.
날씨가 좋으니까 나갑시다. The weather is nice, so let's go out.
(WRONG: 좋아서)

b. Neither –으니까 nor –어서, as a rule, incorporates the tense marker, because the time of the dependent clause is determined by the main (final) clause.

NO TENSE MARKER

날씨가 { 좋으니까 / 좋아서 } 쇼핑 나갔습니다. Since the weather was nice, we went out shopping.

c. -으니까 (but not -어서) may still take -었 (as the marker of the completed state, rather than as the tense marker) if the verb expresses a state after the completion of an action or a process.

COMPLETION MARKER

값이 { 올라갔으니까 / 올라가서 } 살 수 없어요.	Since the price has gone up, I cannot buy it.

d. The reasoning or inference based on some fact is expressed only by -으니까, but not by -어서.

일본말 못하니까 일본사람 아니예요. (WRONG: 못해서)	He is not a Japanese, since he doesn't speak Japanese.
아이가 있으니까 결혼했을 겁니다. (WRONG: 있어서)	Since he has a son, he probably is married.

3. Using Verbs as Noun Modifiers

In any language, verbs are often used as noun modifiers. The verb forms used for this purpose in English are participles (*going* prices, *spoken* words, etc.) and infinitives (time *to go*, things *to do*, etc.). The Korean counterparts will be called prenominal forms, since they always precede a nominal. You have learned two sets of basic prenominal endings, one for action/process verbs and another for stative verbs.

ACTION VERBS/있다	STATIVE VERBS/-이다	
STEM + 는	<NOT USED>	•Present/ Ongoing Action •Generic (timeless)
STEM + 은	STEM + 은	•Past/ Completed Action •Present State of Being
STEM + 을	<NOT COMMON>	•Expected Action or State

The existence verbs 있다/없다 takes -는 like an action verb, but the past form is -던 which will be introduced later in detail.

•Generic Action:	택시 타는 곳	a place to ride a taxi
•Present/Ongoing:	제가 있는데	where I'm staying
•Present State:	비싼 옷	expensive clothes
•Past Action:	내가 본 영화	the movie that I saw
•Completed Action:	결혼한 사람	a married person
•Expected Action:	내일 할 일	things to do tomorrow
•Expected Action:	볼 곳	places to see

•PRENOMINAL PHRASES AND CLAUSES: As you note in some of the above examples, prenominal verb forms often accompany other words to form phrases and clauses. The prenominal clauses in Korean are equivalent to relative clauses in English. Unlike in

English there are no relative pronouns (such as "that, which, who," etc.), and the order of the noun and the modifying clause in Korean is in reverse in English.

제가 배우는 말은 한국말입니다.
The language that I'm learning is Korean.

4. Two Clause in Contrast or Contradiction: -지만

The contrasting or contradicting clauses are connected by -지만. It is generally equivalent to "although" or "but" in English. The sense of contrast or contradiction is stronger than -는데/은데 (Lesson 15). The tense and other modal features are freely incorporated in the connective verb.

어렵지만 배울 수 있어요.
Although it is difficult, you can learn it.

전에 불어를 공부했지만 다 잊어버렸습니다.
I studied French before, but I forgot it all.

잘 모르지만 아마 100원짜리 우표가 필요하실 겁니다.
I am not sure, but you probably need a 100-won stamp.

오늘은 일요일이지만 일해야 해요.
It's Sunday today, but I have to work.

- POLITENESS MARKING IN THE CONNECTIVE: As a rule, the level of politeness is marked only in the sentence-final endings. However, the connective -지만 is one exception. The particle -만 may follow the polite ending -습니다 or -ㅂ니다 to form a connective verb phrase.

장거리 전화는 요금을 받습니다만, 시내 전화는 무료입니다.
We charge for long distance calls, but local calls are free.

미안합니다만 여권 좀 보여 주십시오.
I am sorry, sir, but please show me your passport.

5. A Summary of Postpositions

				English
1. SUBJECT	[4]	(non-focused)-ϕ	(focused) C-이 (focused) V-가	ϕ
2. OBJECT	[8]	(non-focused)-ϕ	(focused) C-을 (focused) V-를	ϕ
3. PLACE	[7]	(location/existence)-에 (event or state) -에서		in/at/on
4. TIME (point)	[3]	-에		in/at/on
5. TIME (duration)	[8] [11]	(non-stressed)-ϕ -동안(에)	(stressed) -을/를	for

6. DATIVE (destination)	[3] [8]	(inanimate noun) -에 (human/animal) -한테	to/for
7. ORIGIN	[7]	(inanimate noun) -에서 (human/animal) -한테서	from
8. MEANS	[10]	C -으로 V/ㄹ-로	by/with
9. DIRECTION	[10]	C -으로 V/ㄹ-로	to toward
10. EXTENT	[10]	-까지	until/up to
11. ACCOMPANY-ING	[11] [12]	-하고 -이랑	and/with
12. COMPARISON	[12]	-보다	than
13. ALTERNATIVE	[13]	-이나	or
14. POSSESSIVE	[14]	-의	of
15. REFERENCE	[15]	-에 대해서	about
16. RESEMBLANCE	[16]	-같이	like

NOTE: 1. ϕ means no markers are used.

2. C- means "after a consonant," V- "after a vowel." V/ㄹ- "after a vowel or ㄹ."
3. The numbers in [ ] (e.g., [4]) shows the lessons in which they are first introduced or explained.
4. Context postpositions (such as -은/는, -도) are not included here.

읽기 · 쓰기 (READING & WRITING)

1. An Article from a Ladies' Magazine

There are many ladies' magazines in Korea, particularly those for housewives, 가정 주부 or simply 주부. The word 가정 is equivalent to "home." Such magazines often contain articles about well-known personalities, as shown below. What follows is about the daily routine of a female TV announcer. Scan the list and follow through the exercises.

강정희 주부의 하루 시간표

6:00	자리에서 일어나, 아침 식사 준비
6:30 - 7:00	조반, 남편 (윤일환 씨) 출근
8:00 - 8:30	청소, 빨래, 설거지
8:30 - 9:00	음악 들으면서 아침 커피
9:00 - 9:30	세수, 목욕, 화장, 외출 준비
10:00	출발! (차안에서 영어 회화 테이프 듣는다)
10:30 - 11:00	수영 (월, 수, 금); 꽃꽂이 (화, 목)
11:30	출근 (방송 자료 준비)
1:00 - 2:00	친구들과 점심 식사
2:00 - 8:30	방송 작업
9:00	퇴근, 집으로!
9:30	귀가, 세수
10:00 - 10:30	간단한 식사, 혹은 부부 티타임
10:30	부부 독서, 혹은 방송 자료 준비
1:00	취침

단어 소개

남편: husband
출근: 일 하러 나가는 것
목욕: taking a bath
외출: 밖으로 나가는 것
퇴근: 일 끝내고 집에 가는 것
간단하다: to be simple
부부: 남편과 아내, married couple
독서: 책 읽는 것
혹은: or (else), otherwise

연습 12. Write answers in Korean to the follwing questions, referring to the information given above.

a. 강 여사는 아침 몇 시에 자리(bed)에서 일어납니까?
b. 강 여사의 남편 되는 분의 이름이 뭣입니까? (남편 되는 분=남편)
c. 이 부부는 같은 시간에 출근합니까? 아니면 다른 시간에 출근 합니까?
d. 점심 식사는 어떻게 합니까?
e. 강 여사는 몇 시에 퇴근합니까?
f. 목욕은 아침에 합니까? 밤에 합니까?
g. 이 부부는 하루에 몇 시간 함께 지냅니까?

2. Postpositions in Formal Style

There are some postpositions in Korean that are somewhat more formal and are used more often in writing than in speech. The following are such postpositions that appear in the clipping below.

Common in Speech	*Common in Writing*	
-하고	-와 (after a vowel) -과 (after a consonant)	"and; with"
-한테	-에게	"to; for"
-한테서	-에게서	"from"

{ 아들과 딸에게 엽서를 보냈다. / 아들하고 딸한테 엽서를 보냈다. } I sent a postcard to my son and daughter.

{ 이것은 남자 친구에게서 받은 선물이다. / 이것은 남자 친구한테서 받은 선물이다. } This is the gift I received from my boy friend.

연습 13. A magazine for young girls carries the quiz below for fun. Scan it and pick your answer.

Q8 여자가 들고 있는 상자 안에 무엇이 들었을까요?

a. 아이에게 줄 생일 선물
b. 바겐 세일에서 싸게 산 물건
c. 그에게서 받은 뜻밖의 선물
d. 드디어 손에 넣은 멋진 드레스

단어 소개

상자	box
들었다	be containd
그	he/she, the person
뜻밖의	unexpected
드디어	finally
손에 넣은	(that) she got
멋진	stylish, good-looking

연습 14. For each word, find a paraphrase from the list on the right, that may define the word. Identify it by the number, as in item a. 방문 (5).

a. 방문	(5)	1. 남편과 아내
b. 부부	( )	2. 일하러 나가는 것
c. 퇴근	( )	3. 책 읽는 것
d. 자리	( )	4. 먼 곳
e. 출근	( )	5. 사람을 찾아가는 것
f. 장거리	( )	6. 밖으로 나가는 것
g. 외출	( )	7. 일을 끝내고 집에 돌아가는 것
h. 독서	( )	8. 앉는 곳

연습 15. For each of the phrases listed below, write a phrase with an opposite meaning.

a. 출근했다 ⟷ ________ d. 남편에게 ⟷ ________

b. 늦게 ⟷ ________ e. 이미 ⟷ ________

c. 형에게서 ⟷ ________ f. 먼 곳 ⟷ ________

연습 16. Complete the following paragraphs by filling in the blank spaces with words listed on the right.

강 여사는 밤 늦게 자지만 아침 6시에 ______ 남편 윤 씨의 아침 식사를 ______ 한다. 윤 씨가 아침 7시에 ______ 하면 강 여사는 집안을 청소하고 빨래도 하고 설거지도 한다. 그리고 9시까지 혼자서 ______ 을 듣고 아침 커피를 마신다. 강 여사는 출근 전에 수영 ______ 꽃꽂이를 한다. 출근은 11시 반에 하고 ______ 은 밤 9시에 한다. 그러니까 윤 씨 ______ 는 함께 지내는 시간이 많지 않다.

출근
퇴근
음악
부부
깨서
혹은
준비

연습 17. Write a similar account of your daily activities.

단어 정리 (VOCABULARY SUMMARY)

Nominals

가정 주부	housewife	상자	box
공중전화	public telephone	시내 전화	local call
그때	at that time	시차	time difference
그림	picture, drawing	어른	adult, senior
남편	husband	엽서	postcard
독서	reading (books)	요금	fee, charge
동전	coin	우체국	post office
로비	lobby	우표	postage stamp
매점	concession store	장거리	long distance
메시지	message	초대	invitation
무료	free of charge	통화	telephone call/ conversation
바보	fool		
법	method; law	파티	party
부부	married couple		

Action/Process Verbs

깨다	to wake up	붙이다	to affix
넣다	to put in, insert	세수하다	to wash (hands and face)
눕다/누워	to lie (down)	일어나다	to get up (from bed)

잊다	to forget	외출하다	to go out (of home)
잊어버리다	to forget (colloquial)	출근하다	to go out to work
목욕하다	to take a bath	퇴근하다	to go off (from work)
손에 넣다	to obtain, get		

Stative Verbs

간단하다	to be simple	-에 들었다	to be contained in
멋지다/멋진	to be stylish		

Adverbs

그 때(에)	at that time	막	just (now)
뜻밖의	unexpected	일찌기/일찍	early

Idioms

수고 하십니다. How are you? (a greeting used in work environment)

또 하나	another	왜 그러세요?	Why do you say/do that?
여보세요.	Hello.		

Bound Nouns

-때	at the time of...	-짜리	(an item) worth...
-때문에	because of...		

Pronouns

그 he/she (written style)

Connectives

혹은 or

연습문제 해답 (ANSWERS TO EXERCISES)

연습 2. a. 배가 고프니까 식당에 갔어요.
b. 손님이 오시니까 집에 있습니다.
c. 날씨가 좋으니까 어디 갑시다.
d. 예약했으니까 방이 있어요.
e. 상점이 가까우니까 택시로 안가요.

연습 3. (Scripts and Answers)

Segment 1. 저는 한국에 오면 일찍 깹니다. 보통 아침 네 시면 깨지요.
그러나 잘 쉬었으니까 고단하지 않습니다.
a. 시차때문에. b. 4시에. c. 아니오.

Segment 2. 침대에 누워서 친구 전화를 기다리고 있었어요.
친구는 11시쯤에 옵니다. 식당에서 만날 겁니다.
a. 전화를 기다렸어요. b. 11시쯤에. c. 식당에서.

연습 4. a. (2) b. (3) c. (1) d. (4)

연습 8. a. 전화로 예약했는데 방 있습니까?
b. 우체국에 갔는데/갔지만 닫혔었습니다.

c. 전화도 있고 텔레비전도 있어요.
d. 늦어서 미안합니다.
e. 늦었으니까 가지 맙시다.
f. 일찌기 일어나서 세수했어요.

연습 9. a. (나한테) 물어 볼 것이 있어요? c. 컴퓨터 쓰는 법 알아요?
b. 떠날 시간이 됐습니다. d. 내가 보낸 엽서 받았어요?

연습 11.

	(Scripts and Answers)	(Key Points)
Segment 1.	한: 여보세요. 누구십니까?	Meet Mr. Min
	민: 저 민입니다.	10:30
	한: 아, 민 선생, 이리 오시겠어요?	Hotel lobby
	민: 네, 10시 반에 가니까 로비에서 기다려 주세요.	
	한: 네, 그러지요. 이따 뵙지요.	
Segment 2.	민: 오늘 저녁 바쁘세요?	A birthday party
	한: 아니오. 왜요?	6 p.m.
	민: 신라 호텔에서 아이 생일파티하는데	Shilla Hotel restaurant
	한 선생 오실 수 있어요?	8th floor
	한: 네, 가지요. 저녁 몇십니까?	
	민: 6시에 8층 식당에 오시지요.	
	한: 네, 알았습니다.	
	민: 잊어버리지 마세요.	
	한: 네. 꼭 가겠습니다.	

EXPLANATION ON "GUESS WHAT IT MEANS": 말도 안 돼 literally means "It doesn't make sense at all." It's an idiom meaning, "No way."

Translation: A: Let's study at home.
B: No way.
It's such a beautiful day. (We should enjoy the sun.)

연습 12. a. 6시 c. 다른 시간에 e. 9시에 g. 4시간
b. 윤일환 d. 1시에 친구와 함께 f. 아침에

연습 14. a. (5) b. (1) c. (7) d. (8) e. (2) f. (4) g. (6) h. (3)

연습 15. a. 퇴근했다 c. 형에게 e. 아직
b. 일찍이 d. 아내에게 f. 가까운 곳

연습 16. 깨서 - 준비 - 출근 - 음악 - 혹은 - 퇴근 - 부부

Communicative Frames in English

Frame 1. Conversing over the Phone

Mun : Hello. Is this Mr. Carson? Are you up?
Carson : Oh, Mr. Mun. Good morning.

I just got up now, and I was washing.

Mun : Did you have a good rest?

Carson : Yes, I had a good rest. But I woke up too early, even though I slept well. So, I was lying on the bed, reading a book.

Mun : It is probably because of the jet lag. I'll be there about 10, so wait for me.

Carson : O.K. I'll be getting ready to go out. See you later.

Frame 2. At the Hotel Lobby

Clerk : Good morning, sir.

Carson : Good morning. There wasn't any message for me, was there?

Clerk : Just a minute, sir... No, there wasn't any.

Carson : Oh, I see. By the way, where can I buy picture postcards?

Clerk : I'm sure they sell them at a concession shop, the shop over there where magazines are sold. But you have to wait until 9:30 because they don't open until then.

Carson : I see. By the way, is the post office far from here?

Clerk : Yes, a little far away. Why do you ask? Do you need stamps?

Carson : I want to mail some postcards to America.

Clerk : Oh, I see. We have stamps here. You just have to put on 300-won stamps. How many shall I give you, sir?

Carson : Give me six, please.

Clerk : Yes, sir.

Frame 3. How to Use the Public Telephone

Carson : I have one other thing that I want to ask you about.

Clerk : Yes, sir.

Carson : What coins do I put in for one call on the public telephone?

Clerk : No. Use the hotel phone. We charge for long distance calls, but local calls are free.

Carson : I know that, but I do this because I must learn how to use the public phone.

Clerk : Yes, you need to, sir. It's 40 won for one call. 10 won- or 50 won-coins will do.

Frame 4. Talking with a Friend over the Phone

Sangbin : Hello. Is this Yong'ok's house?

Adult : Yes, it is.

Sangbin : May I talk to Yong'ok?

Adult : One moment. Yongok! A telephone call for you.

Yong'ok : Yes. Hello. Yong'ok speaking.

Sangbin : It's me, Sangbin. How are you?

Yong'ok : Sangbin! What's up?

Sangbin : I got invited to Haksu's birthday party, but I forgot the date.

Yong'ok : Get invited, and forget the date? You stupid thing! That's coming Friday.

Sangbin : Well, it's because I've been so busy lately. I got it now. Thanks!

제 17 과

상점에서

대화 1 (FRAME 1)

상점에 들어간다

점원: 어서 오십시오. 뭐 찾으십니까?
카슨: 저 바지 좀 보여 주십시오. 저 진열창에 있는 거.
점원: 저 누런 색 바지 말씀이에요?
카슨: 아니, 그 옆의 회색 바지 말이요.
점원: 입어 보시지요. 마음에 드실 겁니다.
카슨: 어디서 갈아 입죠?
점원: 이쪽에 옷 갈아입는 방이 있습니다.
카슨: 알았어요.

단어 공부 (*VOCABULARY STUDY*)

- 바지 — trousers, pants
- 보이다 — to show, let (something) be seen (causative form of 보다)

  This verb is normally used in a compound form with 주다. EX) 보여주세요 "Show me."
- 진열창 — shopwindow (진열=display, 창=window)
- -에 있는 거 — that one (that is) in... ; 거 ← 것

CAUTION! Unlike in English, a location phrase (진열창에) in Korean cannot be placed before a noun to modify it. The verb in a prenominal form, 있는 must be inserted between the location phrase and the noun. This will be explained more later.

- 누렇다/누런/누래 — to be tan (irregular stative verb)
- 색 — color
- 회색 — grey (color)
- -말/말씀이다 — I mean.../I'm talking about... (See Grammar.)
- 입다 — to wear, put on (clothes); 입어보세요. "Try them on."
- 마음에 들다 — to be fond of; to get to like (process verb)
- 갈다/가는/갈아 — to change, exchange

  The verb 갈다 is often used in a compound form with another verb; 갈아 입다 "to change (clothes)"; 갈아 타다 "to change, transfer (vehicles)"
- 옷 갈아 입는 방 — a fitting room (Literally, "a room for changing clothes")

❖ 무슨 색: "WHAT COLOR?"

The basic (native) color expressions in Korean are made with six *stative verbs* (with a stem ending with ㅎ). These verbs express broad categories of colors.

white	yellow	tan	red	green / blue	black
☐	☐	☐	☐	☐	☐
하얗다	노랗다	누렇다	빨갛다	파랗다	까맣다

	☐	☐	☐	☐	☐	☐	☐
	갈색	분홍색	보라색	녹색	청색	남색	회색
Personalized Vocabulary :	brown	pink	purple	green	blue	dark blue	grey

Colors with narrower and more specific hues, listed above in the second row, are *nouns*. When you want to use them as *verbs*, -이다 is suffixed, as in 갈색이다 "to be brown."

연습 1. With your coloring pencils, color the little blocks above while reading each expression aloud.

연습 2. Pick any object in the room, and ask your partner what color it is. Use color words in English if you don't find enough items that you want.

EXAMPLE : 테이블이 무슨 색입니까? — What is the color of the table?
테이블이 갈색입니다. — It's brown.

❖ WHAT DO YOU MEAN? : 무엇 말씀입니까?

Asking for clarification of a topic or responding to such a request is commonly done with the following verbal phrases involving 말/말씀 "word, reference."

Nominal + { 말씀입니까? / 말입니다.	Do you mean...? / I mean...

연습 3. With your partner, have a short conversation after the model below. Start by pointing at some object in the room.

MODEL:	A: 저 책 좀 주세요.	Could you hand me that book?
	B: 이 책 말씀입니까?	Do you mean this book?
	A: 네, 그것 말입니다.	Yes, I mean that.

대화 2 (FRAME 2)

바지를 입어본다

점원: 잘 맞습니다. 이쪽 거울 보시죠.
카슨: 조금 긴 것 같은데.
점원: 조금 짧게 수선해 드리겠습니다.
카슨: 바로 됩니까? 나 다시 못오는데.
점원: 예, 잠깐만 앉아 계세요. 곧 고쳐 드리죠.
고치는 동안에 다른 물건 구경하세요.
저쪽에 구두, 양말, 모자, 안경, 좋은 물건 많습니다.
카슨: 그럼, 그럴까요. 빨리 해 주세요.
점원: 염려 마세요. 15분이내에 됩니다.

단어 공부 (*VOCABULARY STUDY*)

- 맞다 — to fit, match; to be correct
- 거울 — mirror
- 긴 것 같은데 — It seems long; -은 것 같다 "(it) seems..." (See Grammar.)
- 길다/긴/길어 — to be long
- 짧다 — to be short; ㅂ of 짧- is pronounced only when a vowel follows.
- 짧게 — short (adverbial form of 짧다)
- 수선하다 — to repair, refit
- 바로 됩니까? — Will it be done right away?

  Note the use of 되다 "to be ready, done."
- 다시 — again
- 앉아 계세요. — Please be seated.

  The verb 있다/계시다 is used here as a helper verb, denoting the state after an action.

- 고치다 — to repair, fix, alter (=수선하다)
- 곧 — immediately, right away (=바로)
- 고치는 동안에 — while fixing; -는 동안에 while...
- 물건 — thing, item (for sale), merchandise
- 구두 — shoes
- 양말 — socks, stockings
- 모자 — hat
- 안경 — eyeglasses
- 염려하다 — to worry; 염려 마세요. "Don't worry."
- -이내(에) — within (time)

❖ 입다/쓰다/신다 or 벗다 : "TO PUT ON" or "TO TAKE OFF"

Putting on clothes is expressed by three different verbs in Korean.

Items	Put on	Take off
(1) For covering the body 양복 (a suit) 한복 (a Korean dress) 저고리 (a jacket) 바지 (trousers) 치마 (a skirt)	입다	벗다
(2) For wearing on the head or face 모자 (a hat) 안경 (glasses)	쓰다/써	
(3) For covering the feet 구두 (shoes) 양말 (socks)	신다	

CAUTION! All of the verbs above require the use -었 (as the marker of the completed aspect) to describe the state of "wearing something on."

무엇을 입었어요? — What is he wearing?
청색 양복을 입었어요. — He is wearing a blue suit.

연습 4. Describe how your classmates are dressed. The blank spaces will be filled by the names of the students in the class.

a. ______-가 무슨 옷을 입었어요?
b. ______-가 안경을 썼어요?
c. ______-가 모자를 썼습니까?
d. ______-가 저고리를 벗었습니까?
e. ______-가 무슨 구두를 신었습니까?
f. ______-가 늘 같은 옷을 입습니까?

❖ -는/-은/-을 것 같다 : "IT SEEMS..."

STEM + { 는 (Present) / 은 (Past/Completed) / 을 (Expected) } 것 같다 — I think... / It seems...

새 옷을 { 사는 / 산 / 살 } 것 같아요. — I think / It seems } { he *is buying* a new suit. / he *bought* a new suit. / he *will* buy a new suit. }

연습 5. What do you think they are doing? Describe what you think each person doing, by using -것 같다. The pictures may not be very clear as to what each person is doing, but you may use your imagination.

연습 6. What do you think they will do? Looking at the pictures above, describe what they will do next. Use your imagination.

연습 7. What do you think they have just done? Use the same procedures as in 연습 5 and 6.

연습 8. Listen to the conversation, and respond to the questions given below.

a. 무엇이 손님 마음에 들었습니까?
b. 그 물건이 손님한테 잘 맞습니까?
c. 어떻게 고쳐야 합니까?
d. 언제까지 고칠 수 있겠어요?

대화 3 (FRAME 3)

상점에서 돈을 낸다

점원: 다 됐습니다. 다른 거 필요하신 거 없으십니까?

카슨: 아, 여기 양말 두 켤레하고 선글라스 한 개도 주세요.
모두 얼맙니까?

점원: 예, 그러니까, 24만 7천원이 되겠습니다.

카슨: 수표 쓸 수 있죠? 여행자 수표인데.

점원: 그럼요. 여권 있으시죠?
자, 3천원, 거스름 돈입니다.
감사합니다. 상자에다 넣어 드릴까요?

카슨: 아뇨. 그냥 종이백에 넣어 주세요.

단어 공부 (*VOCABULARY STUDY*)

- 다 됐습니다. — It's all done. It's finished.
- 다르다/달라 — to be different; 다른 것 another one
  - A-가 B-하고 다르다. — A is different from B.
- -켤레 — a pair (of shoes or socks)

  This is a counter, as in 구두 한 켤레 "a pair of shoes," 양말 두 켤레 "two pairs of socks."
- 선글라스 — sun glasses
- -개 — a counter for small items
- 모두 — all together
- 그러니까 — so, therefore
- 거스름 / 거스름 돈 — change (coins and notes)
- 상자 — box
- -에 (다) — into

  The postposition -에(다) marks the location of the object, rather than the subject, of a sentence. EX) 내가 구두를 상자에다 넣었어요. "I put the shoes in a box."
- 그냥 — as is, just (without doing anything to it)
- 종이백 — paper bag

대화 4 (FRAME 4)

시장에 가는 길

영옥: 뭐 하니?
소연: 아무 것도 안해.
영옥: 날씨 좋은데, 어디 갈래?
소연: 글쎄, 어디 갈까?
영옥: 동네 시장 갈래? 재미 있어.
소연: 나 살 거 없어. 돈도 없고.
영옥: 나 돈 좀 있어. 맛 있는 거 사 먹자.
소연: 그래, 그럼 오늘은 니가 돈 내라.
영옥: 염려 마. 내가 살께.

단어 공부 (*VOCABULARY STUDY*)

- 아무 것도 안 해. — I'm doing nothing.

CAUTION! The phrase, 아무 + (NOMINAL) + 도 "any (noun)" is always followed by a negative verb.

- 갈래? — Do you want to go?

The colloquial ending 을래 "to want to…" is used to ask or state someone's intention. This blunt form is more common in conversation than its more formal counterpart -겠다.

- 재미(가) 있다 — to be interesting; 재미 "fun"
- 맛(이) 있다 — to be tasty (맛=taste) ; 맛(이) 있는 거 "something tasty"
- 사 먹다 — buy and eat

CAUTION! Note that the connective used here is -어 rather than -고. In other words, you do not say here 사고 먹다. The connective -어 is used when two verbs share the common object.

- 니가 Ⓛ — a colloquial form of 네가 "you"
- 돈(을) 내다/내 — to pay

The verb 내다/내 means "to hand over, issue, put forward." The blunt ending here is -어라, indicating a request.

❖ 아무도/아무 것도 없다 : "THERE IS NOBODY/NOTHING"

The phrase 아무 + noun + 도, followed by a negative verb expresses a total negation, as in 아무 것도 없어요. "I have nothing." or 아무 데도 안 갔어요. "I didn't go to any place."

CAUTION! When no noun is used in this phrase (아무도), it means "no one," as in 아무도 없어요. "No one is here."

연습 9. Respond to the questions with a total negative.

EXAMPLE: 뭐 샀어요?	What did you buy?
아무 것도 안샀어요.	I didn't buy anything.

a. 시장에서 뭐 사 먹었어요?
b. 거기서 누구 만났어요?
c. 무엇이 필요해요?
d. 어제 어디 갔었어요?
e. 종이백에 무엇이 있어요?
f. 무엇이 재미 있었어요?

연습 10. The postposition -에다 marks a place where the object of a sentence is directed, but the last syllable 다 is optional. The following sentences are all complete since the use of -다 is optional. However, for practice, insert 다 wherever applicable.

a. 상자 안에 _____ 무엇이 있습니까?
b. 상자 안에 _____ 양말 한 켤레 넣었어요.
c. 집에 _____ 전화 했습니까?
d. 집에 _____ 아무도 없었어요.

❖ -어 있어요: STATE OF BEING AFTER AN ACTION

You have already learned that the state of being after completion of an action is expressed simply by -었 (marking the completed aspect). The same is also expressed by -어 있다 with some intransitive and passive verbs.

박 선생 여기 와 있어요.	Mr. Pak has come. (He is here.)
미스 리 저기 앉아 있어요.	Miss Lee is sitting there. (She is seated.)
가게 열려 있습니다.	The door is open. (It is left open.)
커피 돼 있어요.	The coffee is done. (It is ready.)

연습 11. Respond to the questions affirmatively, using -어 있다.

EXAMPLE: 커피 됐습니까?	Is the coffee done?
돼 있어요.	It's ready.

a. 은행이 닫혔어요?
b. 저기 누가 섰어요?
c. 일이 많이 밀렸어요?
d. 방이 비었습니까?
e. 미스 김 아직 누워 있어요?
f. 상점이 지금 열렸을까요?

문법 (GRAMMAR)

1. Degrees of Confidence in Conjectures

There are several verb forms that express one's conjecture in Korean, and you have learned two basic forms so far; one using -겠다 and the other using -을 것이다. The combining -겠 and -지요 makes the conjecture a little weaker. They differ from one another in the degree of confidence with which the speaker makes a conjecture. For convenience, we will distinguish three degrees of confidence; "strong," "mild," and "weak."

•STRONG :	날씨가	좋을 겁니다.	*I'm sure* the weather will be nice.
•MILD :		좋겠어요.	*I think* the weather will be nice.
•WEAK :		좋겠지요.	*I guess* the weather will be nice.

The new form introduced in this lesson -을 것 같다 belongs to the MILD type. A detailed explanation for it will be found immediately in the next section.

•MILD : 날씨가 좋을 것 같아요. *I think* the weather will be nice.

CAUTION! The English translations above should not be read to the letter. They are given here only to give you some idea about the notion of "degrees" of confidence.

2. Asking or Stating One's Conjecture: -것 같다

Guessing is not restricted to the *future* event. You can guess what may be the case *now*, or might have been the case in the past. With the first three forms, the future and present are not distinguished, but only the past (what *might have been* the case) is marked by the tense marker -었. For example,

날씨가 좋겠어요.	I guess the weather *is* nice. / I guess the weather *will be* nice.
날씨가 좋았겠어요.	I guess the weather *was* nice.

However, the new form -것 같다 has a different way of marking the tense; -것 is preceded by one of the three prenominal endings (는/은 or 을).

날씨가 좋을 것 같아요.	I think the weather *will be* nice.
날씨가 좋았던것 같아요.	I think the weather *was* nice.

The literal meaning of 같다 is "be the same as," but in this form it means "be like..." Any nominal may be used with the verb 같다 in this sense.

저 분, 김 선생 같아요. She seems like Miss Kim.

3. Three Sets of Prenominal Endings

There are two basic sets of such endings; one for action and process verbs and the other for stative verbs. The third set is an irregular one for the verb 있다/계시다.

ACTION VERBS	STATIVE VERBS (& -이다/아니다)	EXISTENCE VERBS (있다/계시다)	
-는	-은	-는	→ Present/Generic
-은	-던	-던	→ Past/Completed
-을	-을	-을	→ Future/Expected

a. Action Verbs

중국말을 { 배우는 / 배운 / 배울 } 것 같습니다.

It seems she *is studying* Chinese.
It seems she *studied* Chinese.
It seems she *will study* Chinese.

b. Stative Verbs (and -이다/아니다)

{ 지금 바쁜 / 그때 바쁘던 / 내일 바쁠 } 것 같아요.

I think she *is* busy now.
I think she *was* busy then.
I think she *will be* busy tomorrow.

{ 학생인 / 학생이었던 } 것 같아요.

It seems she *is* a student.
It seems she *was* a student.

c. For the Existence Verb (있다/계시다)

집에 { 있는 / 있던 / 있을 } 것 같아요.

It seems she *is* home.
It seems she *was* home.
It seems she *will be* home.

- NEGATION: The negative may be freely incorporated either in the modifier clause or in the final verb. However, the short negative 안- is not used in the final verb.
  집에 없는 것 같아요. — It seems she is *not* home.
  집에 있는것 같지 않아요. — It does *not* seem she is home.
  (WRONG: 있는 것 안 같아요.)

4. The Result of an Action: -어 있다

Certain verbs are used to express a condition resulting from an action as often as these verbs are used to express an *action* itself. You have already learned how to use such verbs in two different ways. For example,

(1) Taking a posture *(action)* : 앉았어요. — I sat down.
(2) Being in a posture *(condition)* : 앉았어요. — I am seated.

The suffix -었 in (1) above marks the past tense while the one in (2) marks the resultant condition of the action. Therefore, the intended meaning can become ambiguous, and it is determined only by the context. However, there is another structure available for exclusive expression of the resultant condition, which may be used to avoid ambiguity.

STEM + 어 있다	to be in a particular condition resulting from the action

The verbs to be used in this structure are generally limited to intransitive verbs of movement and posture such as 가다 "go," 앉다 "sit," etc., and passive verbs such as 열리다 "be opened," 닫히다 "be closed," etc.

• POSTURE VERBS

앉다	to sit	앉아 있어요.	He is seated.
서다	to stand	서 있어요.	He is standing.
눕다	to lie down	누워 있어요.	He is lying.

• MOVEMENT VERBS

가다	to go	거기 가 있어요.	He went and is there.
오다	to come	여기 와 있어요.	He came and is here.

• PASSIVE VERBS

열리다	to be open	문이 열려 있어요.	The door is open.
닫히다	to be closed	문이 닫혀 있어요.	The door is closed.

• OTHERS

차다	to be filled	방이 차 있어요.	The room is full.
비다	to become empty	방이 비어 있어요.	The room is empty.
깨다	to wake up	깨 있어요.	He is awake.

5. Clarification and Restatement of the Topic: -말/말씀이다

A conversation does not always proceed with the smooth giving and taking of information between participants. Breakdowns of communication may often occur, and they require clarification, confirmation or restatement of what was meant. In this lesson, you will learn one common way in Korean of establishing the common reference point between the conversation participants.

NOUN REFERRED + { 말 / 말씀 } 이다	... is what I mean.

어느 스웨터 말씀입니까?	Which sweater do you mean, sir?
베이지 색 스웨터 말입니다.	I mean the beige sweater.
정 선생 말이야?	Do you mean Mr. Chung?
그래, 그 사람 말이야.	Yeah, I mean him.

6. The Irreqular H Verbs

The irregular H verbs are all STATIVE verbs, and their stems are all two or more syllables in length.

어떻다	to be how/somehow	하얗다	to be white
이렇다	to be like this/so	까맣다	to be black
그렇다	to be like that/so	빨갛다	to be red

저렇다	to be like that/so	노랗다	to be yellow
		누렇다	to be tan
		파랗다	to be blue/green

CAUTION! Not all verbs whose stems end in ㅎ are irregular. For example, the following verbs never drop ㅎ in spelling.

좋다	to be good	놓다	to place/put down
		넣다	to insert/put in

In the Vocabulary Summary section, the conjugation of the irregular H verbs are shown in three different forms, as in 하얗다/하얀/하얘. This means that:

	Example	
(a) ㅎ is retained, if a consonant follows:	하얗습니다	하얗고
(b) ㅎ is dropped, if the vowel 으 follows:	하야면	하야니까
(c) the stem and 어 are fused in ...애:	하얘요	하얬어요

7. Location of the Object: -에다/한테다

The place of the object to be directed or located is marked by the particle 다 added to the postposition -에/한테.

구두를 상자에다 넣어 주세요.	Put the shoes in a box, please.
수표를 어디(에)다 놓았어요?	Where did you put the check?
편지를 누구한테다 썼어요?	Whom did you write a letter to?
엽서를 누나한테다 보냈어요.	I sent a postcard to my sister.

NOTE: The use of the extra syllable 다, however, is not absolutely necessary because it is freely dropped without any loss of clarity.

8. A Summary of Sentence Endings

Verb endings used to conclude sentences are summarized below. The honorific forms are not shown here.

a. Sentence Endings Used in Different Moods

	HIGH/MID	LOW
•GENERAL (used in all moods)	-어요.	-어.
•GENERAL (tag questions, etc.)	-지요.	-지.
•QUESTION/STATEMENT (of intention)	-을래요.	-을래.

b. Sentence Endings Used in Specific Moods

•Declarative	-ㅂ/습니다.	-ㄴ/는다.
•Interrogative	-ㅂ/습니까?	-니?
•Asking Opinion	-을까요?	-을까?
•Imperative	-으십시오.	-어라.
•Suggestive	-으십시다.	-자.
•Exclamatory	-네요.	-네.
	-은/는데요.	-은/는데.

읽기 · 쓰기 (READING & WRITING)

1. Bargain Sale Season : 대매출의 시즌

The end of the year (연말) and the coming of the new year (새해 or 신년) along with Christmas (크리스마스 or 성탄) are one of the most festive times, and people exchange gifts at this time. Shopwindows are filled with signs and merchandise (상품), and all stores have big bargain sales to attract shoppers.

Here is a typical greeting expression from the advertisement below : 새해에 복 많이 받으세요 "Happy New Year." Literally, it means "May You Be Blessed with Lots of Luck." The advertisement below also contains three groups of items: those for household (가정용품), those for women (여성용품), and those for men (남성용품). The suffix -품 means "merchandise."

새해 복 많이 받으세요.

안성 백화점

지난해 성원해 주신 고객 여러분들께
진심으로 감사드립니다.
올해에도 더욱 건강하세요.

인기 상품 안내

가정용품

- 밍크 이불 · 전기 담요 · 각종 비타민
- 커피 · 비프저키 · 다이어트 식품 일체
- 각종 슬리퍼 및 실내 화이블, 침대 커버
- 수예품 일절 · 카펫 · 도자기 및 동양화 · 커피세트
- 주발 세트 · 문갑 세트 및 고가구 · 백자 그릇 · 병풍

여성용품

- 각종 화장품 · 고급 핸드백 · 지갑 · 열쇠고리
- 고급 선글라스 · 이태리산 가죽 자켓
- 각종 액세서리 · 속옷 일체 · 각종 블라우스
- 앙고라스웨터 · 자켓 · 파카 만년필

남성용품

- 유명 브렌드 넥타이 · 벨트 · 고급 지갑 · 속옷일체
- 양말 · 고급 면도기

단어 소개

-께	honorific form of -에게 or -한테
올해	this year (금년)
건강하다	to be healthy
인기-	popular
화장품	cosmetic items
속옷	underwear
유명-	famous
고급-	high quality

연습 12. For each category of merchandise advertised above, write down four items that you recognize in Hangul and in English. Note that many items are English loan words.

가정용품: a. ________ c. ________
b. ________ d. ________

여성용품: a. ________ c. ________
b. ________ d. ________

남성용품: a. ________ c. ________
b. ________ d. ________

연습 13. Read the lines below, and guess what type of merchandise/service is being advertised. For your answer, check one of the four categories below.

시원한 여름 세계로 초대합니다.

여름에 더욱 편안한 스타일
여름에 더욱 시원한 스타일

☐ 화장품 (cosmetics)
☐ 식료품 (grocery items)
☐ 수영복 (swimming suits)
☐ 음식점 (restaurants)

2. Formal Honorific Postpositions

In general, postpositions do not change their forms whether or not the given nominal is honorific. 선생님 (honorific form) normally takes the subject postposition -이 like any other plain nominal. However, there are two special postpositions that make the given expression even more honorific. We will call such expressions "formal honorific" for convenience. The first is the subject postposition -께서 (Lesson 14), and the second is the dative postposition ("to" or "for") -께.

	Plain	Honorific	Formal Honorific
Nominative	김 선생이	김 선생님이	김 선생님께서
Dative	김 선생 {한테 / 에게}	김 선생님 {한테 / 에게}	김 선생님께

연습 14. Complete the following paragraphs by filling in the blank spaces with the words listed on the right. Then give the gist of each completed paragraph in English. Note that there are more words listed than the number of blank spaces.

a. 연말에 어머님 _____ 선물로 _____ 스웨터를 하나 사 드렸다. 어머님 _____ 새해에 예순 둘이 되시는데 아주 _____ 하시다.

•고급	•멋진
•-께	•-께서
•건강	•외출

b. 나는 아침에 일어나면 먼저 음악을 들으면서 _____과 같이 커피를 한 잔 한다. 그리고 남편이 _____ 하면 _____을 하고 _____을 한다.

•남편	•아내
•목욕	•화장
•출근	•퇴근

c. 오늘 뜻밖에 남편한테서 선물로 _____을 받았다. 나는 _____과 _____이 더 필요한데 _____들은 그런 것을 잘 모르니까 할 수 없다.

•가정용품	•양말
•남자	•여자
•화장품	•속옷

연습 15. Each set of words below share a common Sino-Korean word builder. Find the common element and guess its meaning.

			Sino-Korean	*Meaning*
a.	외출	going out	外	_____
	외국	foreign country		_____
	해외	oversea		_____
b.	출발	departure	出	_____
	출근	going out to work		_____
	외출	going out		
c.	화장품	cosmetics	化粧	_____
	화장실	rest room		
d.	305호실	Room #305	室	_____
	특실	first class car		_____
	일반실	general class car		_____
e.	상점	store (generic)	店	_____
	음식점	restaurant		_____
	매점	concession shop		_____
	백화점	department store		_____

단어 정리 (VOCABULARY SUMMARY)

Nominals

거울	mirror	안경	eyeglasses
고급	high class	양복	suit (Western style)
구두	shoes	양말	socks
모자	hat	연말	the end of a year
물건	articles, merchandise	올해	this year (= 금년)
상품	merchandise	인기	popularity
색	color	진열창	shopwindow
새해/신년	new year	종이백	paper bag
선글라스	sun glasses	지난해	last year
속옷	underwear (속=inside)	화장품	cosmetic items

Color Nouns (Personalized Vocabulary)

갈색	brown	분홍색	pink
남색	dark blue	청색	blue
녹색	green	회색	grey
보라색	purple		

Action Verbs

갈다/가는/갈아	to change	보이다	to show, let see
고치다	to repair, alter, fix	수선하다 / 수선해	to repair, fix
내다 (돈을)	to pay (money); to hand over, put forward	쓰다/써	to wear (a hat, glasses)
		신다/신어	to wear (shoes, socks)
벗다	to take off (clothes, hats, shoes, etc.)	염려하다	to worry
		입다	to wear (clothes)

Process Verbs

되다/돼	to be done, become ready
맞다	to fit; A-가 B-에 맞다. *A* fits *B*.
마음에 들다	to become fond of; A-가 B-의 마음에 들다. *B* becomes fond of *A*.

Stative Verbs

까맣다/까만/까매	to be black	길다/긴/길어	to be long
노랗다/노란/노래	to be yellow	짧다	to be short
누렇다/누런/누래	to be tan	재미가 있다	to be interesting
빨갛다/빨간/빨개	to be red	맛이 있다	to be tasty
파랗다/파란/파래	to be blue/green	건강하다	to be healthy
하얗다/하얀/하얘	to be white	유명하다	to be famous

Adverbs

곧	immediately, soon (= 바로)
그냥	as is, just (without doing anything to it)
다시	again
모두	all (together)

Counters

(native numeral)+켤레	pairs (of shoes or socks)
(native numeral)+개	pieces (of small tangible items)

Others

-께	to, for
(Stem)+ 는/은/던/을 것 같다.	It seems...
(Stem)+ 는 동안에	while...
(Stem)+ 말/말씀이다.	I/you mean...
(Stem)+ 을래	to want to...
(Stem)+ 어 있다	to be...ed (resultant condition)

Idioms

새해에 복 많이 받으세요!	Happy New Year!

연습문제 해답 (ANSWERS TO EXERCISES)

연습 8. (Scripts and Answers)

A: 어느 것이 마음에 드세요?
B: 이 파란 치마가 좋을 것 같은데 조금 길지 않아요?
A: 조금만 짧게 고쳐 드리죠. 앉아계세요. 기다리시는 동안에 고쳐 드리겠습니다.

a. 파란 치마가 마음에 들었습니다.
b. 조금 길어요.
c. 짧게 고쳐야 합니다.
d. 기다리는 동안에 고칠 수 있어요.

연습 9. a. 아무 것도 안사먹었어요. b. 아무도 만나지 않았어요. c. 아무 것도 필요없어요. d. 아무 데도 안 갔었어요. e. 아무 것도 안 들었어요. f. 아무 것도 재미없었어요.

연습 10. a. ϕ b. -에다 c. -에다 d. ϕ

연습 11. a. 닫혀 있어요. b. 친구가 서 있어요. c. 밀려 있어요. d. 비어 있어요. e. 누워 있습니다. f. 열려 있을 겁니다.

연습 13. 수영복

연습 14. a. 어머님께 - 고급 스웨터를 - 어머님께서 - 건강하시다
I bought an expensive sweater for my mother as a year-end gift. Mother

will be 62 in the new year, but she is very healthy.

b. 남편과 - 출근하면 - 목욕을 - 화장을

As I get up in the morning, I have coffee with my husband while listening to music. Then, after my husband goes to work, I take a bath and do my make-up.

c. 속옷을 - 양말과 - 화장품이 - 남자들은

I unexpectedly received underwear as a gift from my husband. What I really needed are some stockings and some cosmetics, but it can't be helped since men don't know what women need.

Exercise 15. a. 외(外) "out" c. 화장(化粧) "make-up"
b. 출(出) "come out" d. 실(室) "room" e. 점(店) "store"

Communicative Exchanges in English

Frame 1. Going into a Store

Salesman : Please come right in, sir. What can I help you with?
Carson : Could you show me that pair of pants - the ones in the shopwindow?
Salesman : Do you mean brown pants, sir?
Carson : No, I mean the grey ones next to those.
Salesman : Try them on, sir. I'm sure you will like them.
Carson : Where do I change?
Salesman : Over on this side is a fitting room.
Carson : I see.

Frame 2. Trying on a Pair of Pants

Salesman : They fit you well. Look in the mirror here, please.
Carson : They seem a little big.
Salesman : I'll make them a little shorter for you.
Carson : Can it be done right away? I can't come back, you know.
Salesman : Yes, please be seated for a minute. I'll fix them right away. While I fix them, you could check out our merchandise. On that side, there are shoes, socks, hats, glasses — a lot of nice items.
Carson : Well, why not. Could you make it fast?
Salesman : Don't worry, sir. It'll be done in fifteen minutes.

Frame 3. Paying at the Store

Clerk : All ready, sir. Anything else that you need?
Carson : Oh, I'll take two pairs of socks and a pair of sunglasses here. How much are they all together?
Clerk : O.K., so, it comes to 247,000 won.
Carson : I can use a check, I suppose? It's a traveler's check.
Clerk : Surely. You have your passport with you, don't you? Here you are, 3,000 won is the change. Thank you very much, sir. Shall I put them in a box?
Carson : No, just put them in a paper bag, please.

Frame 4. Going to the Market for Shopping

Yong'ok : What are you doing?
Soyon : Nothing.

Yong'ok	:	The weather is nice; do you want to go somewhere?
Soyon	:	Well, where shall we go?
Yong'ok	:	Do you want to go to the neighborhood market? It will be fun.
Soyon	:	I don't have anything to buy. I don't have any money either.
Yong'ok	:	I have some. Let's buy and eat something tasty.
Soyon	:	O.K. Then, you pay today.
Yong'ok	:	Don't worry. I'll buy.

제 18 과

서울 시외 구경

대화 1(FRAME 1)

강화도에 가는 이야기

문 : 오늘은 날씨가 좋은데 시외 구경 하실래요?

카슨: 그거 좋은 생각인데요. 서울 부근에 하루로 갔다 올 수 있는 데가 좋겠지요?

문 : 수원 어때요? 가보신 일 있어요?

카슨: 아, 수원은 지난번 한국에 왔을 때 갔었어요.

문 : 그럼, 강화도는요?

카슨: 아니오. 거긴 가 본 일 없어요. 여기서 얼마나 멉니까?

문 : 서쪽으로 차로 한 시간쯤 갑니다. 서해 바다에 있는 큰 섬이에요.

카슨: 섬이에요? 배를 타고 건너 갑니까?

문 : 아니오. 다리가 있어요. 육지에서 가까워요.

단어 공부 (*VOCABULARY STUDY*)

- 날씨 — weather (=일기)
- 시외 — outside of a city, outskirts (시=city, 외=outside) (antonym : 시내)

- 부근 — vicinity, proximity(=가까운 데)
- -은 일이 있어요? — Have you ever... ed? (See Grammar.)
- 지난번 — last time (지난=past, -번=time, occasion)
- 한국에 왔을 때 — when I came to Korea
- 서쪽으로 — to the west; 서 "west"
- 서해 — the Western Sea (=Yellow Sea)
- 바다 — ocean, sea
- 섬 — island
- 배 — boat, ship
- 건너가다 — to go across; 건너다 "to cross"
- 다리 — bridge
- 육지 — land

연습 1. You are now situated in Seoul. Ask your partner in what directions these places are found? (동쪽 east, 서쪽 west, 남쪽 south, 북쪽 north)

MODEL: 만주가 어느 쪽에 있어요?
북쪽에 있습니다.

a. 부산은···
b. 중국은···
c. 일본은···
d. 북경은···
e. 평양은···
f. 동해 바다는···

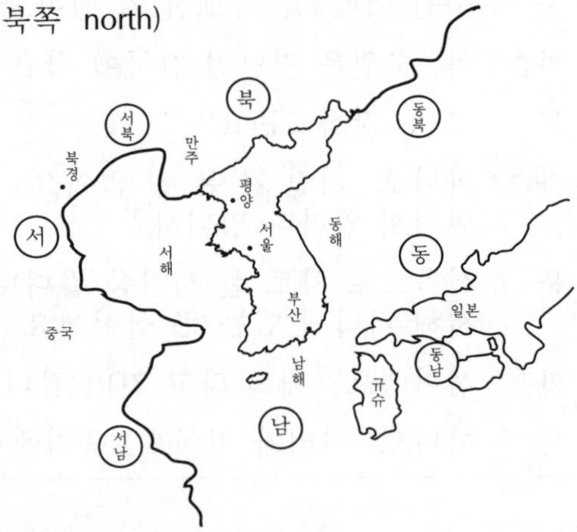

❖ STEM + (었)을 때: "WHEN ONE WAS/DID ..."

The past marker 었 is used in the time clause when the event in the main clause took place clearly *after the completion* of the verb in the time clause. Otherwise, 었 is not normally used even if the clause expresses a past time.

한국에 <u>갔을 때</u> 미스 김을 만났어요. When I went to Korea, I met Miss Kim.
(Going to Korea was PRIOR TO meeting Miss Kim.)

연습 2. Respond to the questions using the time clause with -때. You may choose any one of the suggested phrases or make up one.

EXAMPLE: 김 선생 언제 집에 있었어요?
내가 전화했을 때 집에 있었어요.

a. 언제 그 옷을 샀어요?
b. 언제 안경을 씁니까?
c. 언제 음악을 들어요?

- 공부할 때
- 한국에 갔을 때
- 어머니하고 백화점에 갔을 때

d. 언제 한국말을 배웠어요?
e. 언제 영어를 배웠어요?
f. 그 때 문이 열렸었어요?

- 학교 다닐 때
- 책 읽을 때
- 상점에 갔을 때

❖ -은 일이 있다: ONE'S EXPERIENCE IN THE PAST

STEM + 은 일이 있다

Literally, this phrase means "there is a past event in which..." The English equivalent is the verb phrase "have + past participle," expressing one's experience in the past.

This construction is commonly combined with the form -어 보다.

STEM + 어 본 일이 있다

한국 음식 잡숴 보신 일이 있으세요?	Have you eaten Korean food?
그 사람 바다를 본일이 없습니다.	He has never seen the sea.

연습 3. Respond factually to the follwing questions.

a. 제주도에 가본 일이 있어요?
b. 서울에 간 일이 있습니까?
c. 일본 음식을 먹어 본일 있습니까?
d. 온돌방에서 자 본 일이 있어요?
e. 비행기 타 본 일 있습니까?
f. 골프 쳐 본 일이 있습니까?

연습 4. Say the following sentences in Korean.

a. Have you been to Hawaii?
b. Can you make a day trip there?
c. If you go across the bridge, it will probably take 30 minutes.
d. I went there by boat when I took a trip to the island in 1992.
e. I like to see the outskirts of the city today, since we already saw the city.

연습 5. Guess what it means

동문서답 is a Chinese phrase, and it literally means "Eastern question, and western answer." Guess what it means from the context.

대화 2 (FRAME 2)

시골길을 간다.

카슨 : 좀 천천히 가시죠. 경치도 즐기면서.

문 : 여기서 좀 쉬었다 갈까요?
고단하시죠? 꽤 많이 걸었어요. 우리.

카슨 : 네, 그러세요. 다리가 좀 아픈데요.

문 : 저기 소나무 밑에 앉으십시다.

카슨 : 네… 시골 경치가 참 아름다운데요.
오면서 산에 보라색 꽃을 많이 봤는데
무슨 꽃입니까?

문 : 진달래 꽃이에요. 봄에 가장 먼저 피지요.
예쁘죠?

카슨 : 네, 정말 예뻐요.

단어 공부 (*VOCABULARY STUDY*)

- 천천히 — slowly, leisurely (antonym: 빨리)
- 즐기다 — to enjoy
- -으면서 — while...

CAUTION! The connective -으면서 is used only to connect two simultaneous actions by one subject.

- 쉬었다 가십시다. — Let's have a rest before proceeding.

NOTE: The conjuntive -었다(가) denotes a tentative action (of "resting", here) while proceeding with the main action of walking. The additional particle -가 is optional. The two verbs so connected usually have a sense of reversal or opposite meanings. For example, you have had the same connective in:

갔다 오다 — to go and come back
왔다 가다 — to come and leave

- 걷다/걸어 — to walk

The consonant ㄷ changes to ㄹ when a vowel follows, like 묻다/물어 "to ask"

CAUTION! Unlike its English counterpart "walk", 걷다 cannot be used with a destination phrase (such as Nominal + 에). If the destination is implied, the verb 걷다 should be in a compound form: 걸어 가다, or 걸어 오다.

- 다리 — leg (다리 also means "bridge.")
- 아프다/아파 — to be painful (stative verb)
- 소나무 — pine tree
- 시골 — countryside, rural area

•아름답다/아름다워	to be beautiful, graceful
•산	mountain, hill
•꽃	flower
•진달래	azalea (Common in hills and fields in Korea)
•가장	most (adverb) (= 제일)
•먼저	earlier, prior to others, first (adverb)
•피다	to bloom, blossom

연습 6. Name a kind of flower that bloom in each season, and then describe the color of the flower.

MODEL: 가을에는 무슨 꽃이 펴요?
국화가 핍니다.
국화가 무슨 색입니까?
국화는 노랗습니다.

봄	spring
여름	summer
가을	autumn
겨울	winter

FLOWERS IN SEASONS

봄에 피는 꽃 →	벚꽃	cherry blossom
	진달래	azalea
	개나리	golden bell flower
여름에 피는 꽃 →	무궁화	hibiscus (Korean national flower)
	장미	rose
가을에 피는 꽃 →	국화	chrysanthemum

연습 7. Answer the following questions in Korean.

a. 걷는 것 좋아합니까?
b. 많이 걸으면 어디가 아파요?
c. 무슨 꽃을 좋아해요?
d. 이 부근에 소나무가 있습니까?
e. 진달래꽃을 본 일이 있어요?
f. 겨울에 피는 꽃이 있습니까?

대화 3 (FRAME 3)

날씨 이야기

카슨 : 아이구, 갑자기 하늘이 흐리네요.
비는 안 오겠지요? 우산 안 가지고 왔는데.

문 : 글쎄요. 비 안 오겠지요.

카슨 : 오늘 일기 예보 보셨어요?

문 : 라디오에서 오후는 갠다고 했어요.

카슨 : 그럼 괜찮겠지요.

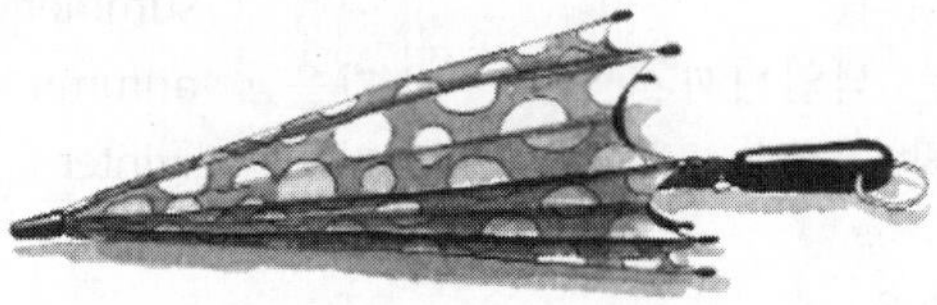

단어 공부 (*VOCABULARY STUDY*)

- 아이구 — Oh my! My Goodness!
- 갑자기 — suddenly
- 하늘 — sky, the heavens; heaven
- 흐리다 — to become cloudy(process verb)
- 비 — rain; 비가 오다 "to rain"
- 우산 — umbrella

  The verb 쓰다 is used in describing the action of holding up an umbrella over one's head.
- 가지다 — to have, possess
- 예보 — forecast
- 라디오 — radio
- 개다/개 — to become clear (process verb)
- 갠다고 했어요. — They said that it will clear up.

  A declarative sentence quoted always ends with the blunt formal ending -(ㄴ/는)다.

갠다고 했어요.	They said that it would be clear.
날씨가 좋다고 합니다.	He says that the weather is fine.
밥 먹는다고 합니다.	He says that he is eating.

❖ USES OF THE VERB 가지다 "TO HAVE"

The verb 가지다 means "to take (something) into possession." It usually implies physical possession rather than abstract possession. The verb is used in the following sentence constructions:

(A-가 B-를 가지다) A takes B into possession.
(A-가 B-를 가졌다= A-가 B-를 가지고 있다) *A* has *B*.

작은 차를 가지고 싶어요.	I want to have a small car.
사전 가졌어요?	Do you have a dictionary?

The verb 가지다 is also used in compound forms with 가다 or 오다 to mean "carry/take along/bring something."

A-가 B-를 가지고 가다=*A* takes *B* along.
A-가 B-를 가지고 오다=*A* brings *B* (to some place).

카메라 가지고 왔어요?	Did you bring a camera with you?
여권을 가지고 가야 해요.	You should carry your passport with you.

연습 8. Ask your partner what he/she would like to have among the things shown below. Use the verb 가지다.

연습 9. The following conversations involve quoting the weather reports in various areas. Write in English the gist of each report.

	AREA	WHEN	CONDITION	WHEN	CONDITION
a.	서울				
b.	부산				
c.	대구				
d.	광주				

연습 10. Convert the following sentences into quotation forms: - 고 합니다.

a. 날씨가 덥습니다.
b. 춥고 비가 옵니다.
c. 내일부터 일기가 좋겠습니다.
d. 비는 안 와요.
e. 일찌기 떠나야 합니다.
f. 일기 예보를 못들었어요.

대화 4 (FRAME 4)

감기때문에 결근하다

인규: 창식이 오늘 못봤는데 회사에 안 나왔었니?
상일: 결근했어. 아침에 결근한다고 전화 왔었어.
인규: 왜 결근한다고 그래?
상일: 몸이 안 좋다고 해. 감기라고 들었어.
인규: 그거 안됐네. 요새 일기가 나빠서
감기 드는 사람 많지. 조심해야 해.

단어 공부 (*VOCABULARY STUDY*)

- 회사 — company, business firm; office, work
- 결근하다 — to be absent (from work) (결=miss, 근=work)

CAUTION! To be absent in school or a meeting is 결석하다. Both 결근하다 and 결석하다 requires the use of 었 to describe the state of being absent at a given time.

임 형은 오늘 결근했어요. — Mr. Yim is absent today.

- 몸 — body; health; 몸이 안 좋다 "to feel sick, be in bad health"
- 감기 — cold (sickness)

A-가 감기가 들다 — *A* catches a cold.

- ...라고 들었어. — I heard that ...

In a quoted sentence, the verb -이다/ 아니다 takes the ending -라.

- 그거 안 됐네 — That's too bad. (an expression of sympathy)

The polite counterpart is 안 됐습니다.

- 나쁘다/나빠 — to be bad (antonym: 좋다)

❖ -이라고/아니라고 한다: "ONE SAYS IT IS/IT IS NOT..."

The equation verb -이다/아니다 is an exception to the general rule; the ending is -라 rather than -다 in a quoted sentence(when 었 or 겠 is not present).

감기입니다 — It's a cold.
감기<u>라고 합니다.</u> — He <u>says it's</u> a cold.
학생이 아니<u>라고 해요.</u> — She <u>says she isn't</u> a student.

비는 안 올 것입니다. — It probably won't rain.

비는 안 올 것이라고 합니다. — They say it probably won't rain.

연습 11. Convert the following sentences into quotation forms.

a. 저 꽃은 진달래입니다.
b. 개나리가 아니예요.
c. 그때 저는 학생이었어요.
d. 비가 올 겁니다.
e. 오늘은 결근 할 것입니다.
f. 아무것도 아닙니다.

A SUMMARY OF QUOTABLE DECLARATIVE FORMS

a. For ALL CASES with the exceptions noted below (b and c)		→ add 다
b. For ACTION or PROCESS VERBS (without 었/겠)	• If the stem ends in a vowel	→ add ㄴ다
	• If the stem ends in a consonant	→ add 는다
c. For -이다/아니다 (without 었/겠)		→ add 라

연습 12. Convert the following sentences into quotation forms.

a. 가 본 일이 있어요.
b. 몸이 좀 아파요.
c. 매일 아침 걸어요.
d. 국화꽃은 가을에 핍니다.
e. 이른 봄이었습니다.
f. 일기 예보 들었어요.
g. 다리를 건너 갔습니다.
h. 갔다오겠습니다.

연습 13. Describe the rural scene, paying attention to landmarks in the picture below.

문법 (GRAMMAR)

1. How to Quote a Statement

When a sentence is quoted within another, the quoted sentence is generally converted to a "blunt" form (shown in the next section). In this lesson, you will learn how to quote a *declarative sentence,* which changes its ending to –다 (with exceptions to be noted below), regardless of what the original utterance actually ended with (polite or blunt). A particle 고 is normally attached to the quoted sentence. This particle is occasionally absent, however. The quoting verb is most commonly 하다 or 그러다, but other verbs may be used.

QUOTED SENTENCE	QUOTING VERB
STEM + (ㄴ/는)다고	하다 그러다 듣다 etc.

집에 간다고 합니다.	He says that he is going home.
날씨가 좋겠다고 그래요.	He says the weather will be fine.
거기 비가 온다고 들었어요.	I heard that it is raining there.

- Occasionally, the quoting verb (say) may be abbreviated (especially when the quotation is repeated).

간다고요?	Did you say that he is going?

- Asking someone to quote a statement takes the following form:

무엇이라고 합니까?	What did he say?

- The word-for-word quotation is not normally used in conversation, but, when it is done as in story-telling, -라고 하다 is used.

"갑니다" 라고 했습니다.	He said, "I am going."

2. Blunt Declarative Forms Used in Quotation

The quotable blunt forms are like the dictionary form; simply add the ending -다, with two notable exceptions.

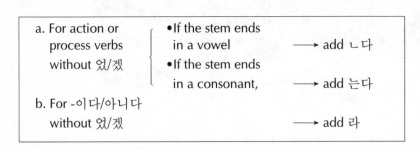

			Example
a. For action or process verbs without 었/겠	• If the stem ends in a vowel	→ add ㄴ다	한다 간다
	• If the stem ends in a consonant,	→ add 는다	먹는다 읽는다
b. For -이다/아니다 without 었/겠		→ add 라	학생이라 아니라

Example

- Action/Process Verbs:

먹는다 / 일한다 / 일했다 / 일하겠다 } 고 합니다.	He says that he is eating. / He says that he is working. / He says that he worked. / He says that he will work.

먹는다 } 고 합니다. — He says that he is eating.
일한다 — He says that he is working.
일했다 — He says that he worked.
일하겠다 — He says that he will work.

- Stative Verbs and 있다/없다

좋다 } 고 합니다. — He says that it is good.
좋았다 — He says that it was good.
좋겠다 — He says that it will be good.
돈이 있다 — He says that he has money.
돈이 있었다 — He says that he had money.
돈이 있겠다 — He says that he probably will have money.

- The Equation Verb (-이다/아니다)

학생이라 } 고 합니다. — He says that he is a student.
학생이었다 — He says that he was a student.
학생이겠다 — He says that he probably is a student.

3. Tenses in Quoted Sentences

Unlike English, the tense of the quoted sentence in Korean does not have to agree with the main (quoting) verb. It remains in the same tense as in its original utterance (as in the direct quotation).

Original Utterance	Quotation
갑니다	간다고 했습니다.
I *will* go.	He said he would go.

The quoting verb ("say") for the *third person* is commonly left tenseless (if it is recent and relevant to the present) unless a specific time phrase (e.g., yesterday) is mentioned or implied in its context.

바쁘다고 합니다.	He says he is busy.
바쁘다고 어제 말했습니다.	He said yesterday he was busy.

However, the *first* or *second* person subject always requires the marking of the real time; 었 if it denotes the past time.

바쁘다고 하셨어요.	You said you were busy.
내가 바쁘다고 했어요.	I said I was busy.

4. The Time Clause: -(었)을 때(에)

The noun 때 "time/occasion" has been used so far with a prenominal modifier as in 그 때 "at that time." It may also be modified by a clause to form a time clause roughly equivalent to "when···" or "at the time when···"

VERB STEM + (었)을 때 (에)	(at the time) when···
공부할 때 사전 씁니까?	Do you use a dictionary when you study?
일본에 있을 때 일본말을 조금 배웠어요.	When I was in Japan, I learned Japanese a little.
작년에 여기 왔을 때 그것을 배웠어요.	I learned it when I came here last year.

❖ -었 IN THE TIME CLAUSE

In most cases, the time clause with -을때 does not require the use of 었 even if the event expressed in it was in the past. This is because the tense of the time clause is determined by the tense of the main clause.

목이 마를 때 맥주 마셨어요.	When we were thirsty, we drank beer.

CAUTION! However, when the time clause expresses a state after the completion of an action, the use of 었 is required.

지난번 한국에 왔을때 수원에 갔어요.	When I came to Korea last, I went to Suwon.
그것이 끝났을 때는 열 시였어요.	When that was finished, it was ten.

❖ POSTPOSITIONS IN TIME CLAUSES

After 때, the postposition -에 is not normally used except for an emphasis, because the succession of two very similar vowels (애 and 에) tends to cancel out the last vowel.

대학에 있을 <u>때에</u> 영어를 배웠어요. (EMPHASIS)	I learned English when I was in college.

The time phrases meaning "until···" and "since···" may be expressed by the use of the postpositions -까지 and -부터.

일이 끝날 때<u>까지</u> 기다릴 수 있어요?	Can you wait until the work is finished?
졸업했을 때<u>부터</u> 일을 했습니다.	I have worked since I graduated from school.

5. Simultaneous Actions: -으면서

When the same person does two actions simultaneously, the connective -으면서 is used to conjoin the two verbs (or clauses). No tense marker is normally used with -으면서.

밥을 먹으면서 얘기 했어요.	We talked while we ate.
음악 들으면서 숙제를 했습니다.	I did my homework as I listened to music.
아침 먹으면서 보통 신문을 읽어요.	I usually read the newspaper while I eat breakfast.
학교에 다니면서 여러가지 일을 했지요.	While attending school I did various kinds of jobs.

CAUTION! Remember that there should be only *one subject* (singular or plural) when two actions are connected by –으면서.

•SECONDARY USAGE: This connective is sometimes used in the sense of "in spite of···" or "even though," but the basic meaning of "one subject doing two actions" should remain in this usage.

알면서 나한테 말 안했어요.	He didn't tell me even though he knew.

6. Expressing Experience or Precedence: –은 일이 있다

You have already learned how to express one's experience with the verb of 보다 (Lesson 15).

강화도 가 봤습니까?	Have you been to Kanghwado?

There is another structure that expresses one's experience or a precedence. The noun 일 used here means "occasion" or "event," and the construction literally means "There is an event where..."

VERB STEM + 은 일이 { 있다 / 없다 }	There was/wasn't an occasion in which··· (= have ···ed)

유 선생은 결근한 일이 없어요.	Mr. Yu has never been absent.
우리 동생 만난 일이 있습니까?	Have you met my brother?
회사에 늦은 일이 없습니다.	I have never been late to work.

STEM + 어 본 일이 { 있다 / 없다 }	This construction is commonly used in conjunction with the verb 보다.

한국에 가 본 일이 있어요?	Have you been to Korea?
일본 음식을 먹어 본 일이 없어요.	I've never eaten Japanese food.

STEM + 는 일이 { 있다 / 없다 }	GENERALIZED STATEMENT: The prenominal ending –는 (generic) may be used in place of -은 (past) to make a general statement on occurrences or non-occurrences.

신 선생은 늦는 일이 있어요.	There are times when Mr. Shin is late.
미스 조는 여기 오는 일 없습니다.	Miss Cho never comes here.
가을에는 여기 비가 오는 일이 없어요.	It never rains in the fall here.

7. A Summary of Irregular Verbs

Irregular verbs in Korean are those whose stems change in writing. Their changes in stems are determined mostly by the first sound of the suffixes. Korean irregular verbs come in several groups, rather than many individually irregular verbs as in English. In the Vocabulary Summary section, most irregular verbs are represented by:

DICTIONARY FORM/ IRREGULAR FORM(S). For example,

어렵다/어려워	to be different
하얗다/하얀/하얘	to be white

Two or three forms for such verbs are shown to represent one basic form (DICTIONARY FORM) and one or more irregular shapes that given verbs may take. You must, of course, know when the irregular shapes occur. All shapes of irregular verbs, *except* the L VERBS (explained in Lesson 14), are determined by how a given suffix starts. Here is a simple test you may want to give.

(1) Does it start with a consonant?	If yes, there is no change.
(2) Does it start with 으?	If yes, the stem usually has the last sound modified.
(3) Does it start with 어?	If yes, the stem often has the last sound modified.

❖ Below is an overview of Korean irregular verbs with the three types of suffixes that determine their shapes. The C type is any suffix starting with a consonant; the 으 type is any suffix starting with 으; and the 어 type is any suffix starting with 어.

	TYPES OF SUFFIXES		
IRREGULAR VERBS	C TYPE	으 TYPE	어 TYPE
(1) 하다/되다	no change	no change	해/돼
(2) LL verbs: 모르다	no change	no change	몰라
(3) U verbs: 바쁘다	no change	no change	바빠
(4) H verbs: 그렇다	no change	그러면	그래
(5) S verbs: 짓다	no change	지으면	지어
(6) P verbs: 춥다	no change	추우면	추워
(7) T verbs: 걷다	no change	걸으면	걸어
(8) L verbs: 살다	•If the first consonant is ㄴ, ㅅ, or ㅂ, drop ㄹ Example: 산, 사는, 사세요, 삽니다 •Otherwise, keep ㄹ (but drop 으). Example: 살고, 살지, 살면, 살러, 살어 (살 + 을) ⟶ 살		

읽기 · 쓰기 (READING & WRITING)

1. Weather Expressions: 날씨에 관한 표현

The Korean expression for "weather" comes in pairs, like so many other terms; one in native Korean and another in Sino-Korean: e. g, 일기 [Sino-Korean], and 날씨 [native Korean]. They are interchangeable in most situations. The list below are some basic weather terms, most of which you have already learned.

비가 오다/와	to rain	날씨가 개다/개	to become clear
눈이 오다/와	to snow	날씨가 흐리다/흐려	to become cloudy
안개가 끼다/끼어	to become foggy	바람이 불다/불어	to be windy
춥다/추워	to be cold	덥다/더워	to be hot

NOTE: The three verbs, 끼다, 개다, 흐리다, are process verbs, which require the completion marker 었 to describe a particular state of being. For example, 날씨가 갰습니다. "It is clear/fine."

연습 14. Scan the weather report below, and answer the questions.

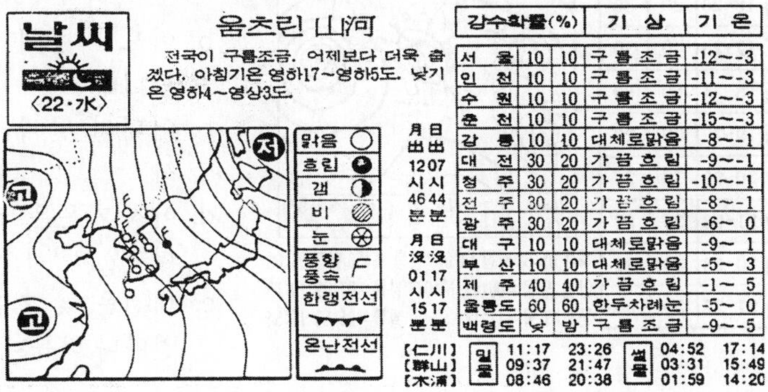
날씨 〈22·水〉

움츠린 山河

전국이 구름조금. 어제보다 더욱 춥겠다. 아침기온 영하17~영하5도. 낮기온 영하4~영상3도.

月出 12시46분 日出 07시44분
月沒 01시15분 日沒 17시17분

	강수확률(%)		기 상	기 온
서 울	10	10	구름조금	-12~-3
인 천	10	10	구름조금	-11~-3
수 원	10	10	구름조금	-12~-3
춘 천	10	10	구름조금	-15~-3
강 릉	10	10	대체로맑음	-8~-1
대 전	30	20	가끔흐림	-9~-1
청 주	30	20	가끔흐림	-10~-1
전 주	30	20	가끔흐림	-8~-1
광 주	30	20	가끔흐림	-6~ 0
대 구	10	10	대체로맑음	-9~ 1
부 산	10	10	대체로맑음	-5~ 3
제 주	40	40	가끔흐림	-1~ 5
울릉도	60	60	한두차례눈	-5~ 0
백령도	낮	밤	구름조금	-9~-5

	밀물		썰물	
【仁川】	11:17	23:26	04:52	17:14
【群山】	09:37	21:47	03:31	15:49
【木浦】	08:46	20:38	01:59	14:20

단어 소개

전국	the entire nation	구름	clouds
기온	temperature	영하	below zero
영상	above zero	-도	degree
대체로	generally	가끔	occasionally
맑다	to be clear, 맑음 (noun)		

a. Write the gist of the nationwide weather forecast in English.

____

____

b. 서울은 구름이 조금 낀다고 합니다. 인천은 어떻겠습니까?
c. 대전은 가끔 흐리겠다고 하는데, 청주는 어떻겠다고 합니까?
d. 대구는 대체로 맑겠다고 하는데, 부산은 어떻겠다고 합니까?
e. 울릉도에는 눈이 오겠다고 하는데, 백령도에는 눈이 오겠습니까?
f. 서울은 기온이 몇도까지 내려가겠습니까?
g. 어느 도시가 제일 춥겠습니까?
h. 내일 기온이 영하로 내려가지 않는 곳이 있습니까?

2. A Sentence ending: -음

In some styles of writing (such as listing or itemizing), verbs often take the ending -음, as in 맑음 "being clear." The ending -음 is a nominalizer (similar to -기) to form a noun. The vowel 으 of 음 is deleted when another vowel precedes it, as in 흐림 "being cloudy." Note more examples below.

연습 15. This is a weather forecast in the summer. Scan it and answer the questions, based on the forecast.

지역	기온	비올확률% 낮	밤
서울	19~27	30	30
인천	19~26	30	30
수원	20~27	30	30
백령	20~25		
대전	20~29	30	20
청주	20~29	30	20
춘천	18~26	30	30
강릉	17~23	40	30
울릉	18~24	60	60
전주	19~29	30	20
광주	20~29	30	20
제주	21~28	30	20
대구	20~28	30	30
부산	21~27	30	30

곳에따라 소나기

날씨 <27일> 전국적으로 흐리고 곳에 따라 소나기가 오겠다. 강원 영동 지방은 비가 온 뒤 점차 개겠음. 아침기온 17~21도, 낮기온 23~29도.

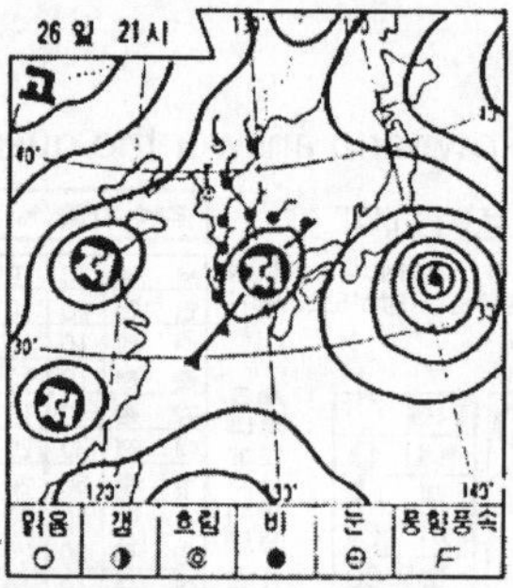

해뜸 05:58 해짐 19:07 달뜸 15:56 달짐 01:06
인천:밀물=00:43 13:04 썰물=07:09 19:13
군산:밀물=11:14 썰물=05:50 17:54

단어 소개

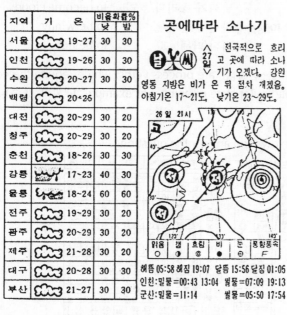

곳에 따라	depending on the place
소나기	shower
지방	area, district

a. 날씨가 전국적으로 어떻겠다고 합니까?

b. 어느 지방에 비가 오겠다고 합니까?

c. 어디의 날씨가 제일 덥습니까?

d. 아침 기온은 몇도까지 내려갑니까?

e. 대전은 낮 기온과 밤 기온이 얼마나 다릅니까?

연습 16. Study on the advertisement, and answer the following questions.

a. What advertisement is this for?

b. The noun form of color verbs appears here. How is it formed?

우산·비옷·가방·장화

비오는 날

비오는 날엔 화려하게 꾸며야 귀엽다.
비옷도 노랑·빨강으로, 우산도 파랑·노랑으로...

연습 17. Complete the following paragraphs by filling in the blank spaces with the words listed on the right. Then, give the gist of each completed paragraph in English. Note that there are more words listed than the numbers of blank spaces.

a. 이 지방은 작년보다 날씨가 추운것 같다.
밤______이 벌써______로 내려가고 아침에는
______가 끼고______이 많이 분다.

기온, 영상, 영하
안개, 바람, 눈

b. 오늘은 몸이 좀 아파서 일찍 ______했다.
내일은 ______해서 집에서 ______쉬고 싶다.
벌써 겨울이니까 ______에 조심해야 하겠다.

결근, 출근, 퇴근
건강, 외출, 편안하게

c. 아버님______는 ______으로 여행하실______이다.
요즈음 그 ______은 날씨가 덥고 비가 자주
오니까 ______을 아버님______ 사 드려야겠다.

-께, 께서, 우산
지방, 예정, 동해안

단어 정리 (VOCABULARY SUMMARY)

Nominals

가을	autumn	예보	forecast
감기	cold (sickness)	우산	umbrella
겨울	winter	육지	land, landmass
꽃	flower	일기	weather (=날씨)
다리	leg; bridge	지난번	last time (occasion)
배	boat, ship	진달래	azalea (bush)
몸	body; health	하늘	sky, the heavens ; heaven
바다	sea, ocean		
부근	vicinity, proximity	회사	company; workplace
비	rain	기온	temperature
산	mountain, hill	-도	degree (suffix)
서해	Western Sea	전국	the entire nation
섬	island	영상	above zero
소나무	pine tree	영하	below zero
시골	rural area, countryside	소나기	shower
시외	outskirts of a city	지방	area, district

Directional Words

동	east	남	south
서	west	북	north

Personalized Vocabulary

강	river	만	bay
고속 도로	highway, speedway	바닷가	beach
논	rice field	밭	cultivated field
들	field, open field	숲	woods, grove
마을	village	절	Buddhist temple

Action Verbs

가지고 오다	to bring	결근하다	to be absent (from work)
건너 가다	to go across	결석하다	to be absent (from school)
걷다/걸어	to walk	즐기다	to enjoy

Process Verbs

개다/개	to become clear	구름이 끼다	to become cloudy
감기가 들다/들어	to catch a cold	바람이 불다	to be windy
비가 오다	to rain	안개가 끼다	to become foggy
흐리다	to become cloudy	맑다	to be clear
피다	to bloom, blossom	눈이 오다	to snow

Stative Verbs

나쁘다/나빠	to be bad
맑다	to be clear
아름답다/아름다워	to be graceful, beautiful
아프다/아파	to be painful

Adverbs

가장	most (=제일)	가끔	occasionally
먼저	early, first	곳에 따라	depending on the place
천천히	slowly	대체로	generally

Idioms

안 됐네. Ⓛ That's too bad. (an expression of sympathy)

연습문제 해답 (ANSWERS TO EXERCISES)

연습 1. a. 부산은 남쪽에 있습니다.
b. 중국은 서쪽에 있습니다.
c. 일본은 동쪽에 있습니다.
d. 북경은 서북쪽에 있습니다.
e. 평양은 북쪽에 있습니다.
f. 동해바다는 동쪽에 있습니다.

연습 4. a. 하와이 가 본 일 있어요?
b. 하루로 거기 갔다 올 수 있어요?
c. 다리를 건너가면 30분쯤 걸릴 겁니다.
d. 1992년에 그 섬에 갔을 때 배로 갔어요.
e. 시내는 봤으니까 오늘은 시외를 구경하고 싶어요.

연습 5. 동문서답 means "giving an irrelevant answer."

연습 9.(Script) a. 서울은 아침에 흐리고 오후에는 비가 온다고 합니다.
b. 부산지방은 오전에 흐렸다가 오후에는 개겠다고 합니다.
c. 대구는 내일 아침에 비가 오고 오후에 갤 것이라고 합니다.
d. 광주는 오늘밤 흐리고 춥지만 내일은 비가 조금 오겠다고 합니다.

(Answers) a. morning: cloudy; afternoon: rainy
b. morning: cloudy; afternoon: clear
c. tomorrow morning: rainy; afternoon: clear

d. tonight: cloudy and cold; tomorrow: rainy

연습 10. a. 날씨가 덥다고 합니다.
b. 춥고 비가 온다고 해요.
c. 내일부터 일기가 좋겠다고 해요.
d. 비는 안 온다고 합니다..
e. 일찌기 떠나야 한다고 합니다.
f. 일기 예보를 못들었다고 합니다.

연습 11. a. 저 꽃은 진달래라고 해요.
b. 개나리가 아니라고 합니다.
c. 그때 학생이었다고 합니다.
d. 비가 올거라고 해요.
e. 오늘은 결근할 것이라고 해요.
f. 아무것도 아니라고 해요.

연습 12. a. 가본 일이 있다고 해요.
b. 몸이 좀 아프다고 합니다.
c. 매일 아침 걷는다고 합니다.
d. 국화꽃은 가을에 핀다고 합니다.
e. 이른 봄이었다고 합니다.
f. 일기예보 들었다고 합니다.
g. 다리를 건너 갔다고 합니다.
h. 갔다 오겠다고 해요.

연습 14. a. Slightly cloudy nationwide; Will be colder than yesterday.
b. 조금 구름이 끼겠습니다.
c. 거기도 가끔 흐리겠습니다.
d. 대체로 맑겠습니다.
e. 아니오. 눈이 안 올 것입니다.
f. 영하 12도까지
g. 춘천
h. 없습니다.

연습 15. a. 전국적으로 흐리겠다고 합니다.
b. 강원 영동지방
c. 대전, 청주, 전주, 광주
d. 17도까지
e. 9도

연습 16. a. For rainwear.
b. The consonant ㅇ replaces the ㅎ of color verbs, as in 빨갛다 ⟶ 빨강, etc.

연습 17. a. 기온이 - 영하로 - 안개가 - 바람이
The weather in this area seems colder than last year.
The temperature at night already goes down below zero, and in the morning it gets foggy and windy.
b. 퇴근 - 결근 - 편안하게 - 건강
I didn't feel well today, so I went home early. I will stay home and rest comfortably tomorrow. It's already winter, and I'll have to be careful about my health.
c. 아버님께서는 - 동해안으로 - 예정이다 - 그 지방은 - 우산을 - 아버님께
Father is planning to go to the east coast. I think I will buy my father an umbrella since it is hot and it rains a lot in that area.

Communicetive Frames in English

Frame 1. Going to Kanghwado

Mun : The weather is nice today. Would you like to go sightseeing to the outskirts of the city?
Carson : That's a good idea. Somewhere near Seoul where we can make one day-trip would be nice, wouldn't it?
Mun : How about Suwon? Have you ever been there?
Carson : Ah, I have been there, when I was in Korea last time.
Mun : Then, how about Kanghwado?
Carson : I haven't been there. How far is it from here?
Mun : You go about one hour by car. It's a big island in the Western Sea.

Carson : An island? Do you go across by boat?
Mun : No, there is a bridge. It's close to the land.

Frame 2. Going through the Countryside

Carson : Let's go a little slower while enjoying the scenery.
Mun : Shall we take a rest here before proceeding?
Tired, aren't you? We have walked quite a lot.
Carson : Yes, let's do that. My legs hurt a little.
Mun : Let's sit down under that pine tree.
Carson : Sure. The rural scenery is quite a sight.
On the way up, I saw many pink flowers; what kind of flowers are they?
Mun : They are azaleas. They bloom earliest in spring. Pretty, aren't they?
Carson : Yes, they are, really.

Frame 3. Talking about the Weather

Carson : Oh, the sky gets cloudy suddenly. I hope it won't rain.
We didn't bring umbrellas.
Mun : Well, I don't think it will rain.
Carson : Did you read today's weather forecast?
Mun : It said over the radio that it will clear up in the afternoon.
Carson : Well, then, it probably will be all right.

Frame 4. A Cold Prevents Him from Going to Work

Inkyu : I haven't seen Changsik today. Didn't he come to work today?
Sangil : He is absent. He called in the morning to say that he would be absent.
Inkyu : Why did he say he would be absent?
Sangil : He says he wasn't feeling well. I heard that he's got a cold.
Inkyu : That's too bad. The weather has been bad lately, so there
are a lot of people ill with a cold. We should be careful.

제 19 과

고속 도로에서

대화 1 (FRAME 1)

고속 도로를 달린다

문	: 돌아 갈 때는 제가 운전하죠.
카슨	: 운전하실 줄 아세요?
문	: 그럼요. 카터 선생만큼 잘 하지는 못하지만요. 피곤하시지 않으세요?
카슨	: 괜찮아요. 저 이 정도 운전은 아무것도 아닙니다.
문	: 그럼 그러세요. 하지만 언제라도 피곤하시면 말씀하세요.
카슨	: 네. 그저 방향과 도로 표지만 잘 봐 주세요.

단어 공부 (*VOCABULARY STUDY*)

• 달리다 — to run; drive (a car)

CAUTION! Like 걷다 "to walk," the verb 달리다 is not used with a destination phrase (어디로). If a destination is mentioned or implied, the compound form 달려가다 or 달려 오다 must be used.

• 운전하실 줄 아세요? — Do you know how to drive? (=운전할 수 있어요?)

The phrasal form -을 줄 알다 means "to know how to," but it is interchangeable with -을 수 있다.

•카터 선생만큼 — as well as Mr. Carter

-만큼 ("as") is a postposition marking a nominal used for comparison. (See Grammar.)

•잘(은) 못해도 — even though I can't do it well

-어도 is a connective meaning "even though," "even if," "although."

•안전히 — safely

•이 정도 — this much, to this extent (정도=degree)

•하지만 — however (=그렇지만, 그러나)

•언제라도 — any time, whenever (used normally in an affirmative sentence)

Question word + 이라도 "any..."

누구라도	anybody	무엇이라도	anything
어디라도	anywhere	어디서라도	at any place
무슨 일이라도	any kind of work		

•피곤하다 — to be tired (=고단하다)

•방향 — direction (orientation)

•-과/와 — and (=하고)

This is a formal or written counterpart to -하고. The latter is more common in conversation. After a consonant, -과 is used, and after a vowel -와.

•도로 표지 — road sign (도로=road, 표지=sign)

연습 1. Respond factually in Korean.

a. 자동차 운전할 줄 압니까?
b. 컴퓨터 쓸 줄 알아요?
c. 영어 할 줄 알아요?
d. 자전거 탈 줄 압니까?
e. 도로 표지 읽을 줄 아세요?
f. 골프 칠 줄 모르세요?

연습 2. Respond to the questions, using a comparative phrase with -만큼 from the list on your right or making up one on your own.

EXAMPLE: 오늘 일기가 어떻습니까? — How is the weather today?
어제만큼 좋지 않습니다. — It's not as good as yesterday.

a. 운전 잘 합니까?
b. 자주 결석해요?
c. 여기 비가 많이 옵니까?
d. 내일 바쁘겠어요?
e. 한국말이 어렵습니까?

•친구만큼
•미국만큼
•서울역만큼
•선생님만큼
•일본말만큼
•오늘만큼

연습 3. Restate each of the following sentences by placing an appropriate clause with -어도 (even though) from the list.

EXAMPLE: 그 사람 안 왔어요. — She didn't show up.
기다려도 그 사람 안 왔어요. — She didn't show up even though I waited.

a. 영어 좀 합니다 •잘은 못해도
b. 다섯 시까지 공항에 가야해요. •자동차가 있어도
c. 이것은 살 수 없어요. •늦어도
d. 저 사람은 늘 걸어 다닙니다. •가고 싶어도
e. 거기 갈 시간이 없습니다. •돈이 있어도

대화 2 (FRAME 2)

교통 순찰차가 지나간다

카슨: 무슨 소리가 들리지 않아요?
문 : 아, 순찰차가 오네요. 빨간 불 켜고.
카슨: 우리때문에 오는 거 아니겠죠?
문 : 아닐 거예요. 우리 빨리 안 달렸어요. 무슨 급한 일 있는 모양이죠.
카슨: 아, 그냥 지나가네요. 아이구, 전 제가 뭘 잘못한 줄 알았어요.
문 : 겁이 많으신데요. 어디서 사고가 난 모양입니다.

단어 공부 (*VOCABULARY STUDY*)

•소리	sound, noise
•들리다	to be heard, audible (passive form of 듣다 "to hear")
•순찰차	highway patrol car; 순찰 "patrol"
•켜다/켜	to light (a lamp)
•급하다	to be urgent
•있는 모양이죠.	I guess there is...

Prenominal ending + 모양이다: "It appears/seems..." (See Grammar.)

•지나다/지나	to pass by

•잘못하다 — to do something wrong, make a mistake

잘못 may be prefixed to any action verb to express "making a mistake in doing something." For example, 잘못 가다 to go a wrong way
잘못 듣다 to hear something wrong.

•잘못한 줄 알았어요. — I thought I did something wrong.

Prenominal ending + 줄 알다 : "to think/believe that..." The verb 알다 has several meanings, and in this construction it means "to assume." (See Grammar.)

CAUTION! The phrase -줄 알다 has a few different meanings. The expression for "know how to" (Frame 1) is always preceded by the ending -을, while the expression of assumption may have any prenominal ending (-는, -은, -을 or -던) to denote the tense of the dependent clause.

•겁 — fear, timidity

겁이 많다 means "to be timid, easily frightened."

•사고 — accident

사고가 나다 means "an accident happens." The verb 나다 means "to occur, happen, emerge."

연습 4. Looking at the pictures below, first, guess what each person is doing and then say it by using -모양이다.

EXAMPLE: 저 여자가 무엇을 하고 있어요?	What is she doing?
남자친구하고 얘기하는 모양입니다.	I guess she is talking with her boy friend.

연습 5. Looking at the pictures above, state the purpose of each activity.

EXAMPLE: 이 사람이 왜 신문을 보고 있습니까?	Why is he reading the newspaper?
좋은 식당을 찾으려고 신문보고 있어요.	He is reading it to find a good restaurant.

Suggested Phrases

•집에 보내려고	•점심 먹으려고	•책을 사려고
•자동차를 팔려고	•여자 친구 만나려고	•버스를 타려고

대화 3 (FRAME 3)

회사 동료 이야기

문 : 미스 양이 오늘 함께 가기로 했었는데 못나왔어요.

카슨 : 왜요? 같이 갔었으면 좋았을텐데.

문 : 운동하다가 발을 다친 모양이에요.

카슨 : 많이 다쳤나요?

문 : 아니오. 대단하지는 않다고 해요.
그러나 걷기가 불편한 모양입니다.

카슨 : 돌아가는 길에 같이 병문안 갈까요?

문 : 뭐, 병이라고는 할 수 있겠어요?
하지만, 원하신다면 들러 보십시다.

단어 공부 (*VOCABULARY STUDY*)

- 가기로 했었는데 — She was to come along, but...
  STEM + 기로 하다 means "to agree/decide to do something."
- 같이 갔었으면 좋았을텐데. — It would have been nice if she went along.
  The use of the past tense conditional form denotes a hypothetical statement contrary to the fact. (-을 텐데<을 터인데, -을 터이다=-을 것이다)
- 운동하다 — to take exercise ; 운동 "physical exercise"
  운동하다가 means "while taking exercise." (See Grammar).
- 발 — foot
- 다치다 — to hurt, get injured
- 대단하다 — to be serious (stative verb)
- 걷기 불편하다 — to be uncomfortable for walking
  STEM + 기 is a noun form derived from a verb. This form is often followed by a stative verb such as 쉽다 "be easy," 어렵다 "be difficult," 편하다 "be comfortable."
- 돌아가는 길에 — on one's way back
- 병문안 가다 — to inquire after someone (병=illness, 문안=inquiry after someone)
- 뭐 — but (interjection used in contradicting someone)
- 원하신다면 — if you wish
- 들르다/들러 — to stop by (on one's way to some place)

❖ PARTS OF BODY

Basic Terms

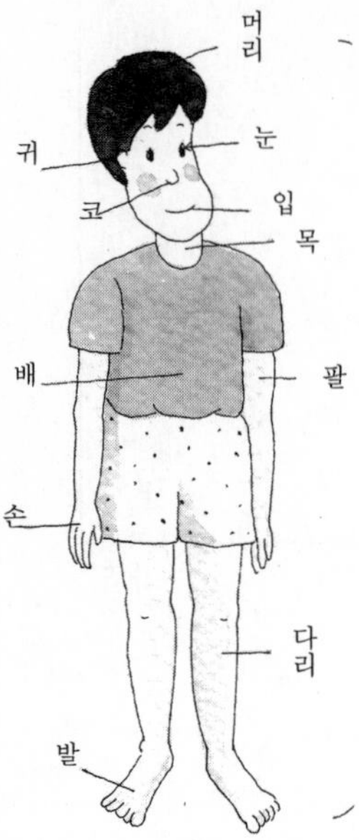

Personalized Vocabulary

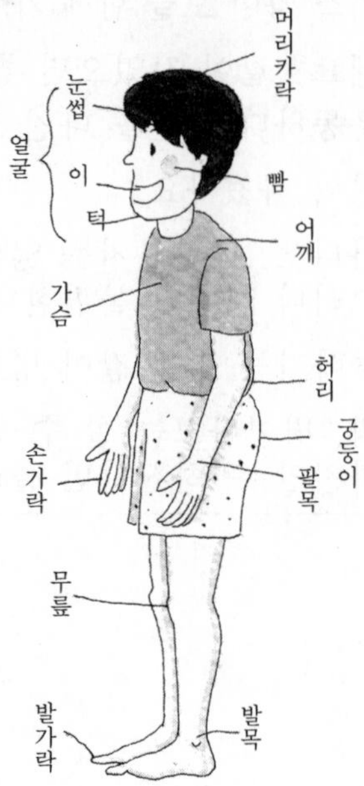

연습 6. Looking at the pictures above, respond to the questions.

a. 사람이 생각할 때 무엇을 씁니까?
b. 사람이 들을 때 무엇으로 듣습니까?
c. 많이 걸으면 어디가 아파요?
d. 말할 때 무엇으로 말해요?
e. 어디가 나쁘면 안경을 씁니까?
f. 구두나 양말은 어디에 신습니까?
g. 글을 쓸 때 무엇으로 써요?
h. 밥을 많이 먹으면 무엇이 불러요?
i. 무거운 물건을 들면 어디가 아파요?
j. 코끼리는 무엇이 깁니까?

연습 7. Ask your partner where he/she has a pain. Your partner will respond by pretending that he/she has a pain in an appropriate part of his/her body.

EXAMPLE:	어디가 아픕니까?	Where do you have a pain?
	머리가 아파요.	I have a headache.

연습 8. Listening to each conversation, write down the key points of information.

	The Location of Pain	The Reason for the Pain
a.	______________________	______________________
b.	______________________	______________________
c.	______________________	______________________
d.	______________________	______________________

대화 4 (FRAME 4)

병문안 전화

문: 여보세요.
양: 여보세요. 양미숙입니다.
문: 미숙 씨, 나야, 문상일.
양: 아, 상일 씨. 강화도 잘 갔다 왔어? 재미 있었어?
문: 응, 그런데 다친 발은 어때? 좀 나아?
양: 거의 다 나았어. 좋은 약을 발랐거든.
문: 우리 잠깐 들를게. 맛있는 과자 사가지고.
양: 그래. 기다릴게.

단어 공부 (*VOCABULARY STUDY*)

- 좀 나아? — Is it a little better?
- 낫다/나으면/나아 — to be better (stative verb); to get better, to recover (process verb)

낫다 is an irregular S verb, which drops ㅅ when followed by a vowel. In writing (the standard form), it drops ㅅ when followed by the vowel 으 of an ending, but the vowel 으 is retained: 낫 + 으면 ⟶ 나으면 (normally pronounced 나면).

- 거의 — almost
- 약 — medicine, drug
- 바르다/발라 — to apply, paste
- 들를게. — We will stop by.

The ending -을게 is another blunt ending expressing the speaker's promissory intention.

- 과자 — sweets, cookies, confectionary

연습 9. Have a short conversation with your partner about pains in some parts of the body, and how he/she got injured.

EXAMPLE: A: 어디가 아파요? — Where does it hurt?
B: 다리가 아파요. — I have a pain in the leg.
달리다가 다리를 다쳤어요. — I hurt my leg while running.

Suggested Sentences:
- 운동하다가 발을 다쳐서 발이 아픕니다.
- 감기가 들어서 머리가 아파요.
- 자동차 고치다가 손을 다쳤습니다.
- 짐을 트럭에 싣다가 어깨를 다쳤어요.

문법 (GRAMMAR)

1. Even though/even if: -어도

The connective -어도 is suffixed to a clause denoting "even if..." or "even though..."

돈이 있어도 살 수 없습니다.	You can't buy it, even if you have money.
어려워도 배울 수 있어요.	You can learn it, even though it is difficult.
늦어도 다섯 시까지 돌아오겠어요.	I'll be back by 5 at the latest (even if I'm late).

• Expressing Permission: The connective -어도 is used in a phrase that experesses one' s permission.

VERB STEM + 어도 좋다/괜찮다	One may...

들어 가도 좋습니까?	May I come in?
여기 앉아도 괜찮아요.	You may sit down here.
여기 차를 세워도 좋습니다.	It's all right to park the car here.
유리창 열어도 괜찮아요?	Is it O.K. if I open the window?

• Non-obligation: The connective -어도 is also used in negating an obligation. (An antonym of STEM + 어야 하다)

NEGATIVE ... + 어도 좋다	One does not have to... (Literally: It's all right if you don't...)

오래 기다려야 합니까?	Do I have to wait long?
아니오. 기다리지 않아도 좋아요.	No, you don't have to wait.

2. To Know How to : -을 줄 알다

The knowledge or skill for performing something is expressed in the following structure.

VERB STEM + 을 줄 {알다 / 모르다}	{One knows / One does not know} how to...

한글 읽을 줄 아세요?	Do you know how to read Han'gŭl?
컴퓨터 쓸 줄 몰라요.	He doesn't know how to use the computer.
우리 거기 갈 줄 압니다.	We know how to get there.
자동차 운전 할 줄 알았었는데.	I used to know how to drive a car.

CAUTION! The same phrase with the bound noun -줄 may be used in entirely different meanings. In Frame 2, you learned a sentence expressing a mistaken assumption.

뭐 잘못한 줄 알았어요. — I thought I did something wrong.

Note in this sentence, the prenominal ending was -은 (rather than -을). In the expression of "assumption," the prenominal ending (-는, -은, -을 or -던) denotes the time of the dependent clause. This and other related usages will be reintroduced later.

3. Expressing a Purpose or Intent: -으려고 (-을려고)

You have already learned how to state a purpose of going or coming using the connective -으러. But it is used only when the main verb is "come" or "go."

홍 선생님 만나러 왔습니다.	I came to see Mr. Hong.

In this lesson, you will learn a similar connective -으려고 that states a purpose, but it is not restricted to the cases where the main verb is 가다 or 오다. The standard (written) form -으려고 is generally spoken with an extra ㄹ (e.g., -을려고) in the Seoul dialect.

VERB STEM + { 으려고 (Written Form) / 을려고 (Spoken Form)	in order to...

무엇을 하려고 컴퓨터 샀어요?	What did you buy a computer for?
영어 공부하려고 영한사전 샀어요.	I bought an English-Korean dictionary in order to study English.
잠을 잘려고 불을 껐습니다.	I turned the light off to sleep.

CAUTION! The connective -으려고 cannot be used in request type of expressions. This is because in a request sentence, the intent of the subject is expressed in a different manner. In this case, the proper connective is -게:

잠을 자게 불을 꺼주세요.	Please turn off the light so that I may sleep.

❖ The connective -으려고 has another important usage: it may simply be followed by 하다 to express an intended or impending action.

VERB STEM + 으려고 하다	One is about to... One is going to... One tries to...

저 결혼 하려고 합니다.	I am going to get married.
비가 오려고 해요.	It is about to rain.
버스가 떠나려고 합니다.	The bus is about to depart.

Unlike -겠 which also expresses the intent, the phrasal form involving -으려고 may express the third person's intent as well as the intent in the past.

갈려고 했는데 못갔어요.	I intended to go, but I couldn't.
선생님한테 전화 하려고 했어요.	She was just about to call you.

CAUTION! The English verb "try" for the -으려고 structure should be used strictly in the sense of "attempting" (with or without success).

• The suffix -으려 is a verb suffix similar to -겠, and it is also commonly used in the form -을래 (Lesson 17) and in -으려고 or -을려면 (in this lesson).

4. Expressing Likelihood: -모양이다

The speaker's conjecture based on his/her observation of something is expressed by the construction below.

MODIFIER CLAUSE + 모양이다	It seems/appears...
사고가 난 모양이다.	Apparently there was an accident. (The scene appears to be so.)
비가 오는 모양입니다.	It looks like raining. (I hear the sounds of rain drops.)
고향이 부산인 모양이지요.	Apparently Pusan is his home town. (He speaks with a southern accent.)
미스 윤을 좋아하는 모양이에요.	He seems to like Miss Yun. (He pays special attention to her.)

CAUTION! The negative of this construction is always incorporated in the dependent clause. In other words, the phrase -모양이다 should always remain in the affirmative form.

비가 안 온 모양입니다.	It doesn't look like it rained. (It seems that it didn't rain.)

- Difference between -것 같다 and -모양이다: The constructions -것 같다 (Lesson 17) has a very similar meaning as -모양이다. Both translate into English "It seems," "It appears," "I think," etc., and they are often interchangeable. However, there is a subtle difference. The former is a simple conjecture, but the latter is a conjecture based on some observed fact. This difference comes from the word 모양이다, which implies that the speaker is using his/her observation as a basis of the conjecture.

5. While Doing Something...: -다(가)

While doing one thing, one may stop it and do something else, or something may happen before finishing the first action. The two actions (by *the same subject*) in the situations of this type are connected by -다(가)

VERB STEM + 다(가)	While ...ing (before completing it)
집에 가다가 문양을 만났어요.	I met Miss Mun on my way home.
책을 읽다 잠이 들었습니다.	I fell asleep while reading a book.
차가 가다가 갑자기 섰어요.	A car, while moving, suddenly stopped.

- In this particular usage, no tense marker is used with -다(가) regardless of the actual time referred to. However, the use of the *perfective* marker 었 with -다(가) has a different meaning, which does not have an English counterpart.

A + 었다(가)	B	Do *A*, and then *B*.

Implications: The action A is considered the opposite in nature of B.

저 갔다 오겠습니다.	I will be back. (go and come back)
어디 갔다 왔어요?	Where have you been? (went and returned)
쉬었다가 갑시다.	Let's have a rest before we resume. (rest and then go)

6. Decision, Agreement, or Arrangement: -기로

Something decided, agreed upon, or arranged is expressed in a noun clause with ending -기로.

VERB STEM + 기로 { 하다 / 되다	(Someone) decides/agrees to... It is arranged/agreed that...

The verbs, 하다 and 되다, may be considered an active-passive pair. While the verb 하다 denotes that someone (subject) makes a decision or arrangement, the verb 되다 simply expresses the end result, not the process.

무엇을 하기로 했어요?	What did you agree to do?
나 그것 안 사기로 했어요.	I decided not to buy it.
무엇 하기로 됐습니까?	What has been agreed (to do)?
우리는 기차로 가기로 됐어요.	We are to go by train.

- In place of 하다 or 되다, other verbs with more explicit meanings such as 약속하다 "to promise," 계획하다 "to plan," etc. may be used.

다시 안 하기로 약속했어요.	He promised not to do it again.

7. The Uses of STEM + 기

STEM + 기, a noun form, is commonly used as part of various constructions rather than being used freely as nouns. (Some nouns are formed with this ending as in 쓰기 "writing," 읽기 "reading," 말하기 "speaking," etc.) This structure is often used as a complement to a stative verb, as in the examples below.

꽃이 보기 좋습니다.	The flower looks beautiful. (It is pleasant to look at.)
음악이 듣기 좋은데요.	The music sounds nice. (It is pleasant to listen to.)
이 길은 걷기 불편해요.	This path is not comfortable to walk on.
한국말은 배우기 쉽습니다.	Korean is easy to learn.
나 저 사람 보기 싫어요.	I hate to see him.

8. To the Same Extent As: 만큼

-만큼 is a bound noun often used as a postposition marking a nominal phrase. It may be translated "as (well) as," where the adverb "well" may be replaced with a qualifying word in the main verb phrase. Since it is a bound noun, -만큼 is also preceded by a modifier as in 이만큼 "this much," or "to this extent."

오늘 일기는 어제만큼 좋지 않아요.	Today's weather is not as good as yesterday's.

버스도 기차만큼 편합니다.	A bus is as comfortable as a train.
저는 선생님만큼 많이 안먹었어요.	I didn't eat as much as you (ate).
이만큼 주세요.	Give me this much (=as much as this).

❖ GUESS WHAT IT MEANS: 어깨 넘어 공부

A: 우리 집사람 중국말 좀 합니다.

B: 그래요? 어디서 배우셨어요?

A: 배운 것 없어요. 남편이 배우니까 어깨 넘어 공부지요.

읽기 · 쓰기 (READING & WRITING)

1. Kanghwa Island: 강화도

Kanghwa Island is a historical (역사적) island situated in the northwest of Seoul. This large island abounds with historical remains (유적) reflecting its long history of resistance (항쟁) against foreign invasions. In the south of the island is the Mount Mani where a Buddhist temple (절), called 전등사, is located. The island is also famous for Kanghwa ginseng products and mushrooms.

Scan the travel guide below taken from a magazine, and follow through the exercises.

곳곳에 항쟁 유적

강화도는 서울 서북쪽으로 자동차로 약 한시간 되는 거리. 서울을 떠나 김포를 통해서 강화대교를 건너 섬으로 들어간다. 이 섬에는 가는 곳마다 외적에 대한 항쟁의 유적이 널려 있다.

▲ 드라이브 안내: 서울 - 김포 - 강화대교 (15Km) - 마니산 입구 - 강화읍 - 외포리 석모도 - 보문사.

▲ 대중교통: 서울 신촌 버스 터미널에서 마니산까지 가는 직행 버스가 있다. 강화에서는 외포리까지 가는 군내 버스를 이용.

▲ 볼만한 곳: 마니산, 보문사, 전등사 등.

▲ 별미: 외포리에 있는 돈대횟집. (☎ 0349-32-2833) 바다를 바라보면서 맛있는 회나 매운탕을 맛볼 수 있다.

▲ 특산품: 강화 인삼, 강화 영지버섯 등.

단어 소개

역사적	historical
유적	historical remains
거리	distance
-을 통해서	through
직행 버스	express bus (직행=going straight)
이용하다	to utilize, use
볼만한 곳	places worth seeing
절	Buddhist temple
-등	etc., and so forth

연습 10. Answer the following questions in Korean.

a. 서울에서 강화도까지의 거리가 얼마나 됩니까?
b. 본토(main land)에서 섬으로 어떻게 건너갑니까?
c. 마니산에 있는 절의 이름이 무엇입니까?
d. 서울에서 강화도에 가는 직행 버스는 어디서 떠납니까?

2. Local Specialty Food

Tasting the local specialty food is an important part of sightseeing trips in Korea. Scan the section with the heading 별미, which means literally "extraordinary taste."

연습 11. Find the meanings of the key words, using a dictionary.

a. 회 ____________ c. 바라보다 ____________
b. 매운탕 ____________ d. 맛보다 ____________

연습 12. Write in English the gist of the specialty food section.

____
____

3. Adjectival Suffix: -적

The suffix -적 is added to some Sino-Korean words to form prenominal adjectives. Adjectives formed in this manner denote "having the characteristics of..." This suffix is generally applied to a limited group of terms that are "modern," "abstract," or "scientific." See the examples below. Related adverbs are derived with the addition of the postposition -으로.

	PRENOMINAL ADJECTIVE	ADVERBIAL FORM
역사 history	역사적 historical	역사적으로 historically
지리 geography	지리적 geographic	지리적으로 geographically
정치 politics	정치적 political	정치적으로 politically
문화 culture	문화적 cultural	문화적으로 culturally
사회 society	사회적 social	사회적으로 socially
경제 economy	경제적 economical	경제적으로 economically
심리 psychology	심리적 psychological	심리적으로 psychologically
수학 mathematics	수학적 mathematical	수학적으로 mathematically

The suffix -적 is also applied to the names of countries and regions.

한국 Korea	한국적 of Korean	한국적으로 in a Korean way
동양 Asia	동양적 of Asian	동양적으로 in an Asian way
세계 world	세계적 of the world	세계적으로 world-wide

A prenominal with -적 may also be used as a stative verb with the equational verb -이다.

버스로 가는 것이 가장 경제적이다.	Taking a bus is the most economical.
한국적인 것은 시골에서 많이 찾을 수 있다.	One can find many things Korean in the countryside.

4. Connectives Often Used in Writing: -으며 and -어

In writing, simple connectives -으며 and -어 are often used in place of -고 and -어서, which are found more in conversation.

a. -(었/겠)으며: It is generally interchangeable with -고, and the tense/aspect marker may be used.

대체로 흐리며 오후에는 눈이 오겠다.
It will be generally cloudy, and it may snow in the afternoon.

b. -어: Mostly used in connecting sequential events with verbs of movement or posture (like-어서). No tense/aspect marker is used.

8시에 서울을 떠나 (<떠나아), 김포에 들러, 강화에는 10시에 도착했다.
We left Seoul at 8, stopped at Kimpo, and arrived at Kanghwa at 10.

연습 13. Complete the following paragraphs by filling in the blank spaces with the words listed on the right. Then give the gist of each completed paragraph in English.

a. 경주는 대구에서 동쪽으로 약 한 시간쯤 가는 _____ 에 있는데, 거기에는 가는 곳마다 _____ 적 유적이 많이 있다. 서울에서는 경주까지 _____ 버스를 _____ 하는 것이 가장 편할 것이다.

직행	역사
거리	경제
이용	유명

b. 내일 날씨는 _____ 으로 흐리고 오후에는 곳에 따라 _____ 가 오겠고, 동북지방은 _____ 이 영하로 내려가며 _____ 이 올 것이라고 한다.

눈	비
기온	바람
지리적	전국적

c. 8월 15일 고국을 _____ 한 정일순 교수는 신라 호텔에서 학생들을 만나, 한국 _____ 에 대해서 이야기하며 한국 학생들은 _____ 인 것을 다시 찾는 것이 _____ 하다고 말했다.

방문	중요
필요	문화
한국적	전국적

연습 14. Pretend that you had a trip to the Kanghwa Island (or any other place that you have visited recently), and write a letter about the trip to your friend. You may mix English words if you don't know enongh Korean words.

단어 정리 (VOCABULARY SUMMARY)

Nominals

겁	fear	손	hand
순찰차	highway patrol car	역사	history
거리	distance	유적	historical remains
귀	ear	약	medicine, drug
눈	eye	입	mouth
머리	head	절	Buddhist temple
문화	culture	정치	politics
문안	inquiry after (someone)	지리	geography
발	foot	직행 버스	express bus
방향	direction	팔	arm
병	illness	표지	sign
사고	accident	코	nose
소리	sound, noise		

Personalized Vocabulary

가슴	chest, breast	손목	wrist
머리카락	hair	얼굴	face
무릎	knee	이	tooth
발가락	toe	어깨	shoulder
발목	ankle	허리	waist; lower back
뺨	cheek	턱	chin
손가락	finger		

Action Verbs

나다/나	to happen, occur; to emerge; to be born
다치다	to get injured
달리다	to run; drive (a car)
들르다/들러	to stop by, stop over (on one's way to somewhere)
바르다/발라	to paste on, apply (medicine)
이용하다	to utilize
운동하다	to take exercise
잘못하다	to do something wrong, make a mistake
지나다	to pass by
켜다	to turn (a light) on; (antonym: 끄다 "to turn off")

Passive Verbs (Processive)

들리다	to be heard, audible (passive form of 듣다 "to hear")

Stative Verbs

급하다	to be urgent, pressing	볼만하다	to be worth seeing
대단하다	to be serious, grave	피곤하다	to be tired (=고단하다)
불편하다	to be inconvenient; uncomfortable		

Adverbs

거의	almost	언제라도	anytime
안전히	safely		

Bound Nouns

-만큼	to the extent, as... as	-등	etc.
-정도	degree, extent		

Connectives

그러나	however	-어	and (= -어서)
-다가	while...ing	-으며	and
-어도	even though, even if	하지만	however
-으려고	in order to...		

Phrasal Forms

-기로 하다	to decide to...	-은 줄 알다	to assume...
-모양이다	It seems...		
-을 줄 알다	to know how to...		

Postpositions

-과/와	and; with (=하고)

Others

-을 통해서	through	-적으로	in the manner of
-적	having the characteristics of		

연습문제 해답 (ANSWERS TO EXERCISES)

연습 6.
a. 머리를 씁니다.
b. 귀를 씁니다.
c. 다리가 아파요.
d. 입으로 말해요.
e. 눈이 나쁘면.
f. 발에 신습니다.
g. 손으로 씁니다.
h. 배가 부릅니다.
i. 팔이 아픕니다.
j. 코가 길어요.

연습 8.
a. (leg; exercise)
철수는 운동하다가 다리를 다쳤어요. 다리가 많이 아파요.
b. (headache; a cold)

영자는 오늘 머리가 아픕니다. 감기가 든 모양입니다.

c. (stomach; ate too much)
인수는 배가 아프다고 해요. 과자를 너무 많이 먹었어요.

d. (eyes; spent too many hours reading)
상일이는 어제 밤에 너무 오래 책을 읽어서 오늘 아침에는 눈이 아프다고 합니다.

연습 10. a. 자동차로 약 한 시간 b. 강화 대교로
c. 전등사 d. 신촌 버스 터미널

연습 11. a. raw fish b. spiced fish soup c. to view d. to taste

연습 12. At the restaurant at Wepori, one can enjoy a raw fish dish or spiced fish soup while viewing the ocean.

연습 13. a. <u>거리</u>에 - <u>역사</u>적 - <u>직행</u> - <u>이용</u>
Kyongju is about one-hour drive toward east from Taegu. There are historical remains everywhere. For a trip from Seoul to Kyongju it would be most convenient to take an express bus.

b. <u>전국적</u>으로 - <u>비</u>가 - <u>기온</u>이 - <u>눈</u>이
Throughout the nation, it will be cloudy tomorrow. Some areas will have rain in the afternoon. In the northeast, the temperature will be below zero, and it will snow.

c. <u>방문</u>한 - <u>문화</u> - <u>한국적</u>인 - <u>중요</u>
Professor Chung, currently visiting his native country, met a group of students at Shilla Hotel. He said rediscovering things truly of Korean character is important for students today.

ANSWER TO "GUESS WHAT IT MEANS"

어깨 넘어 공부 "Studying over someone's shoulders" refers to one's easy way of obtaining knowledge or skill from someone else.

Communicative Frames in English

Frame 1. Driving on the Highway

Mun : I'll drive when we go back.
Carson : Do you know how to drive?
Mun : Of course, although I may not drive as well as you. Aren't you tired?
Carson : I'm O.K. It's nothing for me driving this much.
Mun : Then, so be it. But tell me if you are tired any time.
Carson : Sure. You can just look out for directions and signs for me.

Frame 2. A Highway Patrol Car Passes by

Carson : Don't you hear something?
Mun : Oh, a police car is coming, with a red light on.
Carson : It isn't coming after us, is it?
Mun : I don't think so. We weren't speeding.
I guess he has some urgent business.
Carson : Ah, he is just passing us by. My goodness! I thought I did something wrong.
Mun : You are chicken-hearted, aren't you? Maybe an accident has happened somewhere.

Frame 3. Talking about an Office Colleague

Mun : Miss Yang planned to come along with us today, but she couldn't.
Carson : Why not? It would have been nice if she had come along.
Mun : She seems to have hurt her foot while taking exercise.
Carson : Did she hurt herself badly?
Mun : No, it wasn't serious, I heard. But, walking seems uncomfortable.
Carson : On our way back, shall we visit her to inquire after her?
Mun : But, I don't think you can call her condition a sickness, do you? However, if you would like, let's stop by.

Frame 4. Inquiring after the Ailing Colleague by Phone

Mun : Hello.
Yang : Hello, this is Misuk Yang.
Mun : Misuk, it's me — Sangil Mun.
Yang : Oh, Sangil. You had a good trip to Kanghwado? Was it fun?
Mun : Yeah. But how is your injured foot? Is it better?
Yang : I'm almost O.K. I put a good medicine on it, you know.
Mun : We will stop by your place for a short while. We'll bring some cake that is nice and tasty.
Yang : O.K. I'll be waiting.

제 20 과

음식점에서

대화 1 (FRAME 1)

시골 음식점에 들른다

카슨 : 해가 벌써 지려고 하네요.

문 : 네, 좀 쌀쌀하지요? 바람이 불기 시작했어요. 어디서 식사 하실래요? 서울에 닿을려면 아직 한참 가야 하는데.

카슨 : 다음 휴게소에 들릅시다. 배가 좀 고파요.

문 : 네, 그런데 휴게소보다 더 좋은 데로 제가 모시고 가지요. 저기 주유소 보이죠? 거기 지난 다음에 좌회전 하세요.

카슨 : 이런 데 좋은 식당이 있어요?

문 : 있고말고요. 작은 도시인데 잘 하는 국밥집이 있습니다.

단어 공부 (*VOCABULARY STUDY*)

• 해 sun; year

해가 진다. "The sun sets." The verb 지다 in this usage is limited to 해 and 달 "moon."

• 쌀쌀하다 to be chilly, cool

• 시작하다 to begin, start

The verb phrase -기 시작하다 means "to start doing/being."

- 닿다 — to arrive =(도착하다)
- 한참 — for a while
- 휴게소 — rest area (휴게=rest, 소=place)

The "rest area" along the Korean freeway has souvenir shops, coffee shops, restaurants and other amenities.

- 모시고 가다 — to take (someone) to (some place) (humble form)
- 주유소 — gas station
- 지난 다음에 — after passing

-은 다음에 is a connective construction. (See Grammar.)

- 좌회전 — left turn (antonym: 우회전 "right turn")
- 이런 데 — a place like this; 데 "place"
- 있고 말고요. — There certainly is.

The ending -고 말고요 denotes an emphatic, affirmative response ("surely," "of course") to a question.

- 도시 — city, town

CULTURAL ENCOUNTER 국밥 "rice in soup" is a generic name for thick soup with meat, vegetable and rice. It is favorite meal for working-class Koreans. It was originally served in a rough clay pottery bowl (called 뚝배기). Today, there are many varieties, such as 설렁탕, 곰탕, 꼬리 곰탕, 소머리 국밥, etc.

❖ 가지고/데리고/모시고 가다 : "TO TAKE SOMETHING/SOMEONE WITH ONE"

In English, the verb "to take" or "to bring" is used to express transporting something or accompanying someone to some place. In Korean, there are three verb phrases with 가다 or 오다 (depending on the speaker's orientation) to express the same notions.

Inanimate object	:	카메라를 <u>가지고 갔습니다</u>. I took a camera with me.
Animate object (PLAIN)	:	친구를 <u>데리고 갔습니다</u>. I took a friend with me.
Human object (HUMBLE)	:	선생님을 <u>모시고 갔습니다</u>. I took my teacher with me.

연습 1. Ask your partner to take you to the places listed below.

EXAMPLE: 시장에 데리고 가 주세요. — Would you take me to the market?
네, 거기 모시고 가지요. — Yes, I'll take you there.

a. 음식점에	c. 상가에	e. 극장에	g. 어디라도
b. 시외에	d. 다방에	f. 중국 음식점에	h. 어디 가까운 데

연습 2. Ask your classmate if he/she brought any of the following items to class. Your friend will respond factually (showing the item in question).

EXAMPLE: 책 가지고 왔어요? Did you bring a book with you?

가지고/안 가지고 왔어요. Yes, I did./No, I didn't

Suggested Items: 시계, 돈, 안경, 우산, 가방, 볼펜, 점심, 신문, etc.

대화 2 (FRAME 2)

음식을 주문한다

주인 : 어서 오세요. 방으로 들어가시죠.

문 : 그거 좋겠군요. 방 따뜻합니까?

주인 : 따뜻하고 말고요. 자, 이리 들어 가시죠.

문 : 아줌마, 뭐가 됩니까?

주인 : 벽에 차림표 보시죠. 뭐라도 다 됩니다.

문 : 등심 구이가 있네! 어떻습니까?

카슨 : 전 잘 모르니까 좋으신대로 시켜주세요.

문 : 등심구이가 무엇인지 아세요?

카슨 : 잘 모릅니다. 하여튼 쇠고기 요리죠?

문 : 맞습니다. 잡숴 보세요. 맛이 있어요.
아줌마, 등심구이 2인분이요. 그리고 맥주 큰 병으로 한 병.

단어 공부 (*VOCABULARY STUDY*)

- 따뜻하다 — to be warm
- 아줌마 — auntie (<아주머니); lady (used in shops, in the street)

CAUTION! The expression 아줌마 is often used in addressing a middle-aged lady (over forty) in a friendly manner. It is inappropriate where HIGH LEVEL speech is called for.

- 뭐가 됩니까? — What's available? What do you serve? (뭐가<무엇이)
- 벽 — wall
- 차림표 — menu(=메뉴) (차림=prepared item, 표=chart, display)
- 등심 — sirloin
- 구이 — broiled food (=구은 음식) (<굽다/구워 to broil)
- 소고기/쇠고기 — beef (standard form: 쇠고기) (소=cow, 고기=meat)
- 좋으신대로 — as you please; -대로 "as, according to..."
- 무엇인지 아세요? — Do you know what it is?

  A clause ending with *prenominal form* + 지 is a question included within a sentence. (See Grammar.)
- 하여튼 — anyway, at any rate
- 요리 — dish (prepared food for table); 요리하다 "to cook"

  In a restaurant, 요리 usually implies a main entree for two or three persons at a table.
- 맞습니다. — That's right.
- 이인분 — an order for two persons (이인=two persons, 분=portion)
- 맥주 — beer
- 병 — bottle

❖ -지 알다: "TO KNOW WHAT / HOW / WHETHER"

	Prenominal Ending			Main Clause
• Action/process Verbs (and 있다)	Stem + 는	(Present)	지	알다 / 모르다 / 물어보다 / etc.
	Stem + 었는	(Past)		
	Stem + 을	(Expected)		
• Stative Verbs (and -이다)	Stem + 은	(Present)		
	Stem + 었는	(Past)		
	Stem + 을	(Expected)		

CAUTION! The *past* ending is -었는 (rather than -은/던) for all types of verbs before the bound noun -지.

그 사람이 뭐 하는지 알아요?	Do you know what he does?
그 사람 뭐 했는지 몰라요.	I don't know what he did.
언제 일을 할지 물어보세요.	Ask him when he will work.
나 저 사람 누구인지 모릅니다.	I don't know who he is.
그 사람한테 아팠는지 물어봐요.	Ask her if she was sick.
언제일지 누가 압니까?	Who knows when it will be?

연습 3. Respond factually to the following questions by using a clause ending with -지.

EXAMPLE: 오늘 며칠인지 아세요? — Do you know what day it is?
며칠인지 알지요. 금요일이에요. — I know what day it is. It's Friday.

a. 저 사람이 누구인지 아십니까?
b. 어제 일기가 어땠는지 압니까?
c. 뭐가 되는지 물어 보세요.
d. 주유소가 어디 있는지 알아요?
e. 우회전이 무언지 압니까?
f. 맥주 한 병이 얼마인지 모르지요?

연습 4. Say the following sentences in Korean.

a. The spring is warm in Korea.
b. Anything is available.
c. Beef dishes are not available.
d. I don't know who he is.
e. Any place is O.K. with me.
f. It's of course tasty.

대화 3 (FRAME 3)

건배!

주인	:	자, 기다리시게 해서 미안합니다. 뜨거우니까 불 조심하세요. 맛있게 잡수십시오.
문	:	생선도 있네요! 생선은 안 시켰는데?
주인	:	이건 서비습니다. 좋은 생선이 있어서요.
문	:	아이구, 감사합니다. 잘 먹겠어요.
주인	:	뭐 더 필요하신 게 있으시면 불러 주세요.
문	:	네에. 자, 한 잔 받으시죠.
카슨	:	고맙습니다. 자, 문 선생님도 드세요.
문	:	건배! 선생님의 건강을 위하여!
카슨	:	문 선생 건강을 위하여!

단어 공부 (*VOCABULARY STUDY*)

- 기다리게 해서 — for making you wait
  STEM + 게 하다 means "to make/let (someone) do (something).
- 뜨겁다/뜨거워 — to be (burning) hot
- 맛있게 잡수십시오. — Please enjoy your meal.
  An expression used by the host or hostess to the guest before starting to eat.
- 생선 — fish (as food)
  CAUTION! When fish is not viewed as food, 고기 or 물고기 is the term to be used. For example, 고기 잡으러 갑시다. "Let's go fishing (to catch fish)."
  물고기가 죽었어요. "A fish is dead."
- 서비스 — free service, compliments of the house
- 잘 먹겠어요. Ⓜ — I'll enjoy the food.
  An expression used by a guest to the host or hostess before eating.

- 부르다/불러 — to call, summon; to sing (a song)
- 한 잔 받으세요. — Please accept my offer of drink. (See below.)
- 들다/드세요/들어 — to eat/drink (HIGH); to lift up
- 건배! — Cheers! Bottoms up! (a toast)
- 건강을 위하여 — to your health

  -을 위하여 or -을 위해서 means "for (the sake of)..."

CULTURAL ENCOUNTER At the table in Korea, one is expected to offer his/her cup to a friend and pour liquor 술 (generic term) with two hands, a gesture of respect. The recipient is expected to drink up and then give the glass back and do the same.

❖ 춥다/덥다/서늘하다: DEGREES OF TEMPERATURE

	COLD	COOL		WARM	HOT
•Weather/ atmosphere/ feeling	춥다	쌀쌀하다 서늘하다	신선하다 시원하다	따뜻하다	덥다
•Condition of tangible objects	차다			따뜻하다	뜨겁다

연습 5. Complete the sentences by using appropriate expressions of temperature.

a. 한국은 겨울이 ______.
b. 뉴욕의 여름은 ______.
c. 한국 봄 날씨는 ______.
d. 가을 바람은 ______.
e. 아이스크림은 ______.
f. 여름에 비가 오면 ______.
g. 더울 때 _____ 물을 마시면 ______.
h. 불고기는 _____ 게 먹어야 해요.

❖ STEM+게: "SO THAT IT MAY..."

감기 들지 않게 조심하세요.
Be careful, so you won't catch a cold.

바람이 들어오게 유리창을 열었어요.
I opened the window, so the wind would come in.

연습 6. Complete each of the following sentences by placing a clause that introduces the reason for something just mentioned. Select one from the list.

a. 주소를 공책에 썼어요.
b. 옷을 잘 입으세요.
c. 천천히 말씀해 주세요.
d. 유리창을 닫았습니다.

Suggested Clauses
- 감기 안 들게
- 쇼핑할 수 있게
- 잊어 버리지 않게
- 바람이 안 들어오게

e. 소고기 삼인분 시켰습니다.
f. 은행에서 돈을 찾았어요.

• 둘이 많이 먹게
• 제가 알아 들을 수 있게

❖ STEM+게 하다: "TO LET/MAKE SOMEONE DO..."

The clause ending with -게 may often be followed by the verb 하다, which means "to make, let, or have someone do something." The use of 못- in the 게 clause expresses prohibition.

택시를 밖에서 기다리게 했어요.	I made the taxi wait outside.
선생이 학생들을 집에 가게 했어요.	The teacher let the student go home.
여기서 담배를 못피우게 합니다.	They prohibit smoking here.

연습 7. Complete the following sentences.

a. 그 사람들 _______게 하세요.	Let them come in.
b. 여기 _______ 게 해서 _______.	I'm sorry for making you come here.
c. 아이들을 집에 _______ 했습니다.	I made the children stay home.
d. 너무 오래 _______ 하지 마세요.	Don't make me wait too long.
e. 아무도 _______ 합니다.	They don't let anyone go in.

연습 8. Form a small group, and select one person to be a waiter or a waitress. The rest of the group will be the customers. The waiter or the waitress will welcome the customers, seat them at a table or guide them into the *ondol* room. Show them the menu on the wall and take orders.

1	2	3	4	5	6	7	8	9	10
찌개백반	불고기	갈비	소고기 등심구이	비빔밥	생선구이	돼지갈비	생선찌개	냉면	만두국

1. Rice with stew
2. Barbecued beef
3. Barbecued beef ribs
4. Broiled beef (sirloin)
5. Rice mixed with vegetables
6. Broiled fish
7. Barbecued spare ribs
8. Thick fish stew
9. Cold noodles
10. Soup with dumplings

NOTE: All items are served with 김치 or 깍두기.

대화 4 (FRAME 4)

한국 반찬 이야기

문 : 식기 전에 드시죠. 젓가락 쓸 줄 아시죠?

카슨 : 네, 전 한국에 오기 전부터 쓸 줄 알았어요.

문 : 네에. 불이 뜨겁습니다. 조심하세요.

카슨 : 반찬이 많이 나오는군요. 김치는 꽤 매운데요.

문 : 그건 김치가 아니고 깍두기라고 합니다.
김치보다 더 맵고 짜지요.

카슨 : 그래도 맛이 있어요.

단어 공부 (*VOCABULARY STUDY*)

- 식다 — to cool off, become cool
- 식기 전에 — before it cools down

  STEM + 기 전에 "before ...ing"

  STEM + 기 전부터 "even before ...ing"
- 젓가락 — chopsticks
- 반찬 — side dishes (other than rice and soup)
- 나오다 — to come out; to present itself

  The ending -군요/-는군요 is an exclamatory ending similar to -네요. When an action or process verb without 었/겠 precedes, -는군요 is used. For example,

(a) Action/process Verb:	가시는군요!	So you are leaving!
(b) Otherwise:	가셨군요!	So you did go!
	학생이군요!	So you are a student!
	날씨 좋군요!	It's a nice day!
	좋으시겠군요!	You must be glad!

- 김치 — kimchi (pickled cabbage, spiced with red pepper and garlic)

•맵다/매워	to be hot (spicy)
•깍두기	pickled radish (spiced with red pepper and garlic)
•짜다/짜	to be salty
•그래도	even so

CULTURAL ENCOUNTER A Korean meal (식사) typically includes steamed rice (밥) as a central item. So much so that 밥을 먹다 usually means "to have a meal" even if the rice is not included. Therefore, everything else, except soup (국), is called 반찬 "side dish," which is in the Western concept the main entree. 반찬 usually includes 김치 "pickled cabbage," 깍두기 "pickled radish," seasoned vegetables, and other dishes of 소고기 "beef," 돼지고기 "pork," or 생선 "fish." A spoon (숟가락) is used to eat rice and soup, and chopsticks (젓가락) to eat other solid foods.

STATIVE VERBS INDICATING TASTES

•맵다/매워	to be spicy hot	•달다/단/달아	to be sweet
•짜다/짜	to be salty	•쓰다/써	to be bitter
•싱겁다/싱거워	to be bland, plain	•시다/시어	to be sour

연습 9. Describe one typical food that may be best described by each stative verb above.

연습 10. Write a short paragraph describing a typical Korean meal based on the information given above. Compare your writing against a model shown in the Vocabulary Summary section.

❖ GUESS WHAT IT MEANS: 둘이 먹다가 하나가 죽어도 모른다.

문법 (GRAMMAR)

1. A Question within a Sentence

A question is often treated like a noun phrase within a sentence as in "I don't know *what it is.*" We will call such clauses "included questions" for convenience. In Korean, included questions are noun clauses ending with a particle -지.

INCLUDED QUESTION

VERB STEM + PRENOMINAL ENDING + 지				Main Clause
• Action/Process Verb (and 있다)	Stem + 는	(Present)	지	알다 / 모르다 / 묻다 / etc.
	Stem + 었는	(Past)		
	Stem + 을	(Expected)		
• Stative Verb (and -이다)	Stem + 은	(Present)		
	Stem + 었는	(Past)		
	Stem + 을	(Expected)		

CAUTION! The past action or state in the included question takes -었/는 rather than -은/던 (which is used before a regular noun, as introduced in Lesson 16.)

무엇인지 모르겠어요.	I don't know what it is?
카메라가 어디 있는지 물어 보세요.	Ask him where the camera is.
그사람 언제 올지 누가 압니까?	Who knows when he is coming?
그 분 어디 가셨는지 아세요?	Do you know where he went?
그게 얼마였는지 물어보세요.	Ask him how much it was.

• QUESTIONS WITHOUT A QUESTION WORD: The included question may be of a yes-no type, without any question word. Note that in such cases, the included questions in English start with "if" or "whether."

그 가게 오늘 여는지 알아보세요.	Find out if the store opens today.
집에 있는지 알아야 하겠어요.	We must know whether he is home.

• TWO DERIVED USAGES: When a sentence ends with the 지 clause (without the main clause), it expresses an indirect question equivalent to "I wonder if..." in English.

미스 김이 집에 있는지요.	I wonder if Miss Kim is home.

A weak possibility is expressed by the use of -지도 모른다.

내일 비가 올 지도 몰라요.	It may rain tomorrow.

2. Expressing a Desired Event: -게

When an action is performed in order to have a certain desired effect, that desired effect is expressed in a clause with the ending -게.

DESIRED EFFECT

VERB STEM + 게	+ Main Clause

감기 들지 않게 조심하세요.
Be careful, so you won't catch a cold.
사진 찍게 카메라 가지고 왔어요.
I brought a camera, so we can take pictures.
잊어버리지 않게 공책에 적었습니다.
I wrote it down in my notebook, so that I won't forget it.

CAUTION! The clause expressing a "desired effect" appears very similar to the "purpose" clause (-으러 or -으려고). The difference, however, is that the "desired effect" clause has normally a different subject from that of the main clause. The subject of a clause with -으러 or -으려고 must be the same as that of the main clause.

3. Causative Phrase: -게 하다

The clause ending with -게 may often be followed by the verb 하다, to form a causative construction. It denotes "to make," "to let," or "to allow" someone to do something.

(A-가 B-를 [C …게] 하다) A {makes / lets / has} B [do C].

택시를 밖에 기다리게 했어요.	I made the taxi wait outside.
선생이 학생들을 가게 했습니다.	The teacher let the student go home.
식당에서 담배 피우게 합니까?	Do they let you smoke in the restaurant?
오래 기다리게 해서 미안합니다.	I'm sorry for making you wait so long.

The use of 못- in the 게 clause expresses prohibition.

여기서 담배를 못 피우게 합니다.	They prohibit smoking here.
아무도 못 들어가게 해요.	They don't allow anybody to go in.

4. Another Use of -게

Many adverbs are derived from stative verbs with the use of the ending -게.

반갑다 ⟶ 반갑게	gladly	쉽다 ⟶ 쉽게	easily
이렇다 ⟶ 이렇게	in this way	예쁘다 ⟶ 예쁘게	prettily
어떻다 ⟶ 어떻게	how	크다 ⟶ 크게	in a big way

Phrases may also be made into adverbials.

재미있다 ⟶ 재미있게 with fun
맛이 있다 ⟶ 맛있게 with relish
EX) 맛있게 잡수십시오. "Please enjoy your meal"

There are basically two ways to derive adverbs: (1) add -이 and (2) add -게. The former is restricted to a certain number of stative verbs, and sometimes with additional changes. The latter is open to other stative verbs and has no irregular forms. In the following list are some adverbs with an addition of the vowel 이 (with or without some changes).

바쁘다 ⟶ 바삐	busily		멀다 ⟶ 멀리	afar
많다 ⟶ 많이	much		같다 ⟶ 같이	together
빠르다 ⟶ 빨리	quickly		안전하다 ⟶ 안전히	safely
특별하다 ⟶ 특별히	especially		깨끗하다 ⟶ 깨끗이	clean(ly)
편하다 ⟶ 편히	comfortably			

5. To Begin to Do/Be: -기 시작이다 and -기 시작하다

The verb phrase 시작이다 or 시작하다 may be preceded by a complement clause ending in -기. There are some stylistic difference between 시작이다 and 시작하다, although they are interchangeable.

VERB STEM + 기 시작이다	One begins/starts to ...

• This structure is generally used in the present tense only, and it is typically used in *processive* expressions, those with a non-human subject or those that have a human subject but that are considered not under the subject's control, such as 잠이 오다 "to become sleepy."

비가 오기 시작입니다. — It's beginning to rain.
바람이 불기 시작입니다. — It's beginning to be windy.

VERB STEM + 기 시작하다	One begins/starts to ...

• 시작하다 is generally used in an *action* expression which is considered under the control of a human subject. It may be used in any tenses.

불어를 배우기 시작했어요. — I started learning French.
편지를 읽기 시작했습니다. — She began reading the letter.

6. A Summary of "Time" Clauses

We will review various "time" clauses that are introduced up to this lesson. Most time clauses end with a bound noun, such as -때 "when," -전 "before," -후 "after," and -동안 "during," and they are preceded by a prenominal ending, which *generally does not vary*. The tenses of such clauses are determined by the main clause, not by their own forms. (There are exceptions to be noted below.)

VERB STEM + (었)을 때에	when
VERB STEM + 기 전에	before
VERB STEM + 은 후에/다음에	after
VERB STEM + 는 동안(에)	while/during

비가 올 때는 춥습니다. — It gets cold when it rains.

비가 오기 전에 돌아갑시다. — Let's go back before the rain starts.
비가 온 다음에 바람이 불었어요. — It became windy after the rain.
비가 오는 동안 집에 있었어요. — We stayed at home while it was raining.

❖ FIXED PRENOMINAL ENDING

In most cases, the verb endings before a bound noun (-때, 동안, etc.) do not change as noted above, but there are some exceptions (to be noted below).

한국에 갔을 때 한국말을 배웠습니다.
When I went to Korea (=after I arrived), I learned Korean.

한국에 갈 때 한국말을 배웠습니다.
When I was about to go to Korea(=before arriving there), I learned Korean.

Occasionally, the tense marker -었 is used with certain verbs, such as 있다. But even in this case the use of -었 is optional.

대학에 {있을 / 있었을} 때에 아파트에서 살았습니다.
When I was in college, I lived in an apartment.

❖ 간 동안에: "DURING SOMEONE'S ABSENCE"

Usually 동안 "while" is preceded by -는, but there is an exception: -은 (the completed aspect) may be used with 가다 "to go" to denote "during someone's absence."

내가 간 동안에 전화 왔었어요? — While I was gone, was there any call?
형이 없는 동안에 신 형이 전화 했었어요. — Mr. Shin called while you were away.

❖ DIFFERENCE BETWEEN -동안 AND -동안에

If you add -에 to -동안 it brings about a subtle change of meaning: while -동안 implies "throughout the period," -동안에 implies "at some point within the period."

학교에 다니는 동안 일했어요. — I worked while I was in school. (IMPLIES: throughout the period)
학교 다니는 동안에 김 형 만났어요. — I met Mr. Kim while I was in school. (IMPLIES: a time within the period)

NOTE: The above distinction is so delicate and subtle that a beginning student of Korean probably should not be concerned about it.

❖ -부터 /-까지 IN TIME CLAUSES

More time clauses may be derived from the uses of additional postpositions -부터 "since" and -까지 "until."

STEM + 을 때까지	until (the time)...
STEM + 기 전까지	until (just before)...
STEM + 을 때부터	since (the time)...
STEM + 기 전부터	even (before)...
STEM + 은 후/다음부터	since (after)...

내가 돌아올 때까지 여기 있어요. — Please stay here until I come back.
여기 오기 전까지 그 사람 몰랐어요. — I didn't know him until I came here.
대학 다닐 때부터 알았어요. — I have known him since I was in college.
여기 오기 전부터 알았어요. — I knew him even before I came here.
여기 온 후부터 가까운 친구가 됐어요. — We've been good friends since I came here.

7. Modifying an Indefinite Nominal

Korean has a peculiar rule about modifying *indefinite nominals* (such as "some/any...). The modifier follows the nominal, which is the reverse of the normal order. Then the modifier is followed by a dummy noun (-것, -사람, etc.). Grammatically, it is an apposition (placing two nominal phrases one after another).

NOMINAL + (P)	MODIFIER + Dummy + (P)

(P): space for a postposition

뭐 좋은 것	something good
뭐 먹을 것	something to eat
어디 먼 데	somewhere far away
누구 아는 사람	someone that I know
무엇이라도 필요한 것	anything that you need

❖ THE POSITIONS OF POSTPOSITIONS

Since this type of phrases consist of two small noun phrases, the postposition may be placed after one of the two or both phrases. This possibility creates four variations:

다른 것 필요한 것
다른 것 필요한 것이
다른 것이 필요한 것
다른 것이 필요한 것이
} 없습니까? — Isn't there anything else that you need?

In fact, you have already been using such inverted phrases when an indefinite noun is modified by a number or some quantity expression.

책 다	all the books
의자 몇 개	how many chairs
애들 많이	many children
상자 하나	one box
학생 다섯	five students

읽기 · 쓰기 (READING & WRITING)

1. Importance of Listening Comprehension: 알아 듣기의 중요성

A slightly exaggerated claim on a language learning method (언어 학습 방법) was carried in a newspaper. Listening Comprehension (알아듣기) is undoubtedly an important aspect of language learning. The verb 알아듣다 "comprehend" is a compound of 알다 and 듣다, and it means comprehending something upon hearing. Note that its negative, 못 알아 듣다 is pronounced [modaradŭtta].

귀가 뚫려야 말을 할 수 있다!

영어/일어를 한다고 하는 사람도 상대의 말을 못 알아 듣는 경우가 많습니다. 듣는 능력이 부족하기 때문입니다. 딱 1주일만 검토용 교재로 학습해 보십시오. 힘들게 외우거나, 따라 말할 필요가 없습니다. 학습 방법에 따라 반복해서 듣기만 하십시오. 듣기 훈련을 하는데 해설 강의식 테이프 교재는 필요치 않습니다.

단어소개

뚫리다	to be bored, pierced (passive of 뚫다 "to pierce")	학습하다	to study (=배우다, 공부하다)
		힘들게	in the hard way (=어렵게)
상대	partner, opponent	외우다	to memorize (=기억하다)
경우	situation, case (=때)	-거나	or (a connective ending)
능력	ability (=할 수 있는 힘)	-에 따라	following after.../ according to...
부족하다	to be insufficient (=모자라다)		
교재	teaching material	반복하다	to repeat

연습 11. Scan the clipping above and follow through the exercises.

a. The caption says something must happen before you can speak a language. 귀가 뚫리다 is obviously a metaphor. Guess what it really means.
b. 일어는 어느 나라 말입니까?
c. 무엇이 부족하면 상대의 말을 못 알아듣는 경우가 많습니까?
d. 말하는 능력하고 듣는 능력 중에서 어느 것이 더 중요하다고 생각합니까?
e. 이 학습방법을 쓸 때 무엇이 필요가 없다고 합니까?

연습 12. Below are various captions taken from a newspaper. Write the English equivalents to the clippings. You may use a dictionary for the unknown words.

(A) "저희가 하는 일은
여러분의 사업이
잘되게 돕는 것입니다."

사업	business
즐겁다/즐거워	to be happy
먹되	eat but···
-되	a connective (= -지만)

저희는 여러분을 위해 일하는 것이 즐겁습니다.
저희의 도움이 필요하시면 서슴치 마시고 불러 주십시오.

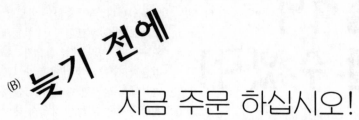

(B) 늦기 전에
지금 주문 하십시오!

(C) 정치적 고려없어

(D) 건강하십니다

싱겁게 천천히 먹되 식사후 10~20분 걸으면 좋아

연습 13. Complete the following paragraphs by filling in the blank spaces with the words listed on the right. Then, give the gist of each completed paragraph in English.

학습	사업
불러	고쳐
언제	도와

a. 여러분의 _____이 잘 되게 _____ 드리는 것이 저희가 하는 일입니다. _____ 라도 저희 도움이 필요하시면 (217) 3384-0884 _____ 주십시오.

-어도	능력
-거나	경우
-되	상대
되는	귀

b. 외국인과 영어로 이야기를 할 때 말은 좀 할 수 있_____, _____ 의 말을 잘 못 알아들을 _____ 가 많다. 외국인이 내가 말하는 것만을 듣고는 내 영어 _____이 얼마나_____ 지 알 수 없어서 말을 빨리 하기 때문일 것이다. 나는 아직 영어에 _____가 뚫리지 않은 것 같다. 이제부터는 미국 영화를 많이 보_____ 자동차 운전할 때 테이프를 많이 들어야 하겠다.

c. 도로 지도를 보 _____, 전화기 사용, 여자들이 스타킹을 갈아 신는 것 등, 사람들이 자동차 운전하_____ 이런 위험한 일을 하는 _____ 가 적지 않_____ 때로는 시속 100 킬로미터 이상으로 _____ 할 때에도 그렇게 한다고 한다. 누구나 이런 일이 얼마나 위험한 _____ 를 알아야 한다.

운전	부족
안전	경우
-지	-(으)며
-거나	-(으)면서

연습 14. Create a caption for each of the paragraphs above.

a. ________________________________
b. ________________________________
c. ________________________________

단어 정리 (VOCABULARY SUMMARY)

Nominals

깍두기	pickled radish	소고기/쇠고기	beef
건강	health	구이	broiled (meat, fish)
건배	a toast ("Bottoms up!")	숟가락	spoon
김치	pickled cabbage	아줌마	auntie; lady (address)
도시	city, town	요리	dish entree
등심	sirloin	이인분	two orders (of dish)
맥주	beer	젓가락	chopsticks
반찬	side dish	주유소	gas station
벽	wall	차림표	menu (=메뉴)
병	bottle	해	sun; year
생선	fish (as food)	휴게소	rest area
경우	case, occasion	상대	partner, the other party
교재	teaching material	학습	study, learning
서비스	free service	능력	ability, capability

Action Verbs

가지고 가다	to take something along with oneself
닿다	to arrive (=도착하다)
데리고 가다	to take/accompany someone to some place (Plain)
들다	to eat/drink
모시고 가다	to take/accompany someone to some place (Humble)
부르다/불러	to call, summon
시작하다	to begin, start
우회전 하다	to make a right turn
좌회전 하다	to make a left turn
반복하다	to repeat
외우다	to memorize

Process Verbs

식다	to cool off	지다	to fade, set (of sun, moon)

Stative Verbs

따뜻하다	to be warm	짜다	to be salty
뜨겁다/뜨거워	to be (burning) hot	즐겁다/즐거워	to be happy
맵다/매워	to be spicy	부족하다	to be deficient
쌀쌀하다	to be chilly, cool	힘(이)들다	to be difficult (=어렵다)

Personalized Vocabulary

달다	to be sweet	선선하다	to be cool
시다	to be sour	서늘하다	to be chilly
쓰다	to be bitter	시원하다	to be refreshing
싱겁다/싱거워	to be bland	차다	to be cold (of things)

Adverbs

하여튼	anyway	힘들게	in the hard way
한참	for a while		

Interjections

그래도	even so

Connectives

-거나	or (a verb ending)	-되	but, and (a connective)

Idioms

맛있게 잡수세요.	Please enjoy your meal.
맞습니다.	That's right.
뭐가 됩니까?	What's available? (at restaurant)
좋으신 대로	as you please
귀가 뚫리다	one's ears get tuned to sound (=to comprehend upon hearing)

Grammatical Forms

-게	so as to...
-게 하다	to let/make/have someone do something
-고 말고요	certainly, of course··· (an emphatic, affirmative response)
-기 전에	before...
-은 후/다음에	after...
-을 위하여	for (the sake of)...
-에 따라(서)	depending on...

연습문제 해답 (ANSWERS TO EXERCISES)

연습 1.

a. 음식점에 데리고 가 주세요.	네, 거기 모시고 가지요.
b. 시외에 데리고 가 주세요.	네, 거기 모시고 가지요.
c. 상가에 데리고 가 주세요.	네, 거기 모시고 가지요.
d. 다방에 데리고 가 주세요.	네, 거기 모시고 가지요.
e. 극장에 데리고 가 주세요.	네, 거기 모시고 가지요.
f. 중국 음식점에 데리고 가 주세요.	네, 거기 모시고 가지요.
g. 어디라도 데리고 가 주세요.	네, 어디라도 모시고 가지요.
h. 어디 가까운데 데리고 가주세요.	네, 모시고 가지요.

연습 4.

a. 한국은 봄이 따뜻합니다.
b. 무엇이라도 다 됩니다.
c. 소고기 요리는 안 됩니다.
d. 저 사람 누구인지 몰라요.
e. 저는 어디라도 좋아요.
f. 맛이 있고 말고요.

연습 5.

a. 추워요 b. 덥습니다. c. 따뜻해요. d. 선선합니다. e. 차요. f. 시원해요. g. 찬, 시원해요. h. 뜨겁

연습 6.

a. 잊어 버리지 않게
b. 감기 안 들게
c. 제가 알아들을 수 있게
d. 바람이 안들어 오게
e. 둘이 많이 먹게
f. 쇼핑할 수 있게

연습 7.

a. 들어오게
b. 오시게 해서 미안해요.
c. 있게
d. 기다리게
e. 못들어 오게

연습 10. A paragraph on a typical Korean meal.

한국 사람은 식사할 때 밥과 김치 또는 깍두기가 있어야 한다. 그래서 밥 먹는다고 하는 말은 밥을 안 먹어도 식사를 한다는 뜻이 된다. 반찬이라는 말은 밥하고 국 외에 나오는 음식을 뜻한다. 대개 소고기, 돼지고기, 생선, 야채 나물 같은 것이 반찬이다. 밥이나 국은 보통 숟가락으로 먹고, 반찬은 젓가락으로 먹는다.

연습 11.

a. "The ears get pierced open." means "One begins to understand utterances upon hearing."
b. 일본
c. 듣는 능력이 부족하면
d. 둘 다 중요하지요.
e. 강의식 테이프 교재

연습 12.

(A) Our business is to assist you so that your business will prosper.
(B) Before it gets (too) late, order now.
(C) No political considerations.
(D) You are in good health.
It will be good (for your health) if you have less salty foods, and take a walk 10-20 minutes after each meal.

연습 13.

a. 사업 - 도와 - 언제 - 불러
What our company does is to help your business prosper. Please call us anytime: (217) 385-0884.

b. 어도 - 상대 - 경우 - 능력 - 되는 - 귀 - 거나
When I talk with a foreigner in English, I can speak fairly well. But I often fail to understand what he says. It is probably because the foreigner speaks too fast, not understanding my knowledge of Enghish simply by

listening to what I have to say. I think I need to either see more American movies or listen to tapes while driving.

c. 거나 - 면서 - 경우 - 으며 - 운전 - 지

Looking at road maps, using a telephone, (ladies) changing stockings, etc. — it's not uncommon for people to do such dangerous things while driving. Sometimes they do these things while driving at over 100 km. People should realize how dangerous these behaviors are.

EXPLANATION ON "GUESS WHAT IT MEANS"

The sentence literally means that "while two people are eating, even if one dies, the other will not notice it." It is a humorous way of saying that the food is so tasty.

Communicative Frames in English

Frame 1. Stopping by a Country Restaurant

Carson : The sun is already about to set.
Mun : Yes, a little chilly, isn't it? It is beginning to be windy. Do you want to eat somewhere? It will be a while before we get to Seoul.
Carson : Let's stop at the next rest area. I'm a little hungry.
Mun : Yes, but I'd like to take you to a better place than the rest area. You see a gas station over there, don't you? Make a left turn after passing that.
Carson : Is there a good restaurant in a place like this?
Mun : There sure is. This is a small town, but there is a good "soup house."

Frame 2. Ordering Dishes

Owner : Come right in, gentlemen. Please go into one of the rooms.
Mun : That will be nice. Is the room warm?
Owner : It certainly is. Well, go right in this way.
Mun : Lady, what's available?
Owner : Please look at the menu on the wall. Everything is available.
Mun : They have broiled sirloin beef! How is that?
Carson : I don't know very well, so please order as you please.
Mun : Do you know what "Deungshim Kui" is?
Carson : I'm not sure. Anyway, it is a beef dish, isn't it?
Mun : Right. You'd better try that. It tastes good. Lady! Two orders of broiled sirloin, please. And one big bottle of beer.

Frame 3. Cheers!

Owner : There, I'm sorry for making you wait. It's hot, please watch out for the fire. Please enjoy your meal.
Mun : We have fish, too! We didn't order fish, did we?
Owner : This is on the house. We happen to have good fish in.
Mun : Oh, thank you very much. We will enjoy it.
Owner : If you have anything else you need, please call me.
Mun : All right. Well, let me fill your glass.
Carson : Thanks. Here, you too.
Mun : Bottoms up! To your health!
Carson : To your health!

Frame 4. Talking about Korean Side Dishes

Mun	: There, please start before it cools off. You know how to use chopsticks, don't you?
Carson	: Yes, I knew how to use them even before coming to Korea.
Mun	: I see. The fire is hot. Please be careful.
Carson	: So many side dishes they serve!. Kimchi is pretty hot.
Mun	: That is not kimchi, but it's called kkakttugi. It's hotter and saltier than kimchi.
Carson	: It's still tasty for me.

제 21 과

가족 이야기

대화 1 (FRAME 1)

문 씨의 고향, 강릉

카슨 : 문 선생은 언제 이 회사에 취직하셨어요?
문 : 취직한 지 2년 됐어요. 아직 배우는 중입니다.
카슨 : 고향은 어딥니까?
문 : 강원도입니다. 강릉이라는 작은 도시예요.
카슨 : 아, 동해안에 있는 도시지요?
문 : 네. 한국 지리에 대해서 잘 아시네요.
카슨 : 알기는요. 한번 가 본일이 있어서 기억이 나요.
문 : 예? 가보셨어요?
카슨 : 작년에 친구가 설악산 가자고 해서
갔었는데 가는 길에 들렀었죠.

단어 공부 (*VOCABULARY STUDY*)

- 취직하다 — to take a job, be employed
- 취직한지 — since I took a job

-은지 "since..." is always followed by a clause expressing a length of time.

- 배우는 중입니다. — I am in the process of learning.

  -는 중이다 "to be in the middle/process of..."
- 고향 — hometown
- 강원도 — Kangwon Province (a province along the east coast)
- 강릉 — a city on the east coast
- 강릉이라는 (도시) — (a city) called Kangnŭng

  -이라는 is a shortened form of -이라고 하는.
- 해안 — coast
- 지리 — geography
- 알기는요. — You say "I am knowledgeable," but not at all.

  STEM+기는(요) is a typical phrase used as a modest denial to compliments.
- 기억이 나다 — to recall, remember (기억=memory)

  (A-가 B-가 기억이 나다) *A* remembers/recalls *B*.
- 예 [↗]? — really? (with a sharp rising tone)
- 가자고 해서 — because he asked me to go along

  -자고 하다 is a quotation form. (Literally, one says "let's....")
- 가는 길에 — on one's way

연습 1. Respond appropriately to the following compliments.

a. 한국말 참 잘 하시네요.
b. 따님이 참 예쁘세요.
c. 골프 아주 잘 치시는데요.
d. 운전 잘 하시는데요.

연습 2. Ask your Korean friend where his/her hometown is, and briefly talk about the city or town. (Pretend that you are a Korean and pick a hometown.)

MODEL: A: 고향이 어디예요?
B: 경기도 인천입니다.
서해안 항구 도시예요.

작은 항구	a small port
농촌	a farm village
어촌	a fishing village
공업 도시	an industrial city

연습 3. Discuss with your partner on what activity your mutual friend has suggested. Use the model below.

MODEL: A: 무엇을 하자고 합니까? — What is he asking you to do?
B: 한국에 가자고 해요. — He asks me to go to Korea.

Suggested Activities:

- 중국어 배우는 것
- 운동 시작하는 것
- 불고기 먹는 것
- 점심 먹으러 나가는 것
- 커피 한 잔 마시는 것
- 택시를 부르는 것

대화 2 (FRAME 2)

카슨 씨의 고향

문 : 카슨 선생은 고향이 어딥니까?

카슨 : 글쎄요. 전 텍사스에서 태어나서 뉴욕에서 자랐거든요.
그래서 고향이 어디냐고 물으면 대답하기 곤란해요.

문 : 그래도 태어난 데가 고향이잖아요?

카슨 : 그렇겠군요. 그런데 전 텍사스는 전혀 모르거든요.

문 : 예. 그럼 뉴욕에서 대학 다니셨어요?

카슨 : 그게 또 우습거든요. 대학은 시카고에서 다녔어요.
부모님은 콜롬비아 대학교에 가라고 하셨는데
젊은 아이들이 부모 말 듣습니까?
아버님이 그 대학교 교수로 계셨거든요.

단어 공부 (*VOCABULARY STUDY*)

- 태어나다/태어나 — to be born
- 자라다/자라 — to grow up, be brought up

  -거든(요) an ending used in explaining something. The close English equivalent may be "..., you see."
- 어디냐고 물으면 — when I was asked where

  -느냐/-으냐 is an interrogative ending used in quotation. The form (-으냐) is used after a stative verb or -이다 without -었 or -겠. (See Grammar.)
- 곤란하다 — to be embarrassing, difficult; to be a problem
- 대답하기 곤란해요. — It is difficult (for me) to answer.
- 고향이잖아요? — Isn't it the hometown?

  -잖아요? is originally a contraction of -지 않아요? However, this phrasal form is used like an ending -지요.
- 그렇겠군요. — That would be so, wouldn't it? (=그러네요.)

  -군(요)/-는군(요) is an exclamtory ending equivalent to -네(요). It is used with a sense of exclamation when the speaker assumes that the addressee has the same opinion.
- 전혀 — (not) at all

  CAUTION! This adverb is used only in a negative sentence, like 별로 좋아하지 않는다. "One doesn't like it particularly."
- 우습다 / 우스워 — to be funny, strange (stative verb)

  This stative verb form is derived from the action verb 웃다 "to laugh; to smile."
- 부모(님) — parents, father and mother
- 가라고 하셨는데 — they said/asked (me) to go

  -으라고 is a form used to quote an imperative sentence. (See Grammar.)

- 젊다 — to be young (adult)

  The consonant ㄹ is pronounced only when a vowel follows.
- 말을 듣다/들어 — to obey
- 교수 — professor
- -으로(서) — as (a status-marking postposition)

❖ VERBS INDICATING YOUNG AND OLD

		Example	
어리다	to be young (as child):	아직 어립니다.	He is still a baby.
	(STATIVE VERB)	어린 아이, 애	a (young) baby
젊다	to be young (as adult):	저 사람 젊어요.	She is young.
	(STATIVE VERB)	젊은이	a young man/woman
늙다	to be old (as adult) :	저 사람 늙지 않아요.	He doesn't get old.
	(PROCESS VERB)	저 사람 늙었어요.	He is old.
		늙은이	an old man/woman

연습 4. Say the following sentences in Korean.

a. Do you have young babies at home?
b. My parents are old, but they walk like young people.
c. I lived in Los Angeles when I was young.
d. My auntie always looks young.
e. Mr. Pak came to America as a student when he was young.
f. I didn't listen to my parents when I was young.
g. The place where you are born is not necessarily (반드시) your hometown.

❖ QUOTING DIFFERENT TYPES OF SENTENCES

There are four ways of quoting sentences.

Sentence Types	Sentence Examples
•STATEMENT :	간다고 합니다. 좋다고 합니다.
•QUESTION :	가느냐고 합니다. 좋으냐고 합니다.
•SUGGESTION :	가자고 합니다.
•REQUEST :	가라고 합니다. 달라고 합니다.

연습 5. Put the following into Korean, paying attention to the quotation forms.

a. He says there is a student.
b. He told me to go home.
c. She asked me if she could go now.
d. I suggested that we wait.

연습 6. Quote each sentence of the conversation. If an utterance does not end with a verb, you should either supply an appropriate verb or use -이라고.

Dialogue 1	*Dialogue 2*
a. 어디 가?	a. 계세요?
b. 백화점에.	b. 네, 어서 들어오세요.
c. 나랑 같이 가자.	c. 커피 한 잔 하시겠어요?
d. 너는 집에 있어.	d. 그러십시다.
e. 왜?	e. 날씨가 참 좋은데요!
f. 전화 오면 받아야지.	f. 네, 오늘 덥겠어요.

연습 7. Supply appropriate postpositions by filling in the blank spaces.

나는 1978년에 학생 _______ 미국에 갔었다. 그때에는 미국 _______ 한국 학생이 지금 _______ 많지 않았다. 내가 다니는 대학 _______ 한국 사람 한 분이 교수 _______ 계셨는데 그분이 나 _______ 많이 도와 주셨다. 나는 뉴욕 _______ 대학교 다니는 동안 그 학교 _______ 매점에서 점원 _______ 일했다.

연습 8. Write a short description of your personal background and your hometown, where you were born and raised, etc. Make up a story to make it more interesting, if you prefer. Then, present it orally to the class.

대화 3 (FRAME 3)

형제에 대해서

카슨 : 문 선생은 형제가 많습니까?
문 : 누님이 한분하고 동생이 하나 있어요.
카슨 : 꼭 가운데시군요. 누님은 결혼하셨겠죠.
문 : 그럼요. 그리고, 동생은 금년에 고3입니다.
카슨 : 네? 못알아 듣겠는데요.
문 : 고등학교 3학년을 고3이라고 합니다.
카슨 : 네에. 고3이 그 뜻이군요.
문 : 네. 내년에 대학교 시험 공부 하느라고 바빠요.

단어 공부 (*VOCABULARY STUDY*)

•형제	siblings, brothers and sisters
•꼭	exactly; without fail
•가운데	middle, center
•뜻	meaning; intention
•알아듣다/들어	to comprehend, understand (by listening)

• 시험 공부 하느라고　　studying for the (entrance) examination (for college)

-느라고 is a form that explains an action, or one that gives an excuse for the action stated in the main clause. The subject of the action must be the same as that of the main clause.

그 사람 공부하느라고 바빠요.	He is busy studying.
옷을 사느라고 돈을 다 썼어요.	She spent all her money buying clothes.

연습 9. After listening to the story, write down answers to questions.

Story 1.

a. 남 씨의 아들은 무슨 학교에 다닙니까?
b. 언제 고3이 됩니까?
c. 무엇 하느라고 바빠요?

Story 2.

a. 미숙이의 언니는 결혼했습니까?
b. 부모님은 무엇이라고 합니까?
c. 언니가 왜 결혼 안합니까?

연습 10. Respond to the questions by using -느라고. You may choose one of the suggested reasons or create one for yourself.

a. 요새 왜 그렇게 바쁘세요?
b. 돈을 어디다 다 썼습니까?
c. 왜 우리집에 놀러 오지 않았어요?
d. 어제 밤에 왜 잠을 못잤습니까?
e. 왜 점심을 안먹었어요?

Suggested Reasons:

• 자동차 고치느라고
• 일 하느라고
• 시험 준비하느라고
• 친구랑 얘기하느라고
• 재미있는 책을 읽느라고

대화 4 (FRAME 4)

사진첩을 보면서

인규 : 요전에 피크닉에서 찍은 사진 볼래?

상일 : 벌써 찾았니? 좀 보자. 야, 단풍 좋다! 요전 주 연휴 때였니?

인규 : 그래. 단풍은 10월이 보통 제일 좋아.

상일 : 너하고 동생 사이에 선 여자는 누구냐?

인규 : 우리 사촌 누나야.

상일 : 야, 미인인데! 애인 있니? 소개해 주라.

인규 : 쓸 데 없네. 벌써 약혼했거든.

상일 : 그래? 그럼, 할 수 없지.

단어 공부 (*VOCABULARY STUDY*)

- 요전 last time (occasion)

  Three demonstratives, 이, 그, and 저 become 요, 고, and 조, respectively, when the speaker uses them with a sense of "smallness, closeness, or endearment": e.g., 요것 "this tiny thing," 고 아이 "that little child."

- 사진을 찍다 to take a picture (photograph)

  찍다 denotes the action "of impressing."

- 단풍 autumnal browns and golds
- 요전 주 the very last week (See the note above on 요전.)
- 연휴 long weekend, continuous holidays (연=continuous, 휴=rest)
- 보통 usually (adverb/prenominal/nominal)
- 사이/새 interval; space (between two points); relationship

명희하고 나는 사이가 좋아요. Myŏnghi and I are on friendly terms.
저 사람들은 사이가 나쁩니다. They are on bad terms.

•사촌	cousin (Literally, "four steps removed" in genealogy.)
•사촌누나/누이	older female cousin
•미인	beautiful woman
•애인	lover (애=love, 인=person)
•소개해 주라.	Introduce (her) to me. (LOW, colloquial)

주라 is a colloquial form used among the young generation today. The standard form is irregular 달라 or 다오 "give me," and 주어라 "give him/her." There is a general tendency to simplify irregular forms (or regularize speech forms) among young generation speakers.

•쓸 데 없어.	It's no use. (쓸 데 literally means "a reason to use.")
•약혼하다	to be engaged (약=promise, 혼=marriage)
•할 수 없지.	There's no help. (Literally, "I can't do anything.")

CULTURAL ENCOUNTER The traditional Korean family often includes three or more generations, even though they may not live under one household. The family members (가족) include grandparents (할아버지, 할머니), parents (아버지, 어머니), sons and daughters (아들, 딸), and grandchildren(손자, 손녀). Since all children of the same generation regard themselves as siblings, the terms of siblings (형, 언니, 오빠, etc.) are applied to each other. The words for uncles and aunts, e.g., the older uncle (큰 아버지), the older aunt (큰 어머니), the younger uncle (작은 아버지), the younger aunt (작은 어머니), reflect the extended meaning of parents. Uncles (especially when they are not married) are also called 삼촌 (three steps removed in genealogy), while the generic terms for "uncle" (아저씨) and for "aunt" (아주머니) are not commonly used within the family today since they have been over-used as terms of address outside the family.

연습 11. Complete the picture of genealogy.

a. Fill in the spaces with appropriate words to be used in calling the members of Insuk's family from her viewpoint.
b. How does Sang'il call his cousins on the right?

연습 12. Talk about your family, describing each member and what he or she does for living. (This exercise may be repeated with some family photographs.)

Personalized Vocabulary

학생	student	목사	pastor, minister
가정부인	housewife	신부	priest (Catholic)
사업을 하다	to run a business	의사	doctor, physician
비서	secretary	간호원	nurse
사무원/회사원	office worker	치과의사	dentist
사장	company president; CEO	약(제)사	pharmacist
군인	soldier/military personnel	기사	engineer
순경/경관	policeman	기술자	technician
공무원	government employee	점원	store clerk
변호사	lawyer	화가	artist (painter)
선생	teacher	음악가	musician
교수	professor	배우	actor/actress
스님	monk (Buddist)	문인/작가	writer

문법 (GRAMMAR)

1. A Summary of Quotation Forms

You have already learned how to quote statements (declarative) and in this lesson you have covered three other types of sentences: questions, suggestions and requests (imperatives). We will now summarize some basic facts about the quotation forms in Korean.

		Example
STATEMENTS		
•Action/Process Verb (without -었/겠)		
after a vowel	⟶ add ㄴ다	간다
after a consonant	⟶ add 는다	먹는다
•Equation Verb (without -었/겠)	⟶ add 이라	책이라
•All Other Cases	⟶ add 다	좋다
QUESTIONS		
•Stative/Equation Verb (without -었/겠)	⟶ add 으냐	좋으냐
•All Other Cases	⟶ add 느냐	가느냐
SUGGESTIONS	⟶ add 자	가자
REQUESTS	⟶ add 으라	먹으라
•Except for the verb 주다 "give" which becomes 달라 when the indirect object ("me, him, etc.) coincides with the speaker.		

NOTE: See Lesson 18 for the tenses of the quoted sentences.

❖ WHAT DOES 달라 MEAN?

The verb 주다 "give" in Korean is a unique verb in that it changes the stem itself in some cases: 달라 "give" when the recipient (the indirect object) is the speaker of the quoted sentence. Compare the following pairs.

선생님이 그 사람한테 그것을 <u>주라고</u> 하셨어요.
The teacher told me to give it to him. (him=someone else)

선생님이 저한테 그것을 <u>달라고</u> 하셨어요.
The teacher told me to give it to him. (him=teacher)

❖ HOW TO QUOTE OTHER TYPES OF SENTENCES

If a sentence does not quite fall in one of the four categories above, you have one of the following two choices:

(1) Choose one of the four that may be interpreted as closest by intent and context.
좋은데요! ⟶ 좋다고 했어요. She said that it's nice.

(2) If a verb is lacking, either supply it based on context, or use the direct quotation form

(-이라고 하다).

건배! ⟶ 건배라고 했습니다. She said "Cheers!"

❖ USES OF THE QUOTATION FORM

The quotation form is not only used for actually quoting someone but also for forming complement clauses which serve to "ask," "suggest," and "tell."

학생이냐고 물었습니다.	He asked me if I was a student.
일하라고 하셨어요.	He told/asked me to work.
같이 가자고 그랬어요.	He asked me to go along.

2. Contracted Forms of Quotation

Quoted structures are so often used that they are frequently shortened. There are two common ways of contraction.

a. *Omission of the main verb.* When the quotation is expected by context (e.g., when a repetition is called for), the main verb, such as (말)하다 "say," is often omitted.

무어라고요?	What (did you say)?
비가 온다고요.	It's raining, (I said).

b. *Quoting a third person.* In the LOW or MID forms, the particle -고 and the main verb 하다 are often shortened, when quoting a third person. In most cases, the stem 하 -is simply dropped, resulting in a succession of two endings, as in the examples below. The honorific form 하시다 is not so contracted.

집에 간다고 합니다.	⟶	집에 간답니다.	He says he is going home.
집에 있으라고 합니다.	⟶	집에 있으랍니다.	He asked me to stay home.
강릉이라고 하는 도시	⟶	강릉이라는 도시	a city called Kangnung

When the quoting verb is in the short form 해 (LOW) or 해요 (MID), the last vowel of the preceding ending changes to 애.

춥다고 해요.	⟶	춥대요.	Ⓜ	He says it's cold.
춥다고 해.	⟶	춥대.	Ⓛ	He says it's cold.

3. An Action Explaining Another: -느라고

The connective -느라고, used with an action verb, is a form that explains or gives an excuse for the action stated in the main clause. The subject and the general time of the two clauses should be the same for both clauses, and no tense marker is used with -느라고.

공부하느라고 바쁩니다.	He is busy studying.
옷을 사느라고 돈을 다 썼어요.	She spent all her money buying clothes.
일하느라고 못들었어요.	I couldn't hear it as I was working.
무엇 하느라고 그렇게 늦었어요?	What made you so late?

4. Since: -은 지(가)

If you wish to mark an event from which a certain time has elapsed, you may use the ending -은 지(가).

STEM + 은지(가) [length of time] { -이다 / 되다 }	It has been [length of time] since...

내가 여기 온 지 벌써 한달입니다.
It's been already one month since I came here.

고향을 떠난지 얼마나 오래 됩니까?
How long has it been since you left your hometown?

그 사람 본지 한참 됐어요.
It's been quite a while since I saw her.

밥 먹은지 두 시간 밖에 안 됐어요.
It's been only two hours since we ate.

NOTE: The present and past tense of 되다 is interchangeable here, but strictly speaking, 됩니다 means "it's getting to be..." while 됐어요 means "has become...."

5. Colloquial Endings with Special Connotations

In colloquial Korean, there are rich varieties of sentence endings, and some of these endings have rather unique connotations.

a. Exclamation as a "Rejoinder"

STEM + (는)	군요	(HIGH/MID)
	군 or 구나	(LOW)

NOTE: -는 is present when the verb is an action/process type (without -었/겠).

This ending is typically used when the speaker assumes that the addressee is aware of what is stated, but *not* when pointing out a new fact to the addressee (where -는데요 should be used). Therefore, it is most often used as a rejoinder to something already mentioned or understood, as in the pairs of sentences below.

비가 오는데요!	(Look,) It's raining! (The addressee is not aware of the fact.)
비가 오는군요!	It's raining (, I see)! (The addressee is aware of the fact.)

Although the two forms are often interchangeable, in the situations below where the addressee is obviously aware of what is stated, only -는군요 is possible (but not -는데요).

한국말 배우시는군요!	So, you are learning Korean!
아드님이 고3이군요!	Your son is a high school senior!
바쁘군!/바쁘구나!	I see, you are busy!

Another way to remember the difference between -는데요 and -는군요 is to remember that -는데요 is "informative" to the addressee while -는군요 is not.

b. Explanatory Ending: -거든(요)

The ending -거든(요) is used when the sentence is used to explain something in the context, about which the speaker is expected to know (e.g., typically about the speaker himself).

저 서울에 대해서 잘 압니다.	I know much about Seoul.
제 고향이 서울이거든요.	My hometown is Seoul, you know.
전화를 받지 못했어요.	I couldn't get the phone call.
집에 없었거든요.	I wasn't home, you know.

c. Reminding Someone: -지 않아요?

You have already learned that the long negative form is used in rhetorical questions, *emphasizing the affirmative.*

저 바로 집에 돌아가지 않았어요?	I went right back home, you know. (Literally, "Didn't I go back home?")

There is, in colloquialism, another similar use of the long negative, but with a slightly different function: *reminding someone of something*. This phrasal form is commonly pronounced like a simple ending: -잖아(요).

태어난 데가 고향이잖아요?	The place of birth is the hometown, isn't it?
날씨가 좋잖아요?	It's a beautiful day, don't you know?
나 동생이 있잖아?	I have a brother, remember? (LOW)

CAUTION! In this usage, the long negative form is treated like a simple ending, i.e., the tense marker is placed before -지 (not in 않다), and it is also suffixed to the verb -이다 or 아니다 as shown in the examples below.

내가 주었잖아요?	I gave it to you, remember?
우리 벌써 밥 먹었잖아요?	We already ate, didn't we?
지금 봄이잖아?	It's spring now, you know? (LOW)
이게 아니잖아?	This isn't it, don't you know? (LOW)

읽기 · 쓰기 (READING & WRITING)

1. Addressing Terms in Korean: 한국어의 호칭

Uses of proper addressing terms, 호칭 (literally "calling titles") in Korean is a delicate matter. Unlike in Western countries, uses of personal names are extremely limited, and surnames with titles are not very easy to use properly. In addition, there is a wide-spread practice of using family/kinship terms (아저씨, 아주머니, etc.) as addressing terms for anybody including strangers at places of business or in the street. A newspaper column deals with common problems caused by such practices. Scan the column, and follow through the exercises.

"아주머니... 할머니..."

얼마전 다방에서 노인들 몇 분이 차를 마시다가 엽차를 달라고 했는데, 다방 주인이 종업원에게 "저 할아버지들에게 엽차 좀 갖다 드려라"라고 시키자 노인들이 몹시 화를 내는 것을 보았다. "손님들께 엽차 좀 드리라고 하면 될텐데 왜 할아버지라고 하느냐? 우리가 당신 할아버지냐?"고 노인들은 말했다. 젊은 다방 주인은 "할아버지를 할아버지라고 부른 것이 무슨 잘못이냐."라는 표정이었지만, 나는 그 노인들의 주장이 옳다고 생각했다.

남자고 여자고 나이 들면서 밖에서 자기를 부르는 호칭 때문에 기분이 상하는 때가 많다. '학생'이라고 불리다가, '아저씨'가 되고, 끝내 '할아버지'와 '할머니'로 불릴 때 남녀를 불문하고 묘한 기분이 된다.

'아주머니' '아저씨' '할머니' '할아버지' 등은 본래 가족간의 호칭이지 사회적인 호칭이 아니다. 그런데 언제부터인지 이 말들이 상대방의 나이를 어림잡아서 적당히 붙이는 호칭으로 사용되고 있다. 나이와 연결되기 때문에 상대방을 약올리기 위해서, 또는 기분을 맞추기 위해서 의도적으로 사용되기도 한다. 물건을 뒤적이다가 안 사고 돌아서는 젊은 여성을 '아줌마'라고 부르거나, 중년이 분명한 여성을 '아가씨'라고 부르며 비위를 맞추는 점원들을 가끔 볼 수 있다.

옛날에는 친한 친구의 부모님도 '아버님'이나 '어머님'으로 부르기가 조심스러웠는데, 요즘에는 백화점에 가도 미장원에 가도 '어머님' 소리를 자주 듣게 된다. "어머님에게는 이 옷이 훨씬 젊어 보입니다." "어머님, 파마를 하세요."라는 소리가 곳곳에서 들린다.

연습 13. Guessing by context.

a. 노인 appears in the first line. Guess what the word means, using the context.

A. 어린 사람
B. 젊은 사람
C. 늙은 사람

b. 주인 means "host" or "owner." The syllable 인(人) of 노인 is the same Sino-Korean as in 주인, 애인, etc. What does the syllable 인(人) mean?

단어 소개

얼마전	a while ago
시키자	as (she) ordered
종업원	employee (=직원)
화를 내다	to get angry
주장	claim, opinion
자기	self; one's own (See note below.)
엽차	green tea
-자(마자)	as soon as
몹시	very (=아주, 대단히)
표정	facial expression
옳다	to be right, correct
기분이 상하다	to feel bad

NOTE ON "자기":

> 자기 is a 2nd/3rd person reflexive pronoun (Mid/Low Level) referring to the earlier subject in the immediate context. For example,
>
> 학생은 자기를 부르는 소리를 못들었다.
> The student didn't hear the voice calling him.
>
> 자기 이름도 못쓰는 사람이 있다.
> There are people who can't even write their own names.
>
> 너는 자기 번호도 잊었니?
> Did you forget your own number?

연습 14. Referring to the newspaper column above, answer the following questions in written Korean.

a. 노인들이 다방에서 무엇을 갖다달라고 했습니까?
b. 다방주인이 그 손님들에게 엽차를 갖다드렸어요?
c. 차를 마시던 노인들이 왜 화를 냈습니까?
d. 모르는 노인을 "할아버지"라고 부르는 것이 맞습니까?
e. 다방 주인이 그 노인들을 어떻게 부르는 것이 옳습니까?
f. 다방 주인이 젊습니까? 늙었습니까?
g. 다방 주인이 자기가 잘못했다고 했어요? 안했어요?
h. 이 글을 쓴 사람은 누가 옳다고 생각했습니까?

여성 잡지 독자란 (Readers' Column)에서

> **나 도 한 마 디**
>
> **독자로 부터**
>
> 전주 월요일에 여자 손님에게 책 두 권을 판 일이 있었다. 그후 며칠이 지나 그 손님에게서 전화가 왔다. 할인권이 있었는데, 그것을 잊고 그냥 책을 샀으니까 지금이라도 할인 해달라고 하는 말이었다. 그날 하루 계산은 끝났으니까 안 된다고 하자 왜 안 되느냐고 화를 낸다.
>
> 한참 "안 된다" "왜 안 되느냐?"를 주고 받고 하다가 할 수 없이 그럼 내가 내 돈으로 차액을 드리겠다고 했더니 그 손님은 그만 두라고 전화를 끊어 버렸다. 그 날은 기분이 몹시 좋지 않았다.

연습 15. After reading the Korean passage above, answer each of the following questions in Korean.

a. 아래의 단어가 무슨 뜻인지 사전을 찾아 알아 보십시오.
  • 할인 ________ • 할인권 ________
b. 이 글을 쓴 사람의 직업이 무엇이겠어요?

c. 이 사람이 가게 주인입니까? 종업원입니까?
d. 그 여자 손님이 무엇을 해 달라고 했습니까?
e. 그 손님이 할인을 받았습니까?

연습 16. Complete the following sentences by filling the open spaces appropriately.

며칠전에 지하철 역에서 어떤 젊은 남자가 어느 여자를 보고 "아주머니"라고 부르 ______ 그 여자가 몹시 ______를 내는 것을 보았다. 나이가 서른이 넘은 것 같______ 아직 미혼인 모양이었다. 아마 그 여자는 ______를 "아가씨"라고 불러 주기를 바랐던것 같지만 그 젊은 청년은 자기보다 나이가 위라고 생각해서 그렇게 부른 모양이었다. ______을 잘못 쓰면 상대의 ______을 상하게 하는 일이 많다. 이런 ______에는 그저 "여보세요"라고 부르고 호칭은 안쓰는 것이 낫겠다.

-되
-자
-거나
화
기분
경우
호칭
부족
자기

a. 그 여성이 결혼한 사람이었습니까?
b. 그 여성이 왜 화를 냈습니까?
c. 그 두 사람중에서 누가 나이가 위였습니까?
d. 그 여성은 자기를 무엇이라고 불러 주기를 바란 것 같았습니까?
e. 아주머니"라고 하는 호칭을 미혼인 (결혼 하지 않은) 여성에게 쓰는 것이 괜찮습니까?

단어 정리 (VOCABULARY SUMMARY)

Nominals

가운데	middle, center	애인	lover
고향	hometown	연휴	long weekend
교수	professor	엽차	green tea
노인	old person	요전	last time (occasion)
단풍	autumnal colors	요전 주	last week
도시	city, town	자기	oneself
뜻	meaning	종업원	employee
미인	beautiful woman	지리	geography
미남	handsome man	표정	facial expression
부모	parents	할머니	grandmother
사이/새	space (between two points)	할아버지	grandfather
사진	photograph	해안	coast, sea coast
사촌	cousin	형제	siblings
아저씨	uncle (generic)	호칭	term of address
아주머니	aunt (generic)		

Personalized Vocabulary

가정부인	housewife	비서	secretary
간호원	nurse	사무원	office worker
순경/경관	policeman	사업	business
고모	aunt (father's sister)	사장	company president
공무원	government employee	삼촌	uncle (father's brother)
군인	military personnel	스님	monk (Buddhist)
기사	engineer	신부	priest (Catholic)
기술자	technician	약(제)사	pharmacist
목사	pastor	음악가	musician
문인/작가	writer	의사	physician
배우	actor/actress	치과의사	dentist
변호사	lawyer	화가	artist (painter)

Action Verbs

기억하다	to remember	사진을 찍다	to take a picture
대답하다	to answer	취직하다	to take a job
알아듣다	to comprehend	주장하다	to insist
약혼하다	to be engaged	화를 내다	to get angry

Process Verbs

기분이 상하다	to feel bad	늙다	to get old
기억이 나다	to recall	자라다	to be raised, grow up
나다	to be born		

Stative Verbs

곤란하다	to be difficult, embarrassing
어리다	to be young (as child)
우습다/우스워	to be funny, strange
젊다	to be young (as adult)
옳다	to be right

Adverbs

꼭	exactly; without fail, for sure
보통	usually
전혀	(not) at all (used in a negative sentence)
몹시	very
얼마전	a while ago

Idioms

말을 듣다/들어	to obey, listen to (someone for advice)
쓸 데 없다	to be of no use
주라.	Give me. (LOW, non-standard colloquial)
할 수 없지.	There's no help for it.

Postpositions

-으로(서)	as (status)

Verb Endings

-(는)군요	Exclamatory ending
-기는요	Ending used as a modest disclaimer
-지 않아요?	Ending used to remind someone of something
-자(마자)	as soon as

Connective Endings

-느라고	for the reason of	-은지(가)	since

Phrasal Forms

-는 중이다	to be in the process of	-이라는	(something) called
-는 길에	on one's way to...		

연습문제 해답(ANSWERS TO EXERCISES)

연습 1.
a. 잘 하기는요.
b. 예쁘기는요.
c. 잘 치기는요.
d. 잘 하기는요.

연습 4.
a. 어린 아이가 집에 있어요?
b. 부모님은 늙으셨지만 젊은 사람같이 걸으세요.
c. 저는 젊었을 때 L.A.에 살았습니다.
d. 우리 아주머니는 늘 젊은 사람 같아요.
e. 박 선생은 젊었을 때 학생으로 미국에 왔어요.
f. 저는 어렸을 때 부모님 말씀을 안들었습니다.
g. 태어난 데가 반드시 고향은 아니지요.

연습 5.
a. 학생이 있<u>다고</u> 합니다.
b. 집에 가<u>라고</u> 합니다.
c. 지금 가도 되<u>느냐고</u> 했어요.
d. 기다리<u>자고</u> 했어요.

연습 6. Quotation Exercise

Dialogue 1.
a. 어디 가느냐고 했습니다.
b. 백화점에 간다고 했어요.
c. 같이 가자고 그랬습니다.
d. 집에 있으라고 말했어요.
e. 왜냐고 물었습니다.
f. 전화를 받아야 한다고 했습니다.

Dialogue 2.
a. 계시냐고 물었어요.
b. 들어오시라고 했습니다.
c. 하시겠느냐고 했어요.
d. 그러자고 했습니다.
e. 좋다고 그랬어요.
f. 덥겠다고 했습니다.

연습 7. 학생으로; 미국에; 지금같이; 대학에는; 교수로; 나를; 뉴욕에서; 학교의; 점원으로

연습 9. Scripts and Answers (Answers)

STORY 1 (Script) 남 씨의 큰 아들은 금년에 고삼이라고 한다. 대학교에 들어가려면 시험을 쳐야 한다. 그래서 그 아이는 요새 시험 공부하느라고 아주 바쁘다.

a. 고등학교에 다닙니다.
b. 금년에요.
c. 시험 공부하느라고 바빠요.

STORY 2 (Script) 미숙이의 언니는 아직 혼자 산다. 미숙이의 부모는 빨리 결혼하라고 하는데 말을 안듣는다. 내년에 다시 대학교에 가겠다고만 한다.

a. 안했습니다.
b. 결혼하라고 합니다.
c. 내년에 대학교 가고 싶어 합니다.

연습 11. a. (1) 할머니 (2) 삼촌/아저씨 (3) 큰 어머니 (4) 사촌 언니
b. 사촌 형, 사촌 누나/누이/누님

연습 13. a. c. 늙은 사람 b. "human"

연습 14. a. 엽차
b. 아니오.
c. 할아버지라고 하니까.
d. 아니오.
e. 손님이라고`
f. 젊어요.
g. 안했어요.
h. 손님들.

연습 15. a. "discount," "discount coupon"
b. 서점 종업원
c. 종업원
d. 할인해 달라고
e. 못받았어요.

연습 16. 부르자 - 화를 - 같되 - 자기를 - 호칭을 - 기분을 - 경우에는
a. 아니오.
b. 아주머니라고 부르니까
c. 여자가
d. 아가씨라고
e. 아니오.

Communicative Frames in English

Frame 1. Kangnŭng, Mun's Hometown
Carson: When did you take up a job in this company?
Mun : It's been two years since I got employed. I'm still (in the process of) learning.
Carson: Where is your hometown?
Mun : It's Kangwon Province. A small city called Kangnung.
Carson: Oh, a city on the East Coast, right?
Mun : Yes. You know well about Korean geography!
Carson: Not really. I've been there once, and so I remember.
Mun : Really? You've been there?
Carson: Last year, a friend of mine asked me to go to Mt. Sorak, and on our way to Mt. Sorak we stopped by Kangnŭng.

Frame 2. Carson's Hometown
Mun : Where is your hometown, Mr. Carson?
Carson: Well. I was born in Texas but grew up in New York, you know.
So, when people ask me where my hometown is, it's difficult to answer.
Mun : But isn't the place of your birth your hometown?

Carson : I guess so. But I know nothing about Texas.
Mun : I see. Then did you go to college in New York?
Carson : That's also weird, you know. I went to college in Chicago. My parents asked me to go to Columbia University, but do young kids listen to their parents? My father was a professor in that university, you know.

Frame 3. Talking about Siblings

Carson : Do you have many brothers and sisters?
Mun : I have one elder sister and one younger brother.
Carson : You're right in the middle, aren't you. I guess she is married.
Mun : Of course. And my brother is a "kosam" this year.
Carson : I beg your pardon? I didn't get it.
Mun : The third grade in high school is called "kosam."
Carson : I see. That's what "kosam"means.
Mun : Yes. He is busy studying for the college entrance examination next year.

Frame 4. Looking at a Photo Album

Ingyu : Do you want to see the pictures I took during the last picnic?
Sangil : Did you get them back already? Let me see them.
Wow. Beautiful autumn colors! Was this the last long weekend?
Ingyu : Yeah. The autumn colors are usually at their best in October.
Sangil : Who is the girl standing between you and your sister?
Ingyu : She is my cousin.
Sangil : Wow, she is a beauty. Does she have a lover? Why don't you introduce me to her?
Ingyu : No use. She is already engaged.
Sangil : Really? Well, there's no help for it.

제 22 과

친구 집 방문

대화 1 (FRAME 1)

새 집에 초대를 받는다

남씨: 이사하셨다고요?

김씨: 네, 괜찮은 아파트 찾았어요.

남씨: 찾아 가 뵈었어야 하는데 요새 바빠서.

김씨: 이번 주말에 꼭 놀러 오세요.

남씨: 네, 그러겠습니다. 주소가 어디죠?

김씨: 청산동이에요. 지하철 역에서 내리시면 바로 뒷 골목입니다. 청산동 매화 아파트 7동 325호.

남씨: 교통이 편리하겠군요.

김씨: 네, 모든 것이 편리해요. 그리고, 산 밑이 돼서 동네가 조용해요. 아내도 기뻐합니다.

남씨: 다행입니다. 우리 집사람도 그런 데에서 살고 싶어하던데요.

김씨: 약도 그려 드리죠.

남씨: 그리고 새 전화번호도 적어 주세요.

김씨: 예, 375의 7360입니다.

단어 공부 (*VOCABULARY STUDY*)

- 방문 — visit, visitation
- 초대 — invitation
- 이사하다 — to move, to change one's residence
- 찾았어요. — I found...

CAUTION! The verb 찾다 basically means "to search, look for." Its past tense form 찾았다 may mean either "to have found" or "to have searched," and the intended meaning is determined by context.

- 뵈었어야 하는데 — I should have (visited and) seen you

The supposition contrary to the fact, "should have," is expressed by the use of 었 in the obligatory form: -었어야 하다.

- 꼭 — without fail, for sure; exactly
- 지하철 역 — subway station
- 골목 — back street, back alley
- 청산동 매화 아파트 7동 325호 — #325, Building 7, Maehwa Apartments, Ch'onggsan-dong (a fictitious name); -동 of 청산동 is a township; -동 of 7동 is a suffix for a building.
- 교통 — traffic
- 모든 — all, every (prenominal)
- 산밑이 돼서 — because it is at the foot of the hill/mountain
- 조용하다 — to be quiet
- 기뻐합니다. — (She) is happy.

CAUTION! The emotional state of a third person is normally expressed in a compound form -어 하다. (See Grammar.)

- 다행이다 — to be fortunate
- 우리 집사람 — my wife (humble form)

우리 "our" here may be rendered in English as "my."

- -던데요 — a verb ending indicating the "witnessed past"
- 약도 — simplified map (compare: 지도 "map")
- 그리다 — to draw (compare: 그림 "picture")
- 적다 — to write, record
- 375의 7360 — 375-7360

[삼칠오의 칠삼육공] is how it is commonly read. Read digit by digit, with 0 to be read 공, meaning literally "empty."

❖ A THIRD PERSON'S FEELING OR DESIRE

Stative verbs expressing personal feelings or desires in Korean are in a compound form, -어 하다, when the subject is a third person.

기쁘시지요?	You are happy, aren't you ?
네, 기쁩니다.	Yes, I am.

아내도 퍽 기뻐합니다. My wife is also very happy.

연습 1. Ask your friend questions about his/her feelings about something. After obtaining an answer, report to the class how he/she feels about the topic.

MODEL: A: 영화 보고 싶어요? Do you want to see movies?
B: 아니오. 보고 싶지 않아요 No, I don't.
A: ____는 영화를 보고 싶어하지 않아요. ____ doesn't want to see movies.

a. 춥습니까?
b. 좀 미안하지요?
c. 고단해요?
d. 친구 만나서 반갑지요?
e. 중국 음식 먹을까요?
f. 취직하고 싶어요?
g. 여행하는 거 좋아요?
h. 운동 싫어요?

연습 2. Respond to each question negatively, and then add that "you should have…"

EXAMPLE: 부인에게 편지 쓰셨어요? Did you write to your wife?
아니오. 안 썼어요. No, I haven't.
썼어야 하는데. I should have written to her.

a. 사진 찍으셨어요?
b. 그 사람 만나셨습니까?
c. 선물 가지고 가셨어요?
d. 점심 많이 잡수셨습니까?
e. 호텔에 예약하셨지요?
f. 대사관에 가 보셨어요?

CULTURAL ENCOUNTER Addresses in Korean are specified from larger to smaller units. Note various suffixes to the city, district, etc.

주소	서울시		종로구		사직동		25번지		123
(ADDRESS)	CITY	>	DISTRICT	>	TOWNSHIP	>	LOT NO.	>	DWELLING NO.

이름	박		종식		선생님
(NAME)	SURNAME	>	GIVEN NAME	>	TITLE

연습 3. Imagine that you are standing in front of 광화문, the main gate to the Kyŏngbok Palace (경복궁). Looking at the map below, listen to the directions to each of the following places and write down the gist in English on how to get there.

a. 세종문화회관 (Sejong Cultural Center) ____________________
b. 독립문 (Independence Arch) ____________________
c. 덕수궁 (Tŏksu Palace) ____________________
d. 사직공원 (Sajik Park) ____________________
e. 시청 (City Hall) ____________________

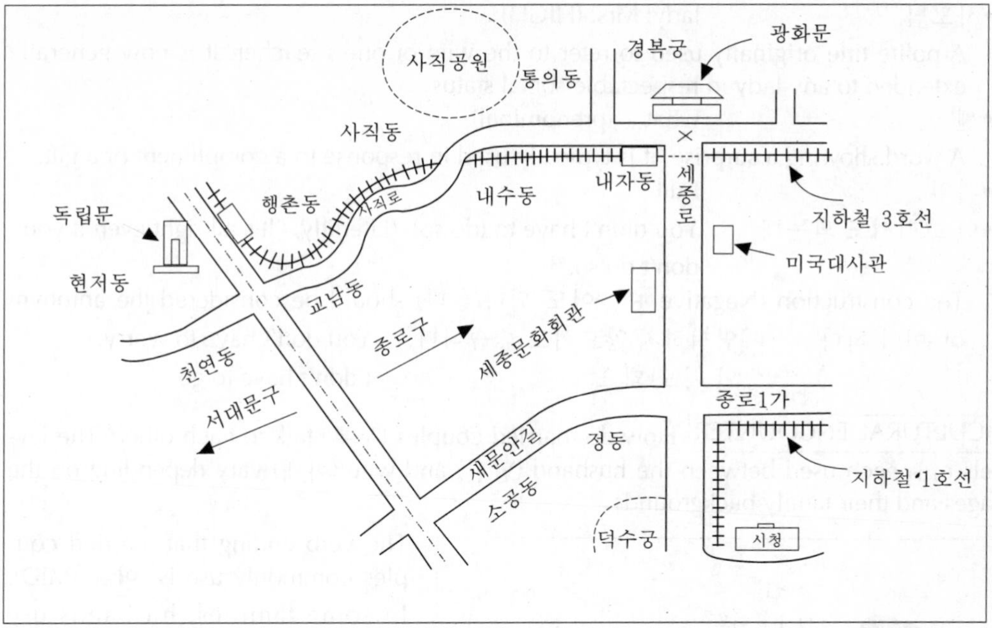

대화 2 (FRAME 2)

친구 집을 방문한다

남씨 : 계세요?
김씨 부인: 네에, 누구시지요?
남씨 : 남관우입니다. 김 선생님 계십니까?
김씨 부인: 아이구, 남 선생, 오셨군요. 기다리고 있었습니다.
어서 들어오세요. 집 찾기 어렵지 않았습니까?
남씨 : 아니오, 적어주신 대로 오니까 간단하던데요.
사모님, 이거 받으시죠.
김씨 부인: 웬 과일을 이렇게 사가지고 오셨어요!
안 그러셔도 되는데.

단어 공부 (*VOCABULARY STUDY*)

- 계세요? Is anybody home? Are you in?
  This is a customary form of greeting used at the entrance of a home one calls at.
- 적어 주신 대로 following your written directions
  -대로 "as..." is a bound noun preceded by a prenominal form.
- 간단하던데요. It was simple.

•사모님 lady; Mrs. (HIGH)

A polite title originally used to refer to the wife of one's teacher. It is now generally extended to any lady in respectable social status.

•웬... what... (prenominal)

A word showing a surprise, it is typically used in response to a compliment or a gift.

•과일 fruit

•안 그러셔도 되는데. You didn't have to (do so). (Literally, "It's all right even if you don't do so.")

The construction (Negative + ...어도 되다/좋다) should be considered the antonym of -어야 하다. 염려하지 않으셔도 좋습니다. You don't have to worry.
안 가도 돼요. I don't have to go.

CULTURAL ENCOUNTER How do married couples (부부) talk to each other? The levels of speech used between the husband (남편) and wife (아내) vary depending on the ages and their family backgrounds.

The verb ending that married couples commonly use is -어요 (MID). In some families, husbands use LOW forms (-어, -지, etc.), while wives use the MID forms (-어요) or HIGH forms (-으세요). The term of endearment between married couples is 여보, and the second-person pronoun for one's spouse is 당신 ("yourself") Younger couples, on the other hand, often use LOW forms to each other. They often use 자기 ("self") instead of 당신.

❖ A SUMMARY OF TERMS REFERRING TO HUSBAND AND WIFE

	REFERRING TO SOMEONE ELSE'S		REFERRING TO ONE'S OWN	
	Husband	Wife	Husband	Wife
HIGH ↓	바깥 어른 바깥 양반 바깥 주인 주인 어른	사모님 안주인 부인	우리 집양반 저의 남편 우리 남편	우리 집사람 제 아내 제 처
MID ↓	부군, 부 남편	처 아내		우리 마누라 우리 여편내
LOW	사내	여편내, 마누라	…아빠	…엄마

연습 4. Respond to the following questions negatively, using the form: NEGATIVE···+어도 되다.

EXAMPLE: A: 집에 가야 해요?
B: 안 가도 됩니다.

a. 주유소에 들러야 돼요?
b. 오래 기다려야 합니까?
c. 여권 가지고 가야 해요?
d. 동네가 조용해야 합니까?
e. 일찍 일어나야 해요?
f. 우표 사야 돼요?
g. 이사해야 합니까?
h. 자동차가 커야 됩니까?

대화 3 (FRAME 3)

거실에서

김씨	:	여보, 날이 더운데 시원한 과일 좀 깎아 와요.
김씨 부인	:	네, 그러죠. 그런데 커피도 준비했는데 드릴까요?
남씨	:	뭘 그러세요? 그저 커피나 한 잔 주세요.
김씨 부인	:	네. 설탕하고 크림은 넣어 드릴까요?
남씨	:	네. 아파트가 밝고 좋습니다. 넓고 깨끗하고. 새로 지은 건물입니까?
김씨	:	아니오. 지은지 5년 됐다고 들었어요.
남씨	:	새 집 같습니다. 좀 구경해도 됩니까?
김씨 부인	:	물론이지요. 여보, 당신이 안내해 드리세요. 전 부엌에서 참외하고 수박 좀 깎아 올테니까.
김씨	:	그래요. 자, 이 쪽으로 들어가 보세요.

단어 공부 (*VOCABULARY STUDY*)

- 거실 — living room
- 여보 — dear, honey

A term used to call attention of one's spouse, derived from 여기 보오 "Please look here."

- 깎다 — to peel (fruit); to trim, cut
  Also used in 머리를 깎다 "to have one's hair cut."
- 뭘 그러세요? — Why do you bother?
  A polite ritualistic expression of humbly declining somene's offer.
- 설탕 — sugar
- 크림 — cream
- 넣다 — to put in
- 밝다 — to be bright (antonym: 어둡다 "to be dark")
  The consonant ㄹ is pronounced only before a vowel.
- 넓다 — to be spacious, wide (antonym: 좁다 "to be narrow")
  The consonant ㅂ is pronounced only before a vowel.
- 건물 — building
- 짓다/지은/지어 — to build (a house)
  Also used in 밥을 짓다 "to cook rice."
- (Nominal) + 같다 — to be like…
- -어도 됩니까? — Is it all right if...?
- 물론이지요. — Of course; Sure.
- 안내하다 — to guide/show (someone) around
- 부엌 — kitchen
- -을 테니까 — since I will…(=-을 것이니까)
  -을 터이다 is another form denoting the speaker's intention or opinion, similar to -을 것이다 or -겠.

연습 5. Referring to the picture below, answer each of the following questions in Korean.

a. 이 집에 침실이 몇개 있습니까?
b. 거실에는 무슨 물건이 있습니까?
c. 마당은 어떻습니까?

d. 화장실은 어디 있어요?
e. 이집의 부엌이 넓어요? 좁아요?
f. 욕실로는 어떻게 갑니까?
g. 온돌방이 없는 것 같은데 있으면 좋겠습니까?
h. 텔레비전은 하나 밖에 없는 것 같은데 어디 있어요?
i. 왜 현관에 신을 벗어 놓았습니까?
j. 벽에 무엇이 걸려 있어요?

연습 6. Show the location of your house in a simplified map that you draw, and then show how the rooms are laid out in the house.

연습 7. Referring to the picture below, answer each of the following questions in Korean.

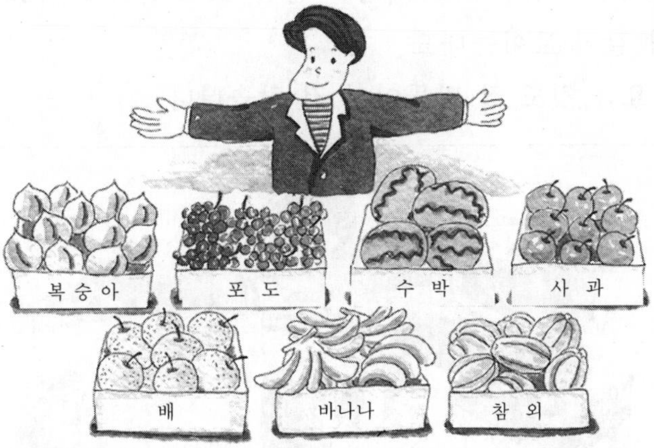

a. 무슨 과일을 가장 좋아합니까?
b. 한국 사람은 사과나 배를 깎아 먹는 것이 보통입니까?
c. 한국 배는 동그랗습니다. 미국 배도 그래요?
d. 포도주는 포도로 만들어요?
e. 수박이나 참외는 어떤 때에 많이 납니까?
f. 과일을 많이 먹는 것이 몸에 좋습니까?

대화 4 (FRAME 4)

집 안을 구경한다

김씨 : 화장실하고 욕실은 이쪽에 있습니다.
남씨 : 네. 모두 신식으로 잘 돼 있네요. 침실은 몇입니까?
김씨 : 침실은 둘인데, 식당 옆에 작은 방이 하나 있어서 서재로 쓰고 있습니다. 보세요.
남씨 : 아, 컴퓨터도 갖다 놓으셨군요.
김씨 : 네. 방이 좀 어둡지만 컴퓨터 쓰기에는 좋아요.
남씨 : 저기 놓인 것은 오래된 이조 자기예요?
김씨 : 아니예요. 가짜지요. 제가 무슨 돈으로 진짜를 사요?
남씨 : 진짜 같이 보이는데요.
김씨 : 네, 요즘 것도 잘 만들어진 것 많습니다.

단어 공부 (*VOCABULARY STUDY*)

•욕실	bathroom (욕= bathing, 실 = room)
•모두	all (adverb, nominal) (= 다)
•신식으로	in a new style (antonym: 구식 "an old fashion")
•돼 있다	is being in a particular way/condition
•서재	study (room), a room for reading and studying
•갖다 놓으셨군요.	You have (it) placed/put in.
•놓다	to put, place, put down

CAUTION! The two verbs 놓다 "to put (on)" and 넣다 "to put (in)" are similar in sound and meaning, but they are different in expressing the place in which a thing is placed; 놓다/놓아 is to place something on some place, while 넣다/넣어 is to place it in or into a container.

- 어둡다/어두워 — to be dark (antonym: 밝다 "to be light, bright")
- 저기 놓인 것 — the thing that is (placed) over there

  The verb 놓이다 "to be placed" is the passive of 놓다.
- 진짜 — real, genuine (colloquial) (antonym: 가짜)
- 이조 자기 — Yi Dynasty pottery

  The Yi Dynasty is the last Korean kingdom (1392-1910), also known as 조선.
- 가짜 — fake, non-genuine, replica (colloquial)
- -같이 보이다 — to look like(something); 보이다 "to appear, be seen"
- 만들어 지다 — to be made (passive form of 만들다 "to make")

연습 8. Complete the sentences below by choosing an appropriate phrase from the list of suggested phrases or by using your own phrase.

a. 아파트가 참 _______ 돼 있습니다.
b. 부엌이 _______ 돼 있는것 같습니다.
c. 침실이 _______ 만들어져 있어요.
d. 마당이 꽤 _______ 돼 있군요.
e. 새 자동차는 아주 _______ 만들어진 것입니다.
f. 거실이 퍽 _______ 돼 있지 않아요?
g. 그림이 정말 _______ 돼 있지요?
h. 이 자기가 참 _______ 만들어졌어요.

Suggested Phrases
- 밝게
- 넓게
- 좁게
- 편리하게
- 예쁘게
- 잘
- 튼튼하게

연습 9. Convert each sentence on the left column to a prenominal form by modifying the noun on the right column.

EXAMPLE: 공부하고 있었어요 ⟶ 공부하던 학생
He was studying. — The student who was studying

a. 과일을 깎고 있었습니다. _______________ 부인
b. 컴퓨터를 쓰고 있었어요. _______________ 사람
c. 결혼 했었어요. _______________ 여자
d. 사진을 찍고 있었지요. _______________ 동생
e. 뒤에 앉았었어요. _______________ 친구
f. 책상 위에 놓여 있었어요. _______________ 책

연습 10. Imagine that you were invited to a friend's house last night. Then, as you look at the picture in Exercise 5, describe how each room was like by using the witnessed past form -던데요.

연습 11. Say the following sentences in Korean, using a "witnessed past" form for any of those parts marked [WITNESSED].

a. I brought a computer into my bedroom so that I can work at night.
b. Peel some fruit and put it in my study, please.
c. He didn't look like a cop [WITNESSED]. Is he a real cop?

d. I'll get my hair cut, so why don't you wait in the tea room.
e. I put a 100-won coin into the telephone (전화기).
f. The kitchen was bright and modern [WITNESSED].

문법 (GRAMMAR)

1. A Summary of Passive Forms in Korean

As you might have noticed, the uses of passive sentences in Korean are not as extensive as in English. There are a few reasons for it. One of them is that there is no standard passive formula (like "be + past participle" as in English) to be used for all transitive verbs. For some verbs, such as 읽다 "read," 배우다 "learn," 묻다 "ask," 만나다 "meet" and many others, there are simply no passive forms available. Where there are passive forms available, several different forms are used, depending on the types and meanings of verbs.

The Korean passive form may be represented as follows:

SUBJECT	AGENT	[Animate] -에게 / 한테 [Inanimate] -에 / 으로	PASSIVE VERB FORM

The agent is either a human that performs the action or an inanimate being which is the cause of the event. The agent, however, is often absent in passive sentences.

도둑이 순경에게 잡혔어요.	The robber was captured by a policeman.
은행이 막 열렸습니다.	The bank is just opened.
커피가 (준비) 됐어요.	The coffee is ready.
열쇠는 책상 위에 놓여 있습니다.	The key is placed on the desk.

CAUTION! If the verb expresses a state of being after the completion of an action, the use of -었 or -어 있다 is required as in the last two examples above.

•TWO TYPES OF PASSIVE FORMS: There are two major types of passive forms: one with an extension of the verb stem (generally with an addition of 이), and the other consisting of a few phrasal forms.

A. Passive Verbs with Addition of 이, 리, 히, or 기

•쓰다 ⟶ 쓰이다	be used/written	NOTE: These types of passive verbs are restricted to a number of native verbs.
•놓다 ⟶ 놓이다	be placed/put	
•보다 ⟶ 보이다	be seen/visible	
•열다 ⟶ 열리다	be opened/open	
•팔다 ⟶ 팔리다	be sold	
•걸다 ⟶ 걸리다	be hung	
•듣다 ⟶ 들리다	be heard/audible	
•부르다 ⟶ 불리다	be called	
•닫다 ⟶ 닫히다	be closed	
•잡다 ⟶ 잡히다	be captured	
•먹다 ⟶ 먹히다	be eaten	
•안다 ⟶ 안기다	be embraced	

CAUTION! Note that the passive verbs 보이다 "be seen" and 들리다 "be heard" are used to express the visibility and audibility as opposed to "active seeing" and "active hearing" (Lessons 10 and 19).

이것 보세요.	Please look at this.
이것이 보입니까?	Do you see this? (visibility)
제말 들으세요.	Listen to me.
제말이 들립니까?	Can you hear me? (audibility)

B. The Passive in Phrasal Forms

With some verbs, several types of phrasal forms are used, but they must be learned individually since there are no general rules for predicting their forms.

(1) A few verbs are converted to the passive with the compound verb form, -어 지다 "become" (either with or without the extended stem).

•알다	know	⟶ 알려 지다	be known
•고치다	repair	⟶ 고쳐 지다	be repaired
•만들다	make	⟶ 만들어 지다	be made

(2) Many 하다 verbs (consisting of a Sino-Korean noun and 하다) may be converted to the passive by replacing 하다 with 되다.

•시작(을) 하다	start	⟶ 시작(이) 되다	get started
•준비(를) 하다	prepare	⟶ 준비(가) 되다	get prepared

(3) Some 하다 verbs with the human object may be converted to the passive with the use of the verb 받다.

•초대(를) 하다	invite	⟶ 초대(를) 받다	be invited
•소개(를) 하다	introduce	⟶ 소개(를) 받다	be introduced

(4) Some verbs with the adverse implications may be converted to the passive with the verb 당하다 "to suffer/undergo."

•파괴(를) 하다	destroy	⟶ 파괴(를) 당하다	be destroyed
•징병(을) 하다	draft	⟶ 징병(을) 당하다	be drafted (into the army)

2. Two Ways of Expressing Feelings

Personal feelings are typically expressed with stative verbs. But for many verbs of emotion and desire, stative verbs are converted to action verbs with the compound form -어하다, which denotes actions or behaviors reflecting the third person's feeling.

반갑습니다.	(STATIVE VERB)	I am glad (to see you).
집사람도 반가워합니다.	(ACTION VERB)	My wife is glad, too.

Listed below are those stative verbs that may be used differently with the third-person subject.

좋다	⟶ 좋아하다	like (something); be happy
싫다	⟶ 싫어하다	dislike

기쁘다	→ 기뻐하다	be happy, glad
반갑다	→ 반가워하다	be happy, glad
미안하다	→ 미안해하다	be sorry
고맙다	→ 고마워하다	be grateful
아프다	→ 아파하다	be painful
배 고프다	→ 배고파하다	be hungry

The compound verb form -고 싶다 expressing one's desire to do something (where 싶다 is a stative verb) is also converted to an action verb form.

집에 가고 싶어요.	I want to go home.
집에 가고 싶어해요.	They want to go home.

The expressions of "liking" and "disliking" are used either way with the first person subject.

운동이 좋아요. 운동을 좋아해요.	I like (taking) physical exercise.
저 생선이 싫어요. 저 생선을 싫어해요.	I don't like fish.

CAUTION! There are cases where a third person's feelings may be expressed without the compound form (-어하다) and those where the speaker's feelings may be expressed with the compound form. To understand why, it is necessary to remember the basic meaning of the compound form with 하다: the expression of one's feeling through his/her *behavior.* The reason for using an action type of expression for the third person subject is that a third person's feelings are normally accessible only through behaviors that are *observable* to the speaker. Therefore, when the speaker uses a conjectural or conditional form, there is no need to use the compound form, -어 하다.

기쁠 겁니다./기쁘겠어요.	I think he is happy.
읽고 싶으면…	If she wants to read it…

3. Witnessed Past : -던데(요)

Korean has a special set of verb endings by which the speaker can state a past event with the implication that he/she has a first-hand experience about the event, not merely through one's belief or hearsay. We will call this type of verb endings "witnessed past" for convenience. (It is also called the "retrospective aspect" by some authors.)

쉽던데요.	It was easy. (I experienced it myself.)
미스 임 일하시던데요.	Miss Yim was working. (I saw her.)
아무도 없던데.	No one was there. (I saw it there.)
간다고 하던데.	He said he was going. (I heard him.)

CAUTION! The grammatical subject of a witnessed past verb form is *not normally* the 1st person (the speaker himself) but the verb ending -던데요 strongly implies that the speaker's first-hand experience is involved here. (See below for exceptions.)

There are other witnessed past endings as shown in the list below. The interrogative forms are used in asking the addressee to report some event as he or she witnessed it. These forms are not frequently used by younger speakers today.

		Declarative	Interrogative
POLITE	:	-습디다 / ㅂ디다	-습디까 / ㅂ디까
BLUNT	:	-더라	-더냐

Exceptions: The witnessed past form is sometimes used with the 1st person subject, when denoting a state or process that is not under the speaker's conscious control.

고단하던데요. I was tired. (E.g., after a hard work)

4. The Prenominal Ending: -던 and -었던

The prenominal ending -던 was first introduced as the past tense form of stative verbs (Lesson 17), but it has wider uses. -던 is originally a witnessed past form, and it may still be used in that sense. However, in most cases, -던 has lost its original meaning, and is used as the past progressive with action or process verbs, and as the past form with stative verbs.

하던 일 끝내야겠어요.	I must finish what I *was* doing.
얘기 하던 사람이 이 씨였어요.	The man who *was* speaking was Mr. Lee.
저기 있던 부인 생각납니까?	Do you recall the lady who was there?
그렇게 덥던 여름이 지나갔어요.	The summer that was so hot is over.

CAUTION! The use of the past form -던 with a stative verb (as in the last example above) is not common because the form emphasizes the fact that the particular state of being is past and is *no more true now.* Normally the ending -은 is sufficient regardless of the time reference.

그렇게 더운 여름이 지나갔어요. The summer that was so hot is over.

The "double past" tense, as in 여기 앉았었어요 "I was sitting here," has its prenominal equivalent in -었던. The double past tense has no English equivalent, and you must find an English translation appropriate to the context.

Double Past Sentences	Double Past in Prenominals
누가 왔었어요. Someone had been here. (He is not here now.)	아까 왔던 손님이 김 선생이었을 겁니다. The visitor who had been here a while ago was probably Mr. Kim.
한국에 갔었습니다. He had gone to Korea. (He isn't there now.)	한국에 갔던 사람 많아요. There are many who had been to Korea.
여기 앉았었어요. She had been sitting here. (But not now.)	여기 앉았던 부인 저 몰라요. I don't know the lady who was sitting here.

CAUTION! The double past form -었던 is generally interchangeable with the simple past form -은 for many verbs. The use of -었던 is crucial *only with those verbs where the* *distinction* between the simple past and double past is clear (such as 결혼하다 "to get married," 앉다 "to sit down," 열리다 "to be opened, "etc.

결혼했어요.	{ He got married. / He is married. }	결혼 한 사람	{ one who got married / a married person }
결혼했었어요.	He had been married.	결혼했던 사람	one who had been married (then)

5. A Summary of Prenominal Endings

Prenominal endings change verbs into noun-modifiers. They are used to form various types of phrases and clauses (Lessons 16). There are altogether five basic forms, determined by the type of verbs and the tense and/or aspect. The existence verb 있다 (including 없다, 계시다, and 안 계시다) has a unique set of prenominal endings.

	Action/Process	Stative & -이다	Existence
(1) Present/Generic	-는	-은	-는
(2) Future/Expected	-을	-을	-을
(3) Past/Completed	-은	-던	-던
(4) Past Progressive	-던	Not applicable	
(5) Double Past	-었던	-었던	-었던

CAUTION! The prenominal endings used in "included questions" are irregular (Lesson 20). The past tense forms used for (3, 4, and 5 above) are replaced by -었는 (past) and -었었는 (double past).

읽기 · 쓰기 (READING & WRITING)

1. Modern Korean Houses: 한국의 현대식 주택

The common types of residential houses (주택) in Korea underwent a radical change after the Korean War in the 1950's. Most city dwellers can no longer easily afford traditional Korean houses (한옥) since the land became an extremely expensive commodity, and instead tall apartment buildings and multiplex dwelling houses became common needs in cities. This brought about changes in arrangement of living spaces within residences from the traditional style to the Westernized style. Today, magazines for housewives frequently include such articles as the one below, discussing how to arrange and decorate the living spaces in typical Westernized dwellings.

거실에서 무엇을 하나?

● **거실의 기능은 막연하다**

'거실에 무엇을 두어야 할까' 라고 생각해 보면 두어야 할 물건의 이미지가 명확하게 머리에 떠오르지가 않는 것이 보통이다.

아마 거실의 기능이 다른 방하고 달리 명확하지 않기 때문일 것이다. 현대 주택에서는 각방의 기능이 대개 명확하다. 예를 들어서 음식을 준비하는 데는 주방, 식사 하는데는 식당, 잠 자는 데는 침실, 책 보고 글 쓰는 데는 서재라고 돼 있으나, 거실에서는 하는 일이 한두 가지가 아니고 막연하니 거실에 무엇을 두어야 할지 얼른 생각이 나지 않는 것 같다.

우리들은 거실에서 잡담도 하고 TV도 보고, 차도 마시고, 과일도 깎아 먹고, 신문도 읽고, 음악을 듣기도 한다. 이렇게 거실이란 대단한 일은 특별히 하는 것이 없으나, 그대신 대단한 일 외의 모든 일이 이루어지는 중요한 방이다.

단어 소개

기능	function	주택	residence (=사는 집)
막연하다	to be vague	예를 들어서	for example
두다	to put, place, store	주방	kitchen (=부엌)
떠오르다	to come up, emerge	-나?	= -느냐?
명확하다	to be clear, definite	-으나	= -지만
달리	differently	-으니	= -으니까
	(adverbial form of 다르다)	얼른	quickly (=빨리)
현대	modern (age)	특별히	especially

연습 12. Referring to the passage above, answer each of the following questions in Korean.

a. 거실의 기능이 다른 방처럼 명확합니까?
b. 부엌을 또 무엇이라고 부릅니까?
c. 책이나 책상 같은 물건은 대개 어느 방에 둡니까?
d. 잠을 자는 방을 뭐라고 합니까?
e. 당신 집의 거실에는 무슨 물건들이 놓여 있습니까? 몇 가지 예를 들으십시오.
f. 거실에 무엇을 두어야 할지를 알려면 무엇을 생각해 보는것이 좋겠습니까?
g. 가족이 함께 거실에서 하는 일이 무엇입니까?

연습 13. Read the Korean captions below and put them into English. Use your English-Korean dictionary for the unknown vocabulary.

(A)

지난 봄 옷장 속에 넣어둔 겨울 옷,
늘 새옷처럼 입는 세탁 손질법

항상 새옷 같아요

부피가 크고 대개가 비싼 소재로 만들어진 겨울 옷들은 세탁하기가 여간 까다롭지 않다.
약간 묻은 얼룩으로 세탁소에 보내자니 그렇고 얼룩 묻은 대로 한 겨울내내 입을 수도 없는 일이다.
세탁소에 맡기지 않고 간단히 집에서 손질할 수 있는 방법을 소개한다.

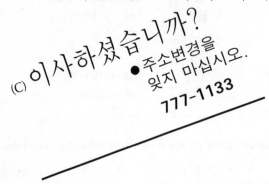

(B)

행복한 가정은
즐거운 부엌에서 시작됩니다.

(C) 이사하셨습니까?
●주소변경을
잊지 마십시오.
777-1133

Sister Words: 놓다, 넣다, 두다, 넣어두다

There are four Korean verbs denoting similar actions of placing things somewhere: 놓다, 넣다, 두다, and 넣어 두다. Let us compare them.

놓다	to put or place something on top of something
넣다	to put or place something in a container
두다	to leave (or store) something somewhere
넣어 두다	to leave (or store) something in a container

연습 14. Complete each of the following sentences by filling in words from the boxes, and then translate the completed sentences into English.

a. 요즈음에는 옛날처럼 전통적인 ________에 사는 ________이 적어졌다. 서울의 땅 값이 비싸져서 보통 사람들은 아파트 같은 현대식 ________에 사는 것이 싸고 ________하기 때문일 것이다.

주택	편리
가족	이용
한옥	

b. 외국어를 배울 때, 단어나 문법의 뜻이 너무 ________해서 잘 배워지지 않을 ________가 많다. 어느 나라 말이나 다른 나라 사람에게는 말의 뜻이 ________한 것이 아니다. 하여튼 단어를 배울 때 단어를 그냥 ________려고 하지 말고 예문을 많이 보고 그런 예문을 ________서 배우도록 하는 것이 가장 좋다.

부족	외우-
명확	통해-
막연	떠오르-
경우	

단어 정리 (VOCABULARY SUMMARY)

Nominals

가짜	fake (thing)	신	shoes (generic term)
거실	living room	신식	modern style
건물	building	아내	wife
골목	back street, alley	약도	simplified map
공원	park	욕실	bathroom
과일 / 과실	fruit	자기	ceramic ware
교통	traffic	지도	map
기능	function	지하철	subway
남편	husband (plain form)	진짜	real, genuine (item)
-동	suffix for a township	주방	kitchen (=부엌)
-동	suffix for a building	초대	invitation
마당	yard, garden	포도	grape
방문	visit	포도주	wine
부엌	kitchen	한옥	Korean-style house
사모님	lady (honorific)	현관	entrance (of a house)
설탕	sugar	현대	modern times
시청	city hall	-호	suffix for a number

Action Verbs

갖다 놓다	to put in, install	방문하다	to visit
그리다	to draw	이사하다	to move (house)
깎다	to trim, peel	적다	to write, record
놓다	to place, put	짓다 / 지어	to build, make
놓이다	to be placed	찾다	to look for; find
넣다	to put (something) in		

Stative Verbs

간단하다	to be simple	밝다	to be bright
기쁘다 / 기뻐	to be happy	어둡다 / 어두워	to be dark
넓다	to be spacious, wide	조용하다	to be quiet
다행이다	to be fortunate	좁다	to be narrow
명확하다	to be clear, definite		

Process Verbs

떠오르다	to come up, emerge (idea)

Adverbs

꼭	without fail; exactly	모두	all (=다)

달리	differently	얼른	quickly (=빨리)

Idioms

뭘 그러세요?	Why do you bother? (a polite phrase for declining one's offer)
찾았어요.	I (have) found.
예를 들어서	for example; 예를 들다 "to cite an example"

Verb Endings

-나?	blunt interrogative ending
-는 대로	as, according to...
-던데요.	witnessed past (See Grammar.)
-으나	= -지만
-으니	= -으니까
-을 테니까	as I will... (=을 터이다; -을 것이다)

Prenominals

모든	all	웬...?	what kind of...?

Interjections

여보	honey, dear (an affectionate term used between husband and wife)

연습문제 해답 (ANSWERS TO EXERCISES)

연습 2.
a. 찍었어야 하는데요.
b. 만났어야 하는데.
c. 가지고 갔어야 해요.
d. 많이 먹었어야 하는데요.
e. 예약했어야 하는데.
f. 가 봤어야 했습니다.

연습 3.
a. 세종문화회관은 광화문에서 남쪽으로 가면 바른 쪽에 있어요.
b. 독립문은 경복궁 앞에서 지하철 3호선을 타시고 다음 역에서 내리시면 됩니다.
c. 덕수궁요? 덕수궁은 세종로로 남쪽으로 가시면 바른 쪽에 있어요. 세종문화회관을 지나서 가세요. 시청 건너 쪽입니다.
d. 사직공원은 가깝습니다. 사직로로 서쪽으로 10분만 가시면 돼요.
e. 시청요? 이쪽으로 곧장 가세요. 왼쪽에 큰 건물이 보입니다. 바로 거기에요. 덕수궁 아세요? 덕수궁 건너 편이에요.

연습 4.
a. 안 들러도 됩니다.
b. 오래 안 기다려도 됩니다.
c. 가지고 가지 않아도 돼요.
d. 조용하지 않아도 좋아요.
e. 일찍 안 일어나도 돼요.
f. 사지 않아도 되겠어요.
g. 이사 안 해도 될것 같아요.
h. 크지 않아도 돼요.

연습 5.
a. 둘입니다.
b. 텔레비전, 의자 같은 것이 있어요.
c. 마당은 좁아요.
d. 이층에 있습니다.
e. 아주 좁습니다.
f. 식당에서 계단으로 올라 갑니다.

g. 있으면 좋지요. h. 거실에 있어요.
i. 한국에서는 집에 들어 갈때 신을 벗어야 하니까요.
j. 그림하고 시계가 걸려 있습니다.

연습 9. a. 과일 깎던 부인 d. 사진을 찍던 동생
b. 컴퓨터를 쓰던 사람 e. 뒤에 앉았던 친구
c. 결혼했던 여자 f. 책상 위에 놓여 있던 책

연습 11. a. 밤에 일하려고 컴퓨터를 침실에 갖다 놓았습니다.
b. 과일을 깎아서 내 서재에 갖다 놓으세요.
c. 순경 같이 안 보이던데요 / 순경 같지 않던데요. 진짜 순경입니까?
d. 나 머리를 깎고 올 테니까 다방에서 기다려 주세요.
e. 전화기에 100원 짜리 동전을 넣었어요.
f. 부엌이 밝고 신식이던데요.

연습 12. a. 아니오. 막연합니다. e. 소파, 테이블 등이 있습니다.
b. 주방이라고도 합니다. f. 거기서 무엇을 하느냐를.
c. 서재. g. 이야기하고 TV를 보는 것 등.
d. 침실이라고 합니다.

연습 13. (A) Last spring you tucked into your dressers those winter clothes; how to wash and care them, so you can always wear them as if they were new. THEY ALWAYS LOOK LIKE NEW.
(B) A happy family starts with a happy kitchen.
(C) Did you move? Don't forget (to inform us of) the change of address.

연습 14. a. 한옥 - 가족 - 주택 - 편리 The number of families living in traditional houses are decreasing nowadays. It may be because the land prices in Seoul have gone up, and living in apartments has become inexpensive and convenient.
b. 막연 - 경우 - 명확 - 외우려고 - 통해서 When you learn a foreign language, the meanings of words and structures are often vague and difficult to learn. No language in this world give clear meanings of words to the non-native speaker. At any rate, it is the best policy to learn words through example sentences rather than simply to memorize them.

Communicative Frames in English

Frame 1. Being Invited to a New Home

Nam : I heard you have moved.
Kim : Yes, I found a nice apartment.
Nam : I should have visited you, but I've been busy lately.
Kim : Come to see us this weekend by all means.
Nam : Yes, I will. What's the address?
Kim : It's Ch'ŏngsan-dong. If you get off at the subway station there, you'll find our place on the back street right there: unit 325, Building 7, Maehwa Apartments, Ch'ŏngsan-dong.
Nam : That's conveniently located for traffic, I'm sure.
Kim : Yes, everything is convenient. And, since it's right at the foot of the hill, the neighborhood is quiet. My wife is happy, too.
Nam : That's fortunate. My wife also says she wants to live in such a location.

Kim : I'll draw a simple map for you.
Nam : And write the new telephone number for me, too.
Kim : Sure. It's 375-7360.

Frame 2. Calling at a Friend's Home
Nam : Is any one home?
Mrs. Kim : Yes. Who is this, please?
Nam : It's Kwanwu Nam. Is Mr. Kim in?
Mrs. Kim : Oh, Mr. Nam, so you are here! We were waiting. Come right in. Wasn't it hard to find the house?
Nam : No, I just followed your directions, and it was simple. Lady, please accept this.
Mrs. Kim : You brought a basket of fruit for us! You shouldn't have done this.

Frame 3. In the Livingroom
Kim : Dear, the weather is hot, could you peel some fresh fruits and bring them over?
Mrs. Kim : Yes, I will. But I have coffee ready, too. Shall I offer you coffee?
Nam : Please don't bother. Just a cup of coffee will do.
Mrs. Kim : All right. Shall I put sugar and cream in it for you?
Nam : Please. The apartment is bright and nice. It's roomy and clean. Has it been recently built?
Kim : No, I heard that it's been five years since it was built.
Nam : It looks like a new house. Is it all right to see the house?
Mrs. Kim : Of course. Dear, why don't you show him around. I will peel apples and pears in the kitchen and bring them out.
Kim : All right. Well, please go right in this way and see.

Frame 4. Walking through the House
Kim : The bathroom and toilet are on this side.
Nam : I see. Everything is modern and well furnished. How many bedrooms are there?
Kim : There are two bedrooms, but we have a small room next to the dining room, so I'm using it as my study. Take a look.
Nam : Oh, you have put in a computer, too.
Kim : Yes. The room is a little dark, but it's good enough for using a computer.
Nam : The thing placed over there, is that a genuine Yi Dynasty ceramic ware?
Kim : No, that's an imitation. How can I afford to buy a real stuff?
Nam : It looks like a real one.
Kim : Yes, there are many modern wares that are well crafted.

제 23 과

친구를 만나서 하는 이야기

대화 1 (FRAME 1)

어느 서점에서

카슨 :	미스 최 아니예요?
미스 최 :	아이구, 카슨 선생님, 깜작 놀랐는데요. 서점에서 선생님 만날 줄은 몰랐어요.
카슨 :	네, 이 부근에 볼 일이 있어서 들렀어요. 날씨가 더워졌죠? 어떻게 지내세요, 요즘?
미스 최 :	늘 무사분주지요.
카슨 :	네? 뭐라고요? 못 알아 들었는데요.
미스 최 :	하는 일없이 바쁘다는 말입니다. 한문이에요.
카슨 :	어려운 말 쓰지 마세요. 초보자 놀리면 안 돼요.
미스 최 :	네에, 잘못했습니다. 죄송해요.

단어 공부 (*VOCABULARY STUDY*)

- •놀라다 — to be surprised (process verb)
- •깜짝 — a symbolic word representing "the blinking of an eye," often used with the verb 놀라다

CAUTION! A surprise is normally expressed with an intransitive verb 놀라다 in Korean. The English verb, "to surprise someone," is a transitive verb, whose equivalent in Korean is 놀라게 하다, a causative verb form.

•서점	bookstore
•더워지다	to become hot (See Grammar on -어 지다.)
•만날 줄은 몰랐어요.	I didn't expect to run into you. (See Grammar on -줄.)
•볼 일	errand, something to attend to
•무사분주	a humorous phrase of Chinese origin. Literally, "Running around busily with little work of any value." (무= no, 사= work, 분= busy, 주= run)
•-없이	without
•-다는 말이다.	It means... (= -다고 하는 말이다) (See Grammar.)
•한문	Classical Chinese (as opposed to 중국어 "modern Chinese")
•초보자	beginner, novice (초= first, 보= step, 자= person)
•놀리다	to tease, make fun of
•죄송하다	to be sorry/guilty (an expression of apology)

❖ -줄 알다 / 모르다: ONE KNOWS/DOES NOT KNOW THAT···

Nominal clauses, equivalent to "the fact that···," usually ends with -것 (Lesson 12), but clauses serving as the object of 알다 "know" and 모르다 "not know" normally end with -줄 rather than -것.

스미스 선생이 미국 사람인 줄 압니다.	I know that Mr. Smith is an American.
비가 올 줄 알았어요.	I knew that it would rain.
저 사람 독일어하는 줄 알았어요?	Did you know that he speaks German?
저 사람 약혼한 줄 몰랐는데요.	I didn't know that she was engaged.

연습 1. For each of the following statements, say that you didn't know that fact by using a nominal clause with -줄.

EXAMPLE: 비가 옵니다 — It's raining!
비가 오는 줄 몰랐어요. — I didn't know that it's raining.

a. 이것이 이조자기 입니다.
b. 저 사람 애인이 있어요.
c. 집이 여기서 가까워요.
d. 김씨는 고향에 갔어요.
e. 형제 사이가 아주 좋아요.
f. 창문이 열렸어요.

연습 2. Answer the following questions, using the phrase -어 지다 "to become..." You may use your own phrase or use one of the suggested phrases listed on the right.

	Suggested Phrases
a. 요새 춥지요?	•바빠 졌어요.
b. 회사 일이 어떻습니까?	•따뜻해진 것 같아요.
c. 여름에 과일 값이 싸요?	•네, 추워졌어요.
d. 요즈음 거기 날씨가 어때요?	•빨개졌어요.
e. 산의 단풍이 빨갛습니까?	•아니오, 젊어지셨는데요.
f. 저 많이 늙었지요?	•싸졌어요.

대화 2 (FRAME 2)

구하는 책

미스 최: 선생님 무슨 책 구하시려고 하세요?

카슨 : 좋은 한영사전이 있을까 해서 들러 봤어요.
특별히 찾는 책은 없습니다. 미스 최는요?

미스 최: 전 골프에 대한 책을 사려고요.

카슨 : 골프하세요? 미스 최 골프하시는 줄 몰랐네요.

미스 최: 하기는요. 배우는 중이에요. 친구들이
모두 골프를 치기 때문에 안 배울 수가 없어요.

카슨 : 그거 좋죠. 운동도 되고 야외에서 신선한 공기를
마시는게 얼마나 좋습니까! 근데 우리 어디 가서
차나 한 잔 같이 하실까요? 시간 있으시죠?

미스 최: 네, 그러세요.

단어 공부 (*VOCABULARY STUDY*)

- 구하다 — to look for (= 찾다)
- -으려고/을려고 하다 — to try/attempt to...

  The connective -으려고 "in order to" is often followed by 하다 to form a compound verb meaning "to try or attempt to do something."
- 한영사전 — Korean-English dictionary
- 있을까 해서 — wondering if there is...

  The question ending -을까 "Shall I?" may be described as a monologue form (thinking to oneself), and -을까 하다 is used in quoting one's own thought.
- 특별히 — especially, particularly; 특별하다 "to be special"
- 골프에 대한 책 — a book on/about golf

CAUTION! The phrasal postposition -에 대해서 "on/about" is always used adverbially. To modify a noun, it must be converted to a prenominal form -에 대한.

- -기 때문에 — because, since (= -으니까)
- 안 배울 수가 없어요. — I cannot help but to learn. (Literally, "It is not possible not to learn.")

CAUTION! Unlike in English, double negation in Korean always leads to an emphatic affirmative.

- 야외 — outdoor (야= field, 외= outside)
- 신선하다 — to be fresh
- 공기 — air
- 마시다 — to breathe (air); to drink (liquid)
- 근데 — a contracted form of 그런데 "but; by the way"

연습 3. You are in a bookstore looking for books on a subject. You may use any subject of your choice, or select one from the list below. Ask the clerk if they have any of the books you want. The clerk will show you where the books are located.

EXAMPLE:	운동에 대한 책 있습니까?	Do you have books on physical exercise?
	네, 저 유리창 옆에 있습니다.	Yes,They are next to that window.

Suggested Subjects:

•음악 music	•역사 history	•심리학 psychology
•컴퓨터 computer	•정치 politics	•언어 languages
•여행 travel	•지리 geography	•과학 science
•예술 arts	•전쟁 wars	
•영화 movie	•종교 religion	•문학 literature
•사진 photography	•철학 philosophy	•요리법 cooking

연습 4. Your friend encountered a word he/she doesn't know. Explain to him/her by choosing one of the definitions listed below or by using your own definitions.

	Suggested Definitions
a. 결근이 무슨 말입니까?	•밥을 먹는다는 말
b. 도착이 무슨 뜻입니까?	•어디에 닿는다는 말
c. 식사가 무슨 뜻이에요?	•하는 일 없이 바쁘다는 말
d. 졸업이 무슨 말이에요?	•좋아 한다는 뜻
e. 결석이 무슨 말입니까?	•일하러 나가지 못한다는 말
f. 무사분주가 무슨 뜻이에요?	•학교에 나가지 않는다는 말
g. 사랑이라는 말은 무슨 뜻이에요?	•꼭 있어야 한다는 말
h. 필요하다는 말은 무슨 뜻입니까?	•학교 공부를 끝낸다는 말

대화 3 (FRAME 3)

어느 다방에서

웨이터 : 뭐 하시겠습니까?

카슨 : 미스 최, 뭐 하실래요? 전 커피 하지요.

미스 최 : 저도 같은 거 주세요.

웨이터 : 커피 두 잔이요. 알았습니다.

미스 최 : 카슨 선생님은 무슨 운동하세요?

카슨 : 별로 하는 거 없어요. 아무 것도 안하고 있으니까 요즘 살이 찌는 것 같습니다. 미스 최처럼 말랐으면 좋겠는데. 테니스나 시작할까 하고 있어요.

미스 최 : 골프 시작하세요, 우리랑 같이.

카슨 : 전 골프 채도 없는데요.

미스 최 : 걱정 마세요. 제 것 빌려 드릴게요.

카슨 : 함께 나가는 사람들이 누구누구입니까?

미스 최 : 미스 윤, 미스터 박, 강 선생 부부, 그리고 민 과장님도 가끔 나오세요. 토요일마다 나가거든요.

카슨 : 네에. 저도 그럼 같이 나가 볼까요?

미스 최 : 그러세요. 아무튼 금요일에 연락 드릴게요.

단어 공부 (*VOCABULARY STUDY*)

- 살 — flesh; skin
- 살이 찌다 — to gain weight, grow fat (process verb) (살 = flesh, 찌다 = to grow)
- -처럼 — like (= -같이)
- 마르다/말라 — to become thin; to dry (process verb)
- -을까 하다 — to be thinking of (do)ing
- 채 — club, stick
- 걱정하다 — to worry (= 염려하다)

The common idiom for "Don't worry." is 걱정마세요 (=염려마세요).

- 빌려 주다/드리다 — to lend (antonym: 빌리다 "to borrow")

CAUTION! Originally, the set of verbs, 빌다 and 빌리다 meant "to borrow" and "to lend," respectively, and they should be considered "written standard." However, in Seoul colloquialism, their meanings have slipped as shown below. You must know both sets.

	Written Standard		Seoul Colloquialism
"borrow"	빌다	⟶	빌리다
"lend"	빌리다	⟶	빌려 주다/드리다

- 누구 누구 — who and who (plural)

Some pronouns and a few short nouns are reduplicated to denote plurality. Some adverbs are reduplicated for emphasis.

내일 누구 누구 옵니까?	Who are coming tomorrow?
무엇 무엇 필요해요?	What items do you need?
어디 어디 갔어요?	What places did you go to?
언제 언제 일하는지 말해주세요.	Tell us what days we are to work on.
사이 사이에 그걸 넣는다.	We put it in at intervals.
곳 곳에 사람들이 보인다.	You can see people here and there.
자주 자주 마십니다.	He drinks very often.
빨리 빨리 해요!	Hurry it up!
얼른 얼른 갑시다.	Let's take off quick.

- 가끔 — once in a while, occasionally
- -마다 — every (postposition)

연습 5. Describe the people in the pictures below, using the suggested phrases.

Suggested Phrases

•살이 쪘다	is fat	•키가 크다	is tall
•말랐다	is thin	•키가 작다	is short
•머리가 짧다	has a short hair	•수염을 길렀다	has a mustache
•머리가 길다	has a long hair	•머리가 까졌다	is bald
•양복을 입었다	is in a suit	•까만 구두를 신었다	is wearing black shoes
•안경을 썼다	is wearing glasses	•모자를 썼다	is wearing a hat

연습 6. Using the form -을까 하다, say what you are thinking of doing this weekend. Use your own words or some of the suggested phrases below.

EXAMPLE:	주말에 뭐 하실래요?	What are you doing this weekend?
	수원에 갈까 합니다.	I'm thinking of going to Suwon.

Suggested Phrases

- 테니스 치다
- 친구집에 놀러 가다
- 바닷가에 가다
- 마당의 풀(grass) 깎다
- 음악회(concert) 가다
- 영화 구경하다

대화 4 (FRAME 4)

친구와 전화 통화

애경 : 미숙이니? 나야. 애경이.
미숙 : 애경아, 웬 일이니?
애경 : 늦게 전화 걸어서 미안해. 자는 걸 깨웠니?
미숙 : 아직 자지는 않았어. 괜찮아. 얘기해.
애경 : 응. 근데, 미스 서 있지? 새로 들어온 여자.
미숙 : 아, 키가 크고 예쁘게 생긴 애 말이야?
애경 : 그래. 근데, 그 애 웃긴다, 너.
미숙 : 왜? 싸웠니?
애경 : 아니. 근데, 내가 뭐 시키니까 울지 않아?
미숙 : 너무 긴장해서 그랬겠지, 뭐.
애경 : 근데 또 갈 때 보니까 나보고 "언니" 하고 웃어.
이상한 애야.
미숙 : 뭐가 이상해? 앞으로 잘 지내도록 해야지.
애경 : 이제 졸리기 시작하는데 자자. 전화 끊는다.
미숙 : 그래. 나도 졸려. 끊자. 안녕.

단어 공부 (*VOCABULARY STUDY*)

- 늦게 — late (adverb)
- 전화를 걸다 — to make a telephone call

  The verb, 걸다 "to hang, to hook up," is used to mean "to make a telephone call."
- 깨우다 — to wake (someone) up (causative of 깨다 "to wake up")
- 미스 서 있지? — This Miss Sŏ, you know.

  The verb form 있지(요)? is idiomatically used to introduce a topic of conversation.
- 키가 크다 — to be tall (키= human height)
- 예쁘게 생긴 애 — pretty-looking girl

  생기다 is a process verb, meaning originally "to happen, come to be." This verb is used in describing the appearance of a person, with an adverb or the adverbial form (-게) of a stative verb preceding.

그 사람 어떻게 생겼어요?	How does he look?
잘 생겼어요.	He is good-looking.

•웃기다	to make (someone) laugh; to be ridiculous, funny (colloquial)
•웃긴다, 너.	She is funny, you know.

너 ("you" the second person pronoun, LOW) is often added in colloquialism to gain more attention; it is equivalent to "..., you know " in English.

•싸우다	to fight, quarrel (noun form: 싸움)
•뭐 시키니까	when I make her do something

시키다, previously introduced as "to order" in a restaurant situation, is a causative verb meaning "to make/let someone do something." (See Grammar.) The connective -으니까 here does not mean "because," but rather "when" or "as." (See Grammar.)

•울다/우는/울어	to cry, weep (antonym: 웃다 "to laugh, smile")
•긴장하다	to get tense, alert (process verb)
•..., 뭐?	an expletive used at the end of a sentence in colloquialism with the implication "what else could it be?"
•나보고	looking at me, to me, at me

-보고 is used here as a postposition (=한테).

•웃다	to smile, laugh (antonym: 울다 "to cry, weep")
•이상하다	to be strange
•뭐가 이상해?	What's so strange? (used when responding with contradiction to something said)
•앞으로	in the future
•잘 지내도록 해야지.	We should try to get along well.

The connective -도록 is synonymous with -게 "so that" (Lesson 20). It is also used in a compound verb form -도록 하다 "to try to..."

•졸리다	to get sleepy
•자자.	Let's go to sleep. 자다 "to sleep"
•끊다	to disconnect, hang up (telephone)

연습 7. Mention someone as a topic to your partner, and then ask what he/she looks like. Use the model and the suggested phrases listed below.

Model	Suggested Phrases	
A: 미스터 송 있지요/알지요?	잘 생겼다	good-looking
B: 네.	못생겼다	homely, ugly
A: 그 사람 어떻게 생겼어요?	예쁘게 생겼다	looks pretty
B: 키가 작고 우습게 생겼어요.	그저 그렇게 생겼다	looks so-so
	우습게 생겼다	looks funny

연습 8. Listen to the two segments of conversation, and answer the questions below. You may answer in English or Korean.

Segment 1. a. 순철이가 왜 울고 있습니까?
b. 순철이가 누구하고 싸웠어요?
c. 어디를 다쳤습니까?

Segment 2. a. 보통 동네 아이들하고 잘 지냅니까?
b. 오늘 아이들이 무엇때문에 싸웠습니까?
c. 순철이를 누가 놀렸어요?
d. 아버지가 어떻게 하라고 말했습니까?

연습 9. Complete the following Korean sentences.

a. _____ 아이들하고 잘 지내_____ 하세요.
Try to get along well with the kids in the neighborhood.

b. 자전거를_____ 주지 않_____ 아이가 울었어요.
As I have refused to lend my bicycle, the boy cried.

c. 날씨가 _____ 지니까 손님도 적어 _____ 습니다.
The (number of) customers got smaller as it got cold.

d. _____ 도 _____ 지 말도록 해요.
Try not to laugh, even if it's funny.

e. 그 여자 _____ 가 작고, _____ 이 크고, _____ 게 생겼어요.
The girl is short, has big eyes, and is cute-looking.

연습 10. Answer the following questions in Korean.

a. What do you say when a friend call after you unexpectedly?
b. You want to talk about a visitor who came to the company this afternoon. How do you start the conversation?
c. How do you apologize for something?
d. Say that you want to get along well with all the co-workers.
e. You want to terminate the telephone conversation. What do you say?

문법 (GRAMMAR)

1. Nominal Clauses with -것 and -줄

The verb 알다 "to know" may take a clause as its object, and such a clause ends with the bound noun -것, which denotes an established fact. The postposition -을 may be used for emphasis.

미스 한이 집에 있는 것 알아요.	I know Miss Han is home. (FACT)
미스 한이 집에 있는 것을 몰랐어요.	I didn't know Miss Han was home. (FACT)

However, the verb 알다 may also mean "think" or "believe." When the verb is used in this sense, the clause expressing a belief or assumption (not a fact) is a complement ending with -줄 rather than -것. Here, the postposition used for emphasis is -로 (not -을).

미스 한이 집에 <u>있는 줄</u> 압니다.	I think Miss Han is home. (BELIEF)
미스 한이 집에 있는 <u>줄로</u> 알았어요.	I thought Miss Han was home. (BELIEF)

The distinction between the two types of clauses, one expressing a *fact* and the other expressing a *belief* is clear enough if the speaker uses -것 and -줄 consistently. In reality, however, Korean speakers commonly use -줄 *for both types of clauses* (for "fact" clauses as well) with only some differences of intonation as shown below.

a. After a "fact" clause, there is a pause (shown by // below), and the verb 알다 is stressed.
b. After a "belief" clause, there is no pause, and the verb 알다 is not stressed.

그 사람 일하는 줄 // 압니다.	I know that he is working. (FACT)
그 사람 일하는 줄 압니다.	I think that he is working. (BELIEF)
그 사람 늦을 줄 // 알았어요.	They knew he would be late. (FACT)
그 사람 늦을 줄 알았어요.	They thought he would be late. (BELIEF)

The above distinction becomes irrelevant when the negative verb 모르다 is used, because then the clause always expresses a *fact*, not a belief.

미스 이가 영어하는 줄 몰랐어요?	Didn't you know Miss Lee speaks English? (FACT)

2. A Summary of Factual and Suppositional Sentences

The three types of sentences with factual and suppositional clauses are summarized below.

Prenominal Ending	-것 (을) // 알다	... know that (FACT)
	-줄 (을) // 알다	
	-줄 (로) 알다	... think that (BELIEF)

See Lesson 16 for a general introduction of prenominal endings, and a summary of prenominal endings for different types of verbs in the Grammar section of Lesson 22.

•NOTE: In "belief" sentences, the past tense form may take either a regular form -은 줄 or an irregular form -었을 줄.

그 사람 집에 {간 / 갔을} 줄 압니다.		I think he went home.

3. Three Different Meanings of the Verb: 알다

The Korean verb 알다 has at least three different meanings, as summarized below. Note, however, that its negative form 모르다 is not used as the negative of (b) "think" and (c) "find out."

a. [A-가 B-를 알다] =A knows B.
나 미스 조 압니다. I know/am acquainted with Miss Cho.
나 그 사람 영어하는 줄 몰랐어요. I didn't know she speaks English.

b. [A-가 (B-를) C-으로 알다] =A thinks (B) is C.
나 그 사람 학생으로 알았어요. I thought she was a student.
나 그 사람 영어 하는 줄 압니다. I think she speaks English.

c. [A-가 B-를 알다] =A finds out/comprehends B.
그 사람 이름 알았어요. I found out her name.
{알았어요? / 알아 들었어요?} Do you understand? / Have you made that out?

4. Stative to Process Verbs: -어지다

Stative verbs may be converted to process verbs by the compound form -어 지다 "to become/get/turn (to be)..."

날씨가 좋아 졌어요.	The weather has become nice.
서울이 달라졌습니다.	Seoul has changed (= become different).
그 여자 예뻐지는데요.	She is getting prettier.
자동차 값이 비싸졌어요.	Prices of cars have got expensive.
선생님 젊어지신 것 같아요.	You seem to have gotten younger.

The compound verb form -어지다 is also used in some useful phrases with some verbs of other types.

•없어지다	to disappear; to run out of something
돈이 벌써 없어졌어요?	Are you out of money already?
•알려지다	to become known, famous
그 사람 잘 알려졌어요.	He has become well known.

5. Talking about an Expression

When one talks about a word or a phrase, it is normally packaged in a quotation form.

•Verbs	-다/ㄴ다/는다/	는 말
•Nominals (or any part of speech other than a verb)	-이라	

가짜라는 말이 무슨 뜻입니까?	What does "가짜" mean?
웃긴다는 말은 우습다는 말입니다.	"웃기다" means "funny."
무사분주라는 말 못들어 봤는데요.	I haven't heard "무사분주" before.
무사분주라는 말은 하는 일없이 바쁘다는 말이에요.	"무사분주" means "being busy without doing anything important.

6. Quoting One's Own Thought

The sentence ending -을까? ("Should I...?," "I wonder if...?") often simulates a monologue or thinking in Korean.

오늘 저녁에 뭘 먹을까?	What shall I eat tonight?
미스 리 집에 있을까?	Will Miss Lee be home?

This sentence ending is followed by the verb 하다 in a construction expressing the speaker's thought. (Literally, the construction is a quoting of the speaker's thinking.)

...을까 하다 { I'm thinking of ...ing / I wonder if...

자동차를 살까 합니다.	I'm thinking of buying a car.
돈을 빌릴까 했어요.	I thought of borrowing money.
댁에 계실까 했지요.	I wondered if you were home.
좋은 한영사전이 있을까 해서 서점에 들렀어요.	I stopped at the book store, wondering if they had a good Korean-English dictionary.

7. One Event Leads to Another: A New Use of -으니까

The connective -으니까, used to introduce the reason for a statement, has another use, somewhat peculiar to Korean: expressing two events occurring in succession. In this usage, the speaker merely suggests a cause-effect relationship between the two events without explicitly so claiming. Common English equivalents of this connective would be "when" and "as."

CAUTION! No tense marker 었 is used with this connective, even though the clause with -으니까, in this sense, always expresses a completed event.

그 후 보니까 나보고 웃어요. (NO TENSE MARKER)	When I saw her later, she smiled at me.
비가 오기 시작하니까 시원하던데요. (NO TENSE MARKER)	As it began raining, it was refreshing.
그 약을 먹으니까 좀 나았어요. (NO TENSE MARKER)	When he took the medicine, he got better.
그 사람한테 물으니까 모른다고 했어요. (NO TENSE MARKER)	As I asked him, he said he didn't know.

8. Expressing the Extent: -도록

A clause ending with the connective -도록 denotes the extent to which the effect of the event in the main clause is to reach. It is similar to and often interchangeable with -게 which denotes a desired effect.

감기 { 들지 않게 / 들지 않도록 } 조심하세요. Take care, so that you won't catch a cold.

However, when the effect of an action is a matter of degree, the use of -도록 is naturally more appropriate as in the examples below.

머리가 아프도록 공부했지요. I studied to the extent that I have a headache.
날이 어두워지도록 기다렸어요. We waited until (the day became) dark.
늦도록 무엇을 했습니까? What did you do until late?

The connective -도록 may be followed by a dummy verb 하다 to form a compound verb expressing an attempt at something ("try to...") or simply a promise for something.

잘 지내도록 해요. Try to get along well.
거기 가도록 하겠어요. I will be there. (I will try my best to go there.)

9. Another Reason Clause : -기 때문에 or -기에

A "reason" clause ending with -기 때문에 is similar to one ending with -으니까. Like -으니까, it may incorporate the tense -었 when expressing a past or completed event. However, unlike -으니까, it is not normally used in a request or suggestion sentence.

친구들이 모두 골프하기 때문에 안 할 수가 없어요. Because all my friends play golf, I can't help but play it.
전화번호를 몰랐기 때문에 전화 못 걸었어요. Since I didn't know your telephone number, I couldn't call you.
그때 돈이 없었기 때문에 돈을 빌려야 했습니다. I had to borrow money because I didn't have money then.

The connective -기 때문에 is sometimes shortened to -기에.

손님이 오셨기에 나가지 못했습니다. I couldn't go out because we had a visitor at home.
일요일이었기에 동해안으로 여행하기로 했어요. Because it was Sunday, we decided to take a trip to the East Coast.

The three types of "reason" clauses and their restrictions are summarized below.

Connectives	Use of tense incorporation	Use in a request or suggestion sentence
-어서	NO	NO
-으니까	YES	YES
-기 때문에	YES	NO

NOTE: The latter two connectives have shorter forms. However, the shorter variants are not as common as the full forms in speech: -으니까 〉 -으니 and -기 때문에 〉 -기에.

10. A Summary of Causative Constructions

The causative form -게 하다 "to let/make someone do something" was introduced in Lesson 20. This phrasal form is useful since you can use any verb in a causative construction, but there are two other types of causative forms available for some verbs. We will summarize all three forms below.

Causative Sentence Formula

A-가	B-를	· · · Verb + Causative

A makes/lets *B* do *C*.

A. Phrasal Form: -게 하다

선생님이 학생들을 집에 가게 했어요.
The teacher let the students go home.

CAUTION! The human object may also take -에게/한테, if the verb accompanies its own object.

선생님이 학생들 {을 / 에게/한테} 책을 읽게 했어요.
The teacher made the students read the book.

B. Causative Verbs with Extended Stems

There are a limited number of verbs that may be converted to causative forms by extending the stems similar to passive forms. (See Lesson 22 for the passive.) Such causative forms often acquire some specialized meanings as shown below.

- 보다 see ⟶ 보이다 make someone see, show
- 먹다 eat ⟶ 먹이다 make someone eat, feed
- 앉다 sit ⟶ 앉히다 make someone sit
- 입다 wear ⟶ 입히다 dress (someone)
- 알다 know ⟶ 알리다 let know, inform
- 살다 live ⟶ 살리다 let live, save someone's life
- 울다 cry ⟶ 울리다 make someone cry
- 자다 sleep ⟶ 재우다 make someone sleep
- 타다 ride ⟶ 태우다 give someone a ride
- 깨다 wake ⟶ 깨우다 wake up someone
- 서다 stand/halt ⟶ 세우다 let stand/park a car/halt someone
- 차다 become full ⟶ 채우다 fill up something
- 비다 become empty ⟶ 비우다 empty some container
- 웃다 laugh/smile ⟶ 웃기다 make someone laugh/smile
- 벗다 take off (clothes) ⟶ 벗기다 undress someone
- 신다 put on (shoes) ⟶ 신기다 make someone put on shoes

C. Nominal + -(을) 시키다

The action verbs, consisting of an action noun and 하다, are converted to the causative with 하다 replaced by 시키다.

<u>걱정 시켜서</u> 미안해요.	I'm sorry for making you worry.
저 사람 <u>운전 시키지</u> 마세요.	Don't let him drive.
아이들을 <u>공부 시켜야지요</u>.	We have to make the children study.
졸리니까 <u>말 시키지</u> 말아요.	I'm sleepy; don't make me talk.

❖ GUESS WHAT IT MEANS: 가는 말이 고와야 오는 말이 곱다.

읽기 · 쓰기 (READING & WRITING)

1. Old Sayings: 옛말

Some old sayings are still alive in daily conversations, and you should be familiar with a number of them already introduced. The caption below uses an old saying to discuss a typical marriage problem. Scan it and follow through the exercises.

부부싸움은 칼로 물 베기…

옛말에 부부싸움은 칼로 물 베기라는 말이 있는데, 그 만큼 부부사이에는 싸움이 자주 있으나 하룻 밤을 자고 나면 언제 싸웠느냐 하는 듯이 풀어진다는 말일 것이다.

우리는 보통 싸우지 않는 부부가 행복한 것으로 생각하기 쉬우나 반드시 그렇지는 않다. 부부싸움이 자주 있다고 해서 부부사이가 반드시 나쁜 것은 아니며, 싸움이 없다고 해서 부부사이에 문제가 없다고 말할 수도 없다. 어떤 경우에는 싸움을 권하고 싶을 때도 있다. 왜냐하면 부부는 부부싸움을 통해서 서로가 서로의 가슴 속에 깊이 숨겨져 있는 감정이나 불평 같은 것을 더욱 잘 이해할 수 있기 때문이다.

단어소개

싸움	fight, quarrel
칼	knife
베다	to cut, slice
옛말	old saying
-는 듯이	as if
풀어지다	to be dissolved
행복하다	to be happy
반드시	necessarily, exactly
권하다	to recommend, offer
왜냐하면	because
속	inside
숨겨지다	to be hidden
감정	emotion
불평	complaint
이해하다	to understand

연습 11. Answer the following questions.

a. What does "cutting the water with a knife" mean?

(1) One shouldn't meddle.
(2) It can't break them apart.
(3) It causes a lot of arguments.
(4) It's no use giving advice.

b. 부부싸움은 보통 어떻게 풀어집니까?

c. 싸우지 않는 부부가 반드시 행복하다고 할 수 있습니까?

d. 부부싸움은 반드시 피할 필요가 있다고 생각해요?

e. 부부싸움을 통해서 무슨 좋은 일이 생길 수 있어요?

f. 부부사이에 무슨 불평이 있을 때 그것을 이야기하는 것이 좋습니까? 안 하는 것이 좋습니까? 어떻게 생각합니까?

연습 12. Gist the following captions, using, when necessary, the Korean-English dictionary.

(A) '맥주를 많이 마시면 살이 찐다! 정말일까요?'

(B) 뚱뚱해서 고민하십니까?
이젠 날씬해질 수 있습니다.

(C) 해외여행가이드
여름휴가 이용한
부부 해외여행
정말 좋군요!
'싸고 알차게 다녀오는 법'

연습 13. Complete the following sentences by filling in words from the boxes, and then translate the completed sentences into English.

a. 〈목감기에는 뜨거운 홍차에 소금을 타서 마신다〉

감기로 목이 _____ 때는 _____ 홍차에 소금을 조금 _____ 마시면 좋다고 한다. 홍차에 _____ 있는 카페인 성분과 소금이 목의 통증을 가라앉게 한다.

넣어 놓아 들어 아플 뜨거운

b. 부부사이에 무슨 _____ 이 있으면 숨기지 말고 _____ 이야기하는 것이 좋다. 그러지 않으면 _____ 가 고쳐야 할 것이 있어도 고치지 못하며, 또 좋지 않은 _____ 이 쌓이면 부부 _____ 가 나빠질 수도 있다.

서로 불평 사이 감정 상대 얼른

c. 대도항공사에서는 "한국 방문의 해"를 맞이하여, 고국을 _____하는 교포와 외국인들을 _____ 특별 국내선 항공료를 할인해주는 프로그램을 시작했는데, 이 프로그램에 _____ 교포와 외국인 방문객들이 국내선을 _____ 할 때 요금을 주중에는 50%, 주말에는 10% _____ 해주며, 김포공항에서 서울 _____ 간의 리무진 버스 이용시에는 15%를 할인해 준다.

방문	국내선
위하여	의하면
관광	도심지
할인	이용

Q 아기가 왜 울고 있을까?

A. 배가 고파서
B. 형이 같이 놀아 주지 않아서
C. 블럭이 망가져서
D. 엄마가 없어서

• 망가지다 to be broken (= 고장이 나다)

단어 정리 (VOCABULARY SUMMARY)

Nominals

공기	air	야외	outdoor, field
누구 누구	who (plural)	채	club, stick
볼 일	thing to do, errand	초보자	beginner
살	flesh; skin	키	height (of a human)
서점	bookstore	한문	classical Chinese
감정	emotion	한영사전	Korean-English dictionary
불평	complaint	옛말	old saying
싸움	fight, quarrel	칼	knife
속	inside		

Action Verbs

걱정하다	to worry (= 염려하다)
걸다	to hang; 전화 걸다 "to make a phone call"
구하다	to look for, obtain
권하다	to recommend, persuade
깨우다	to wake someone up
끊다	to disconnect
놀리다	to tease
마시다	to breathe (air); to drink (liquid)
베다	to cut, slice
빌리다	to borrow (written standard: 빌다)
빌려주다	to lend (written standard: 빌리다)
시키다	to order; make someone do something
싸우다	to fight, have a quarrel
울다	to cry, weep
웃기다	to make someone laugh
웃다	to laugh, smile
이해하다	to understand

Process Verbs

긴장하다	to get tense, alert	놀라다	to be surprized
마르다/말라	to become dry, thin	살이 찌다	to gain weight
생기다	to have looks; to happen	풀어지다	to be dissolved

Stative Verbs

신선하다	to be fresh	이상하다	to be strange, funny
졸리다	to be sleepy (=잠이 오다)	죄송하다	to feel guilty, sorry
숨겨지다	to be hidden	행복하다	to be happy
키가 크다	to be tall (antonym: 키가 작다)		

Adverbs

가끔	once in a while	앞으로	in the future
특별히	especially, particularly	반드시	exactly, necessarily (not)

Interjections

근데	a contraction of 그런데

Postpositions

-마다	every	-보고	at, to (looking at...)
-없이	without	-듯이	as if, as though
-에 대한	about, on (prenominal form of -에 대해서)		

Idioms

무사분주	Being busy without doing anything special.

Sentence Features

..., 너.	..., you know. (LOW)
..., 뭐.	..., (what else could it be) (MID/LOW)
... 있지?	You know... (introducing a topic) (LOW)
왜냐하면	because

Phrasal Forms

-기 때문에	=으니까
-다는 말	a form used in quoting an expression
-도록 하다	to try (one's best) to...
-어 지다	to become/get...
-을까 하다	to think of (do)ing...
-줄 알다	to know/think that...

연습문제 해답(ANSWERS TO EXERCISES)

연습 1.
a. 이조자기인 줄 몰랐어요.
b. 있는 줄 몰랐어요.
c. 가까운 줄 몰랐어요.
d. 간 줄 몰랐어요.
e. 좋은 줄 몰랐어요.
f. 열린 줄 몰랐어요.

연습 2.
a. 추워졌어요.
b. 바빠졌습니다.
c. 싸졌어요.
d. 따뜻해진것 같아요.
e. 빨개졌어요.
f. 아니오. 젊어지신 것 같습니다.

연습 4.
a. 일하러 나가지 못한다는 말입니다.
b. 어디에 닿는다는 말입니다.
c. 밥을 먹는다는 말이에요.
d. 학교공부를 끝낸다는 말입니다.
e. 학교에 안 나간다는 말이에요.
f. 하는 일없이 바쁘다는 말입니다.
g. 좋아한다는 뜻이에요.
h. 꼭 있어야 한다는 말이에요.

연습 8. Scripts & Answers

Segment 1. 아버지: 순철이가 왜 울고 있어요?
어머니: 동네집 아이들하고 싸우다가 팔을 좀 다쳤어요.
아버지: 많이 다쳤어?
어머니: 아니오. 아무것도 아니예요.

Segment 2. 아버지: 동네 애들하고 잘 놀고 지내던데 왜 싸워?
어머니: 보통 잘들 지내던데 이상해요, 오늘은.
아버지: 무엇때문에 싸웠대?
어머니: 한 아이가 자전거를 빌려 달라고 했는데 안빌려 주니까 아이들이 놀린 모양이에요.
아버지: 그놈 바보처럼 울기는 왜 울어? 울지 말라고 해요. 그리고 애들이랑 잘 지내도록 하라고 해요.

Answers: Segment 1.

a. 순철이가 왜 울어요? - 애들하고 싸워서 울어요.
b. 누구하고 싸웠습니까? - 동네집 애들하고.
c. 싸우다가 어떻게 됐습니까? - 팔을 다쳤어요.

Answers: Segment 2.

a. 보통 동네 아이들하고 잘 지내요? - 잘 지냅니다.
b. 왜 싸웠습니까? - 자전거를 안 빌려 주어서.
c. 누가 누구를 놀렸습니까? - 애들이 순철이를.
d. 아버지가 순철이에게 뭐라고 했어요? - 잘 지내도록 하라고 했습니다.

연습 9. a. 동네, -도록 b. 빌려, -으니까 c. 추워, 졌- d. 우스워-, 웃- e. 키, 눈, 예쁘-

❖ EXPLANATION ON "GUESS WHAT IT MEANS": The phrase 가는 말이 고와야 오는 말이 곱다 literally means "When the outgoing words are nice, the incoming words are pleasant also." 곱다/고와 is a stative verb meaning "nice, lovely, pretty." The connective -어야 means "only when," and it was used in the obligatory form -어야 하다/되다. This old saying stresses the importance of nice and kind words in settling differences.

연습 11. a. (2) b. 하룻밤을 자고 나면. c. 아니오. d. 아니오. e. 서로 잘 이해할 수 있어요. f. 이야기하는 것이 좋아요.

연습 12. (A) If you drink a lot of beer, you gain weight. Is it true?
(B) Are you suffering from overweight? Now you can get slim.
(C) Overseas Travel Guide. Isn't it really great! Take advantage of your summer vacation and make a world tour with your spouse. (We know) how to make a quality travel at a low price.

연습 13. (A) 아플 - 뜨거운 - 넣어 - 들어
They say that drinking hot black tea with salt added is good for your sore throat due to a cold. Caffeine contained in tea and salt soothe your sore throat.
(B) 불평 - 얼른 - 서로가 - 감정 - 사이

Any complaints between husband and wife should be openly talked about rather than concealed. Otherwise, they will not be able to correct anything that needs correcting, and if bad feelings accumulate, it may damage the relationship between husband and wife.

c. 방문 - 위하여 - 의하면 - 이용 - 할인 - 도심지

Welcoming the "Visit Korea Year," the Taedo Airlines offers a special discount program for Korean residents overseas and foreigners visiting Korea. This program gives a 50% discount during weekdays and a 10% discount during weekends for domestic flights. It also gives a 15% discount for limousine services between the airport and the downtown locations.

Communicative Frames in English

Frame 1. At a Bookstore

Carson : Isn't this you, Miss Choe?

Miss Choe : My! Mr. Carson! What a surprise. I didn't expect to meet you in a bookstore.

Carson : Well, I dropped in as I had some errand in this neighborhood. The weather has turned warm, hasn't it? How are you getting along these days?

Miss Choe : Always "musa-punju," you know.

Carson : Pardon? What did you say? I didn't get it.

Miss Choe : That means "busy doing nothing." It's a classical Chinese expression.

Carson : Don't use difficult phrases. You mustn't tease a beginner.

Miss Choe : All right. I was wrong. I'm sorry.

Frame 2. The Books That They Are Looking for

Miss Choe : What kind of books are you looking for?

Carson : I wondered if they had a good Korean-English dictionary, so I stopped by here. I don't have any particular book that I'm looking for. How about you, Miss Choe?

Miss Choe : I'm trying to buy a book on golf.

Carson : Do you play golf? I didn't know that you play golf.

Miss Choe : Me playing golf? No. I'm taking lessons. Since all my friends play golf, I can't help but learn it.

Carson : That's good. It'll be a good exercise, and how wonderful it is to breathe fresh air outdoors! But shall we go somewhere and have coffee together? You have time, don't you?

Miss Choe : O.K. Let's do that.

Frame 3. At a Coffee Shop

Waiter : What would you like, sir?

Carson : Miss Choe, what would you like? I'll have coffee.

Miss Choe : I'll have the same, please.

Waiter : Two cups of coffee. Fine, sir.

Miss Choe : What kind of exercise do you do, Mr. Carson?

Carson : I don't have anything special that I do. Since I'm not doing anything, I seem to be gaining weight recently. I wish I were as slim as you are, Miss Choe. I've been thinking of starting tennis or something.

Miss Choe : Why don't you start golf with us?

Carson : I don't even have any golf clubs, you know.

Miss Choe : Don't worry. I'll loan you mine.
Carson : Who are the people going out together?
Miss Choe : Miss Yun, Miss Pak, Mr. and Mrs. Kang. And Section Chief Min comes out once a while. We go out every Saturday, you know.
Carson : I see. Shall I join you?
Miss Choe : By all means. In any case, I'll give you a call on Friday.

Frame 4. Telephone Gossip

Aegyong : Misuk? It's me, Aegyong.
Misuk : Aegyŏng, what's up?
Aegyong : Sorry to call you late. Did I wake you up?
Misuk : I wasn't in bed yet. It's alright. Go ahead and talk.
Aegyong : Yeah. By the way, this Miss Sŏ, you know. The new girl who just joined the company.
Misuk : Oh, the tall and cute-looking one, you mean?
Aegyong : Right. But, she is weird, you know!
Misuk : Why? Did you have a quarrel?
Aegyong : No, but when I told her to do something, she cried, you see?
Misuk : She was too tense. I think that's why.
Aegyong : But, then again, when I saw her after work, she called me "sister," and smiled at me. A funny girl.
Misuk : What's so funny? We'd better get along well in the future.
Aegyong : Now I'm getting sleepy; let's go to bed. I'm gonna hang up.
Misuk : O.K. I'm sleepy, too. Let's hang up. Bye.

제 24 과

한가한 오후

대화 1 (FRAME 1)

다방에서 커피 한 잔

카슨 : 요새 갑자기 추워졌지요?

미스 최 : 네, 눈이 올지도 모르겠어요.

카슨 : 벌써 눈이 와요?

미스 최 : 그럼요. 12월인데 곧 눈도 오고 얼음도 얼지요.

카슨 : 네에.

미스 최 : 그럼, 이제 일어서실까요?

카슨 : 왜 커피 하자마자 가려고 하세요? 볼 일이 있어요?

미스 최 : 아니오. 그게 아니라, 수퍼에 들러 볼까 해서요. 선생님 바쁘시지 않으면 이 동네 상가 구경 안 하시겠어요?

카슨 : 그럴까요?

미스 최 : 같이 가시죠. 재미있는 데 구경시켜 드릴게요.

카슨 : 그러십시다.

단어 공부 (*VOCABULARY STUDY*)

- 한가한 leisurely
- 오후 afternoon
- 눈 snow; 눈이 오다 "to snow"
- 눈이 올 지도 모르겠어요. It may snow.

  -지도 모르다 It may/might (probably)...
- 얼다 to freeze; 얼음 "ice"
- 커피 하자마자 as soon as finishing (one's) coffee

  -자 (마자) as soon as (connective). The second part 마자 may be omitted.
- 그게 아니라 It isn't that,... (a phrase often used in denying a reason already put forward)
- 수퍼/슈퍼 (마켓) supermarket (an American-style grocery store)

  In the Korean usage, the second part 마켓 is often omitted. In Korea, 수퍼 or 슈퍼 also refers to a small grocery store in the neighborhood.

연습 1. Respond to the following questions by using the - 지도 모르다 form.

EXAMPLE: 비가 올까요? Do you think it will rain?
올지도 모르지요. It might.

a. 내일 날씨가 더울까요?
b. 집에 아무도 없을까요?
c. 아침에 얼음이 얼었을까요?
d. 저 여자 결혼했을까요?
e. 가게가 열었을까요?
f. 산에 꽃이 피었을까요?
g. 자동차 빌릴 수 있을까요?
h. 오늘도 바람이 불까요?

대화 2 (FRAME 2)

지하도로 길을 건너면서

미스 최 : 길 건너편이거든요. 저기 사람들 많이 지나가는 것 보세요.

카슨 : 저 육교로 길 건너가나요?

미스 최 : 아니오. 지하도로 건너가십시다. 육교는 바람이 세서 너무 추워요.

카슨 : 아, 저쪽이 지하철 입구이군요.

미스 최 : 네, 오늘이 휴일인데도 저렇게 사람이 많고 혼잡해요. (길 건너서) 저기예요. 저 길 모퉁이 이발관 옆, 저 슈퍼마켓이 이 근처에서 가장 크거든요. 가격이 굉장히 쌀 뿐만 아니라, 물건들이 많고 신선해요.

카슨 : 굉장히 크네요. 미스 최는 늘 여기서 쇼핑하세요?

미스 최 : 대개 그래요. 좀 멀어도 여기까지 와서 장 보지요.

단어 공부 (*VOCABULARY STUDY*)

- 지나가다 — to go past; to pass by

  -는 것을 보다 "to see someone do something"; Note that an action as the object of 보다 or 듣다 takes the ending -는 것.
- 건너가다 — to go across
- -나요? — an interrogative ending
- 세다/세 — to be strong (antonym : 약하다)
- 입구 — entrance (입=enter, 구=mouth) (antonym: 출구)

  This is a Sino-Korean term. The native term for "entrance" is 들어가는 곳; one for "exit" is 나가는 곳.
- 휴일인데도 — even though it is a holiday (-은/는데도 = -지만)
- 혼잡하다 — to be congested
- 모퉁이 — corner (outdoors) (an indoor corner=구석)
- 이발관 — barber shop
- 가까이 — a place nearby

  가까이 is both a nominal and an adverbial form of 가깝다.
- 가격 — price (=값)
- 싸다 — to be inexpensive
- 쌀 뿐만 아니라 — not only inexpensive/low

  뿐만 아니라 above is suffixed to a (stative) verb, but sometimes it may be suffixed to a nominal.

  EX) <u>그것</u> 뿐만 아니라 "not only that…"
- 굉장히 — very, considerably, extremely (an adverbial form of 굉장하다 "to be huge, grand, extreme"
- 장을 보다 — to do shopping ; 장 = 시장 "market"

연습 2. Call the attention of your classmates to each of the scenes shown below, using the construction … -는 것을 보세요 "Look at … do(ing)."

연습 3. Restate the following sentences by replacing the connectives with - 을 뿐만 아니라.

a. 날씨가 춥고 바람도 불어요.
b. 물건이 많고 가격도 싸요.
c. 기차로 가는 것이 빠르고 편합니다.
d. 컴퓨터 배우기가 쉽고 재미도 있어요.
e. 목이 마르고 배도 고픕니다.
f. 오늘은 얼음이 얼고 눈도 왔습니다.

연습 4. Restate the following sentences by replacing the connectives with - 자 마자.

a. 집에 가서 바로 잤습니다.
b. 가게 문이 열려서 곧 들어갔습니다.
c. 식사가 끝나고 커피 하기로 했어요.
d. 대학을 졸업하고 바로 취직했어요.
e. 아침에 깨서 곧 이사 준비했지요.
f. 길을 건너면 바른 쪽으로 가십시오.

연습 5. Say the following sentences in Korean.

a. Did you see Yongsook leaving?
b. I heard him laughing.
c. Because the house is near the beach, it may be windy.
d. The entrance is on the right, and the exit is on the left.
e. As soon as you cross the street, you will see a barber shop.

대화 3 (FRAME 3)

슈퍼에 들른다

카슨 : "대세일" 이라고 써 있는데요.

미스 최 : 광고에는 늘 그러는데 얼마나 싼지 모르죠.
생선이 신선해 보이죠?

카슨 : 금방 새로 들어 왔나 봅니다. 잘 골라 보세요.

미스 최 : 아무거든지 하나 집지요.

미스 최 : (점원을 보고) 아주머니, 이거하고 저거 똑같아 보이는데 어째서 이게 싸지요?

점원 : 그건 어저께 들어온 거예요. 그러니까 세일이 아녜요? 하지만 그것도 신선합니다.

미스 최 : 네에. 근데, 빵이니 과자같은 건 어디 있나요?

점원 : 저쪽 구석에 제과점이 따로 있습니다.

미스 최 : 아, 저기 빵집이 새로 생겼군요!
선생님, 우리 빵집 가서 맛있는 거 먹어요.

카슨 : 그거 좋은 생각인데요. 근데 쇼핑 끝낸 겁니까?

미스 최 : 빵 외에는 살 거 더 없어요.

단어 공부 (*VOCABULARY STUDY*)

- 쇼핑 — shopping; 쇼핑을 하다 "to shop"
- 대세일 — big sale (대=big, grand)
- 써 있다 — is written

  The standard form for "to be written" is 씌어 있다 with the passive form 씌어 < 쓰이어. In conversation, however, 써 있다 is more common.
- 신선해 보이죠? — Don't they look fresh?
- 광고 — advertisement (광=wide, 고=notice)
- 금방 — just now (=막)
- -나 보다 — It seems…

  This ia a form quoting one's own thought; the interrogative ending -나? is followed by 보다. You have already learned a similar phrase, prenominal form + 것 같다 or 모양이다.
- 고르다/골라 — to select, choose
- 아무거든지 — anything (=아무거나, 아무거라도)

  The postposition -이든지 is generally interchangeable with -이나 or -이라도.
- 집다 — to pick up
- 똑같다 — to be exactly alike
- 어째서 — why, for what reason (=왜)
- 빵이니 — bread and…, etc.

  The postposition -이니 is used when two or more objects are mentioned in succession.
- 과자 같은 것 — things like cookies

  The phrase 같은 것 "things like" is added after two or more objects mentioned.
- 구석 — corner (indoors)
- 제과점 — bakery shop (=빵집)
- 따로 — separately
- 생기다 — to happen, come into being
- -외에는 — except

❖ PHRASAL POSTPOSITIONS

{-외에 / -밖에} except	{-내에 / -안에} within
{-중에 / -가운데에} among	

연습 6. Complete the following sentences by supplying appropriate postpositions in blank spaces, and then translate them into English. Suggested postpositions are listed on the right.

a. 상가 ____ 십분 ____ 갈 수 있어요
b. 우리 ____ 미숙이 ____ 가장 키가 커요.
c. 이것 ____ 아무 것 ____ 좋습니다.
d. 야채 ____ 과일 ____ 어디서 팝니까?
e. 아무 책 ____ 한국 역사 ____ 것을 찾습니다.
f. 여기 ____ 아무 ____ 여권 ____ 못 들어가요.
g. 일요일 ____ 친구들 ____ 산에 올라갑니다.
h. 초보자 ____ 박 선생 ____ 잘 하는 사람 없어요.

Suggested Postpositions

•-이/가	•-으로서
•-을/를	•-마다
•-과/와	•-도
•-에는	•-이니
•-내에	•-이든지
•-가운데서	•-이라도
•-없이	•-같은 것
•-처럼	•-에 대한

연습 7. Respond to the following questions by listing more than one object. Use the postposition -니/-이니 and/or the phrase 같은 것.

a. 교실에 무엇이 있습니까?
b. 점심 때 뭐 먹었어요?
c. 상가에는 무슨 가게들이 있어요?
d. 어제 저녁에 누구와 같이 식사 했어요?
e. 슈퍼에서 무슨 물건을 팝니까?
f. 방학동안에 어디 어디 갔다왔습니까?

연습 8. Comment on the pictures below, using -어 보이다. Use one of the suggested phrases if applicable.

a.

c.

e.

b.

d.

f.

Suggested Phrases

- 더워 보이다
- 따뜻해 보이다
- 어려워 보이다
- 맛이 있어 보이다
- 추워 보이다
- 바빠 보이다
- 재미 있어 보이다
- 즐거워 보이다

연습 9. Looking at the pictures above and using your imagination, state your guess as to what these people are doing, using the form -나 보다.

연습 10. Listen to the conversation and answer the questions.

Question 1: 이 사람들이 가는 가게 이름이 뭡니까?
Question 2: 왜 거기 가기로 했어요?
Question 3: 어디에 세일이라고 써 있습니까?
Question 4: 어떻게 하면 싸게 쇼핑할 수 있어요?

대화 4 (FRAME 4)

학교 후배를 만난다

미스 최 : 영희야! 장 보러 왔구나. 아기 업고.
영희 : 오랜 만이에요, 언니.
미스 최 : 아기가 그 새에 저렇게 컸네. 몇 달 됐지?
영희 : 네달 막 넘었어요. 백일이 지났거든요.
미스 최 : 어머, 그렇게 됐구나! 미안해, 가 보지도 못해서.
영희 : 아녜요. 서로 바쁘니까, 그렇게 되죠.
미스 최 : 참 세월도 빠르네. 너 아기 낳은 게 어제 같은데, 그치? 참, 인사드려. 이 분 우리 회사에서 과장으로 계시는 카슨 선생님이야. 선생님, 제 학교 후배예요.
영희 : 처음 뵙겠습니다. 하영희예요.
카슨 : 반갑습니다. 아기가 참 예쁘게 생겼네요.

단어 공부 (*VOCABULARY STUDY*)

- 후배 — a (current or former) school friend younger than you (antonym: 선배)
- -구나! — a blunt exclamatory ending, also shortened to -군!
  Its counterpart on High/Mid level is 군요!
- 아기 — baby (colloquial form: 애기; vocative form: 아가)
- 업다 — to carry (a person) on one's back
  A mother carrying a baby on her back used to be a common sight in Korea. See the picture above.
- 그새에 — already (=그 동안에, 벌써)
  The noun 새 or 사이 (originally "gap" or "space" between two points) has two ex-

tended meanings: (1) relationship between people and (2) time interval between two events:

(1) 형제가 사이가 좋아요. — The brothers get along well.

(2) 선생님 나가신 새에 전화가 왔었어요. — While you were away, there was a telephone call.

• 크다/커 — to grow big (=자라다)

크다 is a process verb ("to grow big") as well as a stative verb ("to be big").

• 넘다 — to pass over, cross over, exceed

네달 넘었어요. It's been over four months. (The standard form is 넉달.)

• 백일 — the Hundredth Day

This is a traditional festive day in Korea for a baby who has enjoyed good health up to this point.

• 막 — just now, just recently

• 서로 — each other; each (of us)

• 낳다/낳아 — to give birth

• 그치? — a contracted form of 그렇지?

• 참 — oh, by the way (interjection)

참 is used here as an interjection, when one is reminded of something forgotten. 참 is also used as an adverb ("really" as in 참 좋아요! "It's really nice!") and an prenominal adjective (e.g., 참말 "truth" as an antonym of 거짓말 "lie, untruth").

• 과장 — section chief

The suffix -장, meaning "chief," is suffixed to the last syllable of the name of an organization, as in 사장 "president of a company (회사)," 회장 "president of an association (회), or a board of directors."

CULTURAL ENCOUNTER The terms 후배 and 선배 carry importance culturally when it comes to social relationships in Korea. In general, 후배 is expected to be deferential to 선배 while 선배 should be generous to 후배 in all aspects of social relationships.

연습 11. After listening to the script, answer the following questions.

Question 1. 누가 애기를 낳았습니까?

Question 2. 그 사람이 애기 낳은지 얼마나 됐어요?

Question 4. 애기가 어떻게 생겼어요?

Question 5. 명애 친구가 왜 장 선배한테 못 갑니까?

연습 12. Talk about your daily life. Try to express yourself in several sentences.

a. 집 가까이 있는 상가에 무슨 가게들이 있어요?

b. 슈퍼마켓에 가면 어떤 물건을 삽니까?그 슈퍼의 물건이나 가격이 어때요?

c. 요새 일기가 어떻습니까?

d. 대세일의 광고가 나면 대개 어떤 물건이 얼마나 싸게 나옵니까?

문법 (GRAMMAR)

1. Conjectural Sentences: A Summary

There are several phrasal verb forms in Korean expressing the speaker's conjecture on some event. They are similar to conjectual sentences in English that use the verbs "seem" and "look." We will summarize them below.

	Example
a. PRENOMINAL + 것 같다 (Lesson 17) • The tense of the clause expressed by 는/은/을/던/었던.	비가 오는 것 같습니다. It seems to be raining.
b. PRENOMINAL + 모양이다 (Lesson 19) • The tense of the clause is expressed by 는/은/을/던/었던.	미스 안은 집에 없는 모양입니다. Miss An doesn't seem to be at home.
c. VERB STEM + 나 보다 (Lesson 24) • The present and past are (with 었) but not future.	눈이 오나 봅니다. It seems it's snowing.
d. STATIVE VERB STEM + 어 보이다 (Lesson 24) • Expresses physical appearance. • The tense of the clause is always the present.	코트가 너무 커 보입니다. The coat looks too big.

The first two forms (a & b) express the tense of the clause (the object event of the conjecture) by selecting one of the PRENOMINAL ENDINGS. (See Lessons 16, 17, and 22 on prenominal endings.)

CAUTION! The verb 보다 in this form is a *stative* verb, rather than an action verb. For this verb, the premise ending is -은데 (not -는데) and the blunt formal ending is -다 (not -ㄴ다).

철수가 자나 본데 깨워요. Ⓜ Cholsu seems to be asleep, so wake him up.
철수가 깼나 보다. Ⓛ Cholsu seems to be awake.

2. Negating Phrasal Forms

For most phrasal verbs (consisting of two verbs), there are two negative forms that are more or less interchangeable. The negative marker used in the first verb of such a phrase is usually the short form (안 -), and it is the long one (-지 않다) for the second verb.

{ **안** 가고 싶어요. / 가고 싶지 **않**아요. } I don't want to go.

❖ *TYPE 1.* Each of the following phrasal forms have two negatives that are generally interchangeable Although sometimes the two forms may be slightly different, but differences are generally negligible.

<NEG> V + V = V + V <NEG>	English
• 안 먹고 있어요. = 먹고 있지 않아요.	I'm not eating.
• 안 닫혀 있어요. = 닫혀 있지 않아요.	It isn't closed.
• 안 보여 줍니다. = 보여 주지 않습니다.	He doesn't show it to me.
• 안 가 봤어요. = 가 보지 않았어요.	I haven't been there.
• 안 가고 싶어요 = 가고 싶지 않아요.	I don't want to go.
• 안 열려 있어요. = 열려 있지 않아요.	It isn't open.
• 안 커 보입니다. = 커 보이지 않아요.	It doesn't look big.

❖ *TYPE 2.* The phrasal forms below have only one negative form for each, and the negative is always placed in the first verb.

<NEG> V + V	English
• 안 그럴 것입니다.	I don't think so.
• 안 그런 줄 압니다.	I don't think so.
• 안 기쁜 모양입니다.	She doesn't seem happy.
• 안 열렸나 봅니다.	It doesn't seem open.
• 안 쌀지도 모르지요.	It may not be cheap.
• 안 갈까 합니다.	I don't think I will go.

❖ *TYPE 3.* Some phrasal forms place the negative only in the last verb.

V + V <NEG>	English
•추워지지 않았습니다.	It hasn't become cold.
•운전할 줄 모릅니다.	I don't know how to drive.

❖ *TYPE 4.* For some phrasal forms, the two negative forms have entirely different meanings. Such phrasal forms usually constitute complex sentences even though their customary English translations may seem like simple auxiliary verbs. This will be illustrated with the two important forms, -어야 하다 "must/have to" and -을 수 있다 "can/be able to."

<NEG> V + V	≠	V + V <NEG>
• 안 가야 합니다. I must not go. (Not to go is necessary.)	≠	가야 하지 않습니다. I don't have to go. (To go is not necessary.)
• 안 갈 수 있어요. I can do without going. (Not to go is possible.)	≠	갈 수 없어요. I can't go. (To go is not possible.)

4. Naming a Series of Nominals: -이니 and 같은 것

The postposition -이니, where the vowel 이 is normally absent when a vowel precedes, is used when naming two or more nominals as samples among many. The last nominal in such a series is often (but not always) followed by the phrase, 같은 + Bound Noun (-것, -데, -사람, etc.).

방에 의자니 테이블 같은 것이 있습니다.
There are chairs, tables, and the like in the room.

미스 홍이니 미스 송 같은 사람이요?
You mean someone like Miss Hong, Miss Song, and the like?

수원이니 대전 같은 데가 좋아요.
I like places like Suwon, Taejon, and others.

Like other connective postpositions, such as -하고, -와/과 "and," -이나 "or," the postposition may also be suffixed to the last nominal mentioned.

책이니 잡지니 어디 놓았어요?
Where did you put things like books and magazines?

5. Two Successive Events: -자 (마자)

The connective -자 마자 or simply -자 is used to connect two successive events. This structure is similar to the connective phrase, "as soon as" or "no sooner than" in English.

내가 사무실에 들어오자 마자 미스 한이 나를 불렀다.
Miss Han called me as soon as I arrived at the office.

집에 가자 마자 낮잠을 자야겠어요.
I'll have to take a nap as soon as I get home.

문이 열리자 사람들이 상점에 들어왔습니다.
No sooner had the door opened than people rushed into the store.

NOTE: This phrasal form is used most commonly in describing a past event. For a future event, -으면 곧 is typically used.

그것을 알아내면 곧 나한테 알려 주세요.
Let me know as soon as you find that out.

6. Anything, Whatsoever: A Summary

a. Any randomly selected item, regardless of kind or quantity, is expressed in a number of different phrasal forms. The postpositions -이나, -이든지, and -이라도 are generally interchangeable.

아무	+	(NOUN)	+	{ 이나 / 이든지 / 이라도 }	any ...

NOTE: The vowel이 is dropped when a vowel precedes.

아무 것이나 (다) 좋아요. Anything will do.

아무 때든지 갈 수 있습니다.	I can go anytime.
아무 곳에라도 갑시다.	Let's go anywhere.

CAUTION! 아무, by itself without any noun following, means always "anybody" or "anyone."

아무나 할 수 있지요.	Anyone can do that.

CAUTION! The notion of 아무 in Korean is *"any and all,"* not just *"any."* For example, "Does *anyone* want coffee?" denotes in English *"someone"* in the group rather than *"everybody."* In such cases, the Korean counterparts do not use 아무.

(누가) 커피 원하세요?	Does anyone want coffee?

b. "Interrogative pronouns" such as 누구, 무엇, 어디, may be used as indefinite pronouns ("some...") as introduced in Lesson 13. They are also used to denote "any" with -이나, -이라도, or -이든지.

QUESTION WORD + 이나/이든지/이라도	any...

누구나 알아야 합니다.	Anyone (=everyone) should know.
무엇이든지 집으세요.	Pick anything.
언제라도 불러 주세요.	Call me anytime.
어디서든지 살 수 있습니다.	You can buy it anywhere.

c. Most examples above did not contain any case postpositions (such as -가, -한테, -으로). It was because the example phrases were mostly either the subject or the object. It is a general rule that the subject or object postposition is absent when a context postposition (-는, -도, -만, etc.) is present in a word or phrase. -이나, -이든지, and -이라도 are to be considered as context postpositions.

However, if the phrase is something other than the subject or object (e. g., -한테, -으로, -에서, etc.), the case postposition should be retained even when the context postposition is present.

아무 상점에서나 살 수 있어요.	You can buy it at any store.
이거 아무한테나 보이지 마세요.	Don't show this (just) to anyboby.
누구하고든지 이야기해요.	He talks with anyboby.
어느 길로라도 갈 수 있지요.	You can get there by any road.

NOTE: In addition to the subject and object postpositions, the postposition -에 ("time" or "place") is also often dropped when the preceding noun ends with a vowel.

아무 가게나 갑시다.	Let's go to any store.

7. Two Ways of Negating "Any"

There are two different ways of negating "any": partial negation (not just any), and total negation (none whatsoever). In Korean, this difference is determined by the postposition, as shown below:

아무 + (NOUN) +	이나/이든지/이라도	Negative (Partial)
	도	Negative (Total)

아무 것이나 먹을 수 없어요. — I can't eat just anything. (PARTIAL)
아무 것도 먹을 수 없어요. — I can't eat anything (at all). (TOTAL)

In "partial negation" sentences, the contrast postposition -는 is normally used to make the difference even more clear. Note the position of -는, attached to the first part of a compound form, in the examples below. In order to apply any postposition to a verb, the verb must be in a compound form. In a negative form of a verb, unless the verb is already in a compound form (such as -올 수 없다), the long negative -지 않다, but not the short 안-, must be chosen in order to apply any postposition to a verb.

아무하고나 얘기하지는 않아요. — He doesn't talk to just anybody. (PARTIAL)

아무하고도 얘기하지 않아요. — He doesn't talk to anybody (at all). (TOTAL)

언제라도 갈 수는 없어요. — I can't go there just anytime. (PARTIAL)

아무때도 갈 수 없어요. — I can't go there anytime (at all). (TOTAL)

읽기 · 쓰기 (READING & WRITING)

1. An Article in Informal Style: 구어체 기사

Some newspaper articles dealing with minor news items may be written in an informal style. Such articles often include colloquial words and structures. The article below, for example, uses a humorous phrase 월요병 [wŏryoppyŏng] "Monday sickness" in the caption, and contains colloquial words such as 꾀병 [kkoebyŏng] "fake sickness," 가짜 "fake" or "false." The noun 골치 "headache" is used as a predicate meaning "causing a problem for someone." Even the quotation form is being used without the final quoting verb.

星港 월요病 환자 골치

"꾀병" 20% 이상이 진단서 요구
"법정病暇 채우자" 연말에 더 늘어

싱가포르 직장인들이 출근하기 싫어 꾀병을 부리는 "월요병 환자"가 늘어 사회 문제가 되어 있다고. 싱가포르 신문 "스트레이츠 타임스"에 의하면 요즈음 병원을 찾는 환자 10명중 2명 이상이 직장에 출근하기 싫어 의사의 진단서만을 요구하는 가짜 환자들이 요즈음 크게 늘어나서 회사와 의사들을 골치 아프게 만들고 있다고 한다.

가짜 환자들은 주로 주말이 낀 월요일과 금요일날 몰려오고 법정 병가 일수를 채울 목적으로 연말이 가까워 질수록 그 수가 늘어나고 있다는 것이다. 이러한 꾀병 환자들은 버스 운전사부터 일반 근로자, 군인, 공무원까지 다양하고 그 수법도 가지가지라고.

단어 소개

단어 소개

환자	patient	직장	workplace
골치	headache, problem	늘다/늘어나다	to increase, expand
꾀병	fake sickness	의사	doctor (physician)
20%	Pronounce 20 퍼센트 or 프로	-에 의하면	according to
…이상	more than…	병원	hospital
진단서	doctor's diagnosis (certificate)	있다고	quoting verb (-하다) is omitted here
요구하다	to request, demand		
직장인	job holder, worker		

연습 13. After reading the passage above, answer the following questions in Korean.

a. 월요병이 무슨 병입니까?
   (1) 감기 같은 병인데 의사들이 가끔 부리는 꾀병입니다.
   (2) 월요일에 의사들이 20% 이상이 걸리는 병입니다.
   (3) 직장인들이 월요일에 많이 부리는 꾀병입니다.
   (4) 주말에 직장인의 20% 이상이 걸리는 병입니다.

b. 이런 환자가 어떤 때에 많이 는다고 합니까?
c. 20% 이상이 그렇다고 하는데, 어떤 사람들의 20% 라는 말입니까?
d. 직장이라는 말은 일하는 자리라는 뜻인데, 직장인이라는 말은 무슨 뜻입니까?
e. 영어에도 "월요병" 같은 말이 있습니까?
f. 이런 환자들은 누구의 골치를 아프게 하고 있습니까?
g. 당신의 직장 혹은 학교에도 월요병 환자들이 있습니까? 있다면 그런 환자가 몇 퍼센트쯤 됩니까?

연습 14. After reading the passage below, answer the questions that follow.

60세이상 영국 노인층 인구의 21%

…영국인들은 과거 보다 장수를 누리고 있으며 60세 이상의 노인층은 전 인구의 21%를 차지하고 있다고 정부통계가 최근 발표.

지난 91년 실시된 국세조사에 근거한 이 정부통계는 60세 이상의 사람수는 지난 81년 이래 8%가 증가하고 85세 이상의 노인층은 지난 10년간 50%가 증가한 것으로 밝혔다.

이 보고서는 60세 이상의 노년층 가운데 여성이 차지하는 비율은 58%이고 남자의 비율은 42%라고 말했다.

단어 소개

층	class, layer
노인층	the aged class
인구	population
과거	past
정부 통계	government statistics
발표하다	to announce
밝히다	to reveal

a. 이 통계에서는 어떤 사람들을 노인층에 넣었습니까?
b. 영국인 인구의 몇 퍼센트가 60세 이상입니까?
c. 지난 10년 동안에 노인층이 몇 퍼센트 늘었다고 합니까?
d. 노인층 가운데 여성은 얼마나 됩니까?

appropriate number in each bracket.

a. 호칭	( )	1. 아파서 의사를 찾아가는 사람
b. 꾀병	( )	2. 매일 나가서 일하는 데
c. 옛말	( )	3. 나이가 많이 들어서 늙은 사람
d. 노인	( )	4. 사람을 부를 때 쓰는 말
e. 환자	( )	5. 같은 말이나 일을 다시 하는 것
f. 진단서	( )	6. 아프지 않은데 아픈 것처럼 하는 것
g. 직장	( )	7. 얼굴에 나타나는 감정
h. 반복	( )	8. 옛날서부터 사람들이 많이 하는 말
i. 표정	( )	9. 의사가 환자의 건강에 대해서 쓴 서류

연습 16. Complete the following sentences by filling in words from the boxes, and then translate the completed sentences into English.

a. 요즘 독감때문에 ____을 찾는 환자가 많아서_____들이 바빠서 큰 일이다. 어떤 병원에서는 입원실이______해서 찾아오는_____를 받지 못하고 있다고.

의사	병원
부족	이용
직장	환자

b. ____ 에 "아는게 병"이라는 말이 있는데 좀 ____ 한 말이다. 모르는 것이 좋을 경우가 있다는 뜻으로____할수도 있고, 잘 모르는 것을 아는척 하지 말라는 뜻으로도 생각할수 있겠다.

명확	막연
반복	이해
옛말	골치

c. 우리 나라의 땅 (land, real estate)값이 미국의 40배 (times) _____ 비싸다고 밝혀졌다. 22일 ____ 는 우리 나라 땅 면적이 미국의 1.1%에 불과하지만 전체 땅 값은 미국 땅 값의 44%가 된다고 ____ 했다.

이상	정보
부족	정부
발표	명확

단어 정리 (VOCABULARY SUMMARY)

Nominals

가격	price (of commodities)(=값)	눈	snow; 눈이 오다 to snow
골치	headache, problem	대세일	big sale
과거	past	모퉁이	corner (outdoor)
과장	section chief	빵	bread; 빵집 "bakery shop"
광고	advertisement	병원	hospital
구어체	informal style	백일	Hundredth Day celebration
기사	article (newspaper)	선배	school friend older
구석	corner (indoor)	수퍼 (마켓)	supermarket, grocery store
꾀병	fake sickness	아기	baby
노인층	the aged class	오후	afternoon
의사	doctor (physician)	제과점	bakery shop (=빵집)

의사	doctor (physician)	제과점	bakery shop (=빵집)
이발관	barber shop	직장인	job holders, worker
이상	more than…	진단서	doctor's diagnosis
인구	population	-퍼센트	per cent
입구	entrance (=들어가는 데)	환자	patient
정부통계	government statistics	후배	school friend younger

Action Verbs

고르다/골라	to choose, select	업다	to carry (a baby) on one's back
낳다/낳아 [naa]	to give birth	장을 보다	to do shopping (grocery)
발표하다	to announce, reveal	집다	to pick (merchandise)
밝히다	to reveal		
요구하다	to demand, request		

Process Verbs

크다/커	to grow (=자라다)	생기다	to happen, come into being
넘다	to go over; to exceed	얼다	to freeze; 얼음 "ice"
늘다	to increase		

Stative Verbs

똑같다	to be exactly the same	한가하다	to be leisurely
싸다	to be cheap	혼잡하다	to be conjested
세다/세	to be strong, violent		

Adverbs

굉장히	tremendously	막	just now (=금방)
그새에	already (=벌써)	서로	each other
금방	just now (=막)	어째서	for what reason (=왜)
따로	separately		

Interjections

그게 아니라	It's not that, but…	그치?	a contraction of 그렇지?

Postpositions

-이니	for naming 2 or more nominals	-외에	except

Sentence Endings

-구나/-군! (Low); -군요! (Mid/High)	exclamatory ending
-나? (Low); -나요? (Mid/High)	interrogative ending

Connectives

-는데도/-은데도	even though (= -지만)	-자 (마자)	as soon as...
-을 뿐만 아니라	not only… but also	-에 의하면	according to

Compound Verb Forms

-나 보다	It seems…	-을지도 모르다	It may…
-어 보이다	It seems…		

연습문제 해답 (ANSWERS TO EXERCISES)

연습 1.
a. 더울지도 모르지요.
b. 없을지도 모릅니다.
c. 얼었을지도 모릅니다.
d. 결혼했을지도 몰라요.
e. 열었을지도 모르겠어요.
f. 피었을지도 모르지요.
g. 빌릴 수 있을지도 몰라요.
h. 불지도 모르겠어요.

연습 3.
a. 추울 뿐만 아니라
b. 많을 뿐만 아니라
c. 빠를 뿐만 아니라
d. 쉬울 뿐만 아니라
e. 마를 뿐만 아니라
f. 얼었을 뿐만 아니라

연습 4.
a. 가자 마자
b. 열리자 마자
c. 끝나자 마자
d. 졸업하자 마자
e. 깨자 마자
f. 건너자 마자

연습 5.
a. 영숙이가 가는 것 봤어요?
b. 그 사람이 웃는 것/소리 들었어요.
c. 집이 바닷가에 가까워서 바람이 많이 불을지도 모르지요.
d. 입구는 오른쪽에 있고 출구는 왼쪽에 있어요?
e. 길을 건너자 마자 이발관이 보입니다.

연습 6.
a. 상가에(는) 십분내에
b. 우리 가운데서 미숙이가
c. 이것 가운데서 아무 것이라도
d. 야채니 과일 같은 것
e. 아무 책이든지 한국 역사에 대한
f. 여기에는 아무도 여권없이
g. 일요일에는 친구들과
h. 초보자로서 박 선생처럼

연습 10. Scripts & Answers

A: 장 보러 가야지? 어느 가게로 갈까?
B: 제일 슈퍼에서 세일 한다고 신문에 났는데 거기 가자.
A: 세일이라고 써 있어도 별로 싸지 않더라.
B: 다 싸지는 않지만 물건 잘 고르면 싸게 쇼핑할 수도 있어. 거기 가.

Q1: 이 사람들이 가는 가게 이름이 무엇니까?	제일 슈퍼
Q2: 왜 거기 가기로 했어요?	세일 하니까
Q3: 어디에 세일이라고 썼습니까?	신문에
Q4: 어떻게 하면 싸게 쇼핑할 수 있어요?	잘 고르면

연습 11. Scripts & Answers

A: 아이구, 명애야. 오랜만인데. 어디 가니?
B: 장 선배님 보러 가는 길이야? 장 선배 애기 낳은거 알지?
A: 장 선배가? 언제?
B: 벌써 3주일 됐을 거아. 딸인데 아주 예뻐. 같이 가자.
A: 나 지금 못 가. 장 보러 가야해.

Q1. 누가 애기를 낳았습니까?	장 선배가.

Q2. 그 사람이 애기 낳은지 얼마나 됐어요? 3주일
Q3. 애기가 남잡니까? 여잡니까? 여자
Q4. 애기가 어떻게 생겼어요? 예쁘게
Q5. 명애 친구가 왜 장 선배한테 못갑니까? 장 보러가야하니까

연습 13. a. (3) c. 환자들의 e. 글쎄요. g.생각해 보십시요.
b. 연말에 d. 직장이 있는 사람들 f. 회사와 의사들

연습 14. a. 60세이상 b. 21% c. 8% d. 58%

연습 15. a. (4) c. (8) e. (1) g. (2) i. (7)
b. (6) d. (3) f. (9) h. (5)

연습 16. a. 병원 - 의사 - 부족 - 환자

Lately doctors are extremely busy with many patients affected by influenza. Some hospitals are reported to be unable to accommodate all visiting patients.

b. 옛말 - 막연 - 이해

An old saying, "Knowledge can bring you trouble," is somewhat ambiguous. It may be understood to mean: "Sometimes it's better not to know something." It may be interpreted as an admonition against "assuming to know all while one has only a bit of knowledge."

c. 이상 - 정부 - 발표

It is reported that the land prices in our country are more than 40 times higher than those in the USA. Although the total area of Korea is no more than 1.1% of the USA, the total land prices of Korea is 44% of those of the USA.

Communicative Frames in English

Frame 1. Having a Cup of Coffee at the Tea House

Carson : It's got suddenly cold lately, hasn't it?
Miss Choe : Yes, it might even snow.
Carson : Snow already?
Miss Choe : Why not? It's December. It will snow and will freeze soon.
Carson : Yeah.
Miss Choe : Well, shall we get up now?
Carson : Why are you hurrying to leave, the minute you finished your coffee? Do you have something to take care of?
Miss Choe : No, it's not that, but I just wanted to stop by the supermarket. If you are not very busy, wouldn't you like to take a look at the shopping mall in this neighborhood?
Carson : Shall I?
Miss Choe : Let's go. I'll show you around interesting places.
Carson : Let's do that.

Frame 2. Crossing the Street by the Underground Passage

Miss Choe : It's across the street. You can see a lot of people crossing the street.
Carson : Do we go across by that land bridge?
Miss Choe : No, let's go by the underground passage. It would be too cold to cross by the land bridge since the wind is strong.

Miss Choe : Yes. Even though it's a holiday today, the streets are so crowded and congested. (*After crossing the street*) Right there. At that street corner, next to the barber shop, there is a supermarket, the biggest one in this area. Not only are the prices very low but you can find a variety of selections nice and fresh in that market.

Carson : It's quite big. Do you always shop here?

Miss Choe : I usually do. It's a little far away, but I come this far to do shopping.

Frame 3. Stopping by the Supermarket

Carson : It says "Big Sale."

Miss Choe : They always say that in their advertisements, but I am not sure whether things are really cheap. The fish look fresh, don't they?

Carson : They seem to have just come in. Take your choices.

Miss Choe : I'll just pick up any.

Carson : (*To a store clerk*) Auntie, these and those look just the same to me, but how come these are cheaper?

Clerk : Those (are the things that) came in yesterday. So they are on sale, you see. But they are fresh, too.

Miss Choe : I see. By the way, where are things like bread and cookies?

Clerk : A bakery shop is separately located in that corner.

Miss Choe : Oh, a new bakery shop is set up there! Mr. Carson, let's go to the bakery shop and have something delicious.

Carson : That's a good idea. But did you finish your shopping?

Miss Choe : Except bread, I don't have any more to buy.

Frame 4. Running into a School Friend

Miss Choe : Yonghi! You're doing grocery shopping, with the baby on your back.

Yonghi : It's been a long time, sister.

Miss Choe : The baby has grown that big already! How many months old now?

Yonghi : Over four months old. Just had the Hundredth Day.

Miss Choe : Wow! Is that so? Sorry that I couldn't go to see (the baby) on that occasion.

Yonghi : Oh, no. That's the way things happen. We're all busy.

Miss Choe : Time really flies. It seems like only yesterday when you had your baby, doesn't it? Oh, I want you to meet this gentleman here, Mr. Carson, who is the section chief in our company. Mr. Carson, meet my school friend.

Yonghi : Glad to meet you, sir. I'm Ha Yonghi.

Carson : Happy to meet you. The baby is really cute-looking.

A Cumulative Vocabulary List

ㄱ

가게	store	133
가격	값, price (of commodities)	196, 407
가깝다/가까워	to bo close	215
가끔	once in a while, occasionally	297, 388
가다	to go	17, 40
가르치다	to teach	217
가방	luggage, suitcase	132
가세요. Ⓗ	Please go.	14
가슴	chest	308
가운데	middle, center	346
가을	autumn	287
가장	most (=제일)	191, 286
가정부인/주부	housewife	258, 350
가족	family	169
-가지	kinds of objects (counter)	113
가지고 가다	to take (something) along with oneself	322
가지고 오다	to bring	112
가짜	fake	371
간단하다	to be simple	258, 365
간호원	nurse	350
갈다/가는/갈아	to change	265
갈비	short ribs	91
갈색	dark brown	265
감기	cold (as illness)	290
감기가 들다/들어	to catch a cold	290
감사합니다.Ⓗ	Thank you.	38
감정	emotion	397
값	price	232
갔다오다/-와	to have been to some place	167
강	river	291
강의	lecture	158
갖다 드리다	to bring (something) to (someone) (Humble form)	106
갖다 주다	to bring (something) to someone) (Plain form)	106
갖다놓다	to bring and put	370
같다	to be the same	90
같이	together	43, 101
개	dog	55
-개	small objects (counter)	113
개다/개	to become clear	288
거기	there (near the addressee)	94
-거나	or (a verb ending)	335
거리	distance	314
거실	living room	367
거울	mirror	266
거의	almost	309
걱정하다	to worry (=염려하다)	387
건강	health	326
건강하다	to be healthy	276
건너가다/건너가	to go across	153, 284
건물	building	368
건배	"Bottoms up!" (toast)	326
걷다/걸어	to walk	286
걸다	to hang; connect	389
걸리다	to take (as of time)	180
겁	fear	306
-것	thing (always preceded by a modifier	56
-게	so as to···	330
-게 하다	let/make/allow someone do something	331
겨울	winter	287
결근하다	to be absent from work	290
결석하다	to be absent from school	290
결혼하다	to marry	217
경우	case, occasion	335
경주	Kyŏngju (city)	107
경치	sight, scenery	180
계단	stairways, steps	167
계세요.	Please stay.	14
계시다	to be there, exist	32
계획	plan	179
-고 말고요	certainly, of course···	322
고국	mother country	223

고급	high class	276
고단하다	to be tired	213
고등학교	high school	217
고려	Koryŏ (medieval Korean kingdom)	20
고르다/골라	to choose, select	409
고맙다/고마워	to be grateful	149
고맙습니다.	Thank you. (= 감사합니다.)	54
고모	aunt (father's sister)	349
고속도로	high way, freeway	291
고치다	to repair, alter, fix	267
고향	hometown	343
곤란하다	to be difficult, embarrassing	344
곧	immediately, right away, soon	98, 105, 267
골목	back street, alley	363
골치	headache	419
골프	golf	162
-곳	place (=데)	182
곳에 따라	depending on the place	298
공기	air	386
공무원	government employee	350
공부하다/해	to study, learn	59
공원	park	364
공중전화	public telephone	250
공항	airport	81
과거	past	418
과일 / 과실	fruit	38, 366
과자	cookies, sweets	38
과장	section chief	412
-과/와	and; with (=하고)	304
관광	sightseeing	206
광고	advertisement	223, 409
광장	plaza, open space	82
괜찮아. Ⓛ	I'm O.K.	16
굉장히	tremendously	407
교수	professor	345
교실	classroom	78
교재	teaching material	335
교통	traffic, transportation	189, 363
교환	exchange	240
교회	church	41
구경하다/해	to sightsee	107
구두	shoes, boots	267
구라파/유럽	Europe	66
구름이 끼다	to become cloudy	297
구석	(indoor) corner	409
구이	broiled (meat, fish)	324
구하다	to look for, obtain	385
-(는)군요	exclamatory ending	344
군인	military personnel	350
궁	palace	82
-권	volumes of books	113
권하다	to recommend, persuade	397
귀	ear	308
귀가 뚫리다.	The ears get tuned to sound (to comprehend).	335
그	he/she (written style)	259
그게 아니라	not that, but	406
그냥	as is, just (without doing anything important to it)	269
그동안	during that time	213
그때	that time	249
그래도	even so	329
그래서	therefore, so	74, 165
그래요?	Is that so?	71
그러나	however	304
그러다/그래	to do so	132
그러세요.	Let's do that.	102
그런데	but, however, by the way	59, 136
그럼	well, then	14
그렇게	so, like that	183
그릇	bowl, dish	90
그리고	and	127
그리다	to draw	363
그림	picture, drawing	249
그새에	already (=벌써)	411
그애	that child	196
그저께	the day before yesterday	201
그치?	a contraction of 그렇지?	412
그-	that...(pointing to something near the addressee)	57
극장	theater	43
근데	a contraction of 그런데	386
근처	vicinity	88
글	writing, sentence	122

글쎄요	an expression of hesitation	179
금년	this year	122
금방	just now (=막)	412
금요일	Friday	108
급하다	to be urgent, pressing	305
-기 전에	before	328
-기는요	ending used as a modest disclaimer	343
기능	function	376
기다리다	to wait	26
-기로 하다	to decide to…	307
기분이 상하다	to feel bad	355
기쁘다 / 기뻐	to be happy	363
기사	driver	147
기사	engineer	350
기술자	technician	350
기억이 나다	to recall	343
기억하다	to remember	343
기온	temperature	297
기차	train	180
긴장하다	to get tense, alert	390
길	street, road, way	103
길다/긴/길어	to be long	266
김치	pickled cabbage	91
까맣다/까만/까매	to be black	265
-까지	up to; until	147
깍두기	pickled radish	91
깎다	to trim, peel	368
깨끗하다	to be clean	232
깨다	to wake up	247
깨우다	to wake someone up	389
-께 Ⓗ	to, for	276
-께서 Ⓗ	subject marker	223
꼭	exactly; without fail, for sure	346, 363
꽃	flower	286
꽤	quite	78
꾀병	fake illness	418
끊다	to disconnect	390
끝	end (noun)	167
끝나다/끝나	to end, be finished	166

ㄴ

나	I (pronoun)	16
-나보다	It seems	409
나가다/나가	to go out	87
나다/나	to emerge; to be born; to happen, occur	309
나라	country, nation	71
나쁘다/나빠	to be bad	290
나흘	four days	231
-나?	blunt interrogative ending	377
날로	daily	223
날씨	weather	199
날짜	date	162
남	South	284
남대문	the South Gate (in Seoul)	120
남동생	younger brother	185
남색	dark blue	265
남자	male person	33
남편	husband	124, 258, 366
남한	South Korea	19
낮	daytime	199
낳다/낳아	to give birth	412
-내	inside (=안)	340
내다 (돈을)	to pay (money); put forward	270
내려가다/-가	to go down	167
내리다/내려	to get off	149
내일	tomorrow	162
냉면	cold noodles	90
너 Ⓛ	you (pronoun)	16
너무	too, excessively	92
너희 Ⓛ	you (plural)	80
넓다	to be spacious, wide	368
넘다	to go over; to exceed	412
넣다	to put in, insert	250, 368
네 Ⓗ	yes	11
-네요	exclamatory ending	73
네./예.	I see.	135
넷	four	74
-년	counter for years	118
노랗다/노란/노래	to be yellow	265
노인	old person	354
녹색	green	265

논	rice field	291
놀다/노세요/놀아	to play; to have a day off	169
놀라다	to be surprized	383
놀리다	to tease	384
놓다	to place, put	370
놓이다	to be placed	370
누가	who (as subject)	107
누구	who	27
누구 누구	who	388
누나	elder sister (of a male person)	185
누렇다/누런/누래	to be tan	265
눈	eye	308
눈	snow	406
눈이 오다	to snow	297
눕다/누워	to lie (down)	247
-느라고	expressing reason or excuse	347
-는	a topic marker as in 너는?	16
-는 길에	on the way	343
-는 대로	as, according to...	365
-는 중이다	to be in the process of	343
-는데도/-은데도	even though (= -지만)	406
늘	always	78
늘다	to increase	418
늙다	to get old	345
능력	ability, capability	335
늦다	to be late	103
니네(들)	you (plural), you guys	169

ㄷ

-다	a blunt declarative ending	138
다	all	76
-다가	while	312
다녀오다/다녀와	to have been to	120
-다는 말	a form used in quoting a word or phrase	384
다니다/다녀	to go, attend	71
다르다/달라	to be different	143
다리	leg; bridge	286
다방	tea house	102
다섯	five	74
다시	again	266
다치다	to get injured	307
다행이다	to be fortunate	363
단풍	autumnal colors	348
닫다	to close	133
닫히다	to be closed	133
달	moon; month	163
달다	to be sweet	329
달리	differently	377
달리다	to run	303
답	answer	219
닷새	five days	231
닿다	to arrive (= 도착하다)	322
-대	machines (counter)	113
대 -	great, big (prefix)	143
대단하다	to be serious, grave	307
대답하다	to answer	344
대사관	embassy	151
대세일	big sale	409
대체로	generally	297
대통령	president (of a country)	158
대한민국	Republic of Korea	143
댁	home, house	122
더	more	135
더럽다/더러워	to be dirty	232
더욱	more (=더)	241
-던데요	"witnessed" past	363
덥다/더워	to be hot (particularly of weather)	199
-데	place	88
데리고 가다	to take/accompany (some-one) to (some place)	322
-도	also; even; too	16, 165
-도	degree (suffix)	297
-도록 하다	to try (one's best) to···	395
도시	city, town	322, 343
도심지	heart of the city	81
도착하다	to arrive	158, 182
독서	reading (books)	258
독일어	German language	67
돈	money	136
돌다/도세요/돌아	to turn (intransitive)	151
돌아오다/-와	to return, come back	107
돕다/도와	to help, assist	215

동	east	284
-동	suffix for a building	363
-동	suffix for a towns	363
동생	younger brother/sister	184
-동안	duration (of time)	230
-동안에	during	169
동양	East, Orient	66
동전	coin	250
동해안	east coast	158
됐어요.	That's O.K.	232
-되	but, and (a connective)	336
되다/돼	to be done, become ready, to become	199, 266
둘	two	74
뒤	behind, back	167
드리다	to give (Humble form)	106
듣다/들어	to listen	234
들	field, open field	291
-들	plural marker	81
들다	to eat/drink	326
들다	to lodge	230
들다/드는/들어	to hold, carry	213
들르다/들러	to stop by, stop over	307
들리다	to be heard, audible (passive of 듣다 "to hear")	305
들어오다/들어와	to come in, enter	29
-듯이	as if, as though	397
-등	etc.	314
등심	sirloin	324
따님Ⓗ	daughter	217
따뜻하다	to be warm	323
따로	separately	409
딸	daughter	121
-때	at the time of...	249
-때문에	because of...	247
떠나다/떠나	to leave, depart	182
떠오르다	to come up, emerge	377
또	again	200
또 하나	another	250
똑같다	to be exactly the same	409
뜨겁다/뜨거워	to be (burning) hot	325
뜻	meaning	346
뜻밖의	unexpected	259

ㄹ

라디오	radio	55
로비	lobby	248

ㅁ

–마다	every	388
마당	yard, garden	368
–마디	words (counter)	113
마르다/말라	to become dry, thin	387
–마리	animals (counter)	113
마시다	to breathe (air); to drink	103, 386
마을	village	291
마음대로	freely	240
마음에 들다	to become fond of	265
마중 나오다	to come out to greet	196
막	just now (=금방)	246, 412
막연하다	to be vague	377
만	bay	291
-만	just, merely, only	61
만	ten thousand	136
만나다/만나	to meet	102
만두	dumplings	90
-만큼	to the extent, as··· as	304
많다/많아	to be many, numerous	76
많이	many; much, a lot	165
말	language; word	71
말씀하다/말씀해Ⓗ	to speak	151
말을 듣다/들어	to obey, listen	345
말하다/말해	to speak	61, 151
맑다	to be clear	297
맛이 있다	to be tasty	270
맛있게 잡수세요.	Enjoy your meal.	325
맞다	to be correct	219
맞다	to fit	266
맞습니다.	That's right.	324
매다/매	to tie, fasten	148
매점	concession store	249
매주	every week	115
매표소	ticket office	181
매표원	ticket agent	181
맥주	beer	324

맵다/매워	to be spicy	329
머리	head	308
머리카락	hair	308
먹다	to eat	88
먼저	early, first	286
멀다/멀어	to be far	215
멋지다/멋진	to be stylish	259
메뉴	menu	91
메시지	message	248
며칠	what day; how many days	162
-명	people (counter)	113
명동	Myŏngdong (a shopping district in Seoul)	153
명확하다	to be clear, definite	377
몇	how many	73
몇 시	what time	87
모두	all (together) (=다)	269, 370
모든	all	370
모레	the day after tomorrow	184
모르다/몰라	not to know	88
모시고 가다	to take/accompany (Humble)	322
-모양이다	It seems···	312
모자	hat	267
모자라다	to be insufficient	136
모퉁이	(outdoor) corner	406
목	throat	197
목사	pastor	350
목요일	Thursday	108
목욕하다	to take a bath	258
목이 마르다/말라	to be thirsty	197
목적	purpose	206
몸	body	290
몹시	very	355
못-	cannot, unable to (negative prefix)	67
무료	free of charge	250
무릎	knee	308
무사분주	busy without having anything special to do	384
무슨···?	what kind of···?	234
무엇	what	39, 60
문	gate, door	82
문안	inquiry after (someone)	307
문인/작가	writer	350
문제	problem	219
문화	culture	315
묻다/물어	to ask	151
물	water	106
물건	articles, merchandise	267
물어보다/물어봐	to ask	151
뭐	Contraction of 무엇	90
뭐가 됩니까?	What's available? (at restaurant)	324
뭘 그러세요?	Why do you bother?	368
뭘요.	Not at all.	183
미스터	Mr.	12
미안하다/미안해	to be sorry	101
미인	beautiful woman	349
밀리다	to be delayed	165
밑	bottom, below	167

ㅂ

바꾸다	to change, exchange	231
바다	sea, ocean	284
바닷가	beach	291
바람	wind	332
바람이 불다	to blow	297
바로	immediately, exactly	165
바르다/발라	to paste on, apply (medicine)	309
바보	fool	252
바쁘다/바빠	to be busy	71
-박	overnight stay	206
밖	outside	168
-밖에	only, no more than	180
반	class	73
반	half	87
반갑다/반가워	to be glad	212
반도	peninsula	19
반듯이	exactly, necessarily	397
반복하다	to repeat	335
반찬	side dish	328
받다	to receive	122
발	foot	307

발가락	toe	308
발목	ankle	308
발전하다	to develop	223
발표하다	to announce, reveal	418
발행	publication	115
밝다	to be bright	368
밝히다	to reveal	418
밤	night	107
방	room	229
방문	visit	206, 363
방문하다	to visit	363
방학	vacation (of a school)	169
방향	direction	304
밭	field (for crops)	291
배	boat, ship	284
배	stomach	198
배가 고프다/고파	to be hungry	198
배우	actor/actress	350
배우다/배워	to learn, study	71
백	hundred	136
백반	"white rice" dish	91
백일	Hundredth Day's celebration	412
백화점	department store	139
-번	occurrences (counter)	113
번호	number (serial)	206, 230
벌써	already	87
법	method; law	250
벗다	to take off	267
베다	to cut, slice	397
벽	wall	324
변호사	lawyer	350
별로	particularly (not)	73
병	bottle	324
병	sickness	307
병원	hospital	418
-보고	(looking) at	390
보내다/보내	to send	121
-보다	than, rather than	179
보다/봐	to see, look at	59
보라색	purple	265
보이다	to be seen; to be visible	152
보이다	to show, let see	264
보통	usually	348
복도	hallway	167
복잡하다	to be complicated, confusing	153
볼 일	thing to do, errand	384
볼만하다	to be worth seeing	314
볼펜	ballpoint pen	55
봄	spring (season)	199
뵙다/뵈워	to see, meet (someone)	36, 102
부근	vicinity	284
부르다/불러	to call, summon	326
부모	parents	344
부부	married couple	258
부엌	kitchen	368
부인/아내	wife	121
부족하다	to be deficient	335
부탁하다	to ask a favor (of someone)	25
-부터	from, since	169
북	north	284
북한	North Korea	19
-분	minutes (counter)	133
-분 Ⓗ	people (Honorific) (counter)	113
분홍색	pink	265
불고기	broiled meat	91
불다	to blow (of wind)	332
불어	French language	60
불편하다	to be inconvenient; uncomfortable	307
불평	complaint	397
붙이다	to attach, add	249
비	rain	288
비가 오다	to rain	297
비다	to become empty	231
비서	secretary	350
비싸다/비싸	to be expensive	138
비행기	airplane	179
빌려주다	to lend	387
빌리다	to borrow	387
빠르다/빨라	to be fast, quick, swift	175, 218
빨갛다/빨간/빨개	to be red	265
빨리	quickly	201
빵	bread	409
뺨	cheek	308

ㅅ

사고	accident	306
사다/사	to buy	121
사람	person, human	76, 113
사모님Ⓗ	lady	366
사무원	office worker	350
사업	business, enterprise	206, 350
사이다	soft drink (similar to 7-up)	38, 197
사이에	between	190
사이/새	space (between)	348
사장	company president	350
사진	photograph	348
사진을 찍다	to take a picture	348
사촌	cousin	349
사회	society, community	223
사흘	three days	231
산	mountain, hill	82, 286
-살	counter for years of age	113,122
살	flesh; skin	387
살다/사는/살아	to live, reside	184
살이 찌다	to gain weight	387
삼촌	uncle (father's brother)	349
상대	partner (the other party)	335
상자	box	259
상점	store	41
상품	merchandise	276
새	new	138
새로	newly, anew	234
새해에 복 많이 받으세요!	Happy New Year!	276
새해/신년	new year	276
색	color	265
생각	thought, idea	219
생기다	to happen, emerge	390, 409
생년월일	date of birth	164
생선	fish (as food)	325
서	west	284
서늘하다	to be chilly	326
서다/서	to stand; to halt, stop	153
서로	each other	412
서비스	free service	325
서양	West	66
서울	Seoul (the capital of South Korea)	47
서점	bookstore	384
서해	Western Sea	284
선	line	189
선글라스	sun glasses	269
선물	gift	121
선배	school friend (older)	411
선생	teacher	12
선생님Ⓗ	teacher	12
선선하다	to be cool	326
설탕	sugar	368
섬	island	284
성	surname	33
성명 Ⓜ	full name	25
성함 Ⓗ	full name	25
성함이 어떻게 되십니까?	What is you name, please?	25
세계	world	66
-세기	century	127
세다/세	to be strong	406
세수하다	to wash (hands and face)	247
세월	time, years	218
셋	three	74
소개하다	to introduce	23
소고기/쇠고기	beef	324
소나기	shower	298
소나무	pine tree	286
소리	sound, noise	305
속	inside	397
속옷	underwear	276
손	hand	308
손가락	finger	308
손님	guest, visitor, customer	107
손목	wrist	308
손에 넣다	to obtain, get	259
수고 하십니다.	How are you? (a greeting in work environment)	248
수선하다/수선해	to repair, fix	266
수요일	Wednesday	108
수퍼(마켓)	supermarket, grocery store	406
수표	check	136
순경/경관	policeman	350

순찰차	highway patrol car	305
숟가락	spoon	329
숨겨지다	to be hidden	397
숫자	number	128
숲	woods, grove	291
쉬다	to rest	232
쉽다/쉬워	to be easy	175, 219
스님	monk (Buddhist)	350
스웨터	sweater	123
승객	passenger	183
-시	hours	113
시간	time	163
시간이 되다	to become time (for···)	200
시골	rural area	286
시내	downtown area	250
시다	to be sour	329
시대	era, period	240
시외	outskirts of a city	283
시원하다	to be refreshing	326
시작하다/-해	to begin, start	165
시장	market place	121
시차	time difference, jet lag	247
시청	city hall	82, 364
시키다	to order; make someone do something	103, 390
시험	test, examination	219
식다	to cool off	328
식당	restaurant	41
식사	meal	92
식품	grocery item(s)	143
신	shoes (generic term)	369
신다/신어	to wear (shoes, socks)	267
신문	newspaper	56
신부	priest (Catholic)	350
신선하다	to be fresh	386
신세계	new world	158
신식	modern style	370
싣다/실어	to load	215
싫어하다	to dislike	234
싱겁다/싱거워	to be bland	329
싸다/싸	to be cheap, to be inexpensive	139, 407
싸우다	to fight, have a quarrel	397
싸움	fight, quarrel	390
쌀쌀하다	to be chilly, cool	321
쓰다	to be bitter	329
쓰다/써	to wear (a hat, glasses)	267
쓰다/써	to write; to use	55, 127
쓸 데 없다	to be of no use	349
-씨	Mr./Miss	13

ㅇ

아가씨	young lady (unmarried)	105
아기	baby	411
아내	wife	366
아니다	nagative of -이다	57
아니오.	No (Ⓛ: 아니).	41
아드님Ⓗ	son	217
아들	son	122
아래	below, lower part	167
아래층	downstairs	167
아름답다/아름다워	to graceful, beautiful	223, 286
아마	perhaps, probably	180
아무것도	anything (used only in a negative sentence)	43
아버님/아버지/아빠	father	107, 124
아이	child	124
아이구	oh, my! (an expression of pain, grief, or surprise)	205
아저씨	uncle; mister (a common term of address)	153, 349
아주	very, extremely	201
아주머니	aunt (generic)	349
아줌마	aunt; lady (a common term of address)	154
아직	yet, still	41, 98, 133
아프다/아파	to be painful	286
아홉	nine	74
-아/야	an extra vowel added to the given name {-야 after a vowel; -아 after a consonant}	16
안	inside	168
안개가 끼다	to become foggy	297
안경	eyeglasses	267

안내하다	to guide, escort	223
안녕히	safely, in peace	14
안됐네.	That's too bad.	290
안부전하다	to give regards to (someone)	200
안전벨트	seat belt	148
안전하다	to be safe	180
안전히	safely	304
안-	a negative prefix	41
앉다 / 앉아	to sit down	47
알다/알아	to know	88
알리다	to inform	232
알아듣다	to comprehend	346
알았습니다.	I understand.	105
앞	front(side)	147, 167
앞으로	in the future	390
애	child, kid	196
애인	lover	349
야외	outdoor, field	386
약	about (with numerals)	118
약	medicine, drug	309
약도	simplified map	363
약속	promise, engagement	101
약혼하다	to be engaged	349
약(제)사	pharmacist	350
양말	socks	267
양복	suit (Western style)	267
양복점	(men') clothes store	121
양품점	boutique shop	121
얘기하다	to talk, chat	183
-어	and (= -어서)	316
-어	language (suffix)	67
-어 보이다.	It seems…	409
-어 지다	to become/get…	393
어깨	shoulder	308
어느	which	71
-어도	even though, even if	310
어둡다 / 어두워	to be dark	371
어디	where	41
어떻게	how	102
어떻게 됩니까?	What is…?	232
어떻다/어때	to be how	102
어렵다/어려워	to be difficult	219
어른	adult	252
어리다	to be young (child)	345
어머님/어머니/엄마	mother	123
어서	please, quickly	29
어제	yesterday	56
어째서	for what reason (=왜)	409
언니	elder sister (of a female person)	184
언어	language	67
언제	when	107
언제라도	anytime	223, 304
얼굴	face	308
얼다	to freeze	406
얼른	quickly (=빨리)	377
얼마	how much	136
얼마 전	a while ago	355
얼마나	how much/long	180
얼마나 오래	how long	118
업다	to carry (a baby) on one's back	411
없다	negative of 있다	54
없이	without	384
-에	in/at/on (time marker); to (destination maker)	40
-에 대한	about, on	386
-에 대해	about, concerning	158
-에 들었다	to be contained in	259
-에 따라(서)	depending on…	335
-에 의하면	according to	418
-에서	from; at (marking the place of an activity)	107
여권	passport	206, 229
여기	here (near the speaker)	55, 94
여덟	eight	74
여동생	younger sister	185
여러분	you (general public)	143
여름	summer	169
여보	hello/dear	367
여섯	six	74
여자	female person	33
여행	travel, trip	135
여행사	travel agency	223
여행자	traveler	136
역	railroad station	82, 147

역사	history	315
연락	contact, correspondence	122
연말	the end of a year	276
연필	pencil	54
연휴	long weekend	348
열	ten	74
열다	to open	133
열리다	to be opened	133
열차	train (=기차)	189
염려하다	to worry	267
엽서	postcard	249
엽차	green tea	355
영상	above zero	297
영어	English language	59
영하	below zero	297
영화	movie (cinema)	201
옆	side	167
예	yes	105
예를 들어서/들면	for example	377
예보	forecast	288
예쁘다/예뻐	to be pretty	138
예약하다	to make a reservation	215
예정	schedule, plan	230
예정이다	to be scheduled	158
옛말	old saying	397
오늘	today	43
오다 / 와	to come	47
오래	for a long time	12, 103
오른 쪽	right side (=바른 쪽)	151
오빠	elder brother (of a female person)	184
오전	before noon (a.m.)	103
오후	afternoon (p.m.)	103, 406
온돌방	floor-heated room	230
올라가다/-가	to go up	172
올리다	to carry up	232
올해	this year = (금년)	276
옳다	to be right	355
옷	garment	138
왕복	round trip	206
왜	why	107
왜 그러세요?	Why do you say/do that?	249
왜냐하면	because (if you ask why)	397

외국어	foreign language	67, 71
-외에	except	409
외우다	to memorize	335
외출하다	to go out (of home)	258
왼쪽	left side	151
요구하다	to demand, request	418
요금	fee, charge	250
요리	dish entree	324
요새	recently, nowadays	199
요전	last time (occasion)	348
요전 주	last week	348
요즈음/요즘	lately, recently	71
욕실	bathroom	370
용산	Yongsan'(a Seoul district north of the Han River)	147
우리	we; us	73
우리 나라말	our language(＝한국말)	183
우산	umbrella	288
우습다/우스워	to be funny, strange	344
우체국	post office	249
우표	postage stamp	249
우회전 하다	to make a right turn	322
운동하다	to exercise (physical)	307
운임	fare	190
운전기사	driver	215
울다/우는/울어	to cry, weep	390
웃기다	to make someone laugh	390
웃다	to laugh, smile	390
-원	won (Korean monetary unit)	136
-월	month (suffix)	142
월요일	Monday	108
웨이터	waiter	90
웬 일이세요?	What brought you here? What's going on?	195
웬…?	what ...? (surprise)	366
위	top, upper part	167
위층	upstairs	167
유명하다	to be famous	276
유적	historical remains	315
육교	overpass, land bridge	153
육지	land, landmass	284
-으러	in order to	86
-으려고	in order to···	311

-으로(서)	as (status)	345
-으며	and	316
-으면	if, when	196
-으십시다. Ⓗ	Let's	87
-으십시오. Ⓗ	Please do	99
-은 줄 알다	One thinks that ...	310
-은 후/다음에	after	322
-은/는	a topic marker	40
-은지(가)	(it's been…) since	343
-을 겁니다	I think…	133
-을 뿐만 아니라	not only… but also	407
-을 위하여	for (the sake of)…	326
-을 줄 알다	to know how to…	303
-을 테니까	as I will...	368
-을 통해서	through	314
-을까 하다	I am thinking of…	387
-을까요?	Do you think…? Shall We/I …?	132
-을지도 모르다.	It may…	406
-을/를	the object marker {-을 after a consonant, -를 after a vowel	121
음식	food	88
음식점	restaurant	96
음악	music	234
음악가	musician	350
응 Ⓛ	yes	16
-의	…'s (possessive)	215
의사	doctor (physician)	350, 418
의자	chair	79
이	tooth	308
-이나	or	196
-이니	postposition for naming 2 or more nominals	409
-이다/이야	to be … (identity)	29
이따/이따가	later, after a while	102
-이라는	(something) called…	343
-이랑	with (someone) (colloquial use) (= 하고)	184
이렇게	so, like this	212
이르다/일러	to be early	92
이리	this way	37
이미	already (=벌써)	175
이발관	barber shop	406
이번	this time (occasion)	165, 217
이분	this person	23
이사하다	to move (house)	363
-이상	more than…	418
이상하다	to be strange	390
이용하다	to utilize	316
이인분	two orders (of dish)	324
이제/인제	now	199
이틀	two days	231
이해하다	to understand	397
이-	this... (pointing to something near the speaker)	57
인구	population	418
인기	popularity	276
인삼차	ginseng tea	38
-일	day (of the month)	142
일곱	seven	74
일기	weather (=날씨)	297
일류	first-class	206
일반실	general class coach	190
일본어	Japanese language	67
일식	Japanese food	91
일어나다	to get up (from bed)	246
일어서다/일어서	to stand up	153
일요일	Sunday	107
일찌기/일찍	early	247
일하다/-해	to work	163
읽다	to read	59
입	mouth	308
입구	entrance	407
입다	to wear (clothes)	265
있다	to be there, exist	30
잊다	to forget	252
잊어버리다	to forget (colloquial)	252

ㅈ

자	well (expression of urging)	213
자기	ceramic ware	371
자기	oneself	356
자다	to sleep	197
자동차	automobile	63

자라다	to be raised, grow up	344
자리	seat	240
자전거	bicycle	55
자주	often	122
-자(마자)	as soon as	355
-자.	Let's⋯ (Blunt)	201
작다/작아	to be small	74
-잔	cups, glasses	113
잘	well, safely	16
잘 부탁합니다.	Happy to be your friend.	25
잘못하다	to do something wrong, make a mistake	305
잠	sleep	213
잠깐	for a moment, for a short while	29
잠이 오다	to become sleepy	213
잠(을) 자다	to sleep (=자다)	213
잡수시다Ⓗ	to eat (Honorific form)	88
잡지	magazine	59
-장	sheets of paper	113, 181
장거리	long distance	250
장을 보다	to do shopping (grocery)	407
재미가 있다	to be interesting	270
저 Ⓗ	I (pronoun)	24
저기	over there	92
저녁	evening	43
저희 Ⓗ	we; us	80
저희/저희들 Ⓗ	we	98
저-	that...(pointing to something away from the speaker)	56
-적	adjectival suffix	315
적다	to write, record	363
-적으로	adverbial suffix	315
전국	the entire nation	297
전송하다	to send off (someone)	196
-전에	before (some event)	103
전혀	entirely (not) (used in a negative sentence)	344
전화	telephone	122
절	Buddhist temple	291
젊다	to be young (adult)	345
젊은이	young man	181
점심	lunch	86

점원	store clerk	135
젓가락	chopsticks	328
정각	exact time, on the hour	182
정도	degree, extent	304
정말	really	103
정보	information	240
정부통계	government statistics	418
정치	politics	315
제 Ⓗ	my	25
제과점	bakery shop (=빵집)	409
제일	most (=가장)	179
조선	Korea (used in North Korea)	19
조용하다	to be quiet	363
졸리다	to be sleepy (=잠이오다)	390
좀/조금	a little, somewhat	61
좁다	to be narrow	368
종업원	employee	355
종이 백	paper bag	269
좋다	to be fine, good	16
좋아하다	to like, be fond of	234
좋으신 대로	as you please	324
좌회전 하다	to make a left turn	322
죄송하다	to feel guilty, sorry	384
–주	week (= 주일)	230
주다	to give	105
주라.Ⓛ	Give me.	349
주로	mainly	127
주말	weekend	49, 107
주문	order (commercial)	198
주문을 받다	to take an order	198
주방	kitchen (=부엌)	377
주소	address	206, 229
주스	juice	103
주유소	gas station	322
주일	week	118
주장하다	to insist	355
준비하다/-해	to prepare	165
–줄 알다	to know/think that ⋯	392
중국어	Chinese language	67
중식	Chinese food	91
중요하다	to be important	191
즐겁다/즐거워	to be happy	336
즐기다	to enjoy	286

-지 않아요?	an ending used in reminding something	344
지금	now	41, 87
지나다	to pass by	305
지난번	last time (occasion)	284
지내다/지내	to get along, spend (time)	107
지다	to fade, set (of sun, moon)	321
지도	map	363
지리	geography	315, 343
지방	area, district	298
지하도	underpass, underground passage	153
지하철	subway	363
-지(요)	an ending for a tag question or an emphatic affirmative response	112
직업	occupation	206
직원	clerk, employee	229
직장인	job holders	418
직접	directly	223
직행	express	314
진단서	doctor's diagnosis	418
진달래	azalea	286
진열창	shop-window	264
진짜	real, genuine	371
질서	order, security	158
집	house, home	41
집다	to pick up	409
집사람	wife (Humble form)	217
짓다 / 지어	to build, make	368
짜다	to be salty	329
-짜리	(an item) worth...	249
짧다	to be short	266
-쯤	approximately	180
찌개	thick stew	91

ㅊ

차	car, motor vehicle	103
차	tea	38
차다	to be cold	326
차다	to become full	231
차림표	menu (메뉴)	324
참	very, extremely	139
찾다	to look for; find	363
찾아가다	to go to visit with (someone)	200
찾았다	to have found (something)	363
채	club, stick	387
책	book	60
처음	for the first time	24
처음 뵙습니다.	I'm happy to meet you.	24
천	thousand	136
천천히	slowly	286
철도	railroad	189
첨단	very modern, advanced	240
첫사랑	the first love	201
청색	blue	265
-초	seconds (counter)	133
초대	invitation	252, 363
초보자	beginner	384
출근하다	to go out to work	258
출발하다	to depart (=떠나다)	189
춥다/추워	to be cold (particularly of weather)	199
취직하다	to take a job	342
층	stratum	418
치과의사	dentist	350
치다	to hit, strike	162
치다 (시험을)	to take (as of a test)	219
친구	friend	25
침대방	room with beds	231

ㅋ

카메라	camera	56
칼	knife	397
커피	coffee	38
커피숍	coffee shop	102
컴퓨터	computer	55
켜다	to turn (a light) on	305
코	nose	308
콜라	Coca-Cola	38
크다/커	to be big, large	73
크다/커	to grow (=자라다)	412
키	height (of a human)	389

키	key (=열쇠)	232
키가 크다	to be tall	389

ㅌ

타다/타	to get on, ride	147
탑	tower	82
턱	chin	308
토요일	Saturday	108
통화	telephone call/conversation	250
퇴근하다	to go home from work	258
특별히	especially,particularly	385
특실	special class coach	190
틀리다	to be wrong	219

ㅍ

파격적이다	to be unprecedented	223
파랗다/파란/파래	to be blue/green	265
파티	party	252
판매	sale	115
팔	arm	308
팔다/파는/팔아	to sell	182
-퍼센트	percent	418
편리하다	to be convenient	215
편안하다/편하다	to be comfortable	242
편지	letter	122
편히	comfortably	232
포도	grapes	369
포도주	wine	369
표	ticket	181
표정	facial expression	355
표지	sign	304
풀어지다	to be dissolved	397
피곤하다	to be tired (고단하다)	304
피다	to bloom, blossom	286
필요하다	to be necessary	232

ㅎ

-하고	and	91
-하고	with (someone)	169
하나	one	74
하늘	sky, heaven	288
하다/해	to do; to have (eat/drink)	39
하루	one day	195, 231
하얗다/하얀/하얘	to be white	265
하지만	however	304
학기	school period, semester	165
학생	student	26
학습	study, learning	335
학원	institution, nightschool	71
한	approximately (=약)	230
한 잔	one cup	38
한가하다	to be leisurely	406
한국	Korea (used in South Korea)	19
한국어/한국말	Korean language	59
한글	Korean script	127
한문	classical Chinese	384
한식	Korean food	91
한영사전	Korean-English dictionary	385
한옥	Korean-style house	376
한인	Koreans (=한국인)	223
한자	Chinese characters	127
한참	for a while	322
-한테	to	121
-한테서.	from	122
할 수 없다.	There's no help.	349
할머니	grandmother	349
할아버지	grandfather	349
함께	together (=같이)	206, 217
항상	always (= 늘)	143
해	sun; year	163, 321
해변	beach (=바닷가)	223
해안	coast, sea coast	343
핸드백	handbag	121
-행	bound for, going to (a place)	181
행복하다	to be happy	397
허리	waist; lower back	308
현관	entrance (of a house)	167, 369
현대	modern time	377
형	elder brother (of a male sibling); Mr.	13, 185
형제	siblings	346
-호	suffix for a number	363
호칭	title (for addressing)	357

호텔	hotel	42
혹은	or	258
혼자(서)	alone	217
혼잡하다	to be conjested	406
홍차	Lipton tea	38
화가	artist (painter)	350
화를 내다	to get angry	355
화요일	Tuesday	108
화장실	restroom, bathroom	167
화장품	cosmetic items	276
화폐	currency	240
확실히	definitely	143
환자	patient	418
회사	company; workplace	290
회색	grey color	265
후배	school friend younger	411
-후에	after (some event)	102
휴게소	rest area	322
흐리다	to become cloudy	288
힘들게	in the hard way	335
힘(이)들다	to be difficult (=어렵다)	335